Network Analysis Using Wireshark 2 Cookbook
Second Edition

Practical recipes to analyze and secure your network using Wireshark 2

Nagendra Kumar Nainar
Yogesh Ramdoss
Yoram Orzach

BIRMINGHAM - MUMBAI

Network Analysis Using Wireshark 2 Cookbook
Second Edition

Commissioning Editor: Vijin Boricha
Acquisition Editor: Rahul Nair
Content Development Editor: Mayur Pawanikar
Technical Editor: Dinesh Pawar
Copy Editor: Vikrant Phadkay, Safis Editing
Project Coordinator: Nidhi Joshi
Proofreader: Safis Editing
Indexer: Priyanka Dhadke
Graphics: Tania Dutta
Production Coordinator: Arvindkumar Gupta

First published: December 2013
Second edition: March 2018

Production reference: 1280318

Published by Packt Publishing Ltd.
Livery Place
35 Livery Street
Birmingham
B3 2PB, UK.

ISBN 978-1-78646-167-4

www.packtpub.com

I would like to dedicate this book to my beloved friend, Suresh Kumar, and his late wife, Dharshana Suresh.

– Nagendra Kumar Nainar

I would like to dedicate this book to my parents, Ramdoss and Bhavani, who have dedicated their life for my success.

– Yogesh Ramdoss

`mapt.io`

Mapt is an online digital library that gives you full access to over 5,000 books and videos, as well as industry leading tools to help you plan your personal development and advance your career. For more information, please visit our website.

Why subscribe?

- Spend less time learning and more time coding with practical eBooks and Videos from over 4,000 industry professionals

- Improve your learning with Skill Plans built especially for you

- Get a free eBook or video every month

- Mapt is fully searchable

- Copy and paste, print, and bookmark content

PacktPub.com

Did you know that Packt offers eBook versions of every book published, with PDF and ePub files available? You can upgrade to the eBook version at `www.PacktPub.com` and as a print book customer, you are entitled to a discount on the eBook copy. Get in touch with us at `service@packtpub.com` for more details.

At `www.PacktPub.com`, you can also read a collection of free technical articles, sign up for a range of free newsletters, and receive exclusive discounts and offers on Packt books and eBooks.

Contributors

About the authors

Nagendra Kumar Nainar (CCIE#20987) is a senior technical leader with RP escalation team in Cisco Systems. He is the co-inventor of more than 80 patent applications and the coauthor of six internet RFCs, various internet drafts and IEEE papers. He is a guest lecturer in North Carolina State University and a speaker in different network forums.

I would like to thank my dear wife, Lavanya, and lovely daughter, Ananyaa, for their understanding and support; my parents, Nainar and Amirtham; brother, Natesh, and family for their support.
Special thanks to my mentor, Carlos Pignataro, and manager, Mike Stallings. Thanks to Arun, Abayomi for the review. Thanks to all my friends Satish, Poornima, Praveen, Rethna, Vinodh, Mani, Parthi, and the publishers.

Yogesh Ramdoss (CCIE #16183) is a senior technical leader in the technical services organization of Cisco Systems. He is a distinguished speaker at CiscoLive, sharing knowledge and educating customers on enterprise/datacenter technologies and platforms, troubleshooting and packet capturing tools, and open network programmability. Co-inventor of patent in machine/behavior learning.

I would like to thank my wife, Vaishnavi, and kids, Janani and Karthik, for their patience and support.
A special mention of and thanks to Dr. V. Abhaikumar, principal of Thiagarajar College of Engineering, Madurai. I am very thankful to my coauthor Nagendra Kumar Nainar, manager Michael Stallings, mentor Carlos Pignataro, and all my friends and family.

Yoram Orzach gained his bachelor's degree in science from the Technion in Haifa, Israel, and worked in Bezeq as a systems engineer in the fields of transmission and access networks. From being the technical manager at Netplus, he is now the CTO of NDI Communications. His experience is with corporate networks, service providers, and internet service provider's networks, and his client companies are Comverse, Motorola, Intel, Ceragon networks, Marvel, HP, and others. His experience is in design, implementation, troubleshooting as well as training for R&D, engineering, and IT groups.

About the reviewer

Abayomi Adefila is a technical leader in services organization of Cisco systems. His array of accomplishments include B.Tech, M.Sc, CCNA, CCDA, CCNP, CCIP, CCDP, CCIE (R&S) along with MPLS L3 VPN, VRF, ISIS, IPv6, BGP4, MP-BGP, OSPFv2&3, RIPng, Eigrpv6, DS1, DS3, Metro-Ethernet, EEM, OER, advanced routing and switching on Cisco network gears, VPN concentrator, GRE, IPSec, Junipere, and so on. He has been awarded with MCI's outstanding performance ovation award at Verizon and Multiple CAP awards for outstanding performances at Cisco.

Jason Morris is a systems and research engineer with 18+ years of experience in system architecture, research engineering, and large data analysis.

He is a speaker and a consultant for designing large-scale architectures, best security practices on the cloud, near real-time image detection analytics with deep learning, and serverless architectures to aid in ETL. His most recent roles include solution architect, big data engineer, big data specialist, and instructor at Amazon Web Services. He is currently the chief technology officer of Next Rev Technologies.

> *I would like to thank the entire editorial and production team at Packt, who work hard to bring quality books to the public, and also to the readers of this publication. May this book aid you in your quest for doing great things.*

Packt is searching for authors like you

If you're interested in becoming an author for Packt, please visit `authors.packtpub.com` and apply today. We have worked with thousands of developers and tech professionals, just like you, to help them share their insight with the global tech community. You can make a general application, apply for a specific hot topic that we are recruiting an author for, or submit your own idea.

Table of Contents

Preface

Wireshark has long since become the market standard for network analysis, and with the growth of the internet and TCP/IP-based networks, it became very popular for network analysis and troubleshooting, as well as for R&D engineering, to understand what is actually running over the network and what problems we face.

This book contains practical recipes on troubleshooting a data communications network. This second edition of the book focuses on Wireshark 2, which has already gained a lot of traction due to the enhanced features that it offers. The book expands on some of the subjects explored in the first edition, including TCP performance, network security, Wireless LANs, and how to use Wireshark for cloud and virtual system monitoring. You will learn how to analyze end-to-end IPv4 and IPv6 connectivity failures for unicast and multicast traffic using Wireshark. The book also includes Wireshark capture files so that you can practice what you've learned. You will understand the normal operation of email protocols and learn how to use Wireshark for basic analysis and troubleshooting. Using Wireshark, you will be able to troubleshoot common applications that are used in an enterprise network, such as NetBIOS and SMB protocols. Finally, you will also be able to measure network parameters, check for network problems caused by them, and solve them effectively. By the end of this book, you'll know how to analyze traffic, how to find patterns of various offending traffic, and how to secure your network from them.

As the name of the book implies, this is a cookbook. It is a list of effective, targeted recipes on how to analyze networks. Every recipe targets a specific issue, how to use Wireshark for it, where to look for it, what to look for, and how to find the cause of the issue. To complete the picture, every recipe provides the theoretical foundations of the subject, in order to give the reader the required theoretical background.

You will see many examples in the book, and all of them are real-world cases. Some of them took me minutes to solve, some hours, and some took many days. But there is one process common to all of them: work systematically, use the proper tools, try to get inside the head of the application writer, and, as someone told me once, *try to think like the network*. Do this, use Wireshark, and you will get results. The purpose of this book is to try and get you there. Have fun!

Who this book is for

This book is for security professionals, network administrators, R&D, engineering and technical support, and communication managers who use Wireshark for network analysis and troubleshooting. It requires a basic understanding of networking concepts but does not require specific and detailed technical knowledge of protocols or vendor implementations.

What this book covers

Chapter 1, *Introduction to Wireshark Version 2*, covers basic tasks related to Wireshark.

Chapter 2, *Mastering Wireshark for Network Troubleshooting*, covers issues that improve the use of Wireshark as a network analysis tool.

Chapter 3, *Using Capture Filters*, talks about capture filters.

Chapter 4, *Using Display Filters*, shows how to work with display filters.

Chapter 5, *Using Basic Statistics Tools*, looks at simple tools that provide us with basic network statistics.

Chapter 6, *Using Advanced Statistics Tools*, covers advanced statistical tools—I/O graphs, TCP stream graphs, and, in brief, UDP multicast streams.

Chapter 7, *Using the Expert System*, teaches you how to use the expert system, a tool that provides deeper analysis of network phenomena, including events and problems.

Chapter 8, *Ethernet and LAN Switching*, focuses on how to find and resolve layer 2-based problems, with a focus on Ethernet-based issues such as broadcast/multicast events, errors, and finding their source.

Chapter 9, *Wireless LAN*, analyzes wireless LAN traffic and diagnoses connectivity and performance problems reported by users.

Chapter 10, *Network Layer Protocols and Operations*, primarily focuses on layer 3 of the OSI reference model and shows how to analyze the layer 3 protocol (IPv4/IPv6) operations. We also cover unicast and multicast traffic flow analysis.

Chapter 11, *Transport Layer Protocol Analysis*, primarily focuses on the transport layer of the OSI reference model, but also teaches you how to analyze various layer 4 protocol (TCP/UDP/SCTP) operations.

Chapter 12, *FTP, HTTP/1, and HTTP/2*, discusses these protocols, how they work, and how to use Wireshark to find common errors and problems in the network.

Chapter 13, *DNS Protocol Analysis*, covers the basic principles of the DNS protocol, the functionality, commonly faced issues, and the use of Wireshark to analyze and troubleshoot the protocol.

Chapter 14, *Analyzing Mail Protocols*, looks at the normal operation of email protocols and how to use Wireshark for basic analysis and troubleshooting.

Chapter 15, *NetBIOS and SMB Protocol Analysis*, teaches you how to use Wireshark to resolve and troubleshoot common applications that are used in an enterprise network, such as NetBIOS and SMB protocols.

Chapter 16, *Analyzing Enterprise Applications' Behavior*, explains how to use Wireshark to resolve and troubleshoot common applications that are used in an enterprise network.

Chapter 17, *Troubleshooting SIP, Multimedia, and IP Telephony*, discusses different protocols and how to analyze audio and video streams using Wireshark.

Chapter 18, *Troubleshooting Bandwidth and Delay Issues*, teaches you how to measure these network parameters, check for network problems caused by them, and solve these when possible.

Chapter 19, *Security and Network Forensics*, starts by differentiating between normal and unusual network traffic. Then, the chapter introduces the various types of attacks, where they come from, and how to isolate and solve them.

To get the most out of this book

You will need to install the Wireshark software. It can be downloaded from www.wireshark.org.

Download the color images

We also provide a PDF file that has color images of the screenshots/diagrams used in this book. You can download it here: https://www.packtpub.com/sites/default/files/downloads/NetworkAnalysisUsingWireshark2CookbookSecondEdition_ColorImages.pdf.

Conventions used

There are a number of text conventions used throughout this book.

CodeInText: Indicates code words in text, database table names, folder names, filenames, file extensions, pathnames, dummy URLs, user input, and Twitter handles. Here is an example: "Add the string tcp.window_size to view the TCP window size."

A block of code is set as follows:

```
tcp[Offset:Bytes]
//Or
udp[Offset:Bytes]
```

Bold: Indicates a new term, an important word, or words that you see onscreen. For example, words in menus or dialog boxes appear in the text like this. Here is an example: "When you go to the configuration menu and choose **Networking**."

Warnings or important notes appear like this.

Tips and tricks appear like this.

Sections

In this book, you will find several headings that appear frequently (*Getting ready, How to do it..., How it works..., There's more...,* and *See also*).

To give clear instructions on how to complete a recipe, use these sections as follows:

Getting ready

This section tells you what to expect in the recipe and describes how to set up any software or any preliminary settings required for the recipe.

How to do it...

This section contains the steps required to follow the recipe.

How it works...

This section usually consists of a detailed explanation of what happened in the previous section.

There's more...

This section consists of additional information about the recipe in order to make you more knowledgeable about the recipe.

See also

This section provides helpful links to other useful information for the recipe.

Get in touch

Feedback from our readers is always welcome.

General feedback: Email `feedback@packtpub.com` and mention the book title in the subject of your message. If you have questions about any aspect of this book, please email us at `questions@packtpub.com`.

Errata: Although we have taken every care to ensure the accuracy of our content, mistakes do happen. If you have found a mistake in this book, we would be grateful if you would report this to us. Please visit `www.packtpub.com/submit-errata`, selecting your book, clicking on the Errata Submission Form link, and entering the details.

Piracy: If you come across any illegal copies of our works in any form on the internet, we would be grateful if you would provide us with the location address or website name. Please contact us at copyright@packtpub.com with a link to the material.

If you are interested in becoming an author: If there is a topic that you have expertise in and you are interested in either writing or contributing to a book, please visit authors.packtpub.com.

Reviews

Please leave a review. Once you have read and used this book, why not leave a review on the site that you purchased it from? Potential readers can then see and use your unbiased opinion to make purchase decisions, we at Packt can understand what you think about our products, and our authors can see your feedback on their book. Thank you!

For more information about Packt, please visit packtpub.com.

Introduction to Wireshark Version 2

1

In this chapter, you will learn about:

- Wireshark version 2 basics
- Locating Wireshark
- Capturing data on virtual machines and on the cloud
- Starting the capture of data
- Configuring the start window
- Saving, printing, and exporting data

Wireshark Version 2 basics

In this chapter, we will cover the basic tasks related to Wireshark. In the *Preface* of this book, we talked a little bit about network troubleshooting, and we saw various tools that can help us in the process. After we reached the conclusion that we need to use the Wireshark protocol analyzer, it's time to locate it for testing in the network, configure it with basic configurations, and adapt it to be friendly.

While setting Wireshark for basic data capture is considered to be very simple and intuitive, there are many options that we can use in special cases; for example, when we capture data continuously over a connection and we want to split the capture file into small files, when we want to see names of devices participating in the connection and not only IP addresses, and so on. In this chapter, we will learn how to configure Wireshark for these special cases.

After this short introduction to Wireshark version 2, we present in this chapter several recipes to describe how to locate and start to work with the software.

The first recipe in this chapter is *Locating Wireshark*; it describes how and where to locate Wireshark for capturing data. Will it be on a server? On a switch port? Before a firewall? After it? On which side of the router should we connect it, the LAN side or on the WAN side? What should we expect to receive in each one of them? The first recipe describes this issue, along with recommendations on how to do it.

The next recipe is about an issue that has become very important in the last few years, and that is the recipe *Capturing data on virtual machines* that describes practical aspects of how to install and configure Wireshark in order to monitor virtual machines that have been used by the majority of servers in the last several years.

Another issue that has come up in recent years is how to monitor virtual machines that are stored in the cloud. In the *Capture data on the cloud* recipe, we have several issues to discuss, among them how to decrypt the data that in most of the cases is encrypted between you and the cloud, how to use analysis tools available on the cloud and also which tools are available from major cloud vendors like Amazon AWS, Microsoft Azure, and others.

The next recipe in this chapter is *Starting the Capture of data*, which is actually how to start working with the software, and configuring, printing and exporting data. We talk about file manipulations, that is, how to save the captured data whether we want to save the whole of it, part of it, or only filtered data. We export that data into various formats, merge files (for example, when you want to merge captured files on two different router interfaces), and so on.

Locating Wireshark

The first step after understanding the problem and deciding to use Wireshark is the decision on where to locate it. For this purpose, we need to have a precise network illustration (at least the part of the network that is relevant to our test) and locate Wireshark.

The principle is basically to locate the device that you want to monitor, connect your laptop to the same switch that it is connected to, and configure a port mirror or in Cisco it is called a **port monitor** or **Switched Port Analyzer** (**SPAN** to the monitored device. This operation enables you to see all traffic coming in and out of the monitored device. This is the simplest case.

You can monitor a LAN port, WAN port, server or router port, or any other device connected to the network.

In the example presented in this diagram, the Wireshark software is installed on the laptop on the left and a server S2 that we want to monitor:

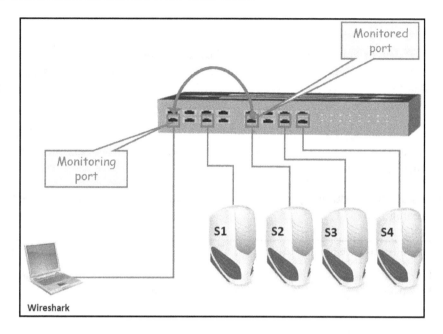

In the simplest case, we configure the port mirror in the direction as in the diagram; that will monitor all traffic coming in and out of server **S2**. Of course, we can also install Wireshark directly on the server itself, and by doing so we will be able to watch the traffic directly on the server.

Some LAN switch vendors also enable other features, such as:

- **Monitoring a whole VLAN**: We can monitor a server's VLAN, telephony VLAN, and so on. In this case, you will see all traffic on a specific VLAN.
- **Monitoring several ports to a single analyzer**: We can monitor traffic on servers **S1** and **S2** together.
- **Filtering**: Filtering consists of configuring whether to monitor incoming traffic, outgoing traffic, or both.

Getting ready

To start working with Wireshark, go to the Wireshark website and download the latest version of the tool.

An updated version of Wireshark can be found on the website `http://www.wireshark.org/`; choose **Download**. This brings you the **Download Wireshark** page. Download the latest Wireshark Version 2.X.X stable release that is available at `https://www.wireshark.org/#download`.

Each Wireshark Windows package comes with the latest stable release of WinPcap, which is required for live packet capture. The WinPcap driver is a Windows version of the UNIX `libpcap` library for traffic capture.

During the installation, you will get the package's installation window, presented in the following screenshot:

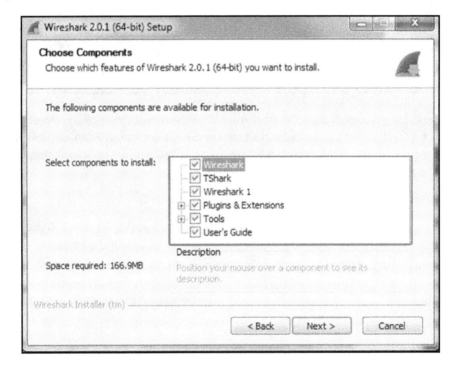

Usually in these setup windows, we simply check all and install. In this case, we have some interesting things:

- **Wireshark**: This is the Wireshark version 2 software.
- **TSark**: A command-line protocol analyzer.
- **Wireshark 1**: The good old Wireshark version 1. When you check this, the legacy Wireshark version 1 will be also installed. Personally, I prefer to install it for the next several versions, so if something doesn't work with Wireshark version 2 or you don't know how to work with it, you always have the good old version available.
- **Plugins & Extensions**:
  - **Dissector Plugins**: Plugins with some extended dissections
  - **Tree Statistics Plugins**: Extended statistics
  - **Mate: Meta-Analysis and Tracing Engine**: User-configurable extension(s) of the display filter engine
  - **SNMP MIBs**: For a more detailed SNMP dissection
- **Tools**:
  - **Editcap**: Reads a capture file and writes some or all of the packets into another capture file
  - **Text2Pcap**: Reads in an ASCII hex dump and writes the data into a pcap capture file
  - **Reordercap**: Reords a capture file by timestamp
  - **Mergecap**: Combines multiple saved capture files into a single output file
  - **Capinfos**: Provides information on capture files
  - **Rawshark**: Raw packet filter

How to do it...

Let's take a look at the typical network architecture, the network devices, how they work, how to configure them when required, and where to locate Wireshark:

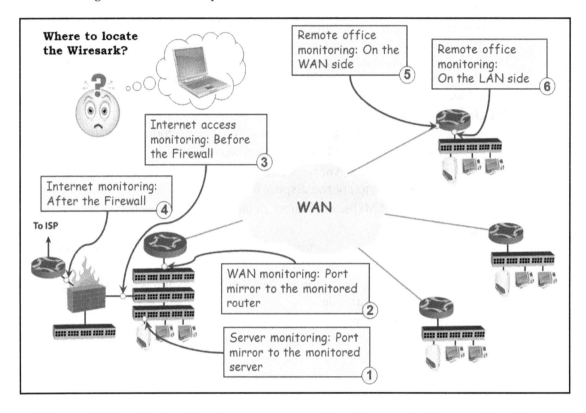

Let's have a look at the simple and common network architecture in the preceding diagram.

Monitoring a server

This is one of the most common requirements that we have. It can be done by configuring the port monitor to the server (numbered 1 in the preceding diagram) or installing Wireshark on the server itself.

Monitoring a router

In order to monitor a router, we can use the following:

Case 1: Monitoring the switch port that the router is connected to:

1. In this case, numbered **2** in the previous drawing, we connect our laptop to the switch that the router is connected to
2. On the switch, configure the port mirror from the port that the router is connected to, to the port that the laptop is connected to

Case 2: Router with a switch module

1. In this case, numbered **5** and **6** in the previous diagram, we have a switch module on the router (for example, **Cisco EtherSwitch®** or **HWIC** modules), we can use it the same way as a standard switch (numbered **5** for the LAN port and 6 for the WAN port, in the previous diagram)

 In general, a router does not support the port mirror or SPAN. In the simple Home/SOHO routers, you will not have this option. The port mirror option is available in some cases on switch modules on routers such as Cisco 2800 or 3800, and of course on large-scale routers such as Cisco 6800 and others.

2. In this case, you will be able to monitor only those ports that are connected to the switch module

Case 3: Router without switch module

1. In this case you can connect a switch between the router port and the **Service Provider** (**SP**) network, and configure the port monitor on this switch, as in the following diagram:

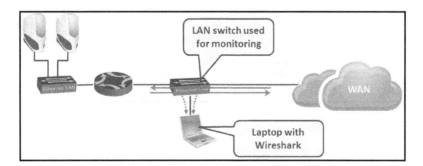

- In this case, configure the port monitor from the port the router is connected to, to the port your laptop is connected to.

 Connecting a switch between the router and the service provider is an operation that breaks the connection, but when you prepare for it, it should take less than a minute.

Case 4: Router with embedded packet capture

In routers from recent years, you will have also an option for integrated packet capture in the router itself. This is the case, for example, in **Cisco IOS Release 12.4(20)T** or later, **Cisco IOS-XE Release 15.2(4)S-3.7.0** or later, and also from **SRX/J-Series** routers from **Juniper**, **Stealhead** from **Riverbed**, and many other brands.

 When using this option, make sure that your device has enough memory for the option, and that you don't load your device to the point you will slow its operation.

When monitoring a router, don't forget this: it might happen that not all packets coming in to a router will be forwarded out! Some packets can be lost, dropped on the router buffers, or routed back on the same port that they came in from, and there are, of course, broadcasts that are not forwarded by the router.

Monitoring a firewall

When monitoring a firewall, it is, of course, different whether you monitor the internal port (numbered 1 in the following diagram) or the external port (numbered 2 in the following diagram):

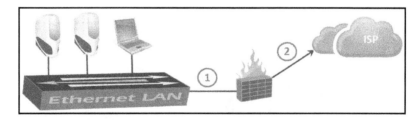

On the internal port, you will see all the internal addresses and all traffic initiated by the users working in the internal network, while on the external port, you will see the external addresses that we go out with (translated by NAT from the internal addresses), and you will not see requests from the internal network that were blocked by the firewall. If someone is attacking the firewall from the internet, you will see it (hopefully) only on the external port.

> In some firewall brands, you also have the option to use an embedded capture engine, as described in the routers, paragraph before.

Test access points and hubs

Two additional devices that you can use are TAPs and Hubs:

- **Test Access Point (TAPs)**: Instead of connecting a switch to the link you wish to monitor, you can connect a device called a **TAP**, a simple three-port device that, in this case, will play the same role as the switch. The advantage of a TAP over a switch is the simplicity and price. TAPs also forward errors that can be monitored on Wireshark, unlike a LAN switch that drops them. Switches, on the other hand, are much more expensive, take a few minutes to configure, but provide you with additional monitoring capabilities, for example, SNMP. When you troubleshoot a network, it is better to have an available managed LAN switch, even a simple one, for this purpose.

- **Hubs**: You can simply connect a hub in parallel to the link you want to monitor, and since a hub is a half-duplex device, every packet sent between the router and the SP device will be watched on your Wireshark. The biggest con of this method is that the hub itself slows the traffic, and therefore it influences the test. In many cases, you also want to monitor 1 Gbps ports, and since there is no hub available for this, you will have to reduce the speed to 100 Mbps that again will influence the traffic. Therefore, hubs are not commonly used for this purpose.

How it works...

For understanding how the port monitor works, it is first important to understand the way that a LAN switch works. A LAN switch forwards packets in the following way:

- The LAN switch continuously learns the MAC addresses of the devices connected to it
- Now, if a packet is sent to a destination MAC, it will be forwarded only to the physical port that the switch has learned that this MAC address is coming from
- If a broadcast is sent, it will be forwarded to all ports of the switch
- If a multicast is sent, and CGMP or IGMP is disabled, it will be forwarded to all ports of the switch (CGMP and IGMP are protocols that enable multicast packets to be forwarded only to devices on a specific multicast group)
- If a packet is sent to a MAC address that the switch has not learned (which is a very rare case), it will be forwarded to all ports of the switch

In the following diagram, you see an example for how a layer 2-based network operates. Every device connected to the network sends periodic broadcasts. It can be ARP requests, NetBIOS advertisements, and others. The moment a broadcast is sent, it is forwarded through the entire layer 2 network (dashed arrows in the drawing). In the example, all switches learn the MAC address **M1** on the port they have received it from.

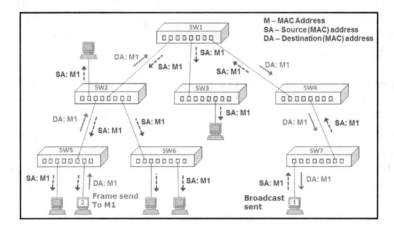

Now, when **PC2** wants to send a frame to **PC1**, it sends the frame to the switch that it is connected to, **SW5**. **SW5** has learned the MAC address **M1** on the fifth port to the left, and that is where the frame is forwarded. In the same way, every switch forwards the frame to the port it has learned it from, and finally it is forwarded to **PC1**.

Therefore, when you configure a port monitor to a specific port, you will see all traffic coming in and out of it. If you connect your laptop to the network, without configuring anything, you will see only traffic coming in and out of your laptop, along with broadcasts and multicasts from the network.

There's more...

There are some tricky scenarios when capturing data that you should be aware of.

Monitoring a VLAN—when monitoring a VLAN, you should be aware of several important issues. The first issue is that even when you monitor a VLAN, the packet must physically be transferred through the switch you are connected to in order to see it. If, for example, you monitor VLAN-10 that is configured across the network, and you are connected to your floor switch, you will not see traffic that goes from other switches to the servers on the central switch. This is because in building networks, the users are usually connected to floor switches, in single or multiple locations in the floor, that are connected to the building central switch (or two redundant switches). For monitoring all traffic on a VLAN, you have to connect to a switch on which all traffic of the VLAN goes through, and this is usually the central switch:

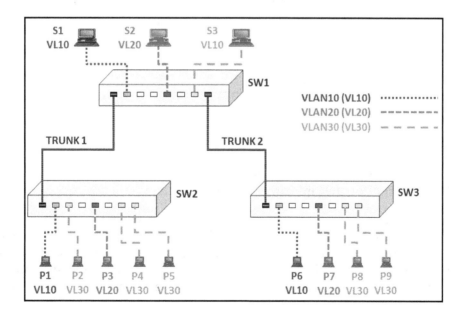

In the preceding diagram, if you connect Wireshark to Switch SW2, and configure a monitor to VLAN30, you will see all packets coming in and out of **P2**, **P4**, and **P5**, inside or outside the switch. You will not see packets transferred between devices on **SW3**, **SW1**, or packets between **SW1** and **SW3**.

Another issue when monitoring a VLAN is that you might see duplicate packets. This is because when you monitor a VLAN and packets are going in and out of the VLAN, you will see the same packet when it is coming in and going out of the VLAN.

You can see the reason in the following illustration. When, for example, **S4** sends a packet to **S2** and you configure the port mirror to **VLAN30**, you will see the packet once sent from **S4** to the switch and entering the **VLAN30**, and then when leaving **VLAN30** to **S2**:

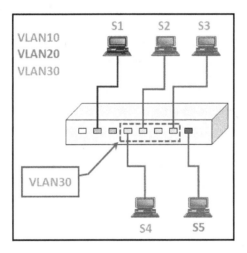

See also

For information on how to configure the port mirror, refer to the vendor's instructions. It can be called **port monitor**, **port mirror**, or **SPAN** from Cisco.

There are also advanced features such as remote monitoring, when you monitor a port that is not directly connected to your switch, advanced filtering (such as filtering specific MAC addresses), and so on. There are also advanced switches that have capture and analysis capabilities on the switch itself. It is also possible to monitor virtual ports (for example, a LAG or EtherChannel groups). For all cases, and other cases described in this recipe, refer to the vendor's specifications.

For vendor information you can look, for example, at these links:

- Cisco IOS SPAN (for catalyst switches):
  `http://www.cisco.com/c/en/us/support/docs/switches/catalyst-6500-serie`
  `s-switches/10570-41.html`
- Cisco IOS Embedded Packet Capture feature:
  `http://www.cisco.com/c/en/us/products/collateral/ios-nx-os-software/io`
  `s-embedded-packet-capture/datasheet_c78-502727.html`
- Check point Packet Sniffer feature:
  `https://www.checkpoint.com/smb/help/utm1/8.2/2002.htm`
- Fortinet FortiOS packet sniffer:
  `http://kb.fortinet.com/kb/viewContent.do?externalId=11186`

Capturing data on virtual machines

Getting ready

In the last few years, a significant amount of servers are moving to virtual environments—that is a large amount of servers on a single hardware device.

First, to put some order in the terms. There are two major terms to remember in the virtual world:

- A virtual machine is an emulation of a computer system that is installed on single or multiple hardware platforms. A virtual machine is mostly used in the context of virtual servers. The major platforms used for server virtualization are **VMware ESX**, **Microsoft Hyper-V**, or **Citrix XenServer.**
- A Blade server is a cage that holds inside server cards and LAN switches to connect them to the world.

In this section, we will look at each one of these components and see how to monitor each one of them.

How to do it...

Let's see how to do it.

Packet capture on a VM installed on a single hardware

A single hardware with virtual machines is illustrated in the following diagram:

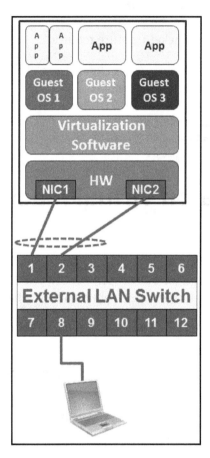

As you see in the preceding diagram, we have the applications that run on the operating systems (guest OS in the drawing). Several guest OSs are running on the virtualization software that runs on the hardware platform.

As mentioned earlier in this chapter, in order to capture packets we have two possibilities: to install Wireshark on the device that we want to monitor, or to configure port mirror to the LAN switch to which the **Network Interface Card** (**NIC**) is connected.

For this reason, in the case of a virtual platform on a single hardware, we have the following possibilities:

1. Install Wireshark on the specific server that you want to monitor, and start capturing packets on the server itself.
2. Connect your laptop to the switch **8**, and configure a port mirror to the server. In the preceding diagram, it would be to connect a laptop to a free port on the switch, with a port mirror to ports **1** and **2**. The problem that can happen here is that you monitor.

The first case is obvious, but some problems can happen in the second one:

1. As illustrated in the preceding diagram, there are usually two ports or more that are connected between the server and the LAN switch. This topology is called **Link Aggregation (LAG)**, teaming, or if you are using Cisco switches, EtherChannel. When monitoring a server, check whether it is configured with **load sharing** or **port redundancy** (also referred to as **Failover**). If it is configured with port redundancy, it is simple: check what the active port is and configure the port mirror to it. If it is configured with load sharing, you have to configure one of the following:
    - Port mirror to LAG interface: that is, port mirror to the virtual interface that holds the two or more physical interfaces. Usually, it is termed by the switch vendor as **Port-Group** or **Port-Channel** interface.

There are various terms for grouping several ports into one aggregate. The most common standard is 802.3ad (LAG), later replaced by 802.3AX LAG. There is also Cisco EtherChannel, and server vendors call it **teaming** or **NIC teaming** (Microsoft), **bonding** (various Linux systems), **Load Based Teaming** (LBT), and other terms. The important thing is to check whether it is a load sharing or redundant configuration. Note that the mechanism used in all the mechanisms is sharing and not balancing, and this is because the load is not equally balanced between the interfaces.

- The server NICs are configured in the port redundancy: the port mirror from one port to two physical ports (in the diagram to ports 1 and 2 of the switch).

- Configure two port mirrors from two interface cards on your PC to the two interfaces on the LAN switch at the same time. A diagram of the three cases is presented here:

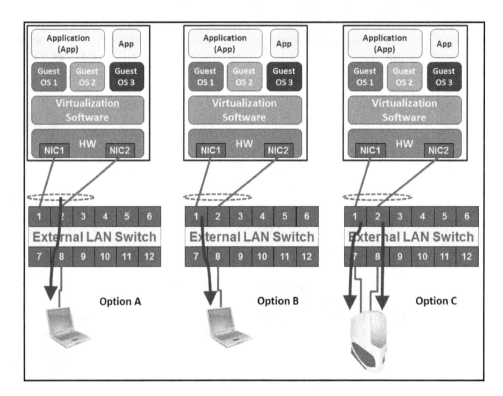

- There is another problem that might happen. When monitoring heavy traffic on ports configured with load sharing, in **Option A** you will have a mirror of two NICs sending data to a single one, for example, two ports of 1 Gbps to a single port of 1 Gbps. Then of course, in case of traffic that exceeds the speed of the laptop, not all packets will be captured and some of them will be lost. For this reason, when you use this method, make sure that the laptop has a faster NIC than the monitored ports or use **Option C** (capture with two interfaces).

 In any case, Wireshark is not suitable for high-rate packet capture and will not suit more then 200-300 Mbps, so when monitoring heavy traffic, configure the capture filters or use commercial software that is suitable.

Packet capture on a blade server

In the case of using a **BLADE Center**, we have the following hardware topology:

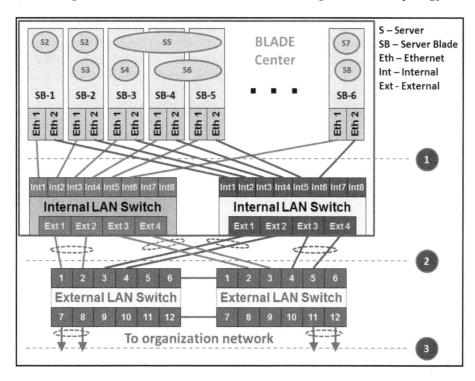

As illustrated, we have a **BLADE Center** that contains the following components:

- **Blade servers**: These are hardware cards, usually located at the front side of the blade.
- **Servers**: The virtual servers installed on the hardware servers, also called **VMs**.
- **Internal LAN switch**: Internal LAN switches that are installed at the front or back of the blade center. These switches usually have 12-16 internal or virtual ports (**Int** in the diagram) and 4-8 external or physical ports (**Ext** in the diagram).
- **External switch**: Installed in the communication rack, and it's not a part of the **BLADE Center**.

Monitoring a blade center is more difficult because we don't have direct access to all of the traffic that goes through it. There are several options for doing so:

- Internal monitoring on the blade center:
    - For traffic on a specific server, install Wireshark on the virtual server. In this case you just have to make sure from which virtual ports traffic is sent and received. You will see this in the VM configuration, and also choose one interface a the time on the Wireshark and see to which one the traffic goes.
    - A second option is to install Wireshark on a different VM and configure the port mirror in the blade center switch, between the server you wish to monitor and the VM with the Wireshark installed on it.
- From servers to blade center switch (**1**) in the previous diagram:
    - For traffic that goes from the servers to the switch, configure, port mirror from the virtual ports the server is connected to, to the physical port where you connect the laptop. Most vendors support this option, and it can be configured.
- For external monitoring, traffic from the internal blade center switch to the external switches:
    - Use a standard port mirror on the internal or external switches

How it works...

As described before, there are several types of virtual platforms. I will explain the way one operates on VMware, which is one of the popular ones.

On every virtual platform, you configure hosts that are provided with the CPU and memory resources that virtual machines use and give virtual machines access to these resources.

In the next screenshot, you see a virtualization server with address **192.168.1.110**, configured with four virtual machines: **Account1**, **Account2**, **Term1**, and **Term2**. These are the virtual servers, in this case, two servers for accounting and two terminal servers:

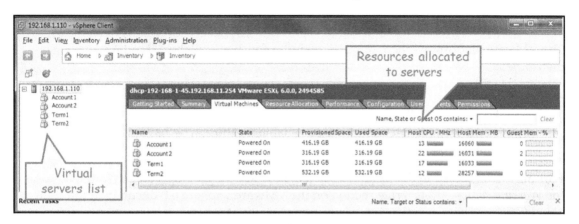

When you go to the configuration menu and choose **Networking**, as illustrated in the next screenshot, you see the **vSwitch**. On the left, you see the **internal ports** connected to the servers, and on the right, you see the **external port**.

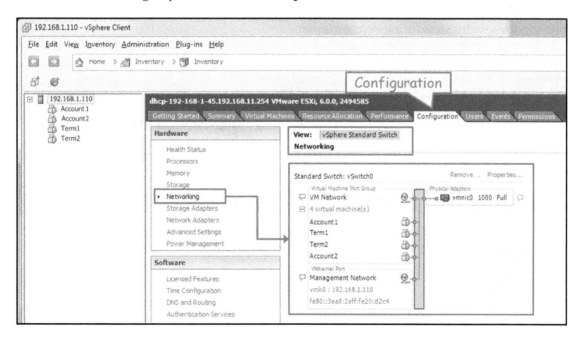

In this example, we see the virtual servers **Account1**, **Account2**, **Term1** and **Term2**; on the right, we see the physical port **vmnic0**.

Standard and distributed vSwitch

The VMware platform vSphere offers two kinds of virtual switches, standard and distributed:

- The **standard vSwitch** is what every vSphere installation has, no matter what license it is running on
- Distributed **vSwitches** are only available for those who have an **Enterprise Plus** license

Port mirror is enabled in distributed **vSwitch**; how to configure it? You can find that out in the *Working With Port Mirroring* section on the VMware vSphere 6.0 documentation center: `http://pubs.vmware.com/vsphere-60/index.jsp#com.vmware.vsphere.networking.doc/G UID-CFFD9157-FC17-440D-BDB4-E16FD447A1BA.html`.

See also

For specific vendor's mirroring configuration:

- For Alteon (now Radware) blade switches: `http://www.bladenetwork.net/ userfiles/file/PDFs/IBM_GbE_L2-3_Applicat_Guide.pdf`
- For Cisco blade switches (called SPAN): `http://www.cisco.com/c/dam/en/us/ td/docs/switches/blades/igesm/software/release/12-1_14_ay/ configuration/guide/25K8411B.pdf`, **Page 340**, *SPAN and RSPAN Concepts and Terminology*

Starting the capture of data

After we have located Wireshark in the network, in this recipe, we will learn how to start capturing data and what we will get in various capture scenarios.

Getting ready

After you've installed Wireshark on your computer, the only thing to do will be to start the analyzer from the desktop, program files, or the quick start bar.

To keep consistency, this book is written for Wireshark version 2.0.2 from February 2016. In general (but not always), if you look at the version number X Y Z, when the X changes it will be a major release (like version 2), that changes every several years and occur the software completely. When the Y changes, it will usually be additional features or significant changes in some features, and if the Z changes, it will usually be bug fixes and new protocol dissectors. Since new minor releases are released usually every few weeks, you can have a quick look at their release notes.

When you do so, the following window will be opened (version 2.0.2):

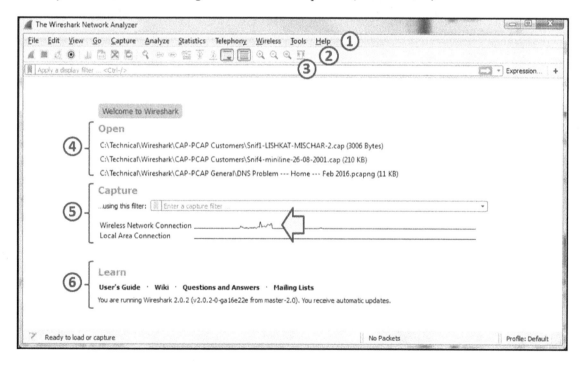

In the start window, you will see the following sections:

- The **main menu**, with file, edit and view operations, capture, statistics, and various tools.
- The **main toolbar** that provides quick access to frequently used items from the menu.
- The **filter toolbar**, it provides access to the display filters.

In the main area of the start window, we have the following items:

- A list of files that were recently opened
- A **Capture** part that enables us to configure a capture filter and shows us the traffic on our computer interfaces

 Seeing traffic on computer interfaces is a nice improvement from version 1, as it enables us to quickly see the active interfaces and start the capture on them.

- The **Learn** part can take us directly to the manual pages

How to do it...

In Wireshark Version 2, it is very simple. When you run the software, down the main window, you will see all the interfaces with the traffic that runs over them. See the following screenshot:

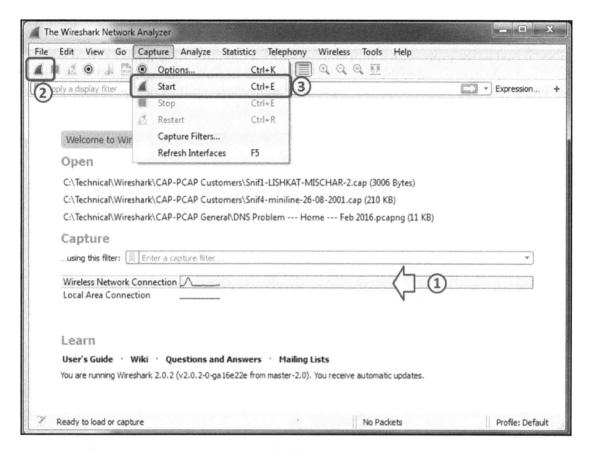

The simplest way to start a simple single-interface capture is simply to double-click on the active interface (**1**). You can also mark the active interface and click on the capture button on the upper-left corner of the window (**2**), or choose **Start** or *Ctrl + E* from the **Capture** menu (**3**).

Capture on multiple interfaces

In order to start the capture on multiple interfaces, you simply use Windows *Ctrl* or *Shift* keys, and left-click to choose the interfaces you want to capture data from. In the following screenshot, you see that the **Wireless Network Connection** and the **Local Area Connection** are picked up:

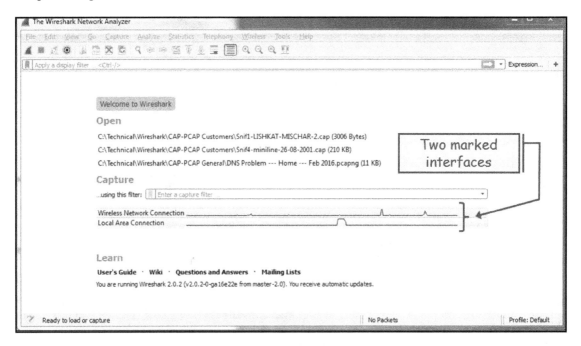

And the traffic that you will get will be from the two interfaces, as you can see from the next screenshot: 10.0.0.4 on the wireless interface, and 169.254.170.91 **Automatic Private IP Address** (**APIPA**) on the LAN interface.

APIPA address is an address allocated automatically when you configure your device to use a DHCP client, and no address is acquired. The APIPA address is like any other address and can be used locally, but it is usually used to notify that your DHCP server is not available.

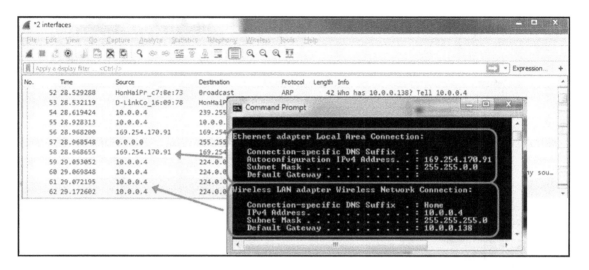

Using capture on multiple interfaces can be helpful in many cases, for example, when you have multiple physical NICs, you can port monitor two different servers, two ports of a router or any other multiple ports at the same time. A typical configuration is seen in the following screenshot:

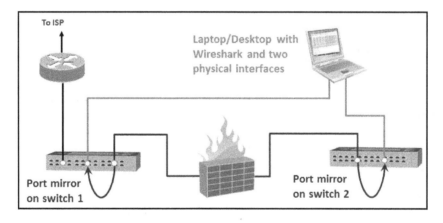

How to configure the interface you capture data from

1. To configure the interface you capture data from, choose **Options** from the **Capture** menu. The following window will appear:

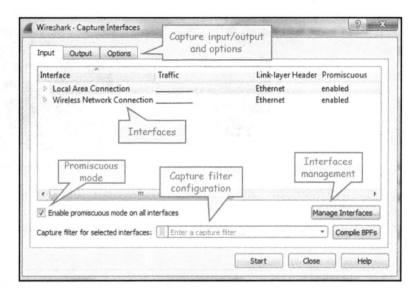

In this window you can configure the following parameters:

2. On the upper side of the window, on the main window, choose the interface on which you want to capture the data from. If no additional configuration is required, click on **Start** to start the capture.

3. On the lower-left side, you have the checkbox **Use promiscuous mode on all interfaces**. When checked, Wireshark will capture all the packets that the computer receives. Unchecking it will capture only packets intended for the computer.

 In some cases, when this checkbox is checked, Wireshark will not capture data in the wireless interface, so if you start capturing data on the wireless interface and see nothing, uncheck it.

4. In the middle of the screen, right below the interfaces window, you can configure the capture filter. We will learn capture filters in Chapter 3, *Using Capture Filters*.

On top of the window, we have three tabs: **Input** (opens by default), **Output**, and **Options**.

Capture data to multiple files

Click on the **Output** tab, and the following window will open:

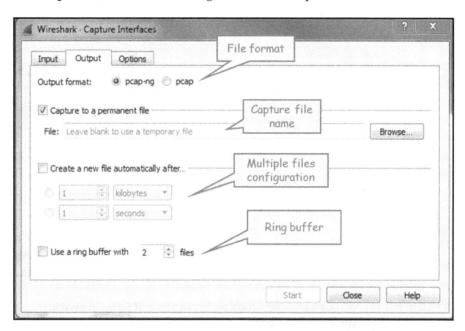

This window enables capture in multiple files. To configure this, write a filename in the **Capture to a permanent file** area. Wireshark will save the captured file under this name, with extensions 0001, 0002, and so on, all under the path that you specify in the **Browse...** button. This feature is extremely important when capturing a large amount of data, for example, when capturing data over a heavily loaded interface, or over a long period of time. You can tell the software to open a new file after a specific amount of time, file size, or number of packets.

Configure output parameters

1. When you choose the **Options** tab, the following window will open.

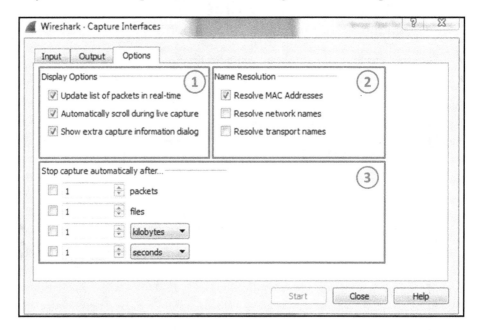

2. On the left (1), you can choose **Display Options**. These options are:
   - **Update list of packets in real-time**: Upon checking this option, Wireshark updates packets in the packet pane in real time
   - **Automatic scroll during live capture**: Upon checking this, Wireshark scrolls down packets in the packet pane as new packets come in
   - **Hide capture info dialog**: By checking this, the capture info dialog is hidden
3. On the right, there is the **Name Resolution** option. Here we can check for:
   - The MAC address resolution that resolves the first part of the MAC address to the vendor ID.
   - The IP address resolution that is resolved to DNS names.
   - TCP/UDP port numbers that are resolved to application names. These are the port numbers; for example, TCP port 80 will be presented as HTTP, port 25 as SMTP, and so on.

There are some limitations to Wireshark name resolution. Even though Wireshark caches DNS names, resolving IP addresses is a process that requires DNS translation, and therefore it can slow down the capture. The process itself also produces additional DNS queries and responses, which you will see on the capture file. Name resolution can often fail, because the DNS you are querying is not necessarily familiar with the IP addresses in the capture file. For all these reasons, although network name resolution can be a helpful feature, you should use it carefully.

Manage interfaces (under the Input tab)

1. As you see in the following screenshot, on the bottom-right, you have the **Manage Interfaces...** button with three tabs; **Local Interfaces, Pipes** and **Remote Interfaces**. These are the options that Wireshark can capture data from:

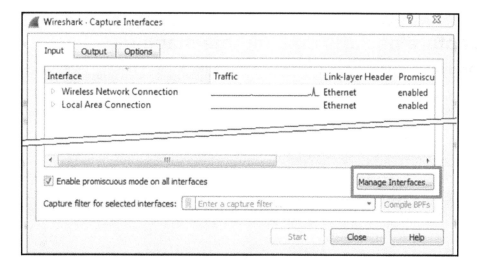

2. When you choose the **Manage Interfaces...** button and the **Input** tab, you will see a list of available local interfaces, including the hidden ones, which are not shown in the other list:

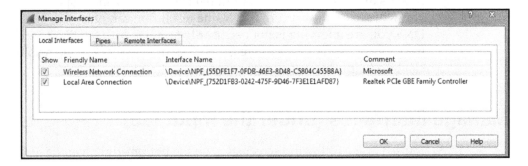

3. Wireshark can also read captured packets from another application in real time.

Capture packets on a remote machine

For capturing data from a remote machine, perform the following actions:

1. Install the **pcap** driver on the remote machine. You can find it at `http://www.winpcap.org/` or install the entire Wireshark package instead.

2. For capturing data on the remote machine, choose **Options | Capture Interfaces | Manage Interfaces | Remote Interface**. The following window will open:

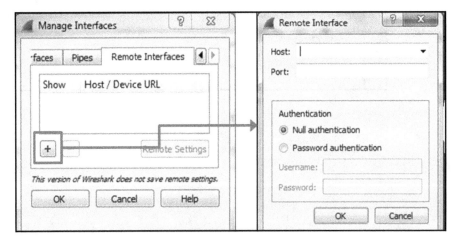

3. On the local machine:

- **Host name**: The IP address or host name of the remote machine
- **Port: 2002:** You can leave it open and it uses the default **2002**
- **Password authentication**: The username and password of the remote machine.

4. On the remote machine:

- Install WinPcap on the remote PCs that you want to collect data from. You can get it from `http://www.winpcap.org/`. You don't need to install Wireshark itself, only WinPcap.
- Configure the firewall is open to TCP port `2002` from your machine.
- On the remote PC, add a user to the PC user list, give it a password, and administrator privileges. You configure this from **Control Panel | Users Accounts and Family Safety | Add or remove user accounts | create a new account**.
- Right-click on the **Start** symbol down to the left of the Windows screen, choose **Open Windows Explorer**, right-click on **Computer**, and choose **Manage**. In the **Manage** window, open the services, as illustrated here:

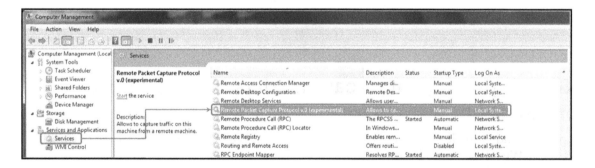

5. You will see the interface you have configured on the remote interfaces, and when you click on **OK**, you will also see it on the local interfaces' list. Now you can capture packets on it as if it was a local interface on your machine.

TIP

This feature can be useful when, for example, you monitor connectivity between your PC and a remote one, or even between two remote machines. When you implement it, you will see the packets that are living on the device; then you will see them arrive (or not!) at the other device, which is a very powerful tool.

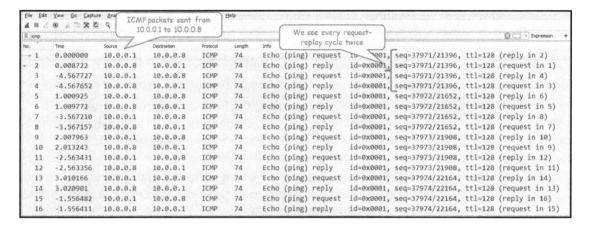

This file is attached as `Cap_B05518_01_01`.

Start capturing data – capture data on Linux/Unix machines

In Linux and Unix devices, we have the good old **TCPDUMP** utility, actually the command that the Wireshark came from.

For using **TCPDUMP**, you have the following commands (the most common ones):

- Capture packets on a specific interface:
    - Syntax is **tcpdump -i <interface_name>**
    - Example is **tcpdump -i eth0**
- Capture and save packets in a file:
    - Syntax is **tcpdump -w <file_name> -i <interface_name>**
    - Example is **tcpdump -w test001 -i eth1**

- Read captured packets' file:
  - Syntax is **tcpdump -r <file_name>**
  - Example is **tcpdump -r test001**

To use capture filters, use the capture filters format described in Chapter 3, *Using Capture Filters*.

Collecting from a remote communication device

In this section, we will describe how to capture data from remote communication equipment. Since there are many vendors that support this functionality, we will provide the general guidelines for this feature for some major vendors, along with links to their website, to get the exact configurations.

The general idea here is that there are some vendors that allow you to collect captured data locally, and then to download the capture file to an external computer.

For Cisco devices, this feature is called **Embedded Packet Capture** (**EPC**), and you can find how to do it in the following link: http://www.cisco.com/c/en/us/support/docs/ios-nx-os-software/ios-embedded-packet-capture/116045-productconfig-epc-00.html. In this link you can find how to configure the capture for Cisco IOS and IOS-XE operating systems.

For Juniper devices, the command is called monitor traffic, and you can find a detailed description of it at http://www.juniper.net/techpubs/en_US/junos14.1/topics/reference/command-summary/monitor-traffic.html.

For check point firewalls, you can use the utility fw monitor, explained in detail at http://dl3.checkpoint.com/paid/a4/How_to_use_FW_Monitor.pdf?HashKey=1415034974_a3bca5785be6cf8b4d627cfbc56abc97&xtn=.pdf.

For additional information, check out the specific vendors. Although capturing data on the LAN switch, router, firewall, or other communication devices and then downloading the file for analysis is usually not the preferred option, keep it in mind and remember that it is there if you need it.

How it works...

Here the answer is very simple. When Wireshark is connected to a wired or wireless network, there is a software driver that is located between the physical or wireless interface and the capture engine. In Windows, we have the WinPcap driver; in Unix platforms, we have the **Libpcap** driver; and for wireless interfaces, we have the **Airpcap** driver.

There's more...

In cases where the capture time is important, and you wish to capture data on one interface or more, and you want to be time-synchronized with the server you are monitoring, you can use **Network Time Protocol** (**NTP**) for this purpose, and synchronize your Wireshark and the monitored servers with a central time source.

This is important in cases where you want to go through the Wireshark capture file in parallel to a server log file, and look for events that are shown on both. For example, if you see retransmissions in the capture file at the same time as a server or application error on the monitored server, then you will know that the retransmissions are because of server errors and not because of the network.

The Wireshark software takes its time from the OS clock (Windows, Linux, and so on). To configure the OS to work with a time server, go to the relevant manuals of the operating system that you work with.

In Microsoft Windows 7, configure it as follows:

1. Go to **Control Panel**
2. Choose **Clock, Language, and Region**
3. Under **Date and Time**, Choose **Set the time and date**. Change to the **Internet time** tab
4. Click on the **Change Settings** button
5. Change the server name or IP address

 In Microsoft Windows 7 and later, there is a default setting for the time server. As long as all devices are tuned to it, you can use it like any other time server.

NTP is a network protocol used for time synchronization. When you configure your network devices (routers, switches, fws, and so on) and servers to the same time source, they will be time synchronized to this source. The accuracy of the synchronization depends on the accuracy of the time server that is measured in levels or stratum. The higher the level is, it will be more accurate. Level 1 is the highest. The higher the level, the lower the accuracy. Usually you will have level 2 to 4.

NTP was first standardized in RFC 1059 (NTPv1) and then in RFC 1119 (NTPv2). The common versions in the last few years are NTPv3 (RFC1305) and NTPv4 (RFC 5905).

You can get a list of NTP servers on various websites, some of them are:
`http://support.ntp.org/bin/view/Servers/StratumOneTimeServers` And `http://wpollock.com/AUnix2/NTPstratum1PublicServers.htm`

See also

You can get more information about the Pcap drivers from:

- For WinPcap visit: `http://www.winpcap.org`
- For Libpcap visit: `http://www.tcpdump.org`

Configuring the start window

In this recipe, we will see some basic configurations for the start window. We will talk about configuring the main window, file formats, and viewing options.

Getting ready

Start Wireshark, and you will get the start window. There are several parameters you can change here in order to adapt the capture window to your requirements:

- Toolbars configuration
- Main window configuration
- Time format configuration
- Name resolution

- Auto scroll in live capture
- Zoom
- Column configuration

First, let's have a look at the menu and the toolbars that are used by the software:

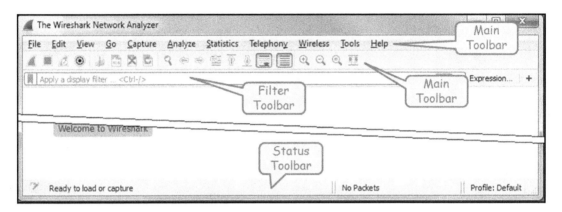

The main menu

Wireshark's main menu is located at the top of the main window. In the main toolbar you have the following symbols:

- **File**: File operations such as open and save file, export packets, print, and so on.
- **Edit**: To find packets, mark packets, add comments, and most importantly, use the preferences' submenu. This will be described in Chapter 2, *Mastering Wireshark for Network Troubleshooting*.
- **View**: For configuring Wireshark display, colorization of packets, zooming, font changes, showing a packet in a separate window, expanding and collapsing trees in packet details, and so on.
- **Go**: To go to a specific packet, for example, to the first packet in the capture, the last packet, a packet number, and so on.
- **Capture**: To configure capture options and capture filters.
- **Analyze**: For analysis and display options like display filter configuration, decode options, to follow a specific stream, and so on.

- **Statistics**: To show statistics, starting from the basic hosts and conversations statistics up to the smart IO graphs and stream graphs.
- **Telephony**: For displaying IP telephony and cellular protocols information, for example, RTP and RTCP, SIP flows and statistics, GSM or LTE protocols, and so on.
- **Wireless**: For showing Bluetooth and IEEE 802.11 wireless statistics, later described in Chapter 9, *Wireless LAN*.
- **Tools**: For Lua operations as described in Appendix 4, *Lua programming*.
- **Help**: For user assistance, sample capture updates, and so on.

The main toolbar

The main toolbar provides quick access to frequently used items from the menu. This toolbar can be hidden using the **View** menu.

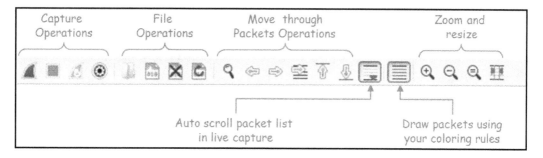

The four left-most symbols are for capture operations, then you have symbols for file operations, *go to packet* operations, auto-scroll, draw packets using coloring rules, zoom and resize.

Display filter toolbar

In the filters toolbar, you have the following symbols:

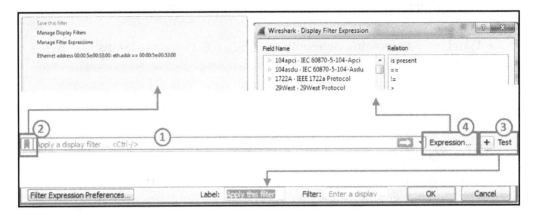

In the display filter toolbar we can:

- Type in a display filter string, with auto complete while showing us previously configured filters
- Manage filter expressions that allow you to bring up filter construction dialog for filter construction assistance
- Configure a new filter and add it to the preferences
- Use filter predefined expressions, and choose a filter

An enhanced description of splay filters is provided in `Chapter 4`, *Using Display Filters*.

Status bar

In the status bar, at the lower side of the Wireshark window, you can see the following data:

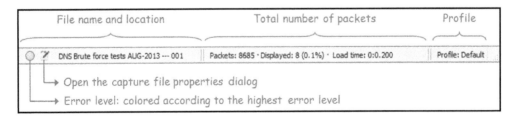

You can see here:

- Any errors in the expert system.
- The **Capture** file properties, including file information, capture time, time and general statistics.
- The name of the captured file (during capture, it will show you a temporary name assigned by the software).
- Total number of captured packets, displayed packets (those which are actually displayed on the screen), and load time, that is, the time it took to load the capture file.
- The profile you work with. For more information of profiles, you can read Chapter 2, *Mastering Wireshark for Network Troubleshooting*.

How to do it...

In this part, we will go step by step and configure the main menu.

Toolbars configuration

Usually for regular packet capture, you don't have to change anything. This is different when you want to capture wireless data over the network (not only from your laptop); you will have to enable the wireless toolbar, and this is done by clicking on it under the view menu, as shown in the following screenshot:

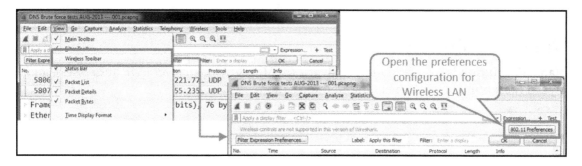

Wireless toolbar

When marking the **Wireless Toolbar** option in the **View** menu, the wireless toolbar opens. The only option available in the current version is to start the preferences' configuration window. There is more about Wireless LAN analysis in Chapter 9, *Wireless LAN*.

Main window configuration

To configure the main menu for capturing, you can configure Wireshark to show the following windows:

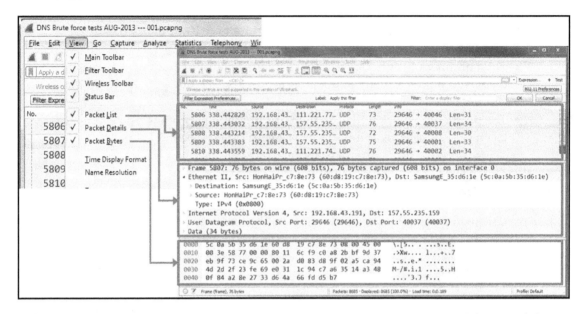

In most of the cases, you will not need to change anything. In some cases, when you don't need to see the packet bytes, you can cancel them, and you will get more space for the packet list and details.

Name resolution

Name Resolution is the translation of layer 2 (MAC addresses), layer 3 (IP addresses), and layer 4 (port numbers) into meaningful information.

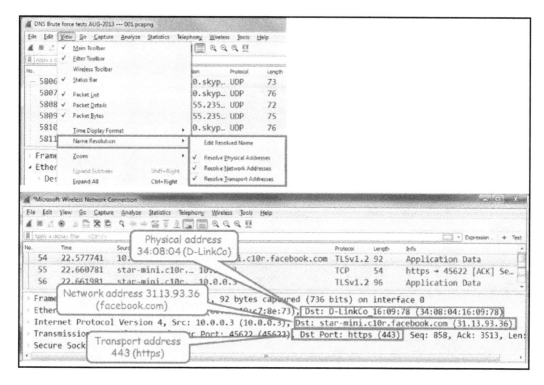

Name Resolution

In the screenshot, we see that the MAC address **34:08:04:16:09:78** (from **D-Link**), the website (that is, `www.facebook.com`), and the HTTPs port number (that is 443).

The MAC address is the most simple translation: Wireshark look at the translation table (stored in `.manuf` file under the Wireshark directory). IP addresses are translated using DNS, and as described earlier in this chapter can cause some performance issues. TCP/UDP port numbers are stored in the **Services** file under the Wireshark directory.

Colorize packet list

Usually you start a capture in order to establish a baseline profile of what normal traffic looks like on your network. During the capture, you look at the captured data and you might find a TCP connection, IP, or Ethernet connectivity that are suspects, and you'll want to see them in another color.

To do so, right-click on the packet that belongs to the conversation you want to color, choose Ethernet, IP, or TCP/UDP (TCP or UDP will appear depending on the packet), and choose the color for the conversation.

In the example, you see that we want to color a TCP conversation.

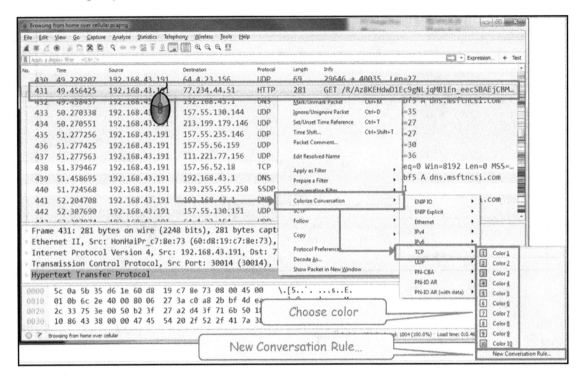

Colorize Conversation

To cancel the coloring rule:

1. Go to the **View** menu
2. In the lower part of the menu, choose **Colorize Conversation** and then **Reset Colorization** or simply click on *Ctrl* + space bar

Zoom

As you see in the following screenshot, for zooming in and out:

1. Go to the **View** menu
2. Click on **Zoom In** on the main toolbar or press *Ctrl++* to zoom in
3. Click on **Zoom Out** on the main toolbar or press *Ctrl +-* to zoom out

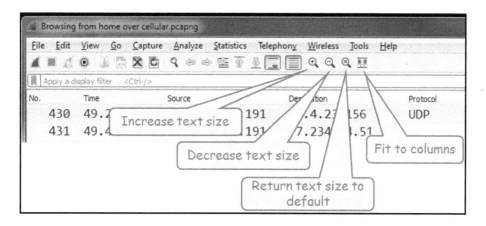

Mastering Wireshark for Network Troubleshooting

2

In this chapter, you will learn about the following:

- Configuring the user interface, and global and protocol preferences
- Importing and exporting files
- Configuring coloring rules and navigation techniques
- Using time values and summaries
- Building profiles for troubleshooting

Introduction

In this chapter, we cover issues that improve the use of Wireshark as a network analysis tool. We start with configuring the user interface, and setting global and protocol preferences. Next, we talk about Wireshark folders, configuration files, and folders and plugins.

We continue with coloring rules and how to configure them. We also talk about the intelligent scrollbar added to Wireshark Version 2, which can be used for traffic patterns and behavior recognition.

We close this chapter with profiles and how to use them. Profiles are sets of display and capture filters, coloring rules, and preferences set for a specific environment, protocols or networking issues that are previously configured to ease network troubleshooting. Profiles are explained, along with helpful profiles that are attached to this book.

Configuring the user interface, and global and protocol preferences

The **Preferences** menu enables us to adapt the display to the way we want to see it, and configuring protocol preferences provides us with the ability to change the way that Wireshark captures and presents common protocols. In this recipe, we will learn how to configure the most common protocols.

Getting ready

Go to **Preferences** in the **Edit** menu, and you will see the following window:

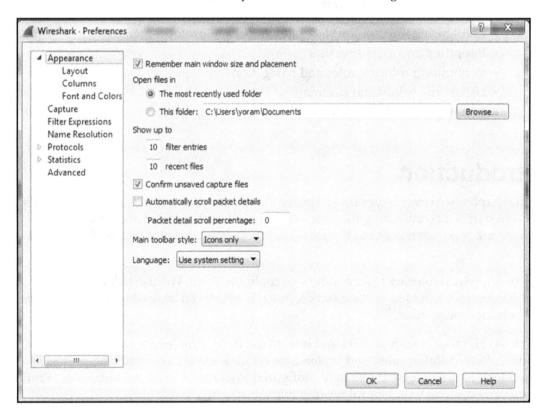

In the **Preferences** window, we have menus from which we choose what we want to configure, while the configuration parameters appear on the right.

How to do it...

In this recipe, we talk about the appearance preferences, along with protocol preferences for the most common protocols. Additional preference configurations will be provided in the relevant chapters later in this book.

Since this book is about recipes to work with and improve the way the reader uses Wireshark for network analysis, we will not talk about all the features of Wireshark. I will leave the simple features for the great manual on the Wireshark website, and focus on the important and special ones that can actually improve the use of the software.

Let's start focusing on the preferences and see how they can help us.

General appearance preferences

In the following screenshot, we see some helpful features that we can configure in the **Preferences** window:

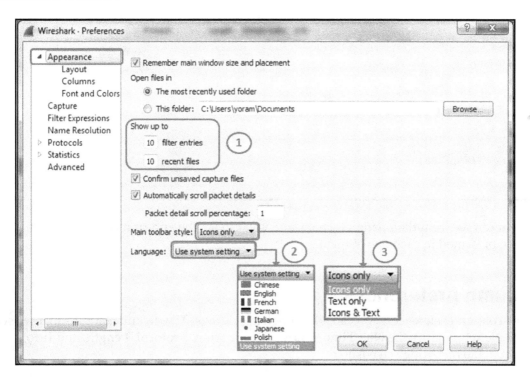

Here, we can configure:

- The size of the display filters and the recent file buffers
- The interface language (more languages will be provided in future versions)
- The main toolbar style—icons, text or icons, and text

Layout preferences

In the layout preferences, you simply set the way that you want Wireshark to present the **Packet Lists**, **Packet Details**, and **Packet Bytes**:

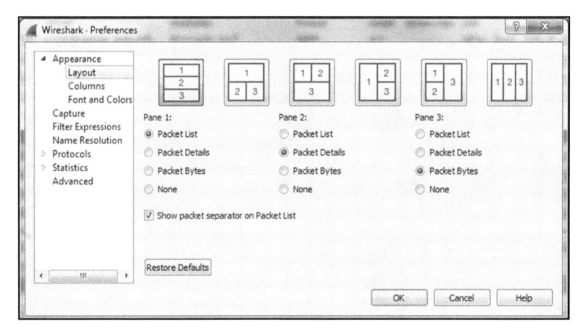

As you can see from the previous screenshot, you can set the appearance of panes and what will be presented in each one of them.

Column preferences

In the column preferences, you can add or delete columns. The default columns that we see in the packet pane are the **No.**, **Time**, **Source**, **Destination**, **Protocol**, **Length**, and **Info**, shown in the following screenshot:

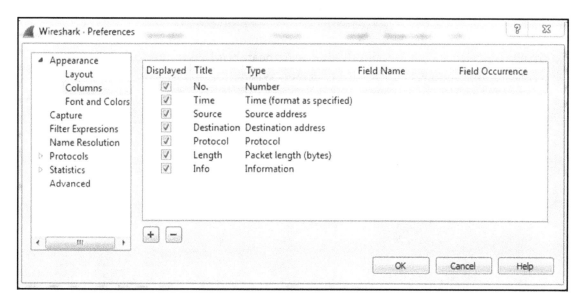

To add a new column to the packet pane:

- You can configure one of the predefined parameters in the **Field Name** to be added as a new column. Among these fields are time delta, IP DSCP value, port numbers, and others.
- A very important feature comes up when you fill in **Custom** in the field type. In this case, you can fill in any filter string for **Field Name**. You can, for example, add the following:
    - Add the string `tcp.window_size` to view the TCP window size (which influences performance)
    - Add the string `ip.ttl` to view the IP **time-to-live** (**TTL**) parameter of every packet
    - Add `rtp.marker` to view every time a marker is set in an RTP packet

To apply a column, you can also choose a field in a packet in the **Packet Details** pane, right-click, and choose **Apply as Column**. The column will be added to the **Packet List** pane.

As we will see in later chapters, this feature will assist us in the fast resolution of network problems.

Font and color preferences

To change font size and shape, simply choose **Appearance** | **Font and Colors** and change the **Main window font**, as you see in the next screenshot:

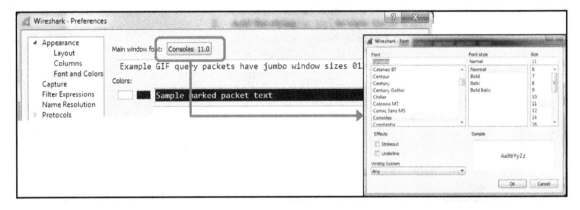

Appearance | Font and Colors

In case you forget how to get back to the default, the default font is Consolas, size 11.0, normal.

Capture preferences

In capture preferences, you can set the default interface to the one that you most commonly use:

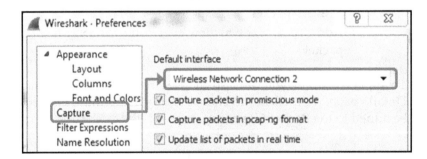

In the previous screenshot, the interface is set to **Wireless Network Connection 2**. Leave all the checkboxes as they are.

Filter expression preferences

In filter expressions, you configure which filter expressions will appear at the right-hand side of the display filters bar at the top of the screen.

To configure display filter expressions, follow these steps:

1. Click on the **Edit** menu and choose **Preferences** and **Filter Expressions**. The following window will come up:

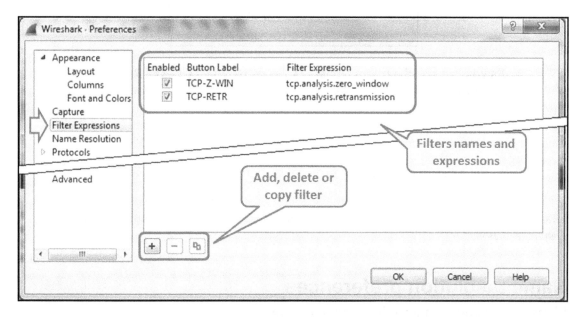

2. Choose Add and configure the **Button Label** and the **Filter Expression**.

3. As you can see in the following screenshot, the **Button Label** will appear at the right-hand side of the display filters bar:

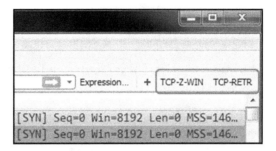

4. As you can see, the filters named **TCP-Z-WIN** and **TCP-RETR** that we have configured in the filters preferences appear in the top-right corner of Wireshark.

 We can configure filter preferences per profile, as described in the *Building profiles for troubleshooting* recipe later in this chapter. By doing so, we can configure profiles for TCP problems, **IP Telephony** (**IPT**) problems, and so on, where each network protocol is configured with their appropriate profile.

Filters should be configured in display filter format, as described in Chapter 4, *Using Display Filters*.

Name resolution preferences

Wireshark supports name resolution in three layers:

- **Layer 2**: By resolving the first part of the MAC address to the vendor name. For example, 14:da:e9 will be presented as AsusTeckC (ASUSTeK Computer Inc.).
- **Layer 3**: By resolving IP addresses to the DNS names. For example, 157.166.226.46 will be resolved to www.edition.cnn.com.
- **Layer 4**: By resolving TCP/UDP port numbers to port names. For example, port 80 will be resolved as HTTP, and port 53 as DNS.

In the following screenshot, you can see how to configure name resolution in the
Preferences window:

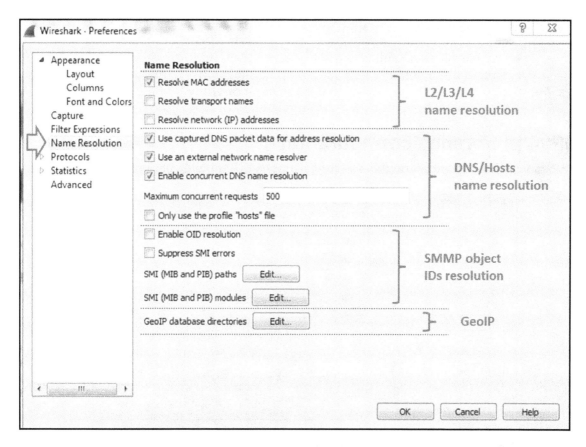

In this window, you can configure, from top to bottom:

- Layer 2, 3, and 4 name resolution.
- How to perform name resolution: by DNS and/or hosts file, and what the
  maximum number of concurrent DNS requests is (so the software will not be
  overloaded).
- **Simple Network Management Protocol** (**SNMP**), object identifiers, IDs, and
  whether we want to translate them to object names.
- GeoIP and whether we want to use it. For further information about this, see
  Chapter 10, *Network Layer Protocols and Operations*.

In TCP and UDP, there is a meaning only to the destination port that the client initially opens the connection. The source port that the connection is opened from is a random number (higher than 1,024) and therefore there is no meaning to its translation to a port name.

- The Wireshark default is to resolve layer 2 MAC addresses and layer 4 TCP/UDP port numbers. Resolving IP addresses can slow down Wireshark due to the large amount of DNS queries that it uses, so use it carefully.

IPv4 preference configuration

When you choose to configure IPv4 or IPv6 parameters, you will get the following window:

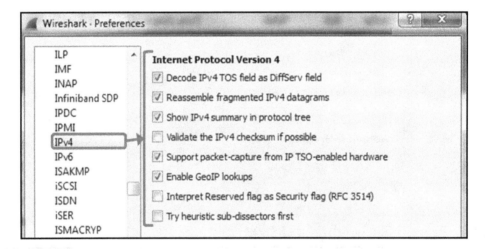

The parameters that you need to change are:

- **Decode IPv4 TOS field as DiffServ field**: The original IP protocol came out with a field called **Type Of Service** (**TOS**) for enabling IP quality of service through the network. In the early 1990s, the **Differentiated Services** (**DiffServ**) standard changed the way that an IP device looks in this field. Unchecking this checkbox will show this field as in the original IP standard.
- **Enable GeoIP lookups**: GeoIP is a database that enables Wireshark to present IP addresses as geographical locations. Enabling this feature in IPv4 and IPv6 will enable this presentation. This feature involves name resolutions and can therefore slow down packet capture in real time. You can see how to configure GeoIP in Chapter 10, *Network Layer Protocols and Operations*.

TCP and UDP configuration

In UDP, there is not much to change; it is a very simple protocol, with a very simple configuration. In TCP, on the other hand, there are some parameters that can be changed:

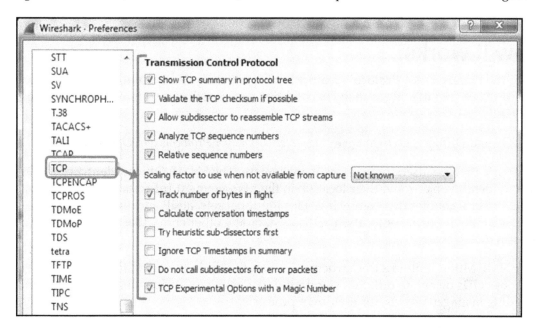

Most of the changes you can make in the TCP preferences are in the way that Wireshark dissects the captured data:

- **Validate the TCP checksum if possible**: In some NICs, you may see many checksum errors. This is due to the fact that TCP checksum offloading is often implemented on NICs. The problem here might be that the NIC actually adds the checksum after Wireshark captures the packet, so if you see many TCP checksum errors, the first thing to do will be to disable this checkbox and verify that this is not the problem.
- **Analyze TCP sequence numbers**: This checkbox must be checked so Wireshark can provide TCP analysis, which is one of its main and most important features.
- **Relative sequence numbers**: When TCP opens a connection, it starts from a random sequence number. When this checkbox is checked, Wireshark will normalize it to zero, so what you will see are not the real numbers, but numbers starting from zero and climbing. In most cases, relative numbers are much easier to handle.

- **Calculate conversation timestamps**: When checking this checkbox, the TCP dissector will show you, in every packet, the time since the beginning of the connection. This can be helpful in cases with a very fast connection when times are critical.

How it works...

Using the **Preferences | Protocols** feature adds more analysis capabilities to Wireshark. Just be careful here not to add too many capabilities, as that will slow down packet capture and analysis.

For TOS and DiffServ, go to `Chapter 10`, *Network Layer Protocols and Operations.*

SNMP is a protocol used for network management. The SNMP **Object Identifier** (**OID**) is used to identify objects and their location in the **Management Information Base** (**MIB**). An object can be a counter that counts interface input packets, an IP address of a router interface, a device name or location, CPU load, or any other entity that can be presented or measured.

The SNMP MIB is built in a tree structure, as you can see in the next diagram. Top-level MIB object IDs belong to different standard organizations. Vendors define private branches, including managed objects, for their own products:

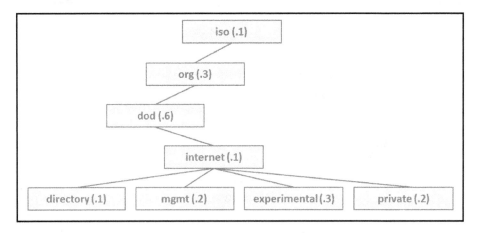

When resolving SNMP MIB, Wireshark shows not only the object ID, but also its name, which helps to understand the monitored data.

There's more...

Concerning GeoIP, go to `http://wiki.wireshark.org/HowToUseGeoIP` for further instructions.

Importing and exporting files

It is quite common to see a need to share the packet capture file with other operational teams or the vendor for root cause analysis. Such capture files may have a lot of packets, while our interest is in only a specific flow or a set of packets. Instead of sharing the entire file, Wireshark allows you to selectively export the packets into a new file, or even modify the format for easier file transportation. In this recipe, we will discuss the import and export options available in Wireshark.

Getting ready

Start Wireshark or open a saved file.

How to do it...

We save or export data as follows.

Exporting an entire or partial file

We can save a whole file or export specific data in various formats and various file types. In the following paragraphs, we will see how to do this.

To save a whole file of captured data, do the following:

- In the **File** menu, click on **Save** (or press *Ctrl* + *S*) to save the file under its current name
- In the **File** menu, click on **Save as** (or press *Shift* + *Ctrl* + *S*) to save the file under a new name

To save a part of a file, for example only displayed data, do the following:

- Navigate to **Export Specified Packets** under the **File** menu. You will get the following window:

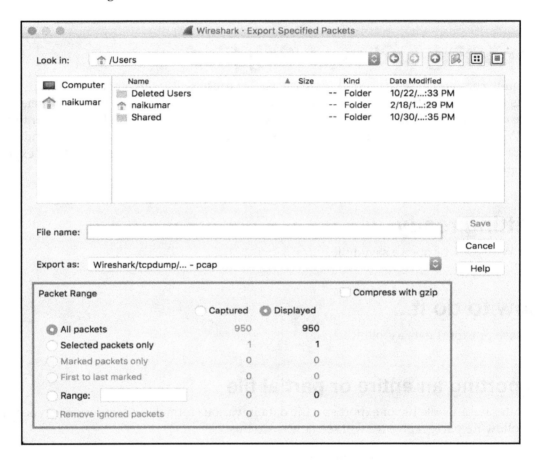

In the bottom-left area of the window, you will see that you can choose which part of the data you want to save:

- To save all the captured data, select **All packets** and **Captured**.
- To save only displayed data, choose **All packets** and **Displayed**.
- To save selected packets from the file (a selected packet is simply a packet that you clicked on), choose **Selected packets only**.

- To save marked packets, that is, packets that were marked by right-clicking on them in the packet list window, choose **Marked packets only** (toggle) from the menu.
- To save packets between two marked packets, select the **First to last marked** option.
- To save a range of packets, select **Range** and specify the range of packets you want to save.
- In the packet list window, you can choose manually to ignore a packet. In the export window you can choose to ignore these packets and not to save them.

To compress the saved file, check **Compress with gzip**.

In all the options mentioned, you can choose the packets from the entire captured file, or from the packets displayed on the screen (packets displayed on the packet list after a display filter has been applied).

Saving data in various formats

You can save the data captured by Wireshark in various formats for further analysis with other tools.

By choosing **Export Packet Dissections** from the **File** menu, you can save the file in the following formats:

- **Plain text (*.txt)**: Export packet data into a plaintext ASCII file.
- **PostScript (*.ps)**: Export packet data into PostScript format.
- **Comma separated values (*.csv)**: Export packet summary into CSV file format, for use with spreadsheet programs (such as Microsoft Excel).
- **C arrays to packet bytes (*.c)**: Export packet bytes into C arrays so that they can be imported by C programs.
- **PSML (*.psml)**: Export packet data into PSML, an XML-based format, including only the packet summary.
- **PDML (*.pdml)**: Export packet data into PDM, an XML-based format, including the packet details.

Printing data

In order to print the data, click on the **Print** button from the **File** menu, and you will get the following window:

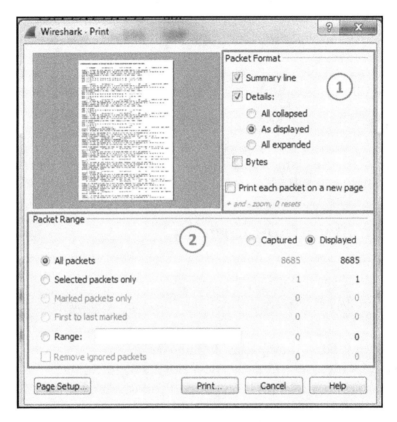

In the **Print** window, you have the following choices:

- In the upper-right part of the window, you choose the file format to be printed. It can be:
  - Only a summary line for every packet. This is what you get from the **Packet List** pane.
  - Packet details. This prints the entire details of the packet, as provided in the **Packet Details** pane.
  - Packet bytes, which you get from the **Packet Bytes** pane.

- In the lower part of the window, you choose what packets to print, as describe in the previous section.

How it works...

The data can be printed in text format, PostScript (for PostScript-aware printers), or to a file. After configuring this window and clicking on print, the regular printing interface will appear and you can choose the printer.

There's more...

To find out what folders Wireshark is stored in, simply choose **Help** from the main menu, then choose **About Wireshark**, and in the window that opens, choose the **Folders** tab. As you can see in the next screenshot, you will see the actual folders that files are stored in, and on the right you can see typical files that are stored in these folders:

Wireshark	Authors	Folders	Plugins	Keyboard Shortcuts	License

Name	Location	Typical Files
"File" dialogs	C:\Technical\Wireshark\CAP-PCAP Customers\	capture files
Temp	C:\Users\yoram\AppData\Local\Temp	untitled capture files
Personal configuration	C:\Users\yoram\AppData\Roaming\Wireshark\	*dfilters, preferences, ethers, ..*
Global configuration	C:\Program Files\Wireshark	*dfilters, preferences, manuf, ..*
System	C:\Program Files\Wireshark	*ethers, ipxnets*
Program	C:\Program Files\Wireshark	program files
Personal Plugins	C:\Users\yoram\AppDat...ing\Wireshark\plugins	dissector plugins
Global Plugins	C:\Program Files\Wireshark\plugins\2.0.2	dissector plugins
Extcap path	C:\Program Files\Wireshark\extcap	Extcap Plugins search path

Clicking on a location will bring us to the folder in which those files are stored.

Configuring coloring rules and navigation techniques

Coloring rules define how Wireshark will color protocols and events in the captured data. Working with the coloring rules will help you a lot with network troubleshooting, since you are able to see different protocols in different colors, and you can also configure different colors for different events.

Coloring rules enable you to configure new coloring rules according to various filters. It will help you to configure different coloring schemes for different scenarios and save them in different profiles. In this way, you can configure coloring rules for resolving TCP issues, rules for resolving SIP and telephony problems, and so on.

 You can configure Wireshark profiles in order to save a Wireshark configuration, for example predefined colors, filters, and so on. To do so, navigate to **Configuration Profiles** from the **Edit** menu.

Getting ready

To start with the coloring rules, proceed as follows:

1. Go to the **View** menu.
2. In the lower part of the menu, choose **Coloring Rules**. You will get the following window:

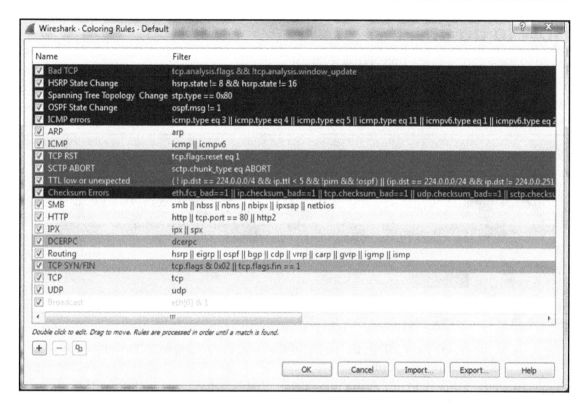

In this window, we see the default coloring rules that we have in Wireshark, including rules for TCP and other protocol events, routing packets, and others.

How to do it...

To go to the coloring rules, proceed as follows:

- For a new coloring rule, click on the new tab, and you will get the following window:

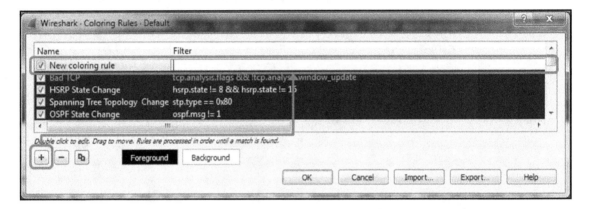

- In the **Name** field, fill in the name of the rule. For example, fill in NTP for the network time protocol.
- In the **Filter** field, fill in the filter string, that is, what you want the rule to show (we will talk about display filters in Chapter 4, *Using Display Filters*).
- Click on the **Foreground** button and choose the foreground color for the rule. This will be the foreground color of the packet in the packet list.
- Click on the **Background** button and choose the background color for the rule. This will be the background color of the packet in the packet list.
- Click on the Delete icon (the minus sign to the left of the plus sign) to delete a coloring rule.
- Click on the Duplicate icon (to the right of the minus button) if you want to edit an existing rule.
- You can also click on the **Import...** button to import an existing color scheme, or click on the **Export...** rule to export the current scheme.

There is an importance to the order of the coloring rules. Make sure that the coloring rules are in the order of implementation. For example, application layer protocols should come before TCP or UDP, so Wireshark will color them in their color and not the regular TCP or UDP color.

How it works...

Like many operations in Wireshark, you can configure various operations on data that is filtered. The coloring rules mechanism simply applies a coloring rule to a predefined filter.

See also

- You can find various types of coloring schemes at `http://wiki.wireshark.org/ColoringRules`, along with many other examples in a simple internet search
- To use one of the coloring rule files listed here, download it to your local machine, select **View | Coloring Rules** in Wireshark, and click the **Import...** button

Using time values and summaries

Time format configuration is about how the time column (second from the left in the default configuration) will be presented. In some scenarios, there is an importance given to this, for example, in TCP connections where you want to see time intervals between packets, or when you capture data from several sources and you want to see the exact time of every packet.

Getting ready

To configure the time format, go to the **View** menu, and under **Time Display Format**, you will get the following window:

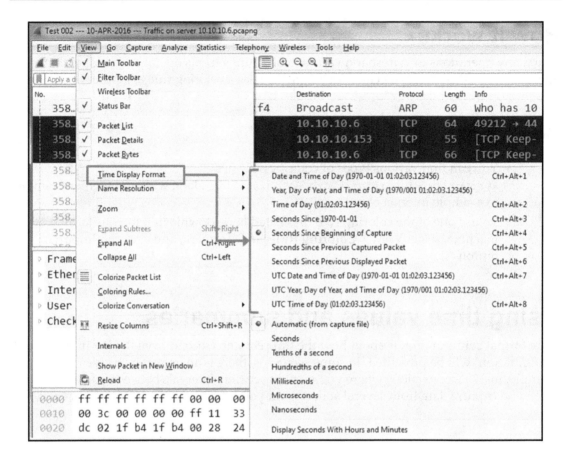

How to do it...

You can choose from the following options:

- **Date and Time of Day**: This will be good to configure when you troubleshoot a network with time-dependent events, for example, when you know about an event that happens at specific times, and you want to look at what happens on the network at the same time.

- **Seconds Since...**: Time in seconds since January 1, 1970. Epoch is an arbitrary date chosen as a reference time for a system, and January 1, 1970 was chosen for Unix and Unix-like systems.

- **Seconds Since Beginning of Capture**: The default configuration.

- **Seconds Since Previous Captured Packet**: This is also a common feature that enables you to see time differences between packets. This can be useful when monitoring time-sensitive traffic such as TCP connections, live video streaming, VoIP calls, and so on when time differences between packets is important.
- **Seconds Since Previous Displayed Packet**: This is a useful feature that can be used when you configure a display filter, and only a selected part of the captured data is presented (for example, a TCP stream). In this case, you will see the time difference between packets, which can be important in some applications.
- **UTC Date and Time of Day**: Provides relative UTC time.

The lower part of the submenu provides the format of the time display. Change it only if a more accurate measurement is required.

You can use also *Ctrl + Alt +* any numbered digit key on the keyboard for the various options.

How it works...

This is quite simple. Wireshark works on the system clock and presents the time as it is in the system. By default, you see the time since the beginning of the capture.

Building profiles for troubleshooting

You can configure Wireshark profiles in order to save Wireshark configuration, for example by setting predefined colors, capture and display filters, and so on. To do so, navigate to **Configuration Profiles** from the **Edit** menu.

Configuration profiles store the following information:

- Preferences, including general and protocol preferences, for example pane sizes, text size and font, column width, and so on
- Capture filters
- Display filters and display filter macros (see `Chapter 4`, *Using Display Filters*)
- Coloring rules
- Customized HTTP, IMF, and LDAP headers (see `Chapter 12`, *FTP, HTTP1, and HTTP2*)
- User-defined decodes, for example a decode as a functionality that enables you to temporarily divert specific protocol dissections

All profiles are saved in the `profiles` directory.

Getting ready

Start Wireshark and open a saved file or start a new capture.

How to do it...

To open an existing profile:

1. Click on **Profile** in the bottom-right of the status bar, and choose the profile you wish to work with:

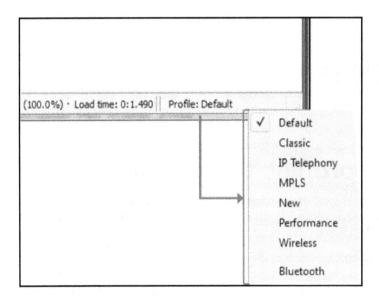

2. Choose **Edit | Configuration profiles** and choose the profile you wish to work with:

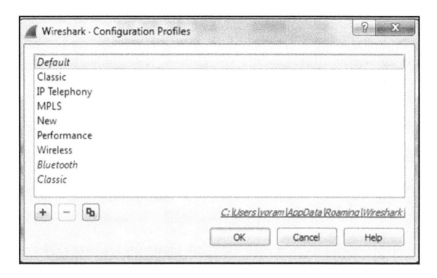

To create a new profile:

1. Right-click on the profile area in the status bar, in the bottom-right corner of the Wireshark window, and choose **New**, or choose **Edit | Configuration profiles** and choose **New**.

2. A new directory will be created in the `profiles` directory:

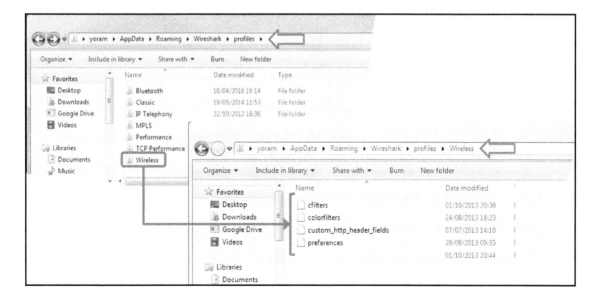

3. In the profile directory, in this example the `Wireless` profile, we have the `cfilter` file, which holds the capture filters; the `colorfilters` file, which holds the coloring rules; the `custom_http_header_fields`, which holds HTTP field configuration; and the `preferences` file, which holds the preference configuration.

How it works...

When you create a new profile, a folder with your profile name is created under `profiles` in your personal configuration directory. When you close Wireshark or load another profile, a file called `recent` is placed in your new profile directory. This file contains the general Wireshark window settings, such as visible toolbars, timestamp display, zoom level, and column widths. If you create capture filters, display filters, and coloring rules while working in a custom profile, additional files will be created and stored in your custom profile's directory (`cfilters`, `dfilters`, and `colorfilters`, respectively).

There's more...

As we saw in the previous section, the files that hold the profile parameters are located in the profile directory. You can of course copy parameters from one profile to another; for example, in the default performance file, you have these filters:

```
####### Filter Expressions ########
gui.filter_expressions.label: SIP
gui.filter_expressions.enabled: FALSE
gui.filter_expressions.expr: sip
gui.filter_expressions.label: RTP
gui.filter_expressions.enabled: FALSE
gui.filter_expressions.expr: rtp
```

If you need one of these filters in another profile, simply copy it to the same file in the profile directory that you need it in.

See also

- Specific profiles will be brought up later in the book, in the relevant chapters. A TCP performance troubleshooting profile will be shown in Chapter 11, *Transport Layer Protocol Analysis*, a wireless LAN analysis profile in Chapter 9, *Wireless LAN*, and so on.

Using Capture Filters 3

In this chapter, we will cover the following topics:

- Configuring capture filters
- Configuring Ethernet filters
- Configuring host and network filters
- Configuring TCP/UDP and port filters
- Configuring structured filters
- Configuring byte offset and payload matching filters

Introduction

In the first and second chapters, we talked about how to install Wireshark, how to configure it for basic and smart operations, and where to locate it on the network. In this chapter and the next one, we will talk about capture filters and display filters.

It is important to distinguish between these two types of filters:

- Capture filters are configured before we start to capture data, so only data that is approved by the filters will be captured. All other data will be lost. These filters are described in this chapter.
- Display filters are filters that filter data after it has been captured. In this case, all data is captured and you configure what data you wish to display. These filters are described in the next chapter.

Capture filters are based on the `tcpdump` syntax presented in the `libpcap/WinPcap` library, while the display filters syntax was presented some years later. Therefore, keep in mind that the display and capture filters have different syntaxes!

In some cases, you need to configure Wireshark to capture only a part of the data that it sees over the interface:

- When there is a large amount of data running over the monitored link and you want to capture only the data you care about
- When you want to capture data only going into and out of a specific server on a VLAN that you monitor
- When you want to capture data only from a specific application or applications (for example, you suspect that there is a DNS problem in the network and you want to analyze only DNS queries and responses to and from the internet)

There are many other cases where you want to capture only specific data and not everything that runs on your network. When using the capture filters, only predefined data will be captured and all other packets will be ignored, so you will get only the desired data.

Be careful when using capture filters. In many cases on a network, there are dependencies between different applications and servers that you are not always aware of; so, when you use Wireshark with capture filters for troubleshooting a network, make sure that you don't filter out some of the connections that causes inaccurate information. A common and simple example of this is to filter only traffic on TCP port 80 for monitoring suspected slow HTTP responses, while the problem could be due to a slow or non-responsive DNS server that is not easily noticeable.

In this chapter, we will describe how to configure simple, structured, byte offset and payload matching capture filters.

Configuring capture filters

We recommend that before configuring a capture filter, you carefully design what you want to capture, and prepare your filter for this. Don't forget—what doesn't pass the filter will be lost.

There are some Wireshark predefined filters that you can use, or you can configure it yourself as described in the next section.

Getting ready

To configure capture filters, open Wireshark, and follow the steps in the recipe.

How to do it...

To configure capture filters before starting with the capture, go through the following steps:

1. To configure a capture filter, click on the Capture options button, fourth from the left, as shown in the following screenshot:

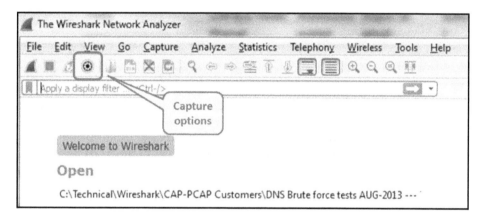

2. The **Wireshark - Capture Interfaces** window will open, as you can see in the following screenshot:

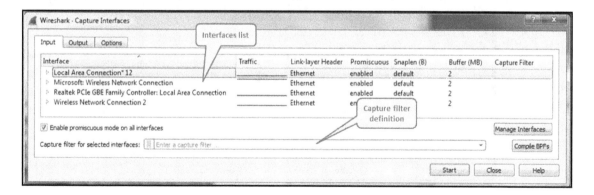

3. Mark the interface you want to capture, and in the **Capture filter for selected interfaces** fill in the filter expression you want to use (you can verify which interface is the active one, as described in Chapter 1, *Introduction to Wireshark Version 2*). As you see in the following screenshot, the filter expression that you wrote will appear in the interface line. In this example, tcp port http will capture all packets with TCP port 80:

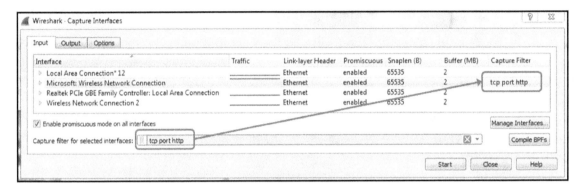

4. After configuring the filter, and making sure the filter box becomes green, indicating the filter string is a legal one, click on the **Start** button and the capture will start.

To configure a predefined filter, see the following steps:

1. To configure a predefined capture filter, choose **Capture Filters...** from the **Capture** menu:

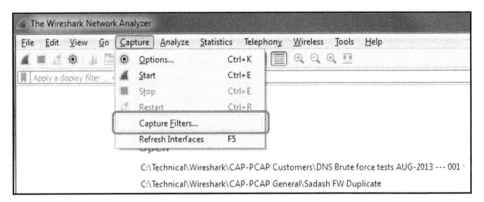

The following window will open:

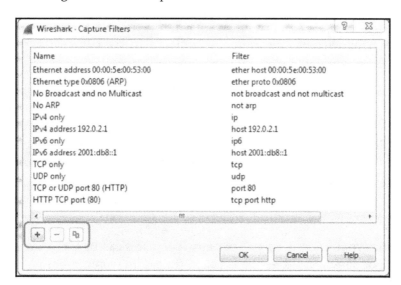

2. In this window you can add, delete, or copy.

How it works...

The **Wireshark - Capture Filters** window enables you to configure filters according to **Berkeley Packet Filter** (**BPF**). After writing a filter string, you can click on the **Compile BPF** button, and the BPF compiler will check your syntax, and if it's wrong you will get an error message.

In addition to this, when you type a filter string in the capture filter textbox, if the filter string is correct, it will become green, and if not, it will become red.

The BPF filter only checks if the syntax is right. It does not check if the condition is correct. For example, if you type the string `host` without any parameters, you will get an error and the string will become red, but if you type `host 192.168.1.1000` it will pass and the window will become green.

BPF is a syntax from the paper *The BSD Packet Filter: A New Architecture for User-level Packet Capture* by Steven McCanne and Van Jacobson from the Lawrence Berkeley Laboratory at Berkeley University from December 1992. The document can be seen at:

`http://www.tcpdump.org/papers/bpf-usenix93.pdf`.

Capture filters are made out of a string containing a filtering expression. This expression selects the packets that will be captured and the packets that will be ignored. Filter expressions consist of one or more primitives. Primitives usually consist of an identifier (name or number) followed by one or more qualifiers. There are three different kinds of qualifiers:

- **Type**: These qualifiers say what kind of thing the identifier name or number refers to. Possible types are `host` for hostname or address, `net` for network, `port` for TCP/UDP port, and so on.
- **Dir (direction)**: These qualifiers specify a particular transfer direction to and/or from ID. For example, `src` indicates source, `dst` indicates destination, and so on.
- **Proto (protocol)**: These are the qualifiers that restrict the match to a particular protocol. For example, `ether` for Ethernet, `ip` for internet protocol, `arp` for address resolution protocol, and so on.

Identifiers are the actual conditions that we test. Identifiers can be the address `10.0.0.1`, port number `53`, or network address `192.168.1` (this is an identifier for network `192.168.1.0/24`).

For example, in the filter `tcp dstport 135`, we have:

- `dst` is the dir qualifier
- `port` is the type qualifier
- `tcp` is the proto qualifier

There's more...

You can configure different capture filters on different interfaces:

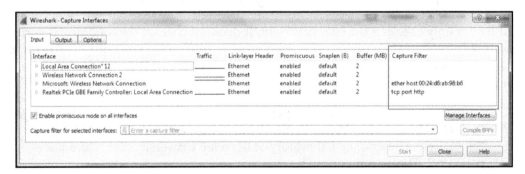

This can be used when you capture traffic on two interfaces of a device and want to check for different packets on the two sides.

The capture filters are stored in a file named `cfilters` in the `Wireshark` directory. In this file you will find the predefined filters, along with the filters you have configured, and you will be able to copy the file to other computers. The location of this directory will change depending on how Wireshark is installed and on what platform.

See also

- Wireshark's capture filters are based on the `tcpdump` program. You can find the reference at: `http://www.tcpdump.org/tcpdump_man.html`.
- You can also find helpful information on the Wireshark manual pages at: `http://wiki.wireshark.org/CaptureFilters`.

Configuring Ethernet filters

When talking about Ethernet filters, we refer to layer 2 filters that are MAC address-based filters. In this recipe, we will refer to these filters and what we can do with them.

Getting ready

The basic layer 2 filters are:

- `ether host <Ethernet host>`: To get the Ethernet address
- `ether dst <Ethernet host>`: To get the Ethernet destination address
- `ether src <Ethernet host>`: To get the Ethernet source address
- `ether broadcast`: To capture all Ethernet broadcast packets
- `ether multicast`: To capture all Ethernet multicast packets
- `ether proto <protocol>`: To filter only the protocol type indicated in the protocol identifier
- `vlan <vlan_id>`: To pass only packets from a specific VLAN that is indicated in the identifier field

For negating a filter rule, simply type the word `not` or `!` in front of the primitive. For example:

`Not ether host <Ethernet host>` or `! ether host <Ethernet host>` will capture packets that are not from/to the Ethernet address specified in the identifier field.

How to do it...

Let's look at the following diagram, in which we have a server, PCs, and a router, connected to a LAN switch. Wireshark is running on the laptop connected to the LAN switch, with port mirror to the entire switch (to VLAN1).

The `/24` notation in the diagram refers to a subnet mask of 24 bits, that is, `11111111.11111111.11111111.00000000` in binary or `255.255.255.0` in decimal:

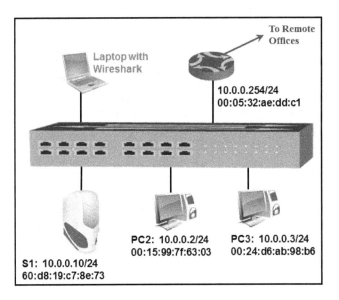

Follow the instructions in the *Configuring capture filters* recipe, and configure the filters as follows:

- To capture packets only from/to a specific MAC address, configure `ether host 00:24:d6:ab:98:b6`.
- To capture packets going to a destination MAC address, configure `ether dst 00:24:d6:ab:98:b6`.

- To capture packets coming from a source MAC address, configure `ether src 00:24:d6:ab:98:b6`.
- To capture broadcast packets, configure `ether broadcast` or `ether dst ff:ff:ff:ff:ff:ff`.
- To capture multicast packets, configure `ether multicast`.
- To capture a specific ether type (number in hexadecimal value), configure `ether proto 0800`. You can also write `ether proto \ip` (the backslash is used when a keyword is used as a value).

How it works...

The way capture filters work with source host and destination host is simple—the capture engine simply compares the condition with the actual MAC addresses, and passes only what is relevant.

A broadcast address is an address in which the destination address is all 1s, that is, `ff:ff:ff:ff:ff:ff:ff`, therefore, when you configure a broadcast filter, only these addresses will pass the filter. Broadcast addresses can be:

- Layer 3 IPv4 broadcast that is converted to layer 2 broadcast; for example, IP packet to `10.0.0.255`, which will be converted to layer 2 broadcast in the destination MAC field
- A network-related broadcast; for example, IPv4 **Address Resolution Protocol** (**ARP**), that sends a broadcast as a part of network operation

> Network-related broadcasts are broadcasts that are sent for the regular operation of the network. Among these are ARPs, routing updates, discovery protocols, and so on.

In a multicast filter, there are IPv4 and IPv6 multicasts:

- In IPv4, a multicast MAC address is transmitted when the MAC address starts with the string `01:00:5e`. Every packet with a MAC address that starts with this string will be considered a multicast.
- In IPv6, a multicast address is transmitted when the MAC address starts with the string `33:33`. Every packet with a MAC address that starts with this string will be considered a multicast.

Ethernet protocol refers to the ether type field in the Ethernet packet that indicates what will be the upper layer protocol. Common values here are `0800` for IPv4, `86dd` for IPv6, and `0806` for ARP and others. An updated list of ether types can be found at: `http://www.iana.org/assignments/ieee-802-numbers/ieee-802-numbers.xhtml`.

There's more...

- To configure a filter for a specific VLAN, use `vlan <vlan number>`
- To configure a filter on several VLANs, use `vlan <vlan number> and vlan <vlan number> and vlan <vlan number>...`

See also

- There are around a hundred ether type codes, most of them not in use. You can refer to `http://www.mit.edu/~map/Ethernet/Ethernet.txt` for additional codes, or simply browse the internet for Ethernet code.

Configuring hosts and network filters

When talking about host and network filters, we refer to layer 3 filters that are IP address-based filters. In this recipe, we will refer to these filters and what we can do with them.

Getting ready

The basic layer 3 filters are:

- `ip` or `ip6`: To capture IP or IPv6 packets.
- `host <host>`: To get a hostname or address.
- `dst host <host>`: To get a destination hostname or address.
- `src host <host>`: To get a source hostname or address.

A host can be an IP address or a hostname related to this number. You can type, for example, a filter host `www.packtpub.com` that will show you all packets to/from the IP address related to the Packt website.

- `gateway <Host name or address>`: Captures traffic to or from the hardware address but not to the IP address of the host. This filter captures traffic going through the specified router. This filter requires a hostname that can be found by the local system's name resolution process (for example, DNS).
- `net <net>`: All packets to or from the specified IPv4/IPv6 network.
- `dst net <net>`: All packets to the specified IPv4/IPv6 destination network.
- `src net <net>`: All packets to the specified IPv4/IPv6 destination network.
- `net <net> mask <netmask>`: All packets to/from the specific network and mask. This syntax is not valid for the IPv6 network.
- `dst net <net> mask <netmask>`: All packets to/from the specific network and mask. This syntax is not valid for the IPv6 network.
- `src net <net> mask <netmask>`: All packets to/from the specific network and mask. This syntax is not valid for the IPv6 network.
- `net <net>/<len>`: All packets to/from the `net` network with `len` length in bits.
- `dst net <net>/<len>`: All packets to/from the `net` network with `len` length in bits.
- `dst net <net>/<len>`: All packets to/from the `net` network with `len` length in bits.
- `broadcast`: All broadcast packets.
- `multicast`: All multicast packets.
- `ip proto <protocol code>`: Captures packets while the IP protocol field equals the `protocol` identifier. There can be various protocols, such as TCP (code 6), UDP (code 17), ICMP (code 1), and so on.

 Instead of writing `ip proto` and protocol code, you can write `ip proto \<protocol name>`, for example `ip proto \tcp`.

- `ip6 proto <protocol>`: Captures IPv6 packets with the protocol indicated in the type field. Note that this primitive does not follow the IPv6 extension headers chain.

 In an IPv6 header, there is a field in the header that can point to an optional extension header, which in turn points to the next extension header, and so on. In the current version, Wireshark capture filters do not follow this structure.

- `icmp[icmptype]==<identifier>`: Captures ICMP packets while the identifier is an ICMP code, such as `icmp-echo` and `icmp-request`.

How to do it...

Follow the instructions mentioned in the *Configure capture filters* recipe, and configure the filters as follows:

- For capturing packets to/from host `10.10.10.1`, configure `host 10.10.10.1`.
- For capturing packets to/from host at `www.cnn.com`, configure `host www.cnn.com`.
- For capturing packets to host `10.10.10.1`, configure `dst host 10.10.10.1`.
- For capturing packets from host `10.10.10.1`, configure `src host 10.10.10.1`.
- For capturing packets to/from network `192.168.1.0/24`, configure `net 192.168.1.0` or `net 192.168.1.0 mask 255.255.255.0` or `net 192.168.1.0/24`.
- For capturing all data without broadcasts or without multicasts, configure `not broadcast` or `not multicast`.
- For capturing packets to/from the IPv6 network `2001::/16`, configure `net 2001::/16`.
- For capturing packets to IPv6 host `2001::1`, configure `host 2001::1`.
- For capturing only ICMP packets, configure `ip proto 1`.
- For filtering only ICMP echoes (pings) you can use ICMP messages or message codes. Configure `icmp[icmptype]==icmp-echo` or `icmp[icmptype]==8`.

How it works...

For host filtering, when you type a hostname, Wireshark will translate the name to an IP address and capture packets that refer to this address. For example, if you configure a filter host `www.cnn.com`, it will be translated by a name resolution service (usually DNS) to an IP address, and will show you all packets going to and from this address. Note that in this case, if the CNN website forwards you to other websites at other addresses, only packets to the first address will be captured.

When writing `icmp[icmptype]`, it checks the ICMP type field in the ICMP header. `icmp-echo` has the code 8, and therefore you can write `icmp[icmptype]==icmp-echo` or `icmp[icmptype]==8`.

There's more...

Some more useful filters:

- `ip multicast`: IP multicast packets
- `ip broadcast`: IP broadcast packets
- `ip[2:2] == <number>`: IP packet size (bytes 3 and 4 of the IP header)
- `ip[8] == <number>`: TTL value (byte 9 of the IP header)
- `ip[12:4] = ip[16:4]`: IP source equal to IP destination address (bytes 13-16 are equal to bytes 17-20)
- `ip[2:2]==<number>`: Total length of IP packet (bytes 3 and 4 equals `<number>`)
- `ip[9] == <number>`: Protocol identifier (byte 10 equals `number`)

These filters are further explained in the *Configuring byte offset and payload matching filters* recipe at the end of this chapter. The principle, as illustrated further, is that the first number in the brackets defines how many bytes there are from the beginning of the protocol header, and the second number indicates how many bytes to watch:

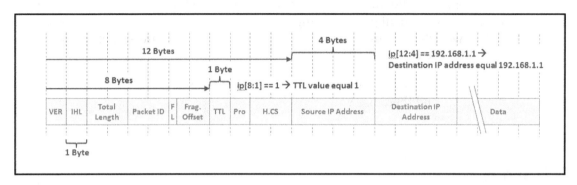

See also

- For more filters, refer to the `tcpdump` manual pages at:
  `http://www.tcpdump.org/tcpdump_man.html`

Configuring TCP/UDP and port filters

In this recipe, we will present layer 4 TCP/UDP port filters and how we can use them with capture filters.

Getting ready

The basic layer 4 filters are:

- `port <port>`: When the packet is a layer 4 protocol, such as TCP or UDP, this filter will capture packets to/from the port indicated in the identifier field
- `dst port <port>`: When the packet is a layer 4 protocol, such as TCP or UDP, this filter will capture packets to the destination port indicated in the identifier field
- `src port <port>`: When the packet is a layer 4 protocol, such as TCP or UDP, this filter will capture packets to the source port indicated in the identifier field

The port range matching filters are:

- `tcp portrange <p1>-<p2>` or `udp portrange <p1>-<p2>`: TCP or UDP packets in the port range of `p1` to `p2`
- `tcp src portrange <p1>-<p2>` or `udp src portrange <p1>-<p2>`: TCP or UDP packets in the source port range of `p1` to `p2`
- `tcp dst portrange <p1>-<p2>` or `udp src portrange <p1>-<p2>`: TCP or UDP packets in the destination port range of `p1` to `p2`

In addition to these filters, the following TCP flags can be used:

- `tcp-urg`: Used for TCP urgent pointer flag
- `tcp-rst`: Used for TCP reset pointer flag
- `tcp-ack`: Used for TCP acknowledgment pointer flag
- `tcp-syn`: Used for TCP sync pointer flag
- `tcp-psh`: Used for TCP push pointer flag
- `tcp-fin`: Used for TCP finish pointer flag

How to do it...

Follow the instructions in the *Configuring capture filters* recipe and configure filters as follows:

- To capture packets to port `80` (HTTP), configure `dst port 80` or `dst port http`
- To capture packets to or from port `5060` (SIP), configure `port 5060`
- To capture all TCP packets that starts a connection (all packets with `syn=1`), configure `tcp-syn != 0`
- To capture the start (`syn` flag) and end (`fin` flag) packets of all TCP connections, configure `tcp[tcpflags] & (tcp-syn|tcp-fin) != 0`

 In `tcp[tcpflags] & (tcp-syn|tcp-fin) != 0`, it is important to note that this is a bitwise AND operation, not a logical AND operation. For example, `010` or `101` equals `111`, and not `000`.

- To capture all TCP packets with the `rst` (reset) flag set to 1, configure `tcp[tcpflags] & (tcp-rst) != 0`
- Length filters are configured in the following way:
  - `less <length>`: Captures only packets with a length less than or equal to the length identifier. This is equivalent to `len <= <length>`.
  - `greater <length>`: Captures only packets with a length greater than or equal to the length identifier. This is equivalent to `<len >= length>`.

For example:

- `tcp portrange 2000-2500`
- `udp portrange 5000-6000`

Port range filters can be used for protocols that work for a range of ports rather than specific ones.

How it works...

Layer 4 protocols, mostly TCP and UDP, are the protocols that connect between end applications. The end node on one side (for example, a web client) sends a message to the other side (for example, a web server), requesting to connect to it. The codes of the processes that send the request and the processes that receive the request are called **port numbers**. Further discussion on this issue is provided in `Chapter 11`, *Transport Layer Protocol Analysis*.

For both TCP and UDP, the port numbers indicate the application codes. The difference between them is that TCP is a connection-oriented, reliable protocol, while UDP is a connectionless, unreliable protocol. There is an additional layer 4 protocol called **Stream Control Transmission Protocol** (**SCTP**), that can be referred to as an advanced version of TCP, which also uses port numbers.

TCP flags are sent in packets in order to establish, maintain, and close connections. A signal is set when a specific bit in the packet is set to 1. The most common flags that are in use are:

- `syn`: A signal sent in order to open a connection
- `fin`: A signal sent in order to close a connection

- `ack`: A signal sent to acknowledge received data
- `rst`: A signal sent for immediate close of a connection
- `psh`: A signal sent for pushing data for processing by the end process (application)

Using capture filters, you can filter packets to/from specific applications, along with filtering packets with specific flags turned on.

 We talked about the filter `tcp[tcpflags] & (tcp-syn|tcp-fin) != 0`, and we saw that we use `&` and not the more common operator `&&`. The difference is that when we write `&` or `|`, these are bitwise operators, that is, the result is calculated bit by bit and not on the entire field.

There's a funny thing here. If you try, for example, the filter `tcp[tcpflags] & (tcp-rst) == 1`, it will come up with no results. This is because the preceding Wireshark filter is instructing to perform a Boolean AND operation of `tcpflags` with `11111111` and check if the result is `1`. TCP packet with `rst` flag set to `1` will be `00000010`. So `00000010` AND `11111111` will result in `00000010` which is not equivalent to `1`.

On the other hand, when we write `tcp[tcpflags] & (tcp-rst) != 0`, we perform a bitwise AND between `00000010` and `11111111`, and the result is again `00000010`, which is not equal to `0`, as configured.

There's more...

Some problematic scenarios (mostly attacks) are:

- `tcp[13] & 0x00 = 0`: No flags set (null scan)
- `tcp[13] & 0x01 = 1`: `fin` set and `ack` not set
- `tcp[13] & 0x03 = 3`: `syn` set and `fin` set
- `tcp[13] & 0x05 = 5`: `rst` set and `fin` set
- `tcp[13] & 0x06 = 6`: `syn` set and `rst` set
- `tcp[13] & 0x08 = 8`: `psh` set and `ack` not set

In the following diagram, you can see how it works. `tcp[13]` is the number of bytes from the beginning of the protocol header, when the values 0, 1, 3, 5, 6, and 8 refer to the flag locations:

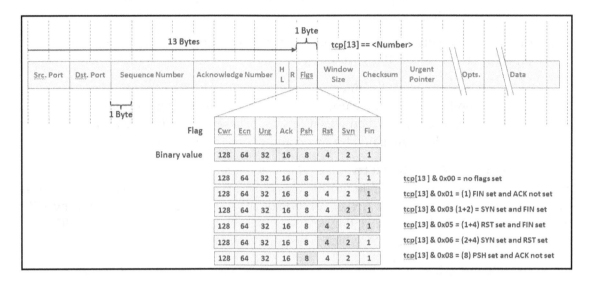

See also

- A deeper description of UDP and TCP is provided in `Chapter 11`, *Transport Layer Protocol Analysis*

Configuring compound filters

Structure filters are simply made for writing filters out of several conditions. It uses simple conditions, such as NOT, AND, and OR for creating structured conditions.

Getting ready

Structured filters are written in the following format:

```
[not] primitive [and|or [not] primitive ...]
```

The following modifiers are commonly used in Wireshark capture filters:

- ! or not
- && or and
- || or or

For bitwise operators, use:

- & for AND operation
- | for OR operation

How to do it...

To configure structured filters, you simply write the conditions according to what we learned in the previous recipes, with conditions to meet your requirements.

Some common filters are:

- For capturing only unicast packets, configure `not broadcast and not multicast`
- For capturing HTTP packets to `www.youtube.com`, configure `host www.youtube.com and port 80`
- For a capture filter for telnet that captures traffic to and from a particular host, configure `tcp port 23 and host 192.180.1.1`
- For capturing all telnet traffic not from `192.168.1.1`, configure `tcp port 23 and not src host 192.168.1.1`
- To capture packets to port `80` (HTTP) on servers `216.58.209.68` and `216.58.209.69`, configure `((tcp) and (port 80) and ((dst host 216.58.209.68) or (dst host 216.58.209.69)))`

How it works...

Some examples for structured filters:

- For capturing data to TCP port `23` (telnet) from a source port range of `5000-6000`, configure `tcp dst port 23 and tcp src portrange 5000-6000`

There's more...

Some interesting examples are as follows:

- `host www.mywebsite.com and not (port xxx or port yyy)`
- `host 192.168.0.50 and not tcp port 80`
- `ip host 10.0.0.1 and not udp`

See also

- `http://www.packetlevel.ch/html/tcpdumpf.html`
- `http://www.packetlevel.ch/html/txt/tcpdump.filters`

Configuring byte offset and payload matching filters

Byte offset and payload matching filters provide us with flexible tools for configuring self-defined filters (filters for fields that are not defined in the Wireshark dissector and filters for proprietary protocols). By understanding the protocols that we work with and understanding their packet structure, we can configure filters that will watch a specific string in the captured packets, and filter packets according to it. In this recipe, we will learn how to configure these types of filters, and we will also see some common and useful examples of the subject.

Getting ready

To configure byte offset and payload matching filters, start Wireshark and follow the instructions in the *Configuring capture filters* recipe at the beginning of this chapter.

String matching filters check a specific string in the packet header. We can configure them in two ways:

- `proto [Offset:bytes]`, where offset is the number of bytes from the beginning of the protocol header. For example, `ip[8:1]` checks byte number 9 of the IP header, and `tcp[8:2]` checks bytes 9-10 of the TCP header.
- `Proto [byte]`, where the byte indicates the byte number to check from the beginning of the protocol. For example, `ip[8]` will also check byte number 9 of the IP header.

With this filter, we can create filters for strings over IP, TCP, and UDP. For payload matching filters, remember also that:

- `proto[x:y] & z = 0`: This matches bits set to 0 when applying mask z to `proto[x:y]`
- `proto[x:y] & z !=0`: Some bits are set to 1 when applying mask z to `proto[x:y]`
- `proto[x:y] & z = z`: All bits are set to z when applying mask z to `proto[x:y]`
- `proto[x:y] = z`: `proto[x:y]` has the bits set exactly to z

How to do it...

1. For IP string-matching filters, you can create the following filter:

   ```
   ip [Offset:Bytes]
   ```

2. For matching application data (that is, to look into the application data that is carried by TCP or UDP), the most common uses of it are:

   ```
   tcp[Offset:Bytes]

   //Or

   udp[Offset:Bytes]
   ```

How it works...

The general structure of an offset filter is:

```
proto [Offset in bytes from the start of the header : Number of bytes to
check]
```

Common examples for string matching filters are:

- For filtering destination TCP ports between 50 and 100, configure (tcp[2:2] > 50 and tcp[2:2] < 100). Here we count two bytes from the beginning of the TCP header, and check the next two bytes are lower than 100 and higher than 50:

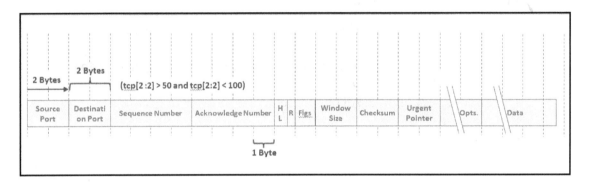

- For checking a TCP window size smaller than 8192, configure tcp[14:2] < 8192. Here we count two bytes from the beginning of the TCP header, and check the next two bytes (the window size) are less than 8192:

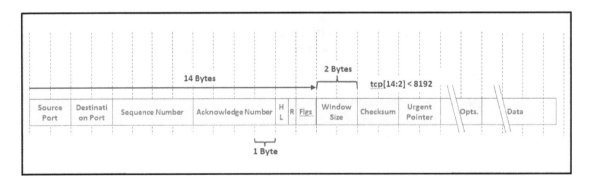

- For filtering only HTTP GET packets, configure port 80 and `tcp[((tcp[12:1] & 0xf0) >> 2):3] = 0x474554`. Here, `tcp[12:1] & 0xf0) >> 2` gives out the TCP header length. Right after it, go and check the strings G, E, T (that is, the HTTP GET command) which have the hex values 47, 45, 54 in the packet bytes pane just after the TCP header.

There's a nice string-matching capture filter generator at: `http://www.wireshark.org/tools/string-cf.html`.

There's more...

You can see additional filters in the `tcpdump` main pages:

- To print all IPv4 HTTP packets to and from port 80 (that is, to print only packets that contain data, not, for example, syn, fin, or ack-only packets), configure the filter: `tcp port 80 and (((ip[2:2] - ((ip[0]&0xf)<<2)) - ((tcp[12]&0xf0)>>2)) != 0)`
- To print the start and end packets (the syn and fin packets) of each TCP conversation that involves a nonlocal host, configure `tcp[tcpflags] & (tcp-syn|tcp-fin) != 0 and not src and dst net localnet`
- To print IP broadcast or multicast packets that were not sent via Ethernet broadcast or multicast, configure `ether[0] & 1 = 0 and ip[16] >= 224`
- To print all ICMP packets that are not echo requests/replies (that is, not ping packets), configure `icmp[icmptype] != icmp-echo and icmp[icmptype] != icmp-echoreply`

See also

- There is a string calculator at `http://www.wireshark.org/tools/string-cf.html`. It doesn't always provide working results, but it might be a good place to start.
- Another interesting blog can be found at: `http://www.packetlevel.ch/html/txt/byte_offsets.txt`.

4
Using Display Filters

In this chapter, you will learn about:

- Configuring display filters
- Configuring Ethernet, ARP, host, and network filters
- Configuring TCP/UDP filters
- Configuring specified protocol filters
- Configuring substring operator filters
- Configuring macros

Introduction

In this chapter, we will learn how to work with display filters. Display filters are filters that we apply after capturing the data (filtered by capture filters or not), and when we wish to display only a part of the data.

Display filters can be implemented in order to locate various types of data:

- Parameters, such as IP addresses, TCP or UDP port numbers, URLs, or server names
- Conditions, such as packet lengths shorter than TCP port ranges
- Phenomena, such as TCP retransmissions, duplicate ACKs and others, various protocol error codes, flag existence, and so on
- Various applications parameters, such as **Short Message Service** (**SMS**) source and destination numbers, **Server Message Block** (**SMB**), **Simple Mail Transfer Protocol** (**SMTP**), server names, and so on

Any data that is sent over the network can be filtered, and once filtered, create statistics and graphs according to it.

As we will describe in the recipes in this chapter, there are various ways to configure display filters, from predefined menus, the packet pane, or by writing the syntax directly.

 When using display filters, don't forget that all the data was captured, and display filters only decide what to display. Therefore, after filtering data, the capture file still contains the original data that was captured. You may later save the whole data or only the displayed data.

Configuring display filters

In order to configure display filters, you can choose one of several options:

- Choosing from the filters menus.
- Writing the syntax directly into the filter window (after working with Wireshark for a while, this will become your favorite).
- Picking a parameter in the packet pane and defining it as a filter.
- With the command line, using `tshark` or `wireshark`. This will be discussed in the appendix.

This chapter discusses the first three options.

Getting ready

In general, a display filter string takes the form of a series of primitive expressions connected by conjunctions (`and|or` and so on) and optionally preceded by `not`:

```
[not] Expression [and|or] [not] Expression...
```

While:

- `Expression` can be any filter expression such as `ip.src==192.168.1.1` (for source address), `tcp.flags.syn==1` for TCP sync flag presence, `tcp.analysis.retransmission` for TCP retransmissions, and so on
- `and|or` are conjunctions that can be used in any combination of expressions, including brackets, multiple brackets, and any length of string

The conditions can be one of the following:

C-like syntax	Shortcut	Description	Example
==	eq	Equal	`ip.addr == 192.168.1.1` or `ip.addr eq 192.168.1.1`
!=	ne	Not equal	`!ip.addr==192.168.1.1` or `ip.addr != 192.168.1.1` or `ip.addr ne 192.168.1.1`
>	gt	Greater than	`frame.len > 64`
<	lt	Less than	`frame.len < 1500`
>=	ge	Greater than or equal to	`frame.len >= 64`
<=	le	Less than or equal to	`frame.len <= 1500`
	Is present	A parameter is present	`http.response`
	contains	Contains a string	`http.host contains cisco`
	matches	A string matches the condition	`http.host matches www.cisco.com`

You can insert a space character between parameter operators or leave it without spaces.

Wireshark colors the display filter area in yellow whenever you use the `!=` operator for combined expressions such as `eth.addr`, `ip.addr`, `tcp.port`, or `udp.port`, but this will not work because when you type a filter expression such as `ip.addr != 192.168.1.100` it must be read, as the packet contains the field `ip.addr` with a value different from `192.168.1.100`. Because an IP datagram contains both a source and a destination address, the expression will evaluate to true whenever at least one of the two addresses differs from `192.168.1.100`. For this reason, you should write `!(ip.addr == 192.168.1.100)`, that is, it displays all the packets for cases where the `ip.addr` field having the value of `1.2.3.4` is not true.

Operators can be as follows:

C-like syntax	Shortcut	Description	Example
&&	and	Logical AND	`ip.src==10.0.0.1 and tcp.flags.syn==1` all SYN flags sent from IP address `10.0.0.1` practically—all connections opened (or tried to be opened) from `10.0.0.1`
||	or	Logical OR	`ip.addr==10.0.0.1 or ip.addr==10.0.02` all packets going in or out the two IP addresses
!	not	Logical NOT	`not arp and not icmp` all packets that are neither ARP nor ICMP packets

How to do it...

For configuring display filters, you can choose one of the preceding methods mentioned.

To use the filters menu, do the following:

1. For choosing from the filters menu, go to the display filter pane at the top of the window and click on the **Expression...** button as you see in the following image:

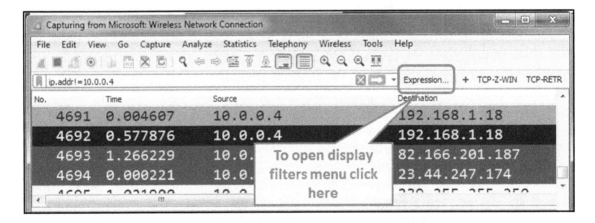

2. When you click the **Expression...** button, the following window will open:

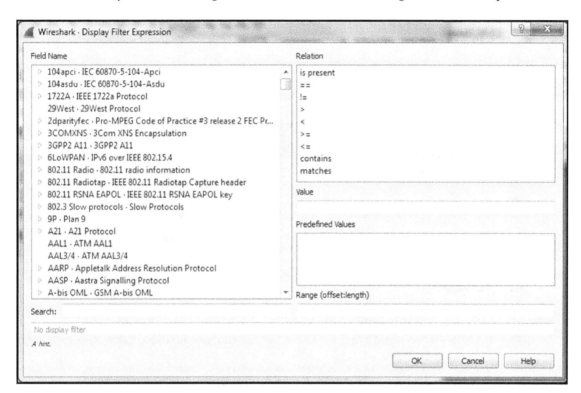

There are four important panes in the **Display Filter Expression** window:

- **Field Name**: In this window, you configure the filter parameter. You can scroll down by typing the protocol name, and get to the protocol parameter by clicking on the **(+)** signs at the left of the list.

  Example 1
  Type the letters `ipv4` to get to the IPv4 protocol, click on the **(+)** sign to see the protocol parameters (or click on *Enter* twice), and choose `ip.addr` to filter a specific IP address.

  Example 2
  Type the letters `tcp` to get to the TCP protocol, click on the **(+)** sign to see the protocol parameters, and choose `tcp.port` for source or destination port number.

- **Relation**: This is the pane that you choose the operator from. You can choose ==
  for equal, != for not equal, and so on.

Example 3

Type the letters sip to get to the SIP protocol, choose sip.Method, and
from the **Relation** window choose ==. In the value window, type invite.
This will filter all SIP invite methods.

- **Value**: Here, you choose the value of the field that you chose before.

Example 4

Type the letters tcp to get to the TCP protocol, click on the **(+)** sign to see
the protocol parameters, choose tcp.flags.syn for a TCP SYN flag, and
in the **Value** field choose 1.

- **Predefined values**: When the value of the field you chose is not Boolean, there
  might be a list of options in this field.

Example 5

Under TCP, there is a field tcp.option_kind. This option relates to TCP
options (for more details go to Chapter 11, *Transport Layer Protocol
Analysis*). You will get a list of the values that are possible here.

- **Search**: A search mechanism that enables you to search for filter expressions. In
  the search box you should write exactly what you are looking for. You can see it,
  for example, in the following screenshot—when you search for ip fragment, it
  brings up OpenFlow and Cisco NetFlow expressions:

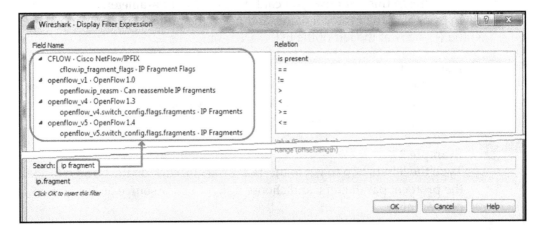

When writing `ipv4 fragment` it will show what we need, that is, IPv4 fragments, as you can see in the following screenshot:

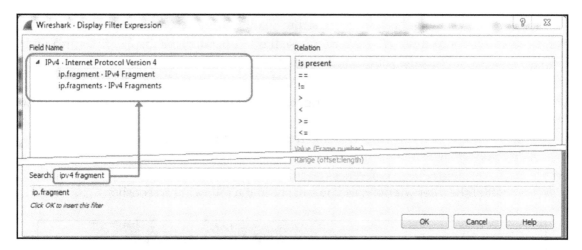

Writing the syntax directly into the filter window is performed as follows:

1. After you get used to the display filters syntax, you might find it easier to type the filter string directly into the filter window, as you see in the following screenshot:

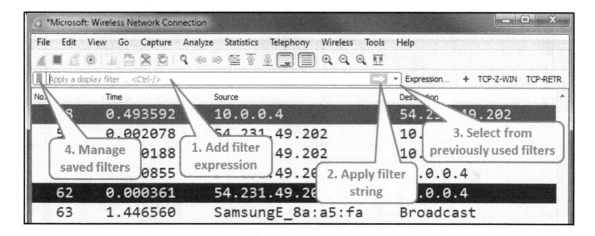

2. In this case, when you write a filter string into the window, the window will light up in one of the following three colors:
   - **Green**: This is when the filter is correct and you can apply it.
   - **Red**: This is a wrong string. Fix the string before you apply it.
   - **Yellow**: Whenever you use the ! = operator, the display filter area will become yellow. It doesn't mean your filter will not work—it is just a warning that it may not work.

3. To apply the filter, click on the right arrow to the right of the filter string window, or use *Enter*.

4. To choose from previously-defined filters, use the scroll-down to the right of the apply arrow.

5. To configure filter preferences and filter expressions, click on the symbol to the left of the filter window, as you can see in the following screenshot:

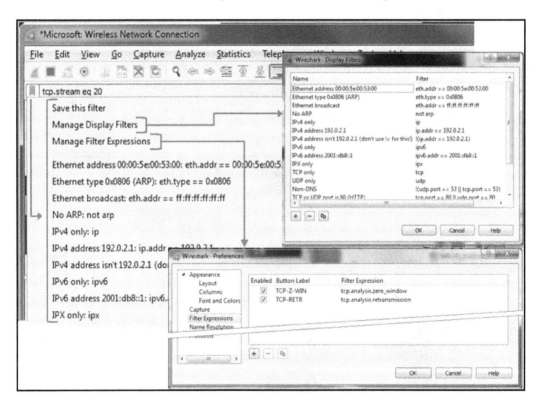

6. Choosing **Manage Display Filters** enables you to add filters for future use (for example, for specific profiles).

7. Choosing **Manage Filter Expressions** enables you to add filter expressions that will appear to the right of the filter window, for more convenient usage of them.

Using the packet pane and defining it as a filter is as follows:

This is a very convenient option. You can choose any field from the packet detail pain in the captured file, right-click it, and you will get the following options, as illustrated in the following screenshot:

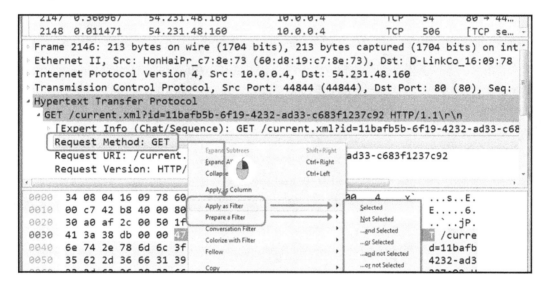

The options are:

- **Apply as Filter**: This will set a filter according to the field you chose, and apply it to the capture data.
- **Prepare a Filter**: This will prepare a filter, but not apply it. It will be applied when you click the **Apply** button on the right-hand side of the filter window.

In both options, you can choose to configure a filter:

- **Selected**: This will choose the selected field and parameter
- **Not selected**: This will choose the not selected fields and parameters

For example, right-clicking on the `http.request.method` field and choosing **Selected** will show the filter string `http.request.method == GET`, while choosing **Not selected** will show the string `!(http.request.method == "GET")`.

You can also choose the options **and selected**, **or selected**, **and not selected**, and **or not selected** for structured filters.

How it works...

The display filters are a proprietary Wireshark language. There are many places that display filters can be used, which will be discussed in following chapters when we talk about protocols. Additional filters will be discussed in following recipes in this chapter.

You can always use the autocomplete feature to complete filter strings. For example, if you type in `tcp.f` as shown in the following screenshot, the autocomplete feature lists possible display filter values that could be created beginning with `tcp.f`, that is, TCP flags (SYN, FIN, RST, and so on):

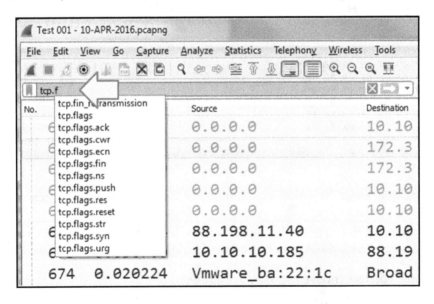

There's more...

Some additional helpful features include the following:

- What is the parameter we filter?
    - Any time you mark a specific field in the packet details pane, you will see the correlating filter string in the status bar, at the lower-left corner of Wireshark:

```
▷ Frame 1: 76 bytes on wire (608 bits), 76 bytes captured (608 bits) on inte
▴ Ethernet II, Src: HonHaiPr_c7:8e:73 (60:d8:19:c7:8e:73), Dst: SamsungE_35:
  ▷ Destination: SamsungE_35:d6:1e (5c:0a:5b:35:d6:1e)
  ▷ Source: HonHaiPr_c7:8e:73 (60:d8:19:c7:8e:73)
    Type: IPv4 (0x0800)
▷ Internet Protocol Version 4, Src: 192.168.43.191, Dst: 157.55.235.159

0000  5c 0a 5b 35 d6 1e 60 d8  19 c7 8e 73 08 00 45 00   \.[5..`. ...s..E.
0010  00 3e 56 10 00 00 80 11  6f 60 c0 a8 2b bf 9d 37   .>V..... o`..+..7
0020  eb 9f 73 ce 9c 65 00 2a  ea 59 d6 ff 02 1a 33 fd   ..s..e.* .Y....3.
0030  4e d1 e4 df 53 8e 2f 4f  4f a6 0f ba 54 c3 7b fe   N...S./O O...T.{.
```
Destination Hardware Address (eth.dst), 6 bytes   Packets: 8685 · Displayed: 8685 (100.0%) · Load time: 0:1.811   Profile: Default

- Adding a parameter column:
    - You can also right-click a parameter in the packet pane. Right-click it and choose **Apply as Column**. This will add a column with the specific parameter. For example, you can choose the `tcp.window_size_value` parameter and add it as a column to the packet list pane, so you will be able to watch the TCP window size online (this influences TCP performance, as we will learn in `Chapter 11`, *Transport Layer Protocol Analysis*).

Configuring Ethernet, ARP, host, and network filters

In these recipes, we will discuss how to configure layer 2-3 filters, that is, Ethernet-based and IP-based filters. We will also discuss **Address Resolution Protocol (ARP)** filters.

Getting ready

In layer 2, we will configure Ethernet-based filters, while in layer 3 we will configure IP filters. For Ethernet, we have filters based on the Ethernet frame and MAC address, while for IP we have filters based on the IP packet and addresses.

Common frame delta filters include the following:

- `frame.time_delta`: For the time delta between the current and previous captured frame (will be used in statistical graphs, in `Chapter 6`, *Using Advanced Statistics Tools*)
- `frame.time_delta_displayed`: For the time delta between the current and previous displayed frame (will be used in statistical graphs, in `Chapter 6`, *Using Advanced Statistics Tools)*

Since the time between frames can influence TCP performance significantly, we will use the `frame.time_delta` parameters in statistical graphs for monitoring TCP performance.

Common layer 2 (Ethernet) filters include the following:

- `eth.addr == <MAC Address>` for displaying a specific MAC address
- `eth.dst == <MAC Address> or eth.src == <MAC Address>` for source or destination MAC addresses
- `eth.type == <Protocol Type (Hexa)>` for Ethernet protocol types

Common ARP filters include the following:

- `arp.opcode == <value>` for ARP requests/responses
- `arp.src.hw_mac == <MAC Address>` for ARP sender

Common layer 3 (IP) filters include the following:

- `ip.addr == <IP Address>` for source or destination IP address
- `ip.dst == <IP Address>` or `ip.src == <IP Address>` for source or destination IP addresses
- `ip.ttl == <value>` or `ip.ttl < value>` or `ip.ttl > <value>` for IP **Time-to-Live (TTL)** values

- `ip.len = <value>` or `ip.len > <value>` or `ip.len < <value>` for IP packet length values
- `ip.version == <4/6>` for IP protocol version (version 4 or version 6)

How to do it...

In this section, we will see some common examples of layer 2/layer 3 filters:

Address format	Syntax	Example
Ethernet (MAC) address	`eth.addr == xx:xx:xx:xx:xx:xx` where x is 0 to f	`eth.addr == 00:50:7f:cd:d5:38`
	`eth.addr == xx-xx-xx-xx-xx-xx` where x is 0 to f	`eth.addr == 00-50-7f-cd-d5-38`
	`eth.addr == xxxx.xxxx.xxxx` where x is 0 to f	`eth.addr == 0050.7fcd.d538`
Broadcast MAC address	`Eth.addr == ffff.ffff.ffff`	
IPv4 host address	`ip.addr == x.x.x.x` where x is 0 to 255	`Ip.addr == 192.168.1.1`
IPv4 network address	`ip.addr == x.x.x.x/y` where x is 0 to 255, y is 0 to 32	`ip.addr == 192.168.200.0/24` (all addresses in the network `192.168.200.0` mask `255.255.255.0`)
IPv6 host address	`ipv6.addr == x:x:x:x:x:x:x:x` `ipv6.addr == x::x:x:x:x` where in the format of nnnn, n is 0 to f (hex)	`ipv6.addr == fe80::85ab:dc2e:ab12:e6c7`
IPv6 network address	`ipv6.addr == x::/y` where x is 0 to f (hex), y is 0 to 128	`ipv6.addr == fe80::/16` (all addressees that start with the 16 bits `fe80`)

The table refers to `ip.addr` and `ipv6.addr` filter strings. The value for any field that has an IP address value can be written the same way.

Ethernet filters:

- Display only packets sent from or to specific MAC addresses:
  - `eth.src == 10:0b:a9:33:64:18`
  - `eth.dst == 10:0b:a9:33:64:18`
- Display only broadcasts:
  - `Eth.dst == ffff.ffff.ffff or Eth.dst == ff:ff:ff:ff:ff:ff`

ARP filters:

- Display only ARP requests:
  - `arp.opcode == 1`
- Display only ARP responses:
  - `arp.opcode == 2`

IP and ICMP filters:

- Display only packets from specific IP addresses:
  - `ip.src == 10.1.1.254`
- Display only packets that are not from a specific address:
  - `!ip.src == 64.23.1.1`
- Display only packets between two hosts:
  - `ip.addr == 192.168.1.1 and ip.addr == 200.1.1.1`
- Display only packets that are sent to multicast IP addresses:
  - `ip.dst == 224.0.0.0/4`
- Display only packets coming from network `192.168.1.0/24` (mask `255.255.255.0`):
  - `ip.src==192.168.1.0/24`
- Display only IPv6 packets to/from specific addresses:
  - `ipv6.addr == ::1`
  - `ipv6.addr == 2008:0:130F:0:0:09d0:666A:13ab`
  - `ipv6.addr == 2006:0:130f::9c2:876a:130b`
  - `ipv6.addr == ::`

Complex filters:

- Packets from network `10.0.0.0/24` to a website that contains the word `packt`:
  - `ip.src == 10.0.0.0/24 and http.host contains "packt"`

- Packets from networks `10.0.0.0/24` to websites that end with `.com`:
  - `ip.addr == 10.0.0.0/24 and http.host matches ".com$"`

- All broadcasts from source IP address `10.0.0.3`:
  - `ip.src == 10.0.0.0/24 and eth.dst == ffff.ffff.ffff`

- All broadcasts that are not ARP requests:
  - `not arp and eth.dst == ffff.ffff.ffff`

- All packets that are not ICMP and not ARP:
  - `!arp || !icmp or not arp&&not icmp`

How it works...

Here are some explanations to the filters we saw in the previous paragraph.

- **Ethernet broadcasts**: For Ethernet, broadcasts are packets that are sent to addresses with all 1s in the destination field, and this is why, to find all broadcasts in the network, we write the filter `eth.dst == ffff.ffff.ffff`.
- **IPv4 multicast**: IPv4 multicasts are packets that are sent to an address in the address range `224.0.0.0` to `239.255.255.255`, that is, in binary, the address range `11100000.00000000.00000000.00000000` to `11101111.11111111.11111111.11111111`.

For this reason, if you look at the binary representation, a destination multicast address is an address that starts with three 1s and a 0, and therefore a filter to IPv4 multicast destinations will be `ip.dst == 224.0.0.0/4`.

That is, an address that starts with four 1s (224), and a subnet mask of four bits (/4) will indicate a network address of 224 to 239 will filter multicast addresses.

- **IPv6 multicasts**: IPv6 multicasts are packets that are sent to an address that starts with `ff` (first two hex digits = `ff`), and then one digit flags and scope. Therefore, when we write the filter `ipv6.dst == ff00::/8`, it means to display all packets in IPv6 that are sent to addresses that start with the string **ff**, that is, IPv6 multicasts.

See also

- For more information on Ethernet, refer to `Chapter 8`, *Ethernet and LAN Switching* and `Chapter 10`, *Network Layer Protocols and Operations*

Configuring TCP/UDP filters

TCP and UDP are the main protocols in layer 4 that provide connectivity between end applications. Whenever you start an application from one side to another, you start the session from a source port, usually a random number equal to or higher than 1,024, and connect to a destination port, which is a well-known or registered port that waits for the session on the other side. These are the port numbers that identify the application that works over the session.

Other types of filters refer to other fields in the UDP and TCP headers. In UDP, we have a very simple header with very basic data, while in TCP we have a more complex header that we can get much more information from.

In this recipe, we will concentrate on the possibilities while configuring TCP and UDP display filters.

Getting ready

As before, we should plan precisely what we want to display, and prepare the filters accordingly.

TCP and UDP port number display filters

For TCP or UDP port numbers, use the following display filters:

- `tcp.port == <value>` or `udp.port == <value>` for specific TCP or UDP ports (source or destination)
- `tcp.dstport == <value>` or `udp.dstport == <value>` for specific TCP or UDP destination ports
- `tcp.srcport == <value>` or `udp.srcport == <value>` for specific TCP or UDP destination ports

TCP header filters

In UDP, the header structure is very simple—source and destination ports, packet length, and checksum. Therefore, the only significant information here is the port numbers.

TCP, on the other hand, is more complex, and uses connectivity and reliability mechanisms that can be monitored by Wireshark. Using `tcp.flags`, `tcp.analysis`, and other smart filters will help you with resolving performance problems (retransmissions, duplicate ACKs, zero-windows, and so on), or protocol operations issues such as resets, half-opens, and so on.

Common display filters in this category are as follows:

- `tcp.analysis`: For TCP analysis criteria such as retransmission, duplicate ACKs, or window issues. Examples for these filters are (you can use the autocomplete feature to get the full list of available filters):
    - `tcp.analysis.retransmission` to display packets that were retransmitted
    - `tcp.analysis.duplicate_ack` to display packets that were acknowledged several times
    - `tcp.analysis.zero_window` to display when a device on the connection end sends a zero-window message (which tells the sender to stop sending data on this connection until the window size increases again)

> `tcp.analysis` fields do not analyze the TCP header, they provide protocol analysis through the Wireshark expert system.

- `tcp.flags`: These filters are used for finding out if flags are set or not:
    - `tcp.flags.syn == 1` to check if the SYN flag is set
    - `tcp.flags.reset == 1` to check if the RST flag is set
    - `tcp.flags.fin == 1` to check if the FIN flag is set
    - `tcp.window_size_value < <value>` to look for small TCP window sizes that are, in some cases, an indication of slow devices

tcp.flags filters—for TCP flags, this will be used to find out whether a specific flag is set or not.

How to do it...

Some examples of filters in TCP/UDP filters are as follows:

- All packets to the HTTP server:
  - tcp.dstport == 80

- All packets from network 10.0.0.0/24 to HTTP server:
  - ip.src==10.0.0.0/24 and tcp.dstport == 80

- All retransmissions on a specific TCP connection:
  - tcp.stream eq 16 && tcp.analysis.retransmission

To isolate a specific connection, place the mouse on a packet on the connection you want to watch, right-click it, and choose **Follow** and **TCP Stream**. A TCP stream is the data that is transferred between the two ends of the transaction from the connection establishment to the tear-down. The string tcp.stream eq <value> will appear in the display filter window. This is the stream you can work on now. In the following example, it came out as stream 6, but it can be any stream number (starting from stream number 1 in the capture file):

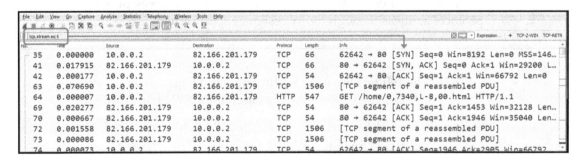

Retransmissions are TCP packets that are sent again. This could be due to several reasons, as explained in `Chapter 11`, *Transport Layer Protocol Analysis*.

 When you monitor phenomena such as retransmissions, duplicate ACKs, and other behavior that influence performance, it is important to remember that these phenomena refer to specific TCP connections.

- All window problems on a specific connection:
    - `tcp.stream eq 0 && (tcp.analysis.window_full || tcp.analysis.zero_window)`
    - `tcp.stream eq 0 and (tcp.analysis.window_full or tcp.analysis.zero_window)`

- All packets from `10.0.0.5` to the DNS server:
    - `ip.src == 10.0.0.5 && udp.port == 53`

- All packets in TCP or protocols in TCP (for example HTTP) that contain the string `cacti` (case-sensitive):
    - `tcp contains "cacti"`

- All packets from `10.0.0.3` that are retransmitted:
    - `ip.src == 10.0.0.3 and tcp.analysis.retransmission`

- All packets to any HTTP server:
    - `tcp.dstport == 80`

- All connections opened from a specific host (if in the form of a scan, can be a warning):
    - `ip.src==10.0.0.5 && tcp.flags.syn==1 && tcp.flags.ack==0`

- All cookies sent from and to a client:
    - `ip.src==10.0.0.3 && (http.cookie || http.set_cookie)`

How it works...

The following are diagrams of the TCP and IP header structure. UDP is quite simple—only source and destination port numbers, length, and checksum:

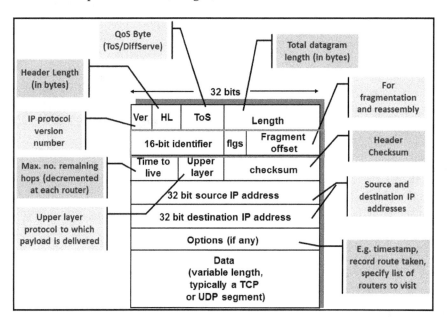

Some important things in the IP packet:

- **Ver**: Version 4 or 6.
- **Header length**: 20 to 24 bytes with options.
- **Type of Service (ToS)**: Usually implemented with **Differentiated Services** (**DiffServ**), and provide priority to preferred services.

 TCP standard (RFC 793 from October 1981) has named this field ToS, and defined its structure. Differentiated Services standards that were published later (RFCs 2474, 2475 from December 1998 and others) are used for the implementation of the ToS byte in the majority of applications.

- **Length**: Total datagram length in bytes.
- **Identifier, flags and fragment offset**: Every packet has its own packet ID. When fragmented, along with the flags and offset, it will enable the receiver to reassemble it.

- **Time to Live**: Start with 64, 128, or 256 (depends on the operating system that sends the packet), when every router on the way decrements the value by one. This prevents packets from traveling endlessly through the network. The router that sees one in the packet decrements it to zero and drops the packet.
- **Upper layer**: The upper layer protocol—TCP, UDP, ICMP, and some others.
- **Internet checksum**: The idea here is that the sender uses an error-checking mechanism to calculate a value over the packet. This value is set in the checksum field, while the receiver of the packet will calculate it again. If the sent value is not equal to the received value, it will be considered a checksum error.
- **Source and destination IP addresses**: As the name implies.
- **Options**: Usually not in use in IP Version 4.

The IP header is followed by TCP header. The format is as follow:

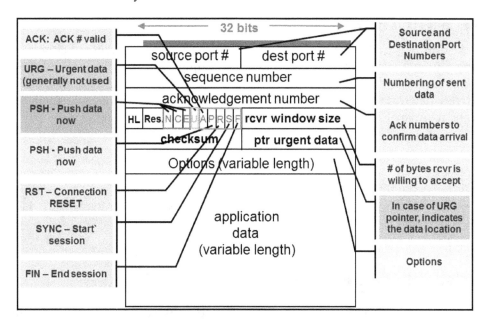

Some important things in the TCP packet:

- **Source and destination ports**: These are the application codes at the two ends.
- **Sequence numbers**: Counts the bytes that the sender sends to the receiver.
- **Acknowledgement number**: ACK's received bytes. We will discuss this in detail in the `Chapter 11`, *Transport Layer Protocol Analysis*.

- **HL**: Header length, indicates whether we use the options field or not.
- **Res**: Reserved (for future flags).
- **Flags**: Flags to start a connection (SYN), close a connection (FIN), reset a connection (RST), and push data for fast processing (PSH). Will be discussed in the TCP analysis chapter.
- **Rcvr window size**: The buffer that the receiver has allocated to the process.
- **Checksum**: Packet checksum.
- **Options**: Timestamps, receiver window enhancement (RFC 1323), and MSS extension. **Maximum Segment Size (MSS)** is the maximum size of the TCP payload. We will discuss this further in Chapter 11, *Transport Layer Protocol Analysis*.

There's more...

The TTL field in IP is quite a helpful field. When seeing a TTL value, it explicitly indicates how many routers the packet has passed. Since operating system defaults are 64,128, or 256, and the maximum number of hops that a packet will cross through the internet is 30 (much less in private networks), if for example we see a value of 120, then the packet has passed 8 routers, and a value of 52 indicates that the packet has passed 12 routers.

See also

- For further information on the TCP/IP protocol stack, refer to Chapter 11, *Transport Layer Protocol Analysis*

Configuring specific protocol filters

In this recipe, we will provide instructions and examples for configuring display filters for common protocols, such as DNS, HTTP, FTP, and others.

The purpose of this recipe is to learn how to configure filters that will help us in network troubleshooting, and we will talk about more in following chapters.

Getting ready

To step through this recipe, you will need Wireshark software and a running capture. No other prerequisites are required.

How to do it...

In this recipe, we will see display filters of some common protocols.

HTTP display filters

Some common HTTP display filters are as follows:

- Display all HTTP packets going to hostname:
    - `http.request.method == <"Request methods">`
- Packets with HTTP GET methods:
    - `http.request.method == "GET"`
- Display URI requested by client:
    - `http.request.method == <"Full request URI">`
    - `http.request.uri == "/v2/rating/mail.google.com"`
- Display URI requested by client that contains a specific string (all requests to Google in this example):
    - `http.request.uri contains "URI String"`
    - `http.request.uri contains "mail.google.com"`
- All cookie requests sent over the network (note that cookies are always sent from the client to the server):
    - `http.cookie`
- All cookie set commands sent from the server to the client:
    - `http.set_cookie`
- All cookies sent by Google servers to your PC:
    - `(http.set_cookie) && (http contains "google")`
- All HTTP packets that contain a ZIP file:
    - `http matches ".zip" && http.request.method == "GET"`

DNS display filters

Some common DNS display filters are as follows:

- Display DNS queries and response:
    - `dns.flags.response == 0` for DNS queries
    - `dns.flags.response == 1` for DNS response
- Display only DNS responses with four answers or more:
    - `dns.count.answers >= 4`

FTP display filters

Some common FTP display filters are as follows:

- FTP request command:
    - `ftp.request.command == <"requested command"> -
      ftp.request.command == "USER"`
- FTP or FTP data—FTP commands (port 21) or data (port 20 or variable):
    - `ftp`
    - `ftp-data`

How it works...

The Wireshark regular expression syntax for display filters uses the same syntax as regular expressions in Perl.

Some common modifiers are as follows:

- `^`: Match the beginning of the line
- `$`: Match the end of the line
- `|`: Alternation
- `()`: Grouping
- `*`: Match zero or more times
- `+`: Match one or more times
- `?`: Match one or zero times

- {n}: Match exactly n times
- {n, }: Match at least *n* times
- {n,m}: Match at least *n* but not more than *m* times

You can use these modifiers for configuring more complex filters. For examples, look for HTTP GET commands that contain ZIP files:

```
http.request.method == "GET" && http matches ".zip" &&
!(http.accept_encoding == "gzip, deflate")
```

Look for HTTP messages that contain websites that end with .com:

```
http.host matches ".com$"
```

See also

- The Perl regular expression syntax list can be found at http://www.pcre.org/, and the manual pages can be found at http://perldoc.perl.org/perlre.html

Configuring substring operator filters

Offset filters are filters in which you actually say *"go to field X in the protocol header, and check if the next Y bytes equal to..."*.

These filters can be used in many cases where a known byte string appears somewhere in the packet and you want to display packets that contain it.

Getting ready

To step through this recipe, you will need Wireshark software and a running capture. No other prerequisites are required. The general representation of an offset filter is as follows:

```
Protocols[x:y] == <value>
X: Bytes from beginning of header
Y: Number of bytes to check
```

How to do it...

Examples of filters that use substring operators are as follows:

- Packets to IPv4 multicast addresses

 `eth.dst[0:3] == 01:00:5e` RFC 1112, section 6.4 allocates the MAC address space of `01-00-5E-00-00-00` to `01-00-5E-FF-FF-FF` to multicast addresses.

- Packets to IPv6 multicast addresses

 `eth.dst[0:3] == 33:33:00` RFC 2464, section 7 allocates the MAC address space that starts with `33-33` to multicast addresses.

How it works...

Wireshark enables you to look into protocols and search for specific bytes in it. This is specifically practical for well-known strings in protocols such as Ethernet, for example.

Configuring macros

Display filter macros are used to create shortcuts for complex display filters that you can configure once and use later.

Getting ready

To configure display filter macros, go to: **Analyze | Display Filter Macros**. You will get the following window:

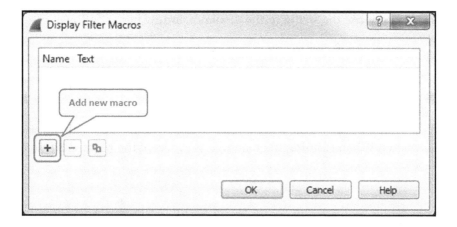

How to do it...

1. In order to configure a macro, you give it a name and you fill in the textbox with the filter string.

2. In order to activate the macro, you simply write the following:

   ```
   $(macro_name:parameter1;paramater2;parameter3 ...)
   ```

3. Let's configure a simple filter name, `test01`, that takes the following parameters as values:

   ```
   ip.src == <value> and
   tcp.dstport == <value>
   ```

4. This will be a filter that looks for packets from a specific source network that goes out to an HTTP port.

   A macro that takes these two parameters would be as follows:

   ```
   ip.src==$1 && tcp.dstport==$2
   ```

5. Now, in order to get the filter results for parameters we do the following:

   ```
   ip.src == 10.0.0.4 and
   tcp.dstport == 80
   ```

6. We should write the string in the display window bar as follows:

```
${test01:10.0.0.4;80}
```

How it works...

Macros work in a simple way—you write a filter string with the sign $ ahead of every positional parameter. When running the macro, it will accept the parameters in order.

Using Basic Statistics Tools

5

In this chapter you will learn about:

- Using the statistics – capture file properties
- Using the statistics – resolved addresses
- Using the statistics – protocol hierarchy menu
- Using the statistics – conversations menu
- Using the statistics – endpoints menu
- Using the statistics – HTTP menu
- Configuring a flow graphs for viewing TCP flows
- Creating IP-based statistics

Introduction

One of Wireshark's strengths is its statistical tools. When using Wireshark, we have various types of tools, starting from the simple tools for listing end-nodes and conversations, to the more sophisticated tools such as flow and I/O graphs.

In the following two chapters, we will learn how to use these tools. In this chapter, we will look at the simple tools that provide us with basic network statistics—that is, who talks to whom over the network, what are the chatty devices, what packet sizes run over the network, and so on. In the next chapter, we'll get into tools such as I/O and stream graphs, which provide us with much more information about the behavior of the network.

There are some tools that we will not talk about—some that are quite obvious (for example, packet sizes), and some that are less common (such as ANSP, BACnet, NCP, and others). Some others we will refer to in the relevant chapter, for example, **Statistics | Service Response Time** or **Statistics | DNS**.

To start statistics tools, start Wireshark, and choose **Statistics** from the main menu.

Using the statistics – capture file properties menu

In this recipe, we will learn how to get general information from the data that runs over the network. The capture file properties in Wireshark 2 replaces the summary menu in Wireshark 1.

Getting ready

Start Wireshark, click on **Statistics**.

How to do it...

1. From the **Statistics** menu, choose **Capture File Properties**:

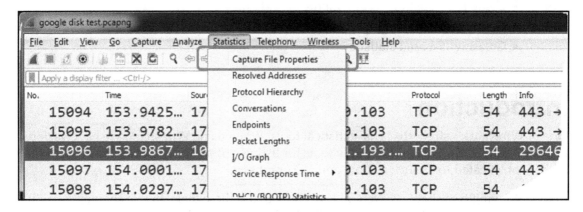

What you will get is the **Capture File Properties** window (displayed in the following screenshot).

2. As you can see in the following screenshot, we have the following:
    - **File**: Provides file data, such as filename and path, length, and so on
    - **Time**: Start time, end time, and duration of capture
    - **Capture**: Hardware information for the PC that Wireshark is installed on

- **Interfaces**: Interface information—the interface registry identifier on the left, if capture filter is turned on, interface type and packet size limit
- **Statistics**: General capture statistics, including captured and displayed packets:

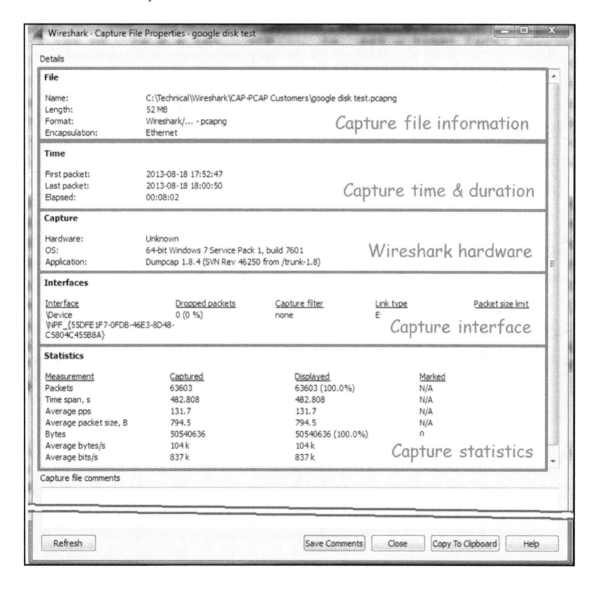

How it works...

This menu simply gives a summary of the filtered data properties and the capture statistics (average packets or bytes per second) when someone wants to learn the capture statistics.

There's more...

From the summary window, you can get the average packets/second and bits/second of the entire captured file, and the same for the displayed data.

Using the statistics – resolved addresses

In this recipe, we will learn a new feature of Wireshark version 2: DNS translations of the captured IP addresses, along with a list of well-known TCP/UDP ports and Ethernet (MAC) addresses vendors.

Getting ready

Start Wireshark, click on **Statistics**.

How to do it...

From the **Statistics** menu, choose **Resolved Addresses**. You will get the following window:

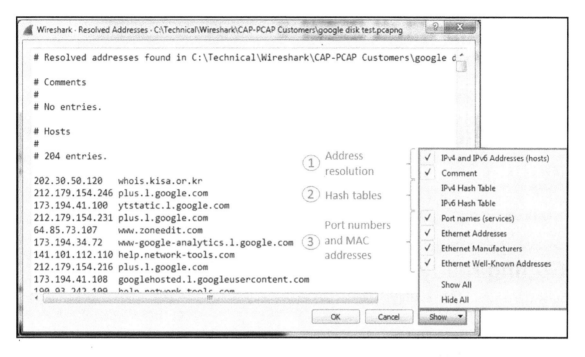

In this window, you have the following information:

- **Address resolution**, which provides DNS names of the captured IP addresses. You can also check **Comment** if you want comments to be seen.
- The **Hash tables** are hash values of the IP addresses.
- **Port names (services)**, **Ethernet Addresses**, **Ethernet Manufacturers**, and **Ethernet Well-Known Addresses** provide Ethernet address information.

How it works...

For IP addresses, Wireshark simply uses your laptop's resolving mechanisms, which are DNS and the Wireshark hosts file, located in the Wireshark home directory.

For the MAC manufacturers, Wireshark uses MAC address translations as defined by the IEEE 802 committee.

TCP and UDP port numbers are defined by the **Internet Assigned Numbers Authority (IANA)** at: http://www.iana.org/assignments/service-names-port-numbers/service-names-port-numbers.xhtml.

There's more

With this new feature of Wireshark, we can gain information that is available on the internet. It is just some more information that is helpful and accessible to us.

Using the statistics – protocol hierarchy menu

In this recipe, we will learn how to get protocol hierarchy information of the data that runs over the network.

Getting ready

Start Wireshark, click on **Statistics**.

How to do it...

1. From the **Statistics** menu, choose **Protocol Hierarchy**:

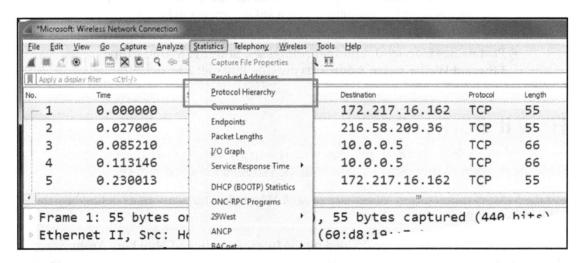

What you will get is data about the protocol distribution in the captured file. You will get the protocol distribution of the captured data.

2. The partial screenshot displayed here depicts the statistics of packets captured on a per-protocol basis:

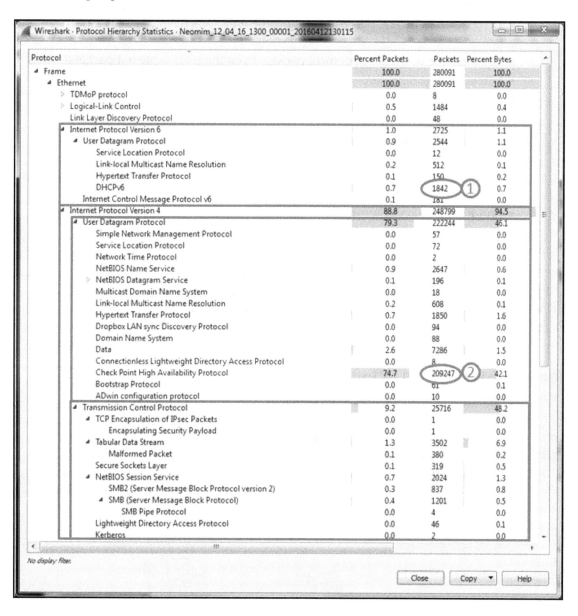

Protocol	Percent Packets	Packets	Percent Bytes
◢ Frame	100.0	280091	100.0
◢ Ethernet	100.0	280091	100.0
▷ TDMoP protocol	0.0	8	0.0
▷ Logical-Link Control	0.5	1484	0.4
Link Layer Discovery Protocol	0.0	48	0.0
◢ Internet Protocol Version 6	1.0	2725	1.1
◢ User Datagram Protocol	0.9	2544	1.1
Service Location Protocol	0.0	12	0.0
Link-local Multicast Name Resolution	0.2	512	0.1
Hypertext Transfer Protocol	0.1	150	0.2
DHCPv6	0.7	1842 ①	0.7
Internet Control Message Protocol v6	0.1	181	0.0
◢ Internet Protocol Version 4	88.8	248799	94.5
◢ User Datagram Protocol	79.3	222244	46.1
Simple Network Management Protocol	0.0	57	0.0
Service Location Protocol	0.0	72	0.0
Network Time Protocol	0.0	2	0.0
NetBIOS Name Service	0.9	2647	0.6
▷ NetBIOS Datagram Service	0.1	196	0.1
Multicast Domain Name System	0.0	18	0.0
Link-local Multicast Name Resolution	0.2	608	0.1
Hypertext Transfer Protocol	0.7	1850	1.6
Dropbox LAN sync Discovery Protocol	0.0	94	0.0
Domain Name System	0.0	88	0.0
Data	2.6	7286	1.5
Connectionless Lightweight Directory Access Protocol	0.0	8	0.0
Check Point High Availability Protocol	74.7	209247 ②	42.1
Bootstrap Protocol	0.0	61	0.1
ADwin configuration protocol	0.0	10	0.0
◢ Transmission Control Protocol	9.2	25716	48.2
◢ TCP Encapsulation of IPsec Packets	0.0	1	0.0
Encapsulating Security Payload	0.0	1	0.0
◢ Tabular Data Stream	1.3	3502	6.9
Malformed Packet	0.1	380	0.2
Secure Sockets Layer	0.1	319	0.5
◢ NetBIOS Session Service	0.7	2024	1.3
SMB2 (Server Message Block Protocol version 2)	0.3	837	0.8
◢ SMB (Server Message Block Protocol)	0.4	1201	0.5
SMB Pipe Protocol	0.0	4	0.0
Lightweight Directory Access Protocol	0.0	46	0.1
Kerberos	0.0	2	0.0

What you will get is the **Protocol Hierarchy** window:

- **Protocol**: The protocol name
- **Percent Packets**: The percentage of protocol packets from the total captured packets
- **Packets**: The number of protocol packets from the total captured packets
- **Percent Bytes**: The percentage of protocol bytes from the total captured packets
- **Bytes**: The number of protocol bytes from the total captured packets
- **Bit/s**: The bandwidth of this protocol, in relation to the capture time
- **End Packets**: The absolute number of packets of this protocol (for the highest protocol in the decode file)
- **End Bytes**: The absolute number of bytes of this protocol (for the highest protocol in the decode file)
- **End Bit/s**: The bandwidth of this protocol, relative to the capture packets and time (for the highest protocol in the decode file)

The end columns counts when the protocol is the last protocol in the packet (that is, when the protocol comes at the end of the frame). These can be TCP packets with no payload (for example, SYN packets) which carry upper layer protocols. That is why you see a zero count for Ethernet, IPv4, and UDP end packets; there are no frames where those protocols are the last protocol in the frame.

In this file example, we can see two interesting issues:

- We can see 1,842 packets of DHCPv6. If IPv6 and DHCPv6 are not required, disable it.
- We see more than 200,000 **checkpoint high availability** (**CPHA**) packets, 74.7% of which are sent over the network we monitored. These are synchronization packets that are sent between two firewalls working in a cluster, updating session tables between the firewalls. Such an amount of packets can severely influence performance. The solution for this problem is to configure a dedicated link between the firewalls so that session tables will not influence the network.

How it works...

Simply, it calculates statistics over the captured data. Some important things to notice:

- The percentage always refers to the same layer protocols. For example, in the following screenshot, we see that logical link control has 0.5% of the packets that run over Ethernet, IPv6 has 1.0%, IPv4 has 88.8% of the packets, ARP has 9.6% of the packets and even the old Cisco ISK has 0.1 %—a total of 100 % of the protocols over layer 2 Ethernet.
- On the other hand, we see that TCP has 75.70% of the data, and inside TCP, only 12.74% of the packets are HTTP, and that is almost it. This is because Wireshark counts only the packets with the HTTP headers. It doesn't count, for example, the ACK packets, data packets, and so on:

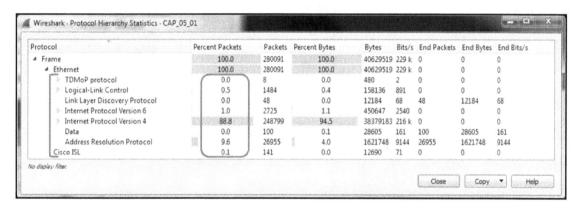

There's more...

In order for Wireshark to also count the data packets, for example, the data packets of HTTP inside the TCP packet, disable the allow subdissector to reassemble TCP streams. You can do this from the **Preferences** menu, or by right-clicking **TCP** in the packet details pane.

Using the statistics – conversations menu

In this recipe, we will learn how to get conversation information of the data that runs over the network.

Getting ready

Start Wireshark, click on **Statistics**.

How to do it...

From the **Statistics** menu, choose **Conversations**:

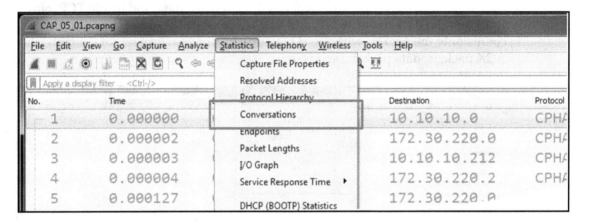

The following window will come up:

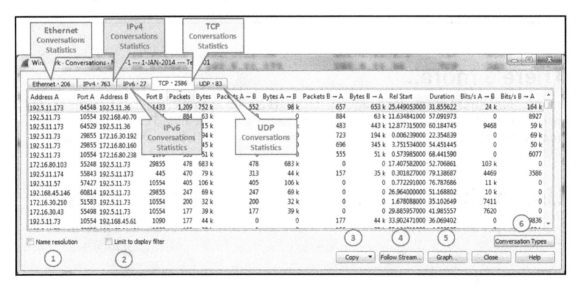

You can choose between layer 2 Ethernet statistics, layer 3 IP statistics, or layer 4 TCP or UDP statistics.

You can use this statistics tools for:

- **On layer 2 (Ethernet)**: To find and isolate broadcast storms
- **On layer 3/layer 4 (TCP/IP)**: To connect in parallel to the internet router port, and check who is loading the line to the ISP

If you see that there is a lot of traffic going out to port 80 (HTTP) on a specific IP address on the internet, you just have to copy the address to your browser and find the website that is most popular with your users.

If you don't get anything, simply go to a standard DNS resolution website (search Google for DNS lookup) and find out what is loading your internet line.

For viewing IP addresses as names, you can check the **Name resolution** checkbox for name resolution (**1** in the previous screenshot). For seeing the name resolution, you will first have to enable it by choosing **View | Name Resolution | Enable for Network layer**.

You can also limit the conversations statistics to a display filter by checking the **Limit to display filter** checkbox (**2**). In this way, statistics will be presented on all the packets passing the display filter.

A new feature in Wireshark version 2 is the graph feature, marked as (**5**) in the previous screenshot. When you choose a specific line in the TCP conversations statistics and click **Graph...**, it brings you to the TCP time/sequence (tcptrace) stream graph. This graph is also available from the **Statistics | TCP Stream Graphs**, and will be explained in the following chapter.

To copy table data, click on the **Copy** button (**3**). In TCP or UDP, you can mark a specific line, and then click on the **Follow Stream...** button (**4**). This will define a display filter that will show you the specific stream of data. As you can see in the following screenshot, you can also right-click a line and choose to prepare or apply a filter, or to colorize a data stream:

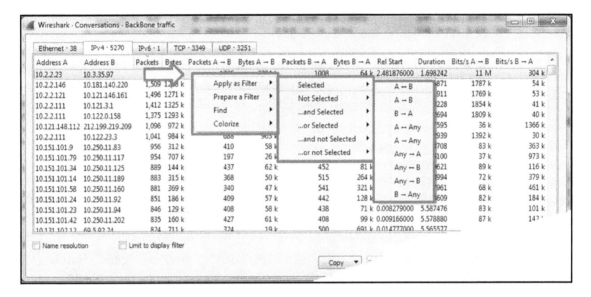

We also see that, unlike the previous Wireshark version, in which we saw all types of protocols in the upper tabs, here we can choose which protocols to see when only the identified protocols are presented by default.

How it works...

A network conversation is the traffic between two specific endpoints. For example, an IP conversation is all the traffic between two IP addresses, and TCP conversations present all TCP connections.

There's more...

There are many network problems that will simply pop up when using the conversations list.

In the Ethernet conversations statistics:

- Look for large numbers of broadcasts—you might be seeing a broadcast storm (a minor one; in a major one, you might not see anything)

> What usually happens in a severe broadcast storm is that, due to thousands, or even tens of thousands, of packets/seconds sent received by Wireshark, the software simply stops showing us the data, and the screen freezes. Only when you disconnect Wireshark from the network will you see it.

- If you see a lot of traffic coming from a specific MAC address, look at the first part of it—this is the vendor ID that will give you a clue to the troublemaker

> Even though the first half of the MAC address identifies the vendor, it does not necessarily identify the PC itself. This is because the MAC address belongs to the Ethernet chip vendor that is installed on the PC or laptop board, and is not necessarily from the PC manufacturer. If you don't get an address that you know where it is coming from, you can ping the suspect and get its MAC address by ARP, find the MAC address in the switches, and if you have a management system use a simple find command to locate it.

In the IP conversations statistics:

- Check the IP addresses with large volumes of packets sent or received and compare the expected behavior. If the address belongs to a server, you might expect to see a large volume of packets. But if it is an end user, it might be a network scan or just generating too much traffic.
- Look for scanning patterns, presented in detail in Chapter 19, *Security and Network Forensics*. It could be a good scan, such as SNMP software that sends a ping to discover the network, but usually scans of the network are not good things.

- You can see a typical scan pattern in the following screenshot:

Address A	Address B	Packets	Bytes	Packets A → B	Bytes A → B	Packets B → A	Bytes B → A	Rel Start	Duration	Bits/s A → B	Bits/s B → A
192.168.110.58	192.170.3.44	1	106	1	106	0	0	1.517110999	0.000000	N/A	N/A
192.168.110.58	192.170.3.45	1	106	1	106	0	0	1.532689000	0.000000	N/A	N/A
192.168.110.58	192.170.3.46	1	106	1	106	0	0	1.548355999	0.000000	N/A	N/A
192.168.110.58	192.170.3.47	1	106	1	106	0	0	1.563934000	0.000000	N/A	N/A
192.168.110.58	192.170.3.48		5	1	106	0	0	1.579562000	0.000000	N/A	N/A
192.168.110.58	192.170.3.49		5	1	106	0	0	1.595191000	0.000000	N/A	N/A
192.168.110.58	192.170.3.50		5	1	106	0	0	1.610806000	0.000000	N/A	N/A
192.168.110.58	192.170.3.51	1	106	1	106	0	0	1.626545000	0.000000	N/A	N/A
192.168.110.58	192.170.3.52	1	106	1	106	0	0	1.642236000	0.000000	N/A	N/A
192.168.110.58	192.170.3.53	1	106	1	106	0	0	1.657772000	0.000000	N/A	N/A
192.168.110.58	192.170.3.54	1	106	1	106	0	0	1.673322000	0.000000	N/A	N/A
192.168.110.58	192.170.3.55	1	106	1	106	0	0	1.690145000	0.000000	N/A	N/A
192.168.110.58	192.170.3.56	1	106	1	106	0	0	1.704616000	0.000000	N/A	N/A
192.168.110.58	192.170.3.57	1	106	1	106	0	0	1.720203999	0.000000	N/A	N/A
192.168.110.58	192.170.3.58	1	106	1	106	0	0	1.735876000	0.000000	N/A	N/A

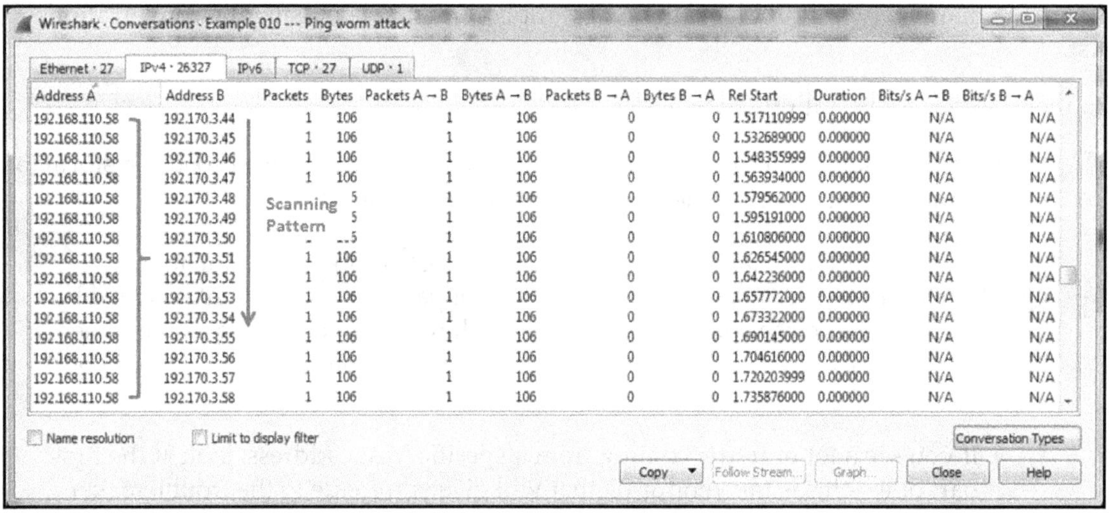

In this example, there is a pattern of a scan. A single IP address, `192.168.110.58`, sends ICMP packets to `192.170.3.44`, to `192.170.3.45`, to `192.170.3.46`, to `192.170.3.47`, and so on (in the picture we see only a very short part of the scan). Then the scan continues to `192.170.4.0`, `192.168.4.1`, and so on. In this case, we had a worm that infected all PCs in the network, and the moment it infects a PC, it starts to generate ICMP requests and sends them to the network, so narrow band links can be easily congested (for example, WAN connections).

In TCP/UDP conversations statistics:

- Look for devices with too many opened TCP connections. 10-20 connections for a PC are reasonable; hundreds are not.
- Look and try to find unrecognized destination port numbers. It might be OK but it can mean trouble. In the following screenshot, you can see a typical TCP scan:

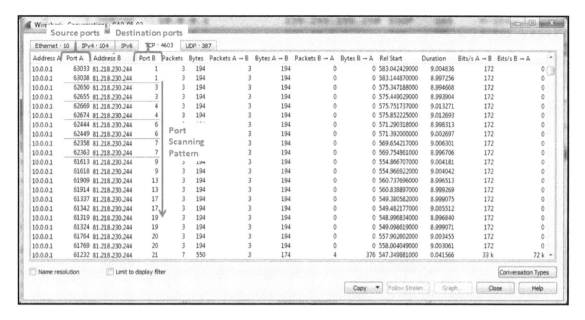

In the preceding screenshot, we see a simple TCP scan pattern. It shows source address `10.0.0.1`, which generates TCP packets to IP address `81.218.230.244` on destination ports 1, 3, 4, 6, 7, and so on.

The scan in this case is in a pattern; `10.0.0.1` sends two packets to every destination port. Two packets are sent from source ports `63033` and `63038` to port 1, two packets from source ports `63650` and `63655` to port 3, and so on.

One of the things that will be recognized immediately when using the conversations tool is that when you click on the source or destination tabs in this window, scanning patterns are seen immediately.

Using the statistics – endpoints menu

In this recipe, we will learn how to get endpoint statistics information of the captured data.

Getting ready

Start Wireshark and click on **Statistics**.

How to do it...

To view the endpoint statistics, follow these steps:

1. From the **Statistics** menu, choose **Endpoints**:

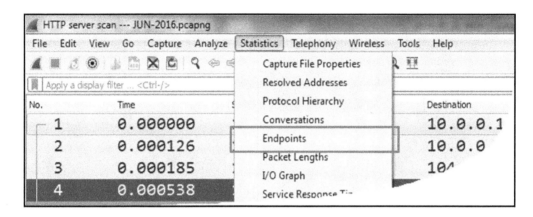

2. The following window will come up:

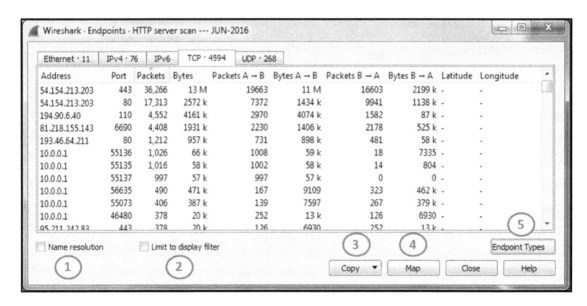

In this window, you will be able to see layer 2, 3, and 4 endpoints, which is Ethernet, IP, and TCP or UDP.

From the left-hand side of the window you can see (here is an example for the TCP tab):

- Endpoint IP address and port number on this host
- Total packets sent, and bytes received from and to this host
- Packets to the host (**Packets A → B**) and bytes to host (**Bytes A → B**)
- Packets to the host (**Packets B → A**) and bytes to host (**Bytes B → A**)
- The **Latitude** and **Longitude** columns applicable with the GeoIP configured as described in `Chapter 10`, *Network Layer Protocols and Operations*.

At the bottom of the window we have the following checkboxes:

- **Name resolution**: Provide name resolution in cases where it is configured in the name resolution under the view menu.
- **Limit to display filter**: To show statistics only for the display filter configured on the main window.
- **Copy**: Copy the list values to the clipboard in CSV or YAML format.
- **Map**: In cases where GeoIP is configured, shows the geographic information on the geographical map. For GeoIP configuration look at `Chapter 10`, *Network Layer Protocols and Operations*.

How it works...

Quite simply, it gives statistics on all the endpoints Wireshark has discovered. It can be any situation, such as the following:

- Few Ethernet (even on) end nodes (that is, MAC addresses), with many IP end nodes (that is, IP addresses)—this will be the case where, for example, we have a router that sends/receives packets from many remote devices.
- Few IP end nodes with many TCP end nodes—this will be the case for many TCP connections per host. Can be a regular operation of a server with many connections, and it could also be a kind of attack that comes through the network (SYN attack).

There's more...

Here we see an example of a capture file taken from a network center, and what we can get from it.

In the following screenshot, we see an internal network where most of the packets go to a Cisco device, probably a router, and an HP device (**1**). Then we see several devices with unresolved MAC addresses (**2**). Next, we see a broadcast (**3**) and spanning tree frames (**4**), IPv4 and IPv6 multicasts (as we will see in Chapter 10, *Network Layer Protocols and Operations*, IPv6 multicasts starts with 33:33:00), and in the last line, these frames from their first six numbers can be one of the presented options—**Cisco Discovery Protocol (CDP)**, **Virtual Trunk Protocol (VTP)** or the other three protocols mentioned:

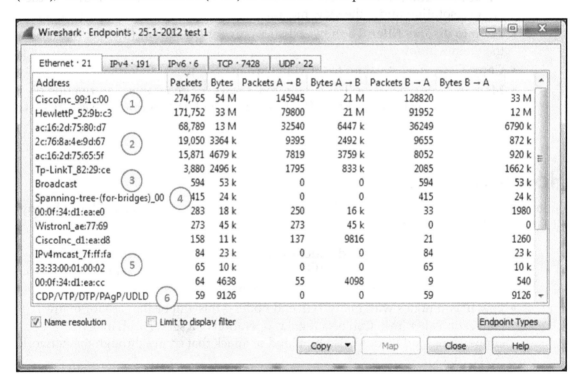

In the next capture file example, taken from a connection to the internet, we see that most of the packets to the internet, 13,031 packets, are sent to the IP address 54.230.47.224:

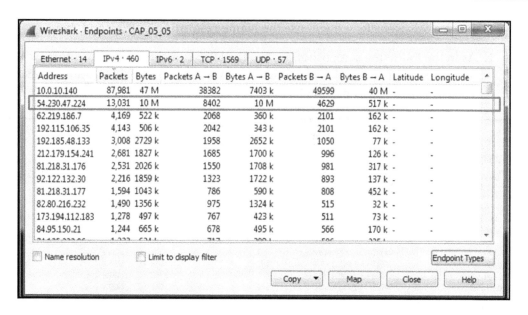

When we try to figure out this website, and we try to simply write its IP address in our browser, we will get errors for both HTTP and HTTPS. We can see this in the following screenshot:

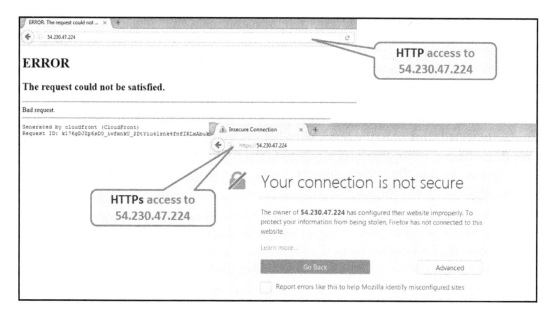

So, in order to see this website, we will use the **Name resolution** button, and then:

1. As in the following screenshot, we see the DNS translation for the address. To see translated addresses you need first to mark **View | Name Resolution | Resolve Network Addresses**, and then to refresh the host table:

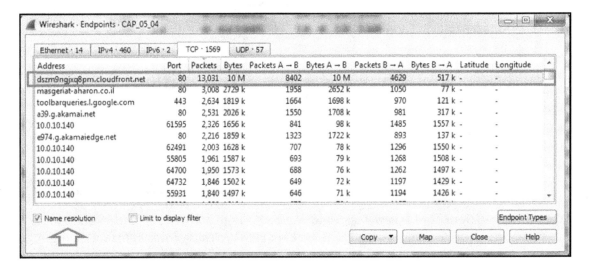

Address	Port	Packets	Bytes	Packets A → B	Bytes A → B	Packets B → A	Bytes B → A	Latitude	Longitude
dszm9ngjxq8pm.cloudfront.net	80	13,031	10 M	8402	10 M	4629	517 k	-	-
masgeriat-aharon.co.il	80	3,008	2729 k	1958	2652 k	1050	77 k	-	-
toolbarqueries.l.google.com	443	2,634	1819 k	1664	1698 k	970	121 k	-	-
a39.g.akamai.net	80	2,531	2026 k	1550	1708 k	981	317 k	-	-
10.0.10.140	61595	2,326	1656 k	841	98 k	1485	1557 k	-	-
e974.g.akamaiedge.net	80	2,216	1859 k	1323	1722 k	893	137 k	-	-
10.0.10.140	62491	2,003	1628 k	707	78 k	1296	1550 k	-	-
10.0.10.140	55805	1,961	1587 k	693	79 k	1268	1508 k	-	-
10.0.10.140	64700	1,950	1573 k	688	76 k	1262	1497 k	-	-
10.0.10.140	64732	1,846	1502 k	649	72 k	1197	1429 k	-	-
10.0.10.140	55931	1,840	1497 k	646	71 k	1194	1426 k	-	-

Some windows in Wireshark refresh automatically when the operation you make requires it, and some not. In our case, in version 2.0.3, it does not. In this case, you can simply check the **Limit to display filter** checkbox and the window will be refreshed. Then, if you don't need the filter, uncheck it.

2. Right-click on the line with the host you want to check, choose **Apply a filter | Selected**, and go to the main Wireshark window.
3. In the main Wireshark window, go to the **Packet Detains** pane. Click on the address with the name you want to copy. Choose **Copy | Description**. You can also use *Ctrl + Shift + D*:

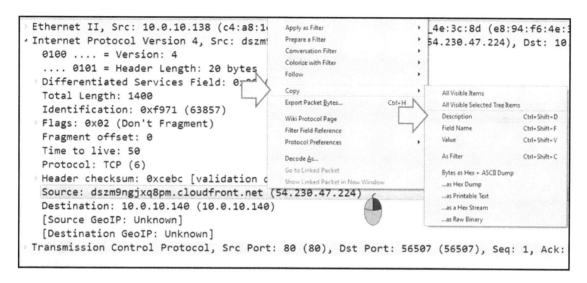

4. Copy the value without the IP address to your web browser, and you will get the required website:

With the DNS name, the website will come up.

Using the statistics – HTTP menu

In this recipe, we will learn how to use HTTP statistical information of the data that runs over the network.

Getting ready

Start Wireshark, click on **Statistics**.

How to do it...

To view the HTTP statistics, click on the **Statistics** menu and choose **HTTP**. The following window will appear:

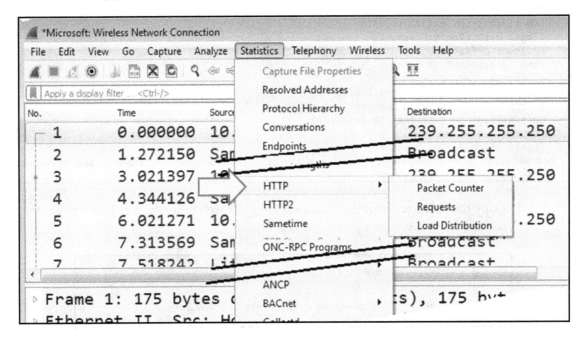

In the HTTP menu, we have the following:

- **Packet Counter**: Provides us with the number of packets to each website. This will help us see how many requests and responses we've had.
- **Requests**: To see request distribution to websites.
- **Load Distribution**: To see load distribution between websites.

Viewing packet counter statistics:

1. Choose **Statistics | HTTP | Packet Counter**.
2. The following window will open:

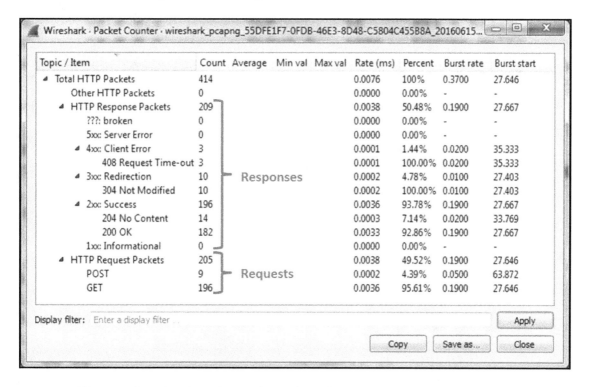

This window displays the total number of HTTP requests and responses.

3. In order to see HTTP statistics for a specific node, you can configure a filter to it, using a display filter format. This can be configured in the **Display filter** window.

Viewing HTTP requests statistics:

1. Choose **Statistics** | **HTTP** | **Requests.** The following window will appear:

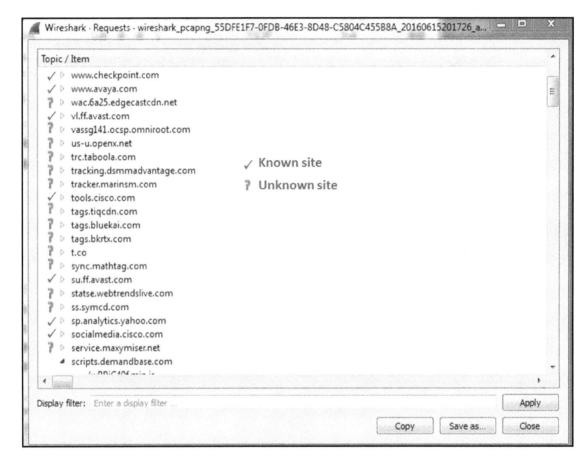

2. To get statistics to a specific HTTP host, you can set a filter `http.host contains <host_name>` or `http.host==<host_name>` (depends if you need a hostname with a specific name or a hostname that contains a specific string), and you will see statistics to this specific host.
3. For example, configuring the filter `http.host == www.ndi-com.com`, you will get the statistics to the website of `www.ndi-com.com` (in the following screenshot):

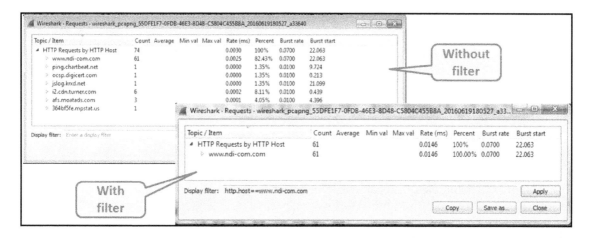

To see load distribution to the web or a specific website:

1. Choose **Statistics | HTTP | Packet Load Distribution**.
2. The following window will appear (narrowed down for explanation):

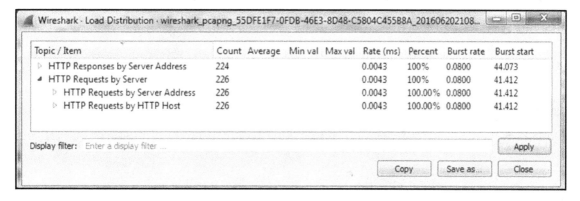

3. When opening the table items, you get the list of servers by:
   - IP address
   - Server address
   - HTTP hostname

In `Chapter 12`, *FTP, HTTP/1, and HTTP/2*, you will see how to use these tools for HTTP analysis.

How it works...

When we open a website, it usually sends requests to several URLs. In this example, one of the websites we opened was www.cnn.com, which forwarded us to edition.cnn.com. In view of this, we have sent several requests to the root URL for breaking news and to two other locations on the home page.

There's more...

For deeper HTTP analysis, you can use specific-purpose tools. One of the most common ones is Fiddler. You can find it at: http://www.fiddler2.com/fiddler2/.

Fiddler is a software tool developed for HTTP troubleshooting, and therefore it provides more data with a better user interface for HTTP.

Configuring a flow graph for viewing TCP flows

In this recipe, we will learn how to use the flow graph feature.

Getting ready

Open Wireshark, click **Statistics**, and choose **Flow Graph** around the middle of the statistics menu.

How to do it...

Choosing flow graph, the following window will open:

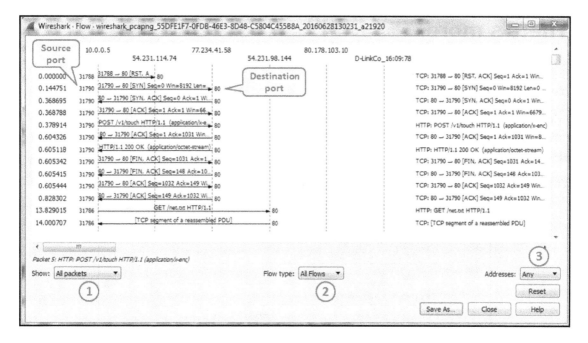

In the window, we see the packet time on the left, the originating and destination addresses of the packets, as well as the port numbers on the two sides of the flow arrows.

Clicking on one of the session arrows will bring you to the packet in the Wireshark main window packet list pane.

You can choose from several options in the flow graph window:

- Show all the captured packets or just displayed packets, filtered by display filter.
- Show all flows or just TCP flows. This will show only TCP operation, for example, in HTTP requests it will show that it is a TCP PUSH (explained in Chapter 12, *FTP, HTTP/1, and HTTP/2*), and the fact that it is an HTTP GET command.
- Show any type of address, for example MAC addresses, or only network addresses (practically, this will show only IP addresses).

How it works...

Simply by creating simple statistics from the captured file.

There's more...

Understanding TCP problems is sometimes quite complex. The best way to do it, most of the time, is to use graphical software that has a better graphical interface, or simply take a piece of paper and different colored pens and draw it yourself.

Friendly software that can do the job includes the Cascade Pilot package from the developers of Wireshark: http://www.riverbed.com/us/products/cascade/wireshark_ enhancements/cascade_pilot_personal_edition.php.

You can see an example of a self-made graph in the following diagram:

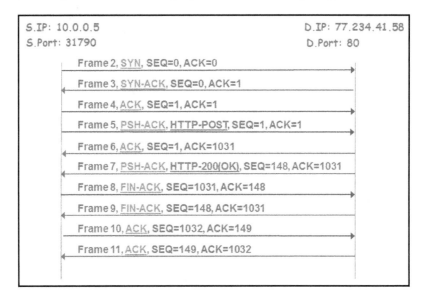

You can clearly see how a TCP connection is set (frames 2-4), how the client 10.0.0.5 sends the HTTP POST command and gets 200 (OK) from the server 77.234.41.58 (frames 5-7), and how a connection is orderly closed (frames 8-11).

We will see more of these self-made graphs later in Chapter 12, *FTP, HTTP/1, and HTTP/2*, and in other applications chapters. After a few graphs, you will know this like the back of your hand.

Creating IP-based statistics

In this recipe, we will learn how to create some IP-based statistics. IP statistics are actually several tools based on the same data, that is, source and destination IP addresses, and the packets that are sent between them.

Getting ready

Open Wireshark and click on the **Statistics** menu. Right at the bottom of the **Statistics** menu, we see the following statistics tools:

- **IPv4 Statistics**
- **IPv6 Statistics**

The following displays the options under the IPv4/IPv6 statistics sections:

- **All Addresses**
- **Destinations and Ports**
- **IP Protocols Types**
- **Source and Destinations Addresses**:

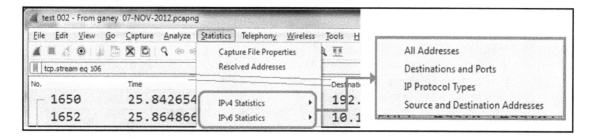

How to do it...

To get the statistics, follow these steps:

To get all IP addresses:

1. Go to **Statistics** | **IPv4 Statistics** | **All Addresses**.
2. Alternatively, go to **Statistics** | **IPv6 Statistics** | **All Addresses**. The following window opens:

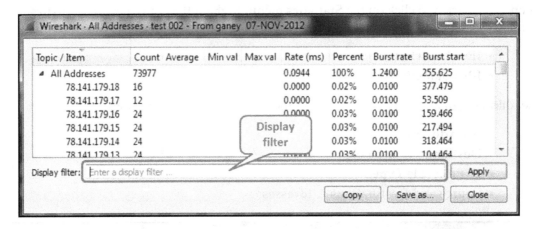

3. So far, it is obvious. The interesting stuff here is that you can configure a filter, for example (in this example), the filter `tcp.analysis.retransmission` shows us that most of the retransmissions are to the address `10.10.10.30` and there are 1,262 retransmissions to this address:

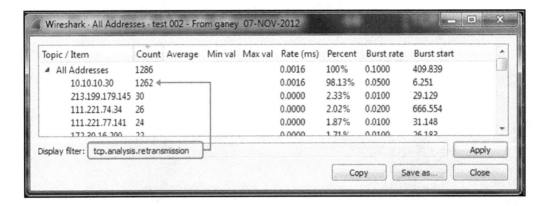

4. There are other tools that can show us the same information, for example, **Statistics | Conversations**, which we talked about earlier in this chapter, or simply use display filters on the main Wireshark window.

To get IP and TCP/UDP destinations statistics:

1. Go to **Statistics | IPv4 Statistics | Destinations and Ports**.
2. Alternatively, go to **Statistics | IPv6 Statistics | Destinations and Ports**. The following window is where you choose the filter you want to use, for example, `tcp.analysis.zero_window`, as in the following screenshot:

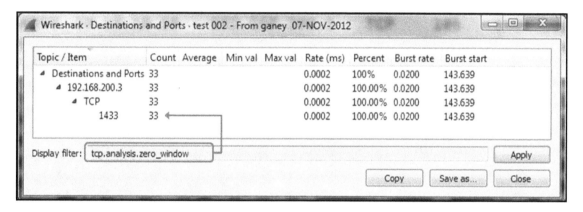

To get IP protocol types:

1. Go to **Statistics | IPv4 Statistics | Protocol Types**
2. Alternatively, go to **Statistics | IPv6 Statistics | Protocol Types**

Nothing much to get from here.

To get IP source and destination addresses:

1. Go to **Statistics | IPv4 Statistics | Source and Destination Addresses**
2. Alternatively, go to **Statistics | IPv6 Statistics | Source and Destination Addresses**

Nothing much to get from here either.

The file that was presented as an example here is `CAP_05_08`.

How it works...

It works simply by creating statistics over the captured file.

There's more...

There are various options in Wireshark that give you quite similar statistics; these are conversations, protocol hierarchy, and endpoints that were discussed at the beginning of this chapter. You can use them in conjunction with the previous.

6
Using Advanced Statistics Tools

In this chapter, we will learn about the following topics:

- Configuring I/O graphs with filters for measuring network performance issues
- Throughput measurements with I/O graphs
- Advanced I/O graphs configurations with advanced y axis parameters
- Getting information through TCP stream graphs – time/sequence (Steven's) window
- Getting information through TCP stream graphs – time/sequence (TCP-trace) window
- Getting information through TCP stream graphs – throughput window
- Getting information through TCP stream graphs – round-trip-time window
- Getting information through TCP stream graphs – window-scaling window

Introduction

In Chapter 5, *Using Basic Statistics Tools*, we discussed the basic statistical tools—that is, the list of end users, list of conversations, the capture summary, and others. In this chapter, we will look at the advanced statistical tools—the I/O graphs, TCP stream graphs, and, in brief, also UDP multicast streams.

The tools we will talk about here enable us to have a better look at the network. Here, we have two major tools:

- The I/O graph, which enables us to view statistical graphs for any predefined filter—for example, the throughput on a single IP address, the load between two or more hosts, application throughput, TCP phenomena distribution, time between frames, time between TCP sequence numbers and acknowledgement, and more.
- TCP stream graphs. In examining these, we will have a deeper look at a single TCP connection, and learn how to isolate TCP problems and what causes them.

Wireshark Version 2 has significantly improved the I/O graphs and the TCP stream graphs. In this chapter, we will learn how to use the tools; we will need them for deeper protocol analysis in the chapters that deal with protocols.

Configuring I/O graphs with filters for measuring network performance issues

In this recipe, we will learn how to use the I/O graph tool, and how to configure it for network troubleshooting.

Getting ready

Under the **Statistics** menu, open the I/O graph. You can do this during an online file capture or on a file you've captured before. When using the I/O graph on a live capture, you will get live statistics on the captured data.

How to do it...

Run the I/O graph, and you will get the following window:

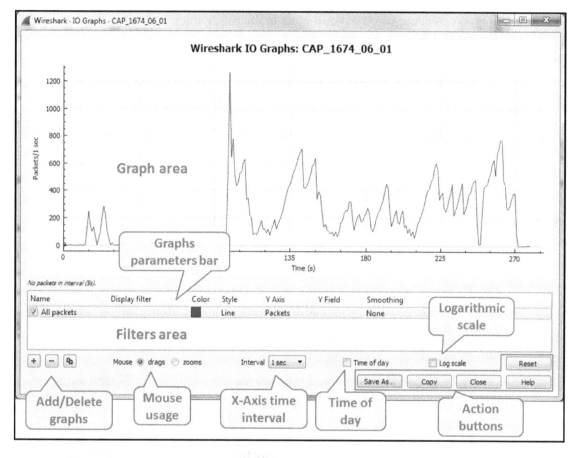

On the upper part of the window, you see the graph area. On the lower-left side, you have the filters area, which enables you to configure display filters that will enable specific graphs. The default, as you can see in the preceding screenshot, is packets per second on the *y* axis and time in seconds on the *x* axis.

You can configure the following parameters for the window's display:

- The +/- and copy buttons in the lower-left corner of the window are used to add/delete and copy graphs.
- Use the mouse usage checkboxes to drag or zoom. You can drag a graph across the window and use the zoom function to zoom in or out. Use the **Reset** button in the lower-right corner of the window to go back to the initial window state.

On the x axis, you can configure the parameters in the following ways:

- Choose the **Interval**. The scale can be between 1 millisecond and 10 minutes

 If, for example, we get a peak of 1,000 packets/second when the x axis is configured with a 1 second interval, it means that in the last second, we've received 1,000 packets. When we change the x axis to a 0.1 second interval, the peak will be different because now we can see how many packets were captured in the last 0.1 seconds.

- Mark the **Time of day** checkbox for choosing the time of day format instead of the time since the beginning of capture

On the y axis configuration, you can make the following change:

- Mark the **Log scale** checkbox to see the graphs in logarithmic scale

Graph configuration:

- In the graph window, you can add/delete/copy and change graphs. Simply go through the following steps:
    1. When you start the I/O graphs, all packet graphs are presented by default.
    2. To add an additional graph with a filter, click on the + sign in the lower-left corner of the I/O graph window. A new line will be added.
    3. Give the graph a name in the **Name** column.
    4. Configure the required filter in the **Display filter** column. As the name indicates, the filter is in display filter syntax with autocomplete.
    5. Configure (or leave as default) the **Color** and **Style** columns.
    6. In the **Style** column, you can configure the **Line**, **Impulse**, **Bar**, **Stacked bar**, **Dot**, **Square** and **Diamond** parameters. **Line**, for example, is good for a traffic graph, while **Dot** is suitable for event graphs such as TCP analysis, retransmission, duplicate ACK, or others.
    7. Choose **Smooth** if you want to see the running average—that is, when, in every tick-interval, you see the average of the past ticks. You can choose values from 4 to 1024, to smooth the graph.

In the following example, CAP_1674_06_02, you see a traffic graph with all packets, tcp.analysis.duplicate_ack, and tcp.analysis.fast_retransmission filters:

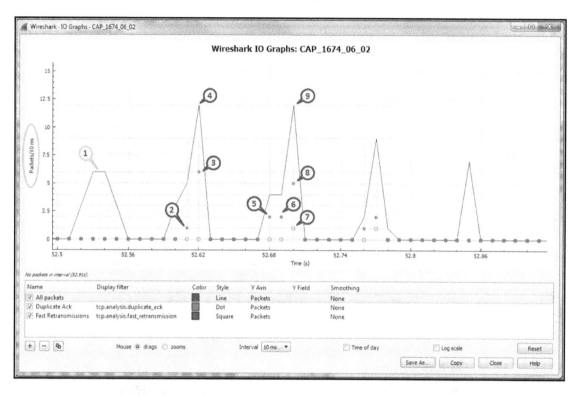

In the example, you can see that the x axis scale is in 10 ms (milliseconds) and the y axis scale is in packets/10 ms. In the first graph, **All packets** is the total traffic without any filter presented with a **Line** style; the second graph using the filter tcp.analysis.duplicate_ack is presented using a **Dot** style, and the third graph with the filter tcp.analysis.fast_retransmission is presented with a **Square** style. The graph is presented with a zoomed-in focus on the time between **52.5** to **52.86** seconds since the beginning of capture.

The traffic starts with a peak of 6 packets per 10 ms (**1**) from 52.53 to 52.54, and the next two peaks are of 12 packets per 10 ms (**4** and **9**).

For duplicate acknowledge, we see one event at 52.61 seconds (**2**), six events at 52.62 seconds (**3**), two events at 52.68 seconds (**5**), and two more at 52.69 seconds (**6**), and at 52.60 seconds, we see five duplicate ACK (**8**) events and one fast retransmission event (**7**).

As we can see from the following screenshot that an event at a specific time means that the event that happened at the time specified—for example, six events at the time 52.62 means that six events happened at the time 52.62:

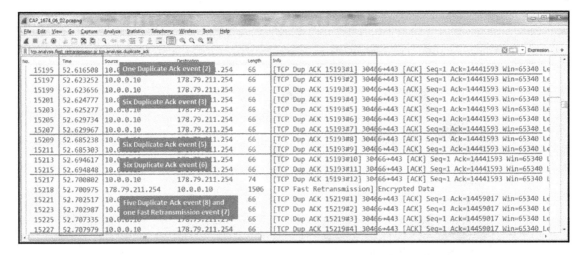

Later, in the chapters dealing with protocols, we will see the importance of the accuracy we talked about here, and where and when to use it.

How it works...

The I/O graph feature is one of the important Wireshark tools that enable us to monitor online performance along with offline captured file analysis.

When you are using this tool, the important thing to remember is to configure the right filter with the right *x* axis and *y* axis parameters.

There are two types of parameters that we can measure in the *y* axis. The first type is the numeric parameter—packets, bytes, and bits that are measured in relation to the time scale in the *x* axis. As shown in the following screenshot, the second type of parameter is **SUM**, **COUNT FRAMES**, **COUNT FIELDS**, **MAX**, **MIN**, **AVG**, and **LOAD**, which are used for counts in which the *y* axis does not necessarily display a number, as described in the section on advanced I/O graph configurations with advanced *y* axis parameters later in this chapter:

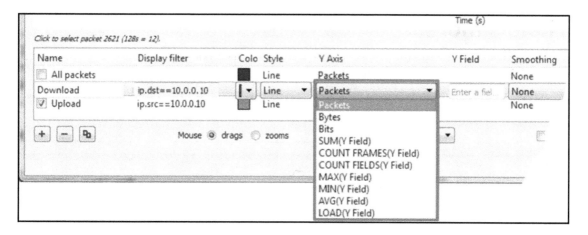

Another important feature to bear in mind is the smoothing column to the left of the window, as shown in the following screenshot. The term **smoothing** means that it will not graph the value per sample, but will accumulate the latest 10, 20, 50, 100, and 200 samples, build an average of those readings, and graph this average (of 10, 20, 50, 100, and so on):

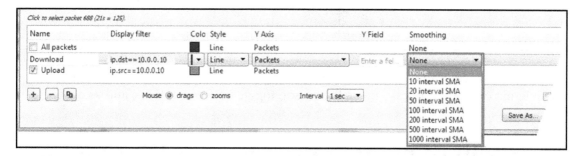

As we will see later, this can be used for bandwidth/throughput measurements.

There's more...

To see the list of shortcuts for the I/O graph window, place your mouse on the space between the graph window and the filter window:

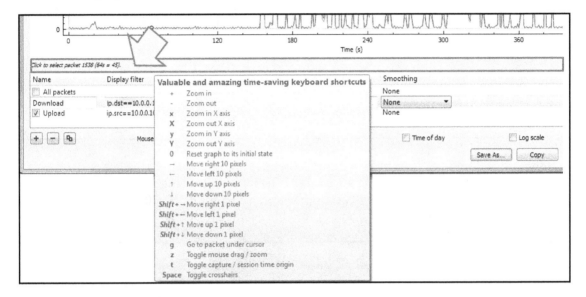

In this window, you can change this display in any way you see fit—for example, you can zoom in/out on the *x* or *y* scale, move the cursor, toggle between options, and so on.

Throughput measurements with I/O graphs

The I/O graph feature is a convenient tool for measuring throughput through the network. We can use it to measure the traffic and throughput of any predefined filter. In this recipe, we will see some examples of how it can be used to measure throughput in a network.

Getting ready

Connect your laptop to the network with Wireshark, with the port mirror to the link you want to measure, as you learned in `Chapter 1`, *Introduction to Wireshark Version 2*. Start a new capture or open an existing file, and then open the I/O graphs from the **Statistics** menu.

When measuring the throughput, we can measure it on a communication line between end devices (PC to server, phone to phone, PC to the internet) or to a specific application:

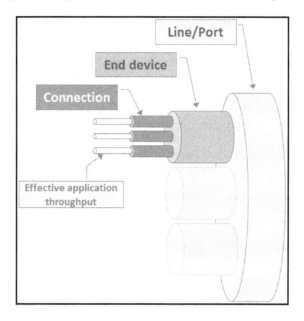

The process of isolating network problems starts from measuring traffic over a link, between end devices, or on single connections to see where it comes from.

Some typical measurements are host-to-host traffic, all traffic to a specific server, all traffic to a specific application on a specific server, all TCP performance phenomena on a specific server, and so on.

How to do it...

In this recipe, we will provide some basic filters for measuring traffic throughout the network.

Measuring download/upload traffic

Let's have a look at the next two graphs, in which a PC with an IP address of 10.0.0.10 is browsing the internet, watching a movie on http://www.youtube.com. The graph is configured on file CAP_1674_06_03.

In these two I/O graphs, we have configured two filters:

- The first graph shows all traffic to the IP address `10.0.0.10`—this is the `ip.dst==10.0.0.10` filter, colored in red (the upper line). This is the graph of the download (downstream) traffic.
- The second graph shows all traffic from the IP address `10.0.0.10`—this is the `ip.src==10.0.0.10` filter, colored in green (the lower line). This is the graph of the upload (upstream) traffic.

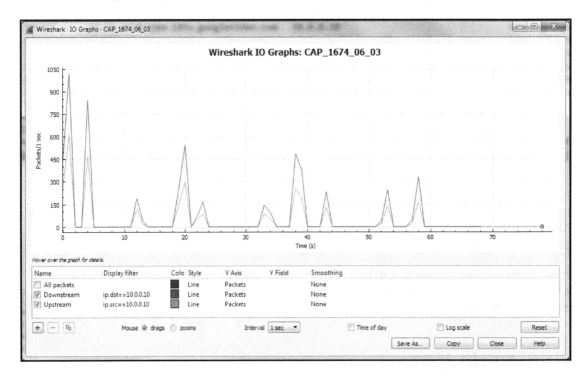

In the first graph, we can see that we've measured the traffic when the *x* axis is configured to an interval of 1 second, and the *y* axis scale is configured to packets/second. The results that we've got show that while the user is watching a movie, the upload is about one half of the total download:

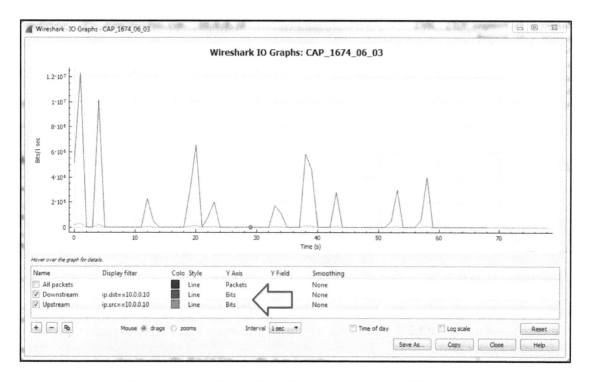

In the second graph, we can see the traffic in bits/second for watching a movie in a reasonable quality. In this example, the movie is being watched on http://www.youtube.com. As you can see, the traffic is 10 Mbits/second for the initial download (this is when you see the little rounded arrow when you open the movie window), and 6 Mbits/second when the movie is being watched continuously from that point on.

We can also see that the traffic is strongly asymmetric, with most of the traffic coming from the download. In the following screenshot, you can see why:

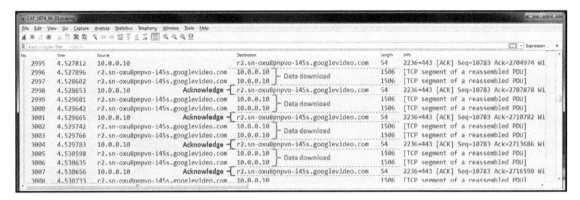

Here, we can see that for every two downstream packets from googlevideo.com to 10.0.0.10 there is one upstream acknowledgment, and this is why we see a ratio of 1:2. On the other hand, when we look at the packet length, we can see that the two packets in the download traffic are 1,506 bytes long, while the upstream acknowledge packet is a short 54-bytes-long packet.

Measuring several streams between two end devices

To measure the throughput between devices at endpoints, simply configure a display filter between their IP addresses.

Let's look in the CAP_1674_06_04 file from **Statistics | Conversations.** In this file, we can see that the three busiest connections are as follows:

- One connection from a terminal server client 192.168.1.192 to the terminal server at 172.30.0.10
- Two connections from the terminal server 172.30.0.10 to the database server at 172.30.0.22

In the following screenshot, we can see the **Conversations** window:

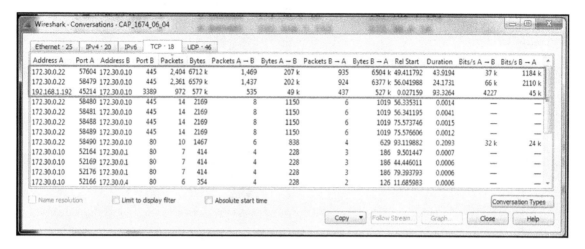

The parameters set in the filter fields are as follows:

- `ip.addr==172.30.0.22 && tcp.port==57604 && ip.addr==172.30.0.10 && tcp.port==445`

- `ip.addr==172.30.0.22 && tcp.port==58479 && ip.addr==172.30.0.10 && tcp.port==445`

- `ip.addr==192.168.1.192 && tcp.port==45214 && ip.addr==172.30.0.10 && tcp.port==3389`

As we can see in the following screenshot, when we look at the I/O graphs, we can see two peaks from the terminal server `172.30.0.10` to the database server `172.30.0.22`. The Client-Server Traffic 1 in brown peaks on the right, while Client-Server Traffic 2 in green peaks on the left:

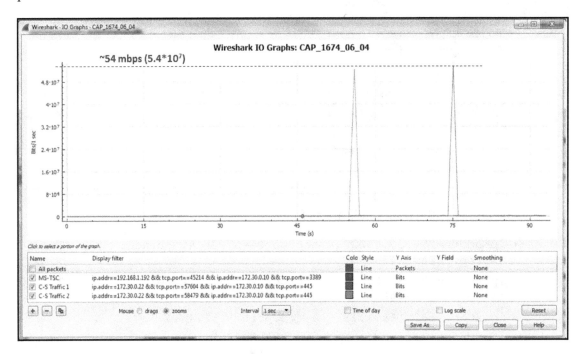

Since the bandwidth of the two bit-streams from the terminal server to the database server are much higher than the terminal server stream, we don't see the last one on this window (dashed line has been added to the screenshot). In order to see it, we disable the two higher bit-stream checkboxes, and what we get is the following:

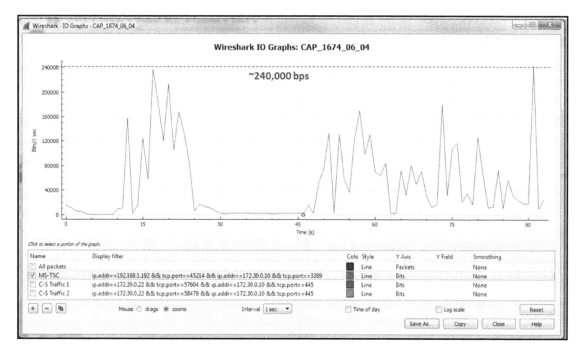

Here, we can see that the highest peaks in the terminal server traffic are around 400,000 bits per second (a dashed line has been added in the preceding screenshot).

Measuring application throughput

In order to configure the performance measurement of a specific application, you can configure a filter that contains specific port numbers or a specific connection.

There are several ways to isolate an application graph:

- In the captured data, click on any packet that belongs to the traffic stream. In TCP, it will be a specific connection; in UDP it will be just a stream between an IP/port pair.
- Right-click it and choose **Follow TCP stream** or **Follow UDP stream**.
- You will get `tcp.stream eq <number>`or `udp.stream eq <number>`. The `<number>` is simply the number of the stream in the capture file.

- Copy the string to the filter window in the I/O graph and you will get the graph of the specific stream:

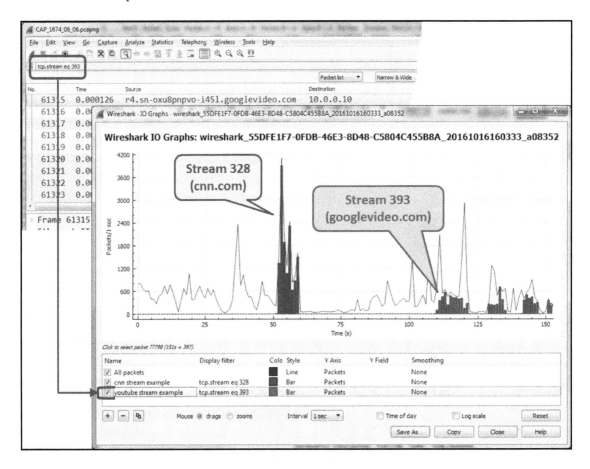

Measuring a TCP stream with TCP event analysis

To measure a specific stream in order to find the events that are disturbing this stream, use I/O graphs as follows:

1. Open the capture file (or start a new capture) and start the I/O graphs. In this example, we use the `CAP_1674_06_06` file.

2. In the first filter, configure the stream number—in this example, we are looking at `tcp.stream eq 0`. This will give you the traffic on this stream.

3. In the first filter, configure the stream number and
   `tcp.analysis.retransmissions: tcp.stream eq 0,` and
   `tcp.analysis.retransmissions.` This will show all TCP retransmission
   phenomena on the specific stream (indicating a slow end device).

In the following screenshot, we see stream number 0 in the first line graph and the
retransmissions on this stream in the second dot graph:

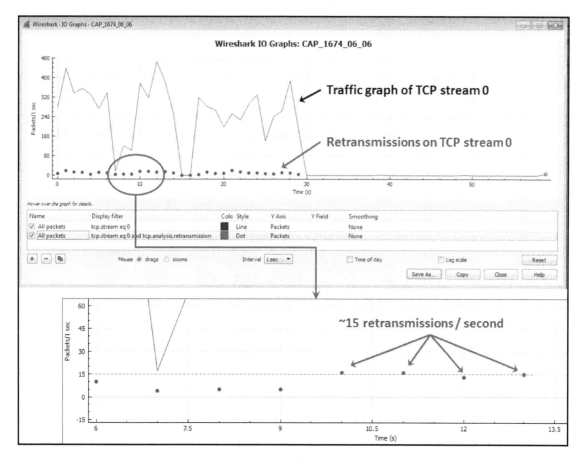

In `Chapter 10`, *Network Layer Protocols and Operations*, we will see how to use these features
for in-depth analysis of TCP traffic.

How it works...

The power of the I/O graph tool comes from the fact that you can configure any display filter and see it as a graph, in various shapes and configurations. Any parameter in a packet can be filtered and monitored in this way.

There's more...

You can configure an I/O graph on any parameter that can be filtered by a display filter string, which makes this a very strong tool. Let's see some examples.

We can use a graph to find SMS messages that have been sent by a specific subscriber (CAP_1674_06_07):

1. To configure the filter, choose **Short Message Peer-to-Peer** (SMPP) protocol packets with the Submit_SM command. This is the SMPP command that sends the SMS.

2. Type the smpp.source_addr == phone number filter. The smpp.source_addr == 0529992525 filter was applied in the example:

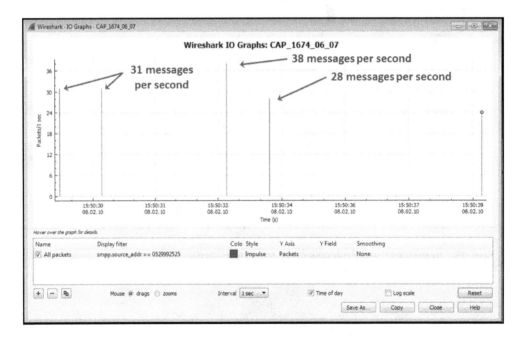

We can also use a graph to show a number of HTTP requests (CAP_1674_06_08):

1. Open the I/O graph. You can do this during capture to view online statistics, or you can open a saved capture file.
2. Configure the http.request filter on the **I/O Graphs** window.
3. You will get the following graph:

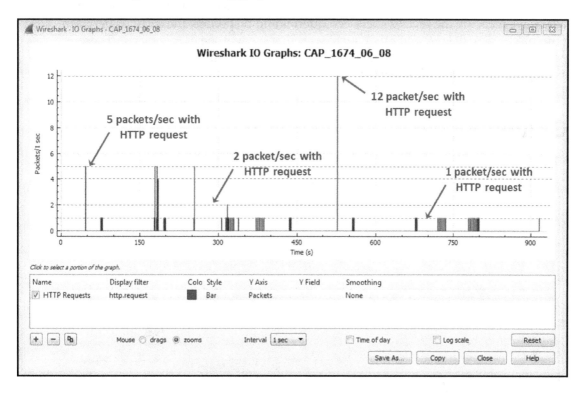

The graph shows the number of packets that contain HTTP requests per second.

The purpose of this recipe is to show the capabilities of the I/O graph tool. Later, in the chapters dealing with protocols, we will use them for deeper protocol analysis.

Advanced I/O graph configurations with y axis parameters

In standard measurements using I/O graphs, we measure the performance of the network when the *y* axis is displayed in units of packets/second, bytes/second, or bits/second. There are some types of data that are not measured with these parameters—for example, cases where we measure the seconds between queries and responses, the seconds between Ethernet frames, delays, and other such cases that we will see in this recipe. These parameters are described in the next section. These capabilities are called **Advanced** in the *y* axis options in Wireshark version 1.

Getting ready

Open the drop-down menu under the *y* axis, as shown in the following screenshot:

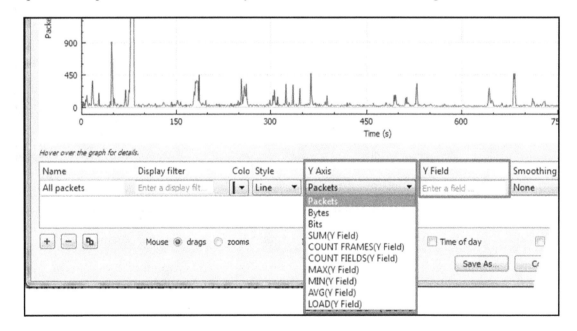

You will get the following options for the *y* axis:

- **SUM (Y Field)**: Draws a graph with the summary of a parameter in the tick interval
- **COUNT FRAMES (Y Field)**: Draws a graph that counts the occurrence of the filtered frames in the time interval
- **COUNT FIELDS (Y Field)**: Draws a graph that counts the occurrence of the filtered fields in the time interval
- **MAX (Y Field)**: Draws a graph with the average of a parameter in the time interval
- **MIN (Y Field)**: Draws a graph with the minimum of a parameter in the time interval
- **AVG (Y Field)**: Draws a graph with the average of a parameter in the time interval
- **LOAD (Y Field)**: Used for response time graphs

In the **Y Field**, you can set the parameters that you want to view.

How to do it...

To start using the I/O graphs with the *y* axis configuration options' feature, go through the following steps:

1. Start the I/O graph from the **Statistics** menu
2. In the **Y Axis** drop-down menu, choose the parameter you want to be presented in the *y* axis
3. You will see a new drop-down menu with the string **SUM (Y Field)**
4. Choose the following fields: **SUM (Y Field)** / **COUNT FRAMES (Y Field)** / **COUNT FIELDS (Y Field)** / **MAX (Y Field)** / **MIN (Y Field)** / **AVG (Y Field)** / **LOAD (Y Field)**
5. Configure the appropriate filter in the **Y Field** column

Let's see some useful examples.

Monitoring inter-frame time delta statistics

The time delta between frames can influence TCP performance and badly influence interactive applications such as voice and video and more. For this reason, there are various options that you can use. One of these is using the `frame.time_delta` for the time delta between all frames or `frame.time_delta` for the time delta between displayed packets.

Let's look at the following capture file (file `CAP_06_09`):

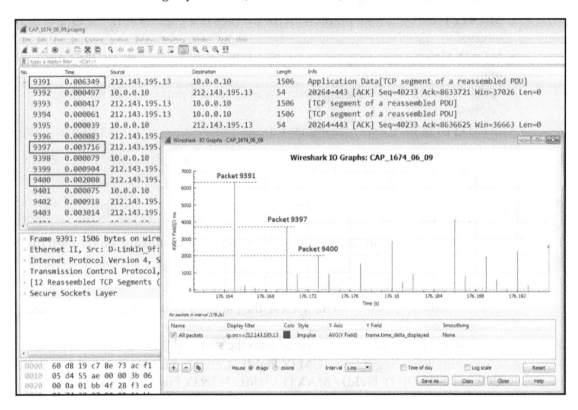

As we can see in the previous screenshot, the following parameters are configured:

- In the **Display filter** column, the filter **ip.src==212.143.195.13**. This is used to see frames coming from this website to our PC.
- In the **Y Axis** field, **AVG (Y Axis)** is used to show the average inter-frame times.
- In the **Y Field** column, the `frame.time_delta_displayed` filter is used to show the inter-frame times.

The interval in this example is configured to be 1 millisecond, with the zoomed-in view centered at 176 seconds since the beginning of capture.

The time values in the *y* axis are presented in microseconds—for example the inter-frame time between frame 9391 and the previous frame is shown as 6349 microseconds.

To see the minimum, average, and maximum values, we can use three graphs, as you can see in the following screenshot.

We can view the maximum, average, and minimum values of the `frame.time_delta` filter, as we can see in the next screenshot. Bear in mind the following points:

- For the first graph:
    - In the **Display filter** column, the `ip.src==212.143.195.13` filter depicts frames that are coming from this website to our PC
    - In the **Y Axis** field, **AVG (Y Axis)** is used to show the average inter-frame times
- For the second graph:
    - In the **Display filter** column, the `ip.src==212.143.195.13` filter depicts frames that are coming from this website to our PC
    - In the **Y Axis** field, **MIN (Y Axis)** is used to show the average inter-frame times
- For the third graph:
    - In the **Display filter** column, the `ip.src==212.143.195.13` filter depicts frames that are coming from this website to our PC

- In the **Y Axis** field, **MAX (Y Axis)** is used to show the average inter-frame times

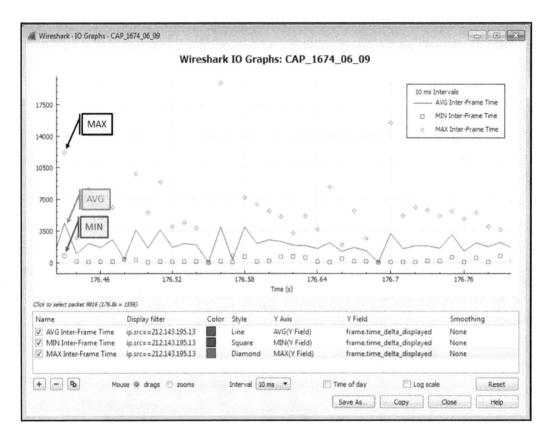

As configured in the **Style** column, we can see the minimum as **Squares**, the maximum as **Diamonds** and the average as a **Line**. What should we do with these graphs, and how should we use them for network debugging? This we will learn in Chapter 10, *Network Layer Protocols and Operations* to Chapter 19, *Security and Network Forensics*, which deal with protocols.

Monitoring the number of TCP events in a stream

TCP events can be of many types—retransmissions, sliding window events, ACKs, and so on. To see the number of TCP events over time, we can use the I/O graph with the advanced feature and **COUNT (Y Axis)** parameter.

In the following example, `CAP_1674_06_10`, we have two TCP streams:

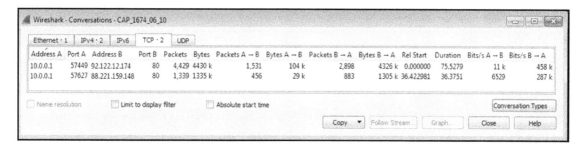

To configure the I/O graph, go through the following steps:

1. Open the IO graph from the **Statistics** menu.
2. Configure the display filter columns; in this example, these are as follows:
    - The first graph: `ip.addr==10.0.0.1 && tcp.port==57449 && ip.addr==92.122.12.174 && tcp.port==80`
    - The second graph: `ip.addr==10.0.0.1 && tcp.port==57627 && ip.addr==88.221.159.148 && tcp.port==80`

> To configure the filters, you can right-click on the stream line in the conversations window, prepare a filter that will appear in the display filter window, and copy it to the I/O graph window. You can also right-click on one of the packets in the stream and choose to follow the TCP stream.

3. Configure the **Y Axis** parameters:
    1. Configure **COUNT FRAMES (Y Field).**
    2. On the **Y Field**, configure the filter—in this example, this is `tcp.analysis` for all TCP events, but it can be any specific filter, such as `tcp.analysis.retransmissions`, `tcp.analysis.zero_window`, or any other.

3. In this example, you will get the graph shown in the following screenshot:

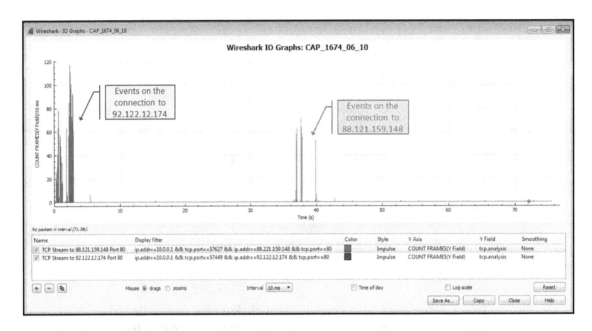

In the last screenshot, we can see two periods of events. We can zoom in on one of them—for example, on the first group of events—and we will get the next screenshot.

Monitoring the number of field appearances

The variable **COUNT FIELDS (Y Field)** counts the appearance of a specific field in the capture file, or in information filtered by a filter configured in the display filter column.

The principle of this is as follows:

- In the **Display filter** columns, you configure a filter to the traffic that should be checked
- In the **Y Axis** column, you configure **COUNT FIELDS (Y Field)**
- In the **Y Field** column, you specify the field whose appearances you want to count

In the following screenshot (file `CAP_1674_06_11`), you see an example of how it is used:

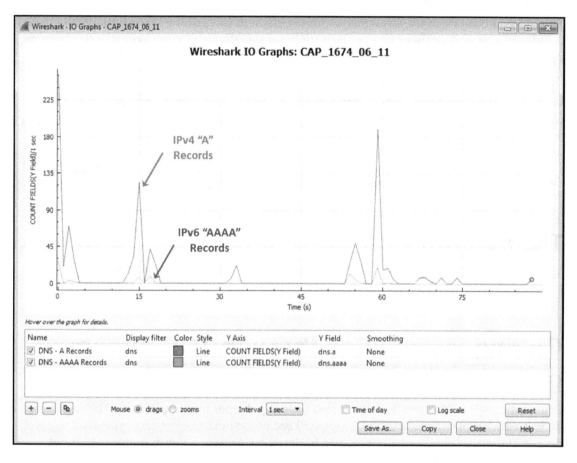

Here, we can see that we checked the number of appearances of A records and AAAA records: the upper graph is for the IPv4 A records, and the lower graph is for the IPv6 AAAA records.

How it works...

The I/O graph is one of the strongest and most efficient tools of the Wireshark. While the standard I/O graph statistics can be used for basic statistics, the y axis configuration can be used for in-depth monitoring of response times, TCP analysis of a single stream or several streams, and more.

When we configure a filter on the left, we will filter the traffic between hosts, traffic on a connection, traffic on a server, and so on. The y axis configuration feature provides us with more details about the traffic. For example:

- On the left—TCP stream. On the right—time delta between frames in the stream
- On the left—video/RTP stream. On the right—occurrence of a marker bit

There's more...

You can always click on the I/O graphs, and it will bring you to the reference packet in the packet pane.

Getting information through TCP stream graphs – time/sequence (Steven's) window

One of the tools in Wireshark that enables us to dig deeper into applications' behavior are TCP stream graphs. These graphs, as we will see in the next few recipes, enable us to get the details of the application's behavior, and in doing so, present us with the possibility of locating problems with it.

Getting ready

Open an existing capture or start a new capture. Click on a specific packet in the capture file. Even though you can use this feature on a running capture, it is not meant for online statistics, so it is recommended that you start a capture, stop it, and then use this tool.

How to do it...

For viewing TCP stream graph statistics, do the following:

1. Click on a packet on the stream you want to monitor.

> The TCP stream shows a **directional** graph, so when you click on a packet, it should be in the direction in which you want to view the statistics. If, for example, you download a file, and you want to view the download statistics, click on a packet on the download direction.

2. From the **Statistics** menu, choose **TCP Stream Graphs | Time Sequence Graph (Stevens)**.

The following window will open:

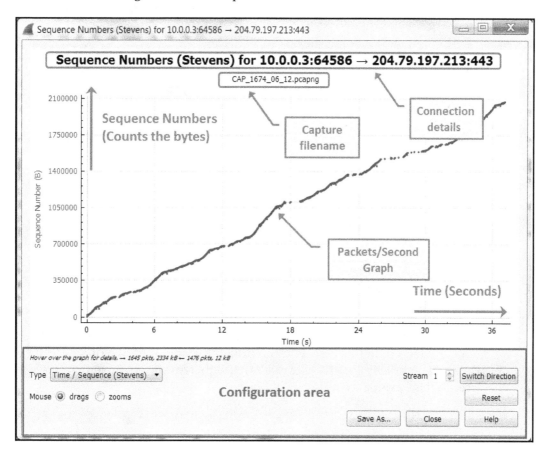

The graph shows the progress of the amount of byte transference over time. In this example, we can see a continuous diagonal line, with some plateaus in the transfer.

The **Y-Axis** in the graph is for sequence numbers, while in the graph I wrote packets/second graph. It actually means the same—each dot in the graph refers to a packet, when its value is the first sequence number in the TCP packet (see in the *How it works...* section later in this recipe).

In Chapter 10, *Network Layer Protocols and Operations*, we will learn what this graph indicates, and some cases that it helps to solve.

3. In the case of a file transfer, to measure its throughput, simply calculate the bytes transferred in a unit of time, as seen in the following screenshot:

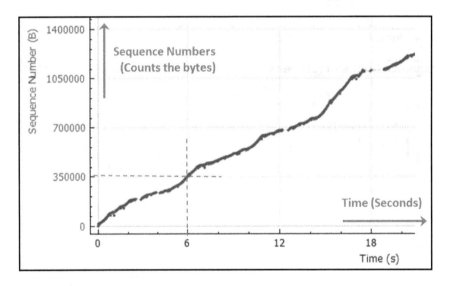

4. We can see that the transfer rate is 350,000 bytes in 6 seconds—that is roughly 58,000 bytes/second, or 58 kilobits/second.

5. By default, the **Drags** checkbox, in the lower-left corner of the stream graph menu, is checked. In this case, you can drag the graph up/down or stretch the *x* axis-*y* axis right/left. For example, we can use this feature to move the graph closer to the *y* axis to see a specific value.

With when the **Mouse** checkbox is set to **drag**, you can use *Ctrl* + the mouse wheel to zoom in and out on the TCP stream graph.

6. When we check the **Zoom** checkbox, to the right of the **Mouse** checkbox, we change the setting to zoom. In the next screenshot, we can see how we can zoom-in twice to the graph to get more details on a specific time period—in this case, we are looking at a point in time that is roughly between 16 to 19 seconds since capture started:

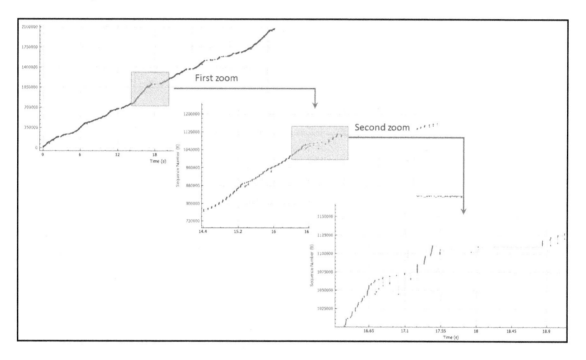

7. The other graph configuration buttons are as follows:
   - Type of graph (lower-left corner, right above the drag/zoom checkboxes). You can choose between the various types of TCP graphs (shown in the following screenshot): **Time / Sequence (Stevens)**, **Round Trip Time**, **Throughput**, **Time / Sequence (tcptrace)**, **Window Scaling**.

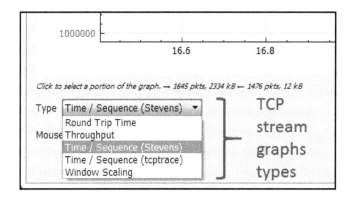

   - **Stream number**, on the lower-right corner of the window. This shows the number of the stream in the capture file.
   - **Switch direction**, to the right of the stream number. Clicking on this shows the opposite direction of the stream. If we choose a stream direction on the download from the server to us, the opposite direction is the packets on the same stream on the way back from us to the server—in this case, the acknowledgments.
   - **Reset**, below the **Switch Direction** checkbox. This brings the graph back to the default view.
   - **Help** brings up the software manual.
   - **Save As...** saves the graph in the `.pdf`, `.png`, `.bmp`, or `.jpg` formats.

How it works...

The time-sequence graph (Stevens) is a simple graph that counts the TCP sequence numbers over time. Since TCP sequence numbers count the bytes sent by the TCP, these are actually application bytes (including application headers) sent from one side to the other.

In the graph, we actually see a point for every packet, when the point is located on the y axis, on the sequence value of the first byte in the packet, as shown in the following diagram:

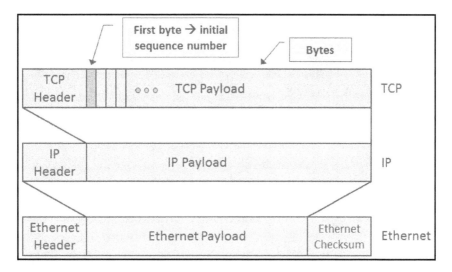

This graph (as we will learn in the chapters looking at TCP and applications) can give us a good indication of the application's behavior. For example, a diagonal line means a good file transfer, while a diagonal line with interruptions shows a problem in the transfer. A diagonal line with a high gradient indicates fast data transfer, while a low gradient indicates a low rate of transfer (depending on the scale, of course).

There's more...

When the mouse is set to the drags option in the lower-left corner of the window, clicking on a dot brings you to the matching packet in the capture window. As you can see in the following screenshot, a sequence number slightly higher than 872,000 is transmitted in packet 8119, about 15.24 seconds after the start of capture, and then again in packet 8191 at 15.35 seconds after capture start:

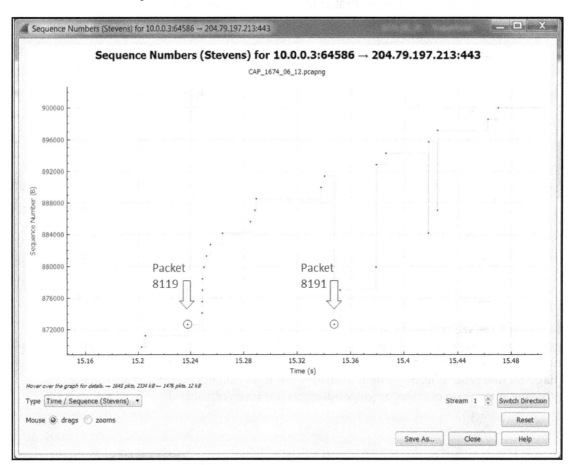

In the following screenshot, we can see the result of clicking on these two dots in the time-sequence graph. The first packet, packet 8119, has the sequence number 872674 at 15.248 seconds since capture started:

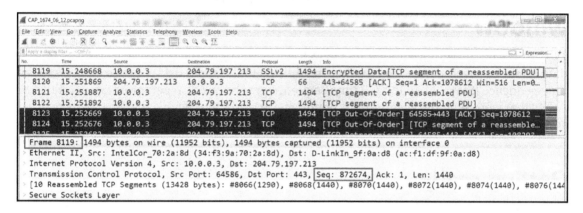

In the following screenshot, you can see the second packet, with the same sequence number, at 15.25 seconds after the start of capture. When a sequence number repeats itself, this is called TCP retransmission, and will be covered in `Chapter 10`, *Network Layer Protocols and Operations*.

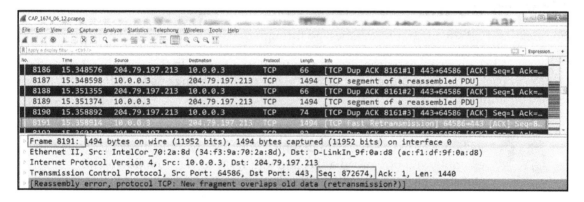

When viewing a graph, the important thing is to know what the application is. A graph that indicates a problem in one application can be perfect network behavior for another application.

Getting information through TCP stream graphs – time/sequences (TCP-trace) window

TCP time/sequence graphs, based on UNIX's tcpdump command, provide us with more data on the connection that we monitor. In addition to the standard sequence/seconds in the time-sequence (Stevens), with TCP time/sequence graphs, we also get information on the ACKs that were sent, retransmissions, window size, and more details that enable us to analyze problems with the connection.

Getting ready

Open an existing capture, or start a new capture. Click on a specific packet in the capture file. Even though you can use this feature on a running capture, it is not meant for online statistics, so it is recommended that you start a capture, stop it, and then use this tool. In this recipe, we use the example files CAP_1674_06_05 and CAP_1674_06_14.

How to do it...

For viewing TCP stream graph statistics, go through the following steps:

1. Click on a packet on the stream you want to monitor. In this example, I clicked on packet 100 on capture file CAP_1674_06_05. This brings us to TCP stream number 0.

> The TCP stream shows a directional graph, so when you click on a packet, it should be in the direction in which you want to view the statistics. If, for example, you download a file, and you want to view the download statistics, click on a packet in the download direction.

2. From the **Statistics** menu, choose **TCP Stream Graphs Time Sequence (tcptrace)**.

3. The following window will be opened. The capture filename is listed as a subtitle at the top of the graph:

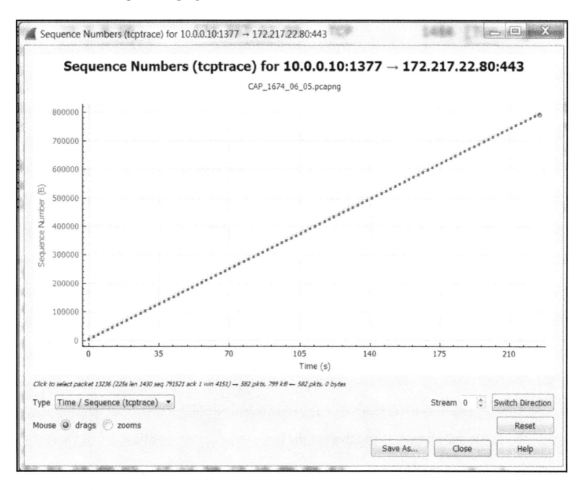

4. Zooming in to the graph gives us the following:

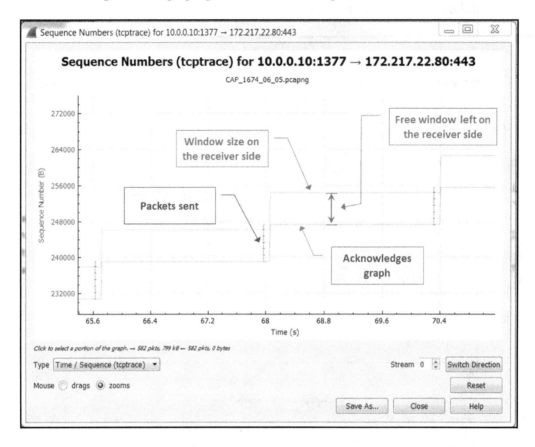

5. The graph shows the progress of the byte transference over time. What we see is the following:

- The short, vertical blue lines show the packets sent over the connection.
- The lower brown graph shows the acknowledgments sent for the received packets.
- The upper green line shows the window size. The space between the two lines—that is, the upper green line and the lower brown line—indicate the size of the TCP buffer that is left, which enables the TCP to keep sending bytes. When the two lines get closer and touch each other, this is a window-full phenomenon that does not enable greater data transference.

6. When we zoom deeper into the graph, we see the following screenshot:

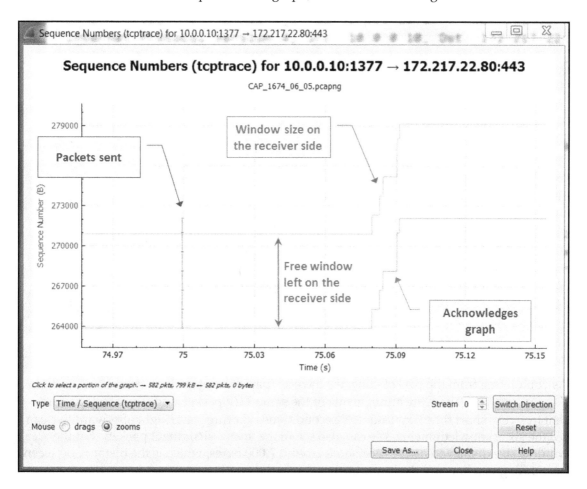

Here, we can see that:

- Several packets were sent 75 seconds since the start of capture
- These packets were acknowledged from 75.08 to 75.09, which is roughly 80-90 milliseconds after they were sent
- We also see that the free receiver window is around 7,000 bytes, which is 271,000-264,000 sequences on the *y* axis

To view these on the packet capture pane, click on **Mouse | drags**, and then, with the mouse clicked on one of the dots, the relevant packet will be marked on the packet pane:

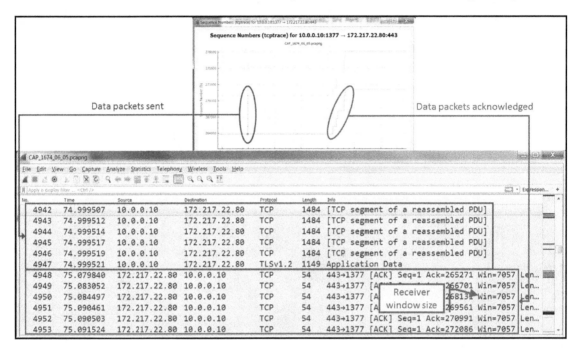

As you can see from the packet pane, we have six packets that are sent from 10.0.0.10 to 172.217.22.80. These are all segments of the same TCP packet, and they are, therefore, sent in a very short time, just under 75 seconds since capture start. Right afterward, we can see the six acknowledgments. We can also see in the acknowledgment packets that the window size displayed by the receiver is around 7,000 bytes, which is the distance between the upper green line and the lower brown line in the graph.

How it works...

The time-sequence (tcptrace) is taken from UNIX's tcpdump command, which also refers to the window size published by the receiver (this is the buffer size allocated by the receiver to the process), along with the retransmitted packets and ACKs.

Working with this graph provides us with a lot of information that we will use later for network debugging. Phenomena such as a window that is getting full faster than expected, too many retransmissions, and so on, will be made apparent by this graph, and this will help us solve these issues.

There's more...

In some cases, especially in high-speed data transfer, the graph might look like a perfectly straight line, but when you zoom in, you will see the problems.

In the following screenshot, we can see the capture file `CAP_1674_06_14`:

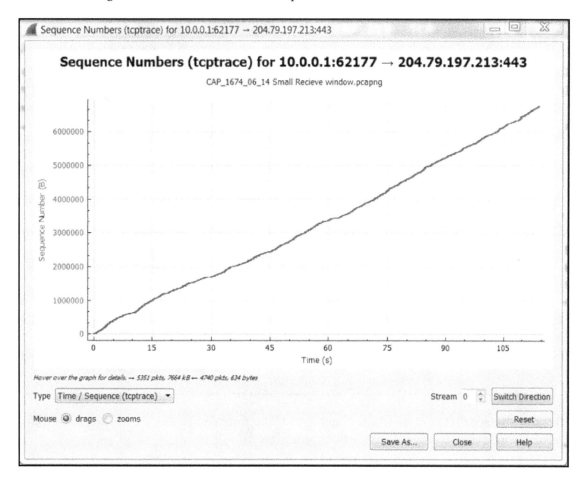

Zooming in shows us that there are time gaps, retransmissions, and other problems:

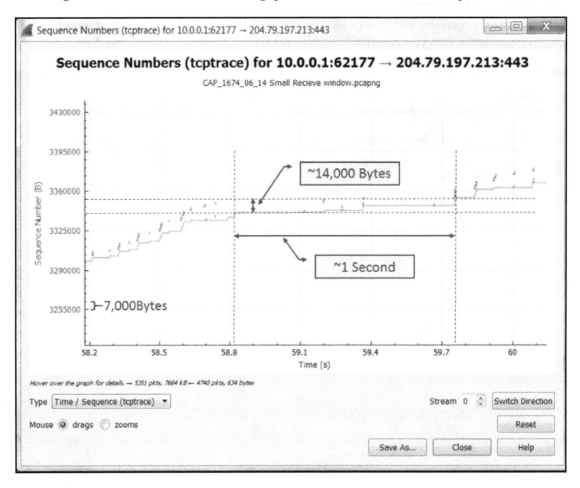

You can also see that in one second, roughly 14,000 sequences (bytes) are transferred—that is quite slow in relation to the rest of the connection.

A bar is an indication to a packet (which carries data between the initial and final sequence number). A bar that is not in the regular graph and looks like it has run away from it is a retransmission, and a gray bar is a duplicate ACK. We will learn about these phenomena in the forthcoming chapter dealing with TCP analysis.

Getting information through TCP stream graphs – throughput window

The throughput windows of the TCP stream graphs enable us to look at the throughput of a connection. With this graph, we can also check for instabilities, depending on the application.

Getting ready

Open an existing capture, or start a new capture. Click on a specific packet in the capture file. Even though you can use this feature on a running capture, it is not meant for online statistics, so it is recommended that you start a capture, stop it, and then use this tool.

How to do it...

To view TCP stream graph statistics, go through the following steps:

1. Click on a packet on the stream you want to monitor.
2. From the **Statistics** menu, choose **TCP Stream Graph** | **Throughput Graph**.

3. The following window will be opened:

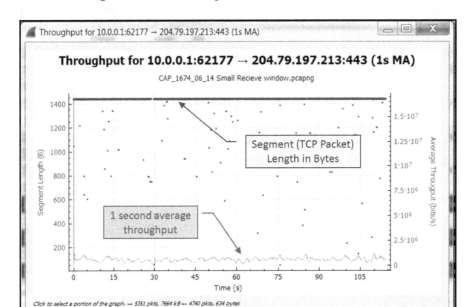

Here, we can see the example CAP_1674_06_14, stream 0. In the graph, we can see the following:

- The TCP connection throughput. We see here that it is roughly around 700-800 kilobits/second.
- The TCP segment length. This is the TCP size.

The formal definition of a data unit in data networks varies based on the OSI layer it belongs to—frame to layer 2, for example Ethernet frame, packet to layer 3, for example, IP packet, segment to layer 4 TCP and datagram to layer 4 UDP. The protocol data unit, or PDU, is a general name for all such units. In most cases, the terms are used in place, and I have tried to do so in this book, but in many other cases there is confusion between them. In any case, the important thing is to understand which layer we are talking about, no matter what the formal definition is.

This graph does not seem as much use as the TRP time/sequence graph does, but it can still show us any sudden degradation in throughput that can indicate a problem.

How it works...

The throughput graph simply counts the TCP sequence number over time, and since sequence numbers are actually application data, this gives us the application throughput in bytes per second.

There's more...

A stable file transfer should look similar to a central value, as shown on the left-hand side of the following graph. An unstable file transfer can look like the graph on the right, where the throughput graph is jumping up and down:

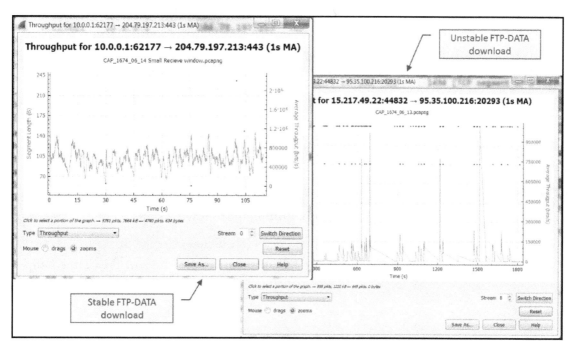

You can also see the throughput in the I/O graph. The main point to note is that the I/O graph shows you the throughput of all the traffic in the trace file, in both directions, while the TCP stream throughput graph shows only the throughput from one TCP stream in one direction, based on the selected packet. If you filter the I/O graph so that it is looking at the same traffic as the throughput graph, you'll see the same values for bytes/second.

Getting information through TCP stream graphs – round-trip-time window

The round-trip-time windows of the TCP stream graphs enable us to look at the round trip between sequence numbers and the time they were acknowledged. Along with the other graphs, it provides us with a look at the performance of the connection.

Getting ready

Open an existing capture, or start a new capture. Click on a specific packet in the capture file. Even though you can use this feature on a running capture, it is not meant for online statistics, so it is recommended that you start a capture, stop it, and then use this tool.

In the following example, we use the CAP_1674_06_13 file for TCP stream number 8, which is the TCP connection that starts in packet 85.

How to do it...

For viewing TCP stream graph statistics, go through the following steps:

1. Click on a packet on the stream you want to monitor.
2. From the **Statistics** menu, choose **TCP Stream Graph | Round Trip Time Graph**.

3. The following window will be opened:

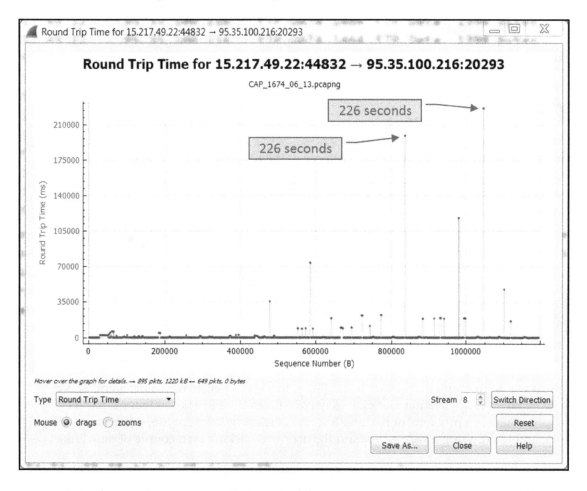

4. In the graph, we can see that most of the sequence numbers were acknowledged in a short time, but there is some instability, and this will influence TCP performance.

5. If you want to see this graph in the I/O graphs, use the `tcp.analysis.ack_rtt` filter.

6. To view the sequence so that you can see acknowledge the graph's progress for smaller denominations of time, use the **Mouse - Zoom** function.

How it works...

What we see in the graph is the TCP sequence numbers versus the time that it took to acknowledge them. This is the time between a packet being sent and the ACK for this packet being received.

There's more...

You can see the value of the `tcp.analysis, ack_rtt` filter in the packet details' pane further down the TCP packet, as you can see in the following screenshot:

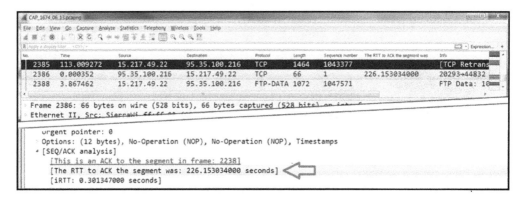

When you see a graph that shows instabilities, this is not necessarily a problem. This could well be how the application works. It may have taken time to acknowledge a packet because there is a problem, or because a server is waiting for response, or because a client was simply browsing a web server and the user was clicking on a couple of new links.

In Wireshark version 2, you can choose between graph types in a scroll-down menu in the lower-left corner of the window.

Getting information through TCP stream graphs – window-scaling window

The window-scaling graph of the TCP stream graphs enables us to look at the window size published by the receiving side, which is an indication of the ability of the receiver to process data. Along with the other graphs, it provides us with a look at the performance of the connection.

Getting ready

Open an existing capture, or start a new capture. Click on a specific packet in the capture file. Even though you can use this feature on a running capture, it is not meant for online statistics, so it is recommended that you start a capture, stop it, and then use this tool.

How to do it...

To view TCP stream graph statistics, go through the following steps:

1. Click on a packet on the stream you want to monitor.
2. From the **Statistics** menu, choose **TCP Stream Graph | Window Scaling Graph**.
3. The following window will be opened:

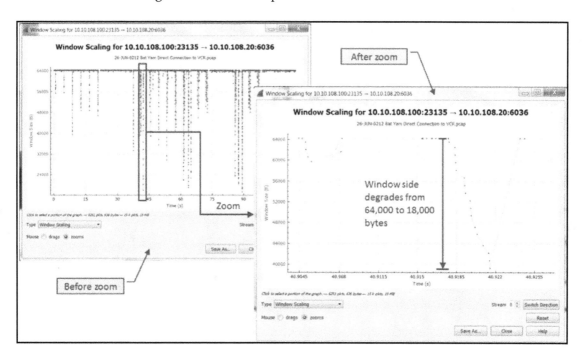

In this graph, we can see instability, caused by one of the sides. This can be an indication of a slow server or client, which cannot process all the data it receives, and therefore, by reducing the received window size, it tells the other side to send less data.

How it works...

The software here simply watches the window size on the connection and draws it. In `Chapter 10`, *Network Layer Protocols and Operations*, we will look at this in more detail.

There's more...

When the window size decreases, so should the application throughput. The window size is completely controlled by the two ends of the connection—for example, a client and a server—and variations in window size do not have anything to do with network performance.

Using the Expert System

In this chapter, we will learn about the expert system, a tool that provides us deeper analysis of network phenomena, including events and problems. We will talk about:

- The expert system window and how to use it for network troubleshooting
- Error events and what we can understand from them
- Warning events and what we can understand from them
- Note events and what we can understand from them

Introduction

One of Wireshark's strongest capabilities is the ability to analyze network phenomena and suggest a probable cause for it. Along with other tools, it gives us detailed information on network performance and problems. In this chapter, we will learn how to use this tool. Later in this book, we will provide detailed recipes on using the expert system, along with other tools, to find and resolve network problems.

The expert information option can be used when we first come to check a network, communication link, host servers, and so on, and we wish to get the first filling of the network. We will be able to see if there are events that can indicate a problem before we get into a deeper analysis. We should look for events to hold on to: things like TCP retransmissions, Ethernet checksum errors, DNS problems, duplicate IPs, and so on.

In the first recipe, we will learn how to work with the expert info window. In the next recipe, we will learn about the probable causes for the majority of events that you might expect.

The expert system window and how to use it for network troubleshooting

The expert window provides a list with events and network problems discovered by Wireshark. In this recipe, we will learn how to start the expert system and how to refer to the various events.

Getting ready

Start Wireshark, and start a live capture or open an existing file.

How to do it...

To start the expert window, click on the **Analyze** menu; choose **Expert Information**:

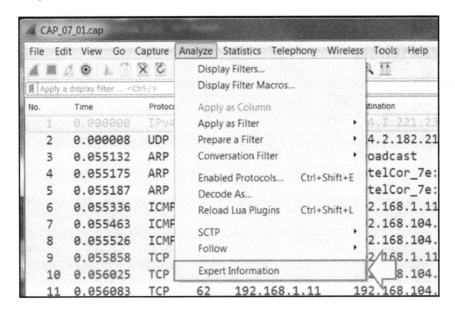

The following window will open:

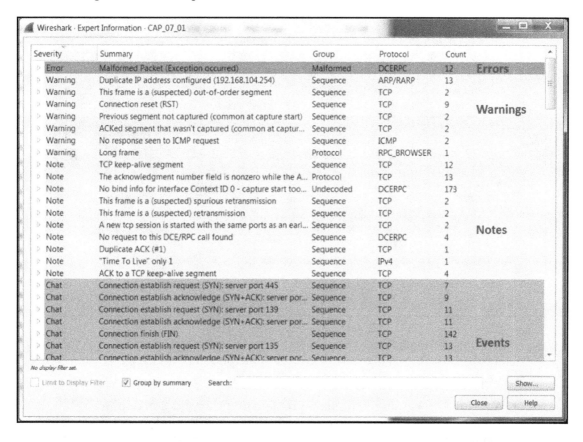

All valid events are presented in this order (if any): **Errors**, **Warnings**, **Notes**, and so on...

The number on the right-hand side of the bar shows the number of events in this category.

The upper bars give you the following information:

- **Errors**: Serious problems can be Ethernet checksum errors, malformed packets, or missing fields in a protocol header. These can be malformed packets of various types, such as malformed SPOOLSS, GTP, or others. They can also be bad checksum errors, such as IPv4 bad checksum. In the following screenshot, you can see Ethernet checksum errors:

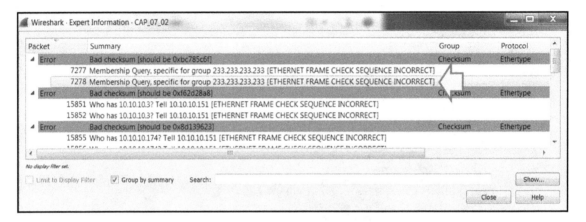

Clicking on the small arrow to the left of the error group opens the error list under this category. To see the specific packet in the packet pane, click on the packet line.

- **Warnings**: A warning indicates a problem in the application or in communications: things like TCP zero-window, TCP window-full, previous segment not captured, out-of-order segment, and any issue that is unnatural to the protocol behavior. You can see an example of this in the following screenshot:

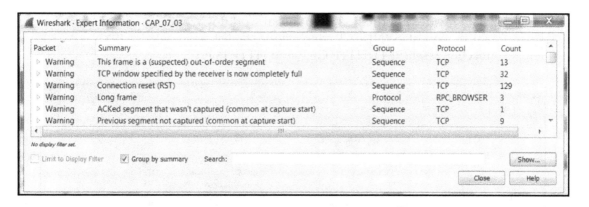

- **Notes**: A note is when Wireshark indicates an event that may cause a problem but is still inside the normal behavior of the protocol. TCP retransmission, for example, will be displayed here, because even though it is a critical problem that slows down the network, it is still under the normal behavior of TCP. Other events here are duplicate ACK, fast retransmission, and many more. In the following screenshot, you can see retransmissions and duplicate acknowledgements; they can be an indication of slow communications but are still normal behavior of the TCP protocol:

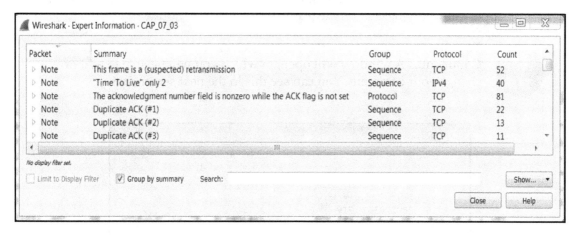

- **Chats**: Provides information about usual workflow, for example TCP connection establish request (SYN), TCP connection establish acknowledge (SYN + ACK), connection reset (RST), HTTP GET, and HTTP POST:

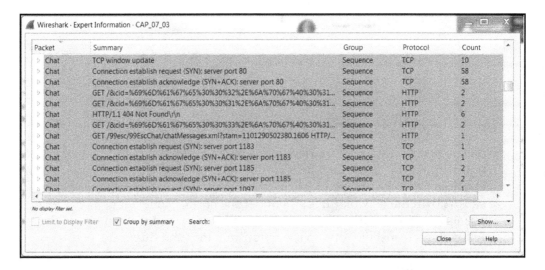

- **Packet comments**: You can manually add a comment to every packet. This will appear down to the chat on the expert information window.

To add a comment to a packet, right-click on it and choose **Packet Comment...**. A window will open, in which you will be able to add or change your comment. You can see this in the next screenshot.

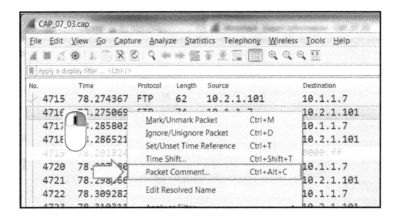

General operation notes:

- At the bottom of the **Expert Information** window, you have the options to **Limit to Display Filter** and to **Group by summary** (marked by default), and you can also search for specific words in an event.
- To go to the event in the packet capture pane, simply click on the packet under the event in the expert window, and it will lead you to it.

> It is important to note that a warning event may have no importance while a note event may influence the network badly. Always get into the problem details, and see where it is coming from and what the meaning of it is.

- The three columns to the right of the table indicate the group of the event. In the following screenshot, you can see that the first line belongs to the group sequence in the protocol TCP (**1**). The next line belongs to the group protocol. The protocol is RPC browser (**2**). The last marked event belongs to a sequence group; the protocol is IPv4 (**3**). The group holds events from the same category, for example, Sequence events that refer to sequenced parameters, and it indicates on which protocol the event happened.

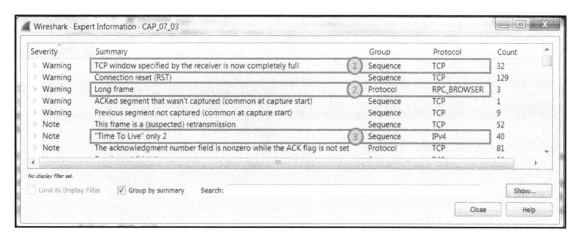

How it works...

The **Expert Information** window is an expert system that provides us information about problems in the network, and in some cases also suggestions to the probable cause of it. Although it gives reasonable results, always verify its findings.

There are cases in which Wireshark finds problems that are not real ones, and vice versa—cases in which Wireshark does not show real problems that exist.

 Don't forget that the best troubleshooting tool is your brain (and your knowledge of networking!). Wireshark is a very smart tool, but still, it is just a tool.

It could be that you started the capture during data transfer, and so you see previous segment loss messages or even more sophisticated problems when, for some reason (good or not!), you have captured only part of the data. Wireshark refers to it as it is a complete stream of data and shows you many errors about it. We will see many examples of these issues later in the book.

There's more...

Expert severities can also be filtered and presented in the packet pane by display filters. To view events according to display filters:

1. Choose the expression on the right-hand side of the display filter window.
2. Scroll down to get the expert messages (you can just type the work expert and you will get there).
3. As illustrated in the following screenshot, you will get the following filters—expert.message, expert.group, and expert.severity:

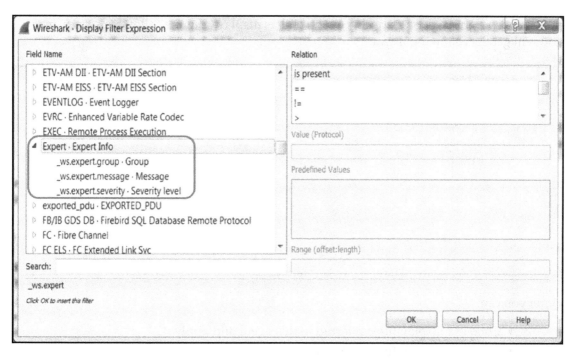

The preceding filters are explained here:

- The `expert.group` refers to expert message groups, for example, checksum errors group, sequence group, malformed group, and so on.
- The `expert.message` refers to specific messages. Here, for example, you can configure a filter that displays a message that contains or matches a specific string.
- The `expert.severity` refers to messages with specific severities, that is, error, warning, note and so on.

You can also right-click on a specific event, and as displayed in the following screenshot, you will get the following menu:

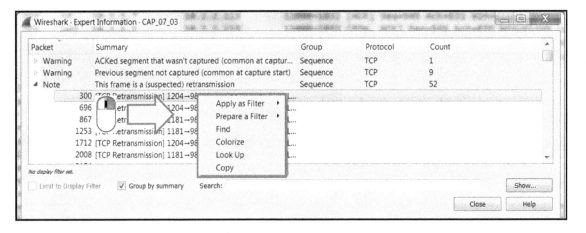

Here, you can:

- Choose a display filter referred to this event and apply it
- Choose a display filter referred to this event and only prepare it
- Find the specific packet on the packet pane
- Configure a colorization rule for the event
- Lookup the internet for the event information
- Copy the event text

See also

- Chapter 8, *Ethernet and LAN Switching* and the protocols chapters

Error events and what we can understand from them

In this recipe, we will dive into error and event types, checksum errors, malformed packets, and other types of errors.

Getting ready

Start a capture, or open an existing file and start the expert system.

How to do it...

1. From the **Analyze** menu, open **Expert Information**. Errors are listed at the top of the window:

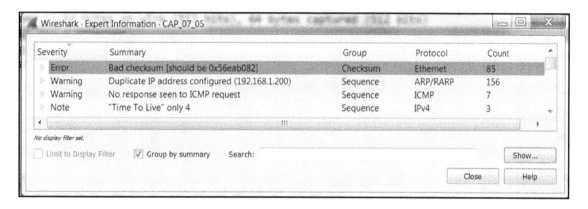

In the preceding window that is brought as an example, you can see checksum errors; in this case, it can be because of real errors or offload.

2. Clicking on a specific error takes us to the packet pane to see the error in the packet itself. This is presented in the following screenshot:

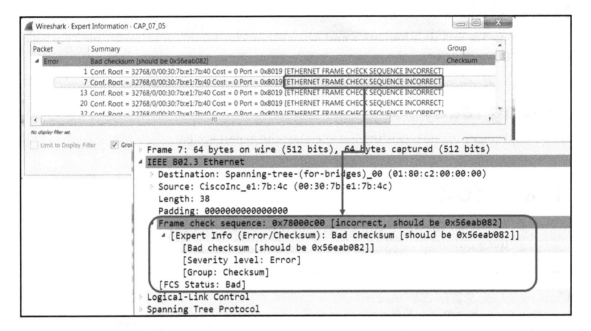

What you see in this event is a checksum error, and that the checksum is incorrect. In this case (file CAP_07_05), we see that all errors are coming from a single device, which is a good point to start to look where the problem is coming from. More about Ethernet and Ethernet errors later, in Chapter 8, *Ethernet and LAN Switching*.

How it works...

Checksum is an error-checking mechanism that uses a byte or sequence of bytes inserted in the packet to implement a frame verification algorithm. The principle of error-checking algorithms is to calculate a formula over the entire message (layer 4), packet (layer 3), or frame (layer 2). They insert the result in the bytes inside the packet, and when the packet arrives at the destination, they calculate it again. If we get the same result, it is a good packet, and if not, there is an error. The error-checking mechanism can be calculated over the entire packet or over just the header; it depends on the protocol.

Offload mechanisms are mechanisms on which the IP, TCP, and UDP checksums are calculated on the NIC just before they are transmitted to the wire. In Wireshark, these show up as error packets, because Wireshark captures packets before they are sent to the network adapter; therefore it will not see the correct checksum, as it has not been calculated yet.

For this reason, even though it might look like severe errors, in many cases checksum errors are Wireshark errors of misconfiguration. If you see many checksum errors on packets that are sent from your PC, it is probably because of the offload.

For canceling the checksum validation:

- For IPv4, when you see many checksum errors and you are sure they are due to the offload, go to **Edit | Preferences**, and under **Protocols | IPv4**, unmark the radio button: **Validate the IPv4 checksum if possible**
- For TCP, when you see many checksum errors and you are sure they are due to the offload, go to **Edit | Preferences**, and under **Protocols | TCP**, unmark the radio button: **Validate the TCP checksum if possible**

There's more...

For malformed packets, these can be a Wireshark bug or a real malformed packet. Use other tools to isolate the problem. Suspected bugs can be reported on the Wireshark website.

When you see many malformed packets of checksum errors, it is probably because of offload or dissector errors. Networks with more that 1%-2% errors of any kind will cause many other events (retransmissions, for example) and will become much slower than expected; therefore, you cannot have a high error rate with a functioning network!

See also

- Chapter 8, *Ethernet and LAN Switching* and the protocols chapters

Warning events and what we can understand from them

As described earlier, warnings events indicate a problem in the application or in communications. In this recipe, we will describe the main events in this category.

Getting ready

Start a capture, or open an existing file and start the expert system.

How to do it...

1. From the **Analyze** menu, open **Expert Information.**

2. Warning events will be presented second from the top. If there are no error events, then warnings will be first. You can see an example in the next screenshot (file CAP_07_04):

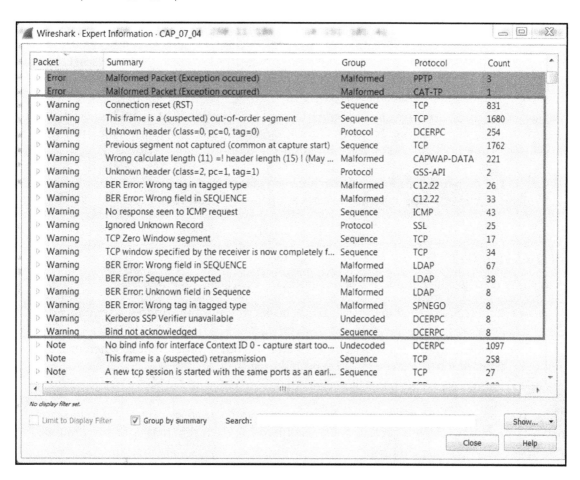

You will see several event categories here:

- Reassembly problems, mostly unassembled packets. Usually indicate a Wireshark dissector problem.
- TCP window problems, mostly zero window and window full. Usually indicate slow end devices (servers, PCs, and so on).
- Connection reset, not necessarily a problem. The TCP reset mechanism is further explained in `Chapter 11`, *Transport Layer Protocol Analysis*.
- Previous segment not captured, previous segment loss, and out of order message, indicating TCP issues further explained in `Chapter 11`, *Transport Layer Protocol Analysis*.

3. For more information on a specific event, right-click on the event and choose **Lookup**; this will take you to relevant pages on the internet.

How it works...

Wireshark watches the parameters of the monitored packets:

- It watches TCP window sizes, and checks whether the window size reduced to zero
- It looks for TCP packets (segments) that are out of order, that is, whether they were sent before or after the expected time
- It looks for ACKs for TCP packets that were not sent

These parameters, along with many others, provide you a good starting point to look for network problems. We will get to the details of it in `Chapter 11`, *Transport Layer Protocol Analysis*.

There's more...

Don't forget that warning events are those that Wireshark refers to as non-critical but not a normal behavior of a protocol. Here, you have events such as these:

- **TCP resets**: They are part of the TCP protocol, but a connection should end with a TCP FIN and not with a TCP reset. So, in this case, it can be due to a problem, or just because the TCP developer has chosen to close a connection in this way.
- **TCP zero window**: An indication to a slow end device on the connection; here we have another behavior of the protocol that can be due to a problem on one of the sides of the connection, but this is still how TCP works.

Messages like unknown header, BER error: wrong tag in tagged type, and so on. These messages indicate that there are problems in the packet structure. Like all kinds of errors and events, the important thing is to understand it, and not the category or the color.

See also

- Chapter 8, *Ethernet and LAN Switching* and the protocols chapters

Note events and what we can understand from them

As described earlier, when Wireshark indicates an event that may cause a problem but is still inside the normal behavior of the protocol, it will be under the note category. TCP retransmission, for example, will be displayed under the notes bar, because even though it is a critical problem that slows down the network, it is still under the normal behavior of TCP.

Getting ready

Start a capture, or open an existing file and start the expert system.

How to do it...

1. From the **Analyze** menu, open **Expert Information**.
2. The notes events are presented third from the top on the **Expert Information** window:

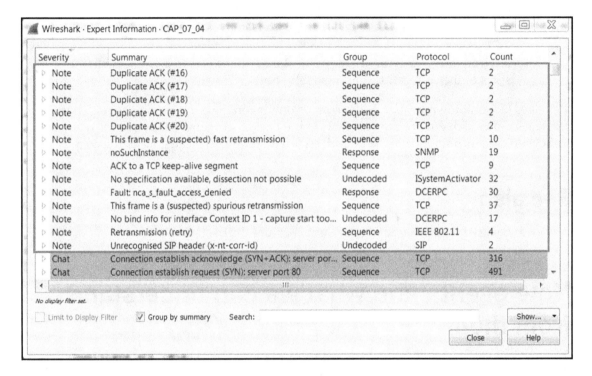

You will see here several event categories:

- Retransmissions, duplicate ACKs, fast retransmissions usually indicate slow network, packet loss, or very slow end devices or applications
- Keep-alive indicates TCP or application problems
- Time to live and routing events, in most cases, indicate routing problems

Additional events will be discussed in the relevant TCP and applications chapters.

How it works...

Wireshark watches the parameters of the monitored packets:

- It watches TCP sequence and acknowledgement numbers. It checks for retransmissions as well as other sequencing problems.
- It looks for IP time to live with value of 1 coming from a remote network, and tells you it is a problem.
- It looks for keep-alive; that can be a normal condition but can also indicate a problem.

These parameters, along with many others, provide you a good starting point to look for network performance problems.

There's more...

Many symptoms that are seen here can be indications of several types of problems. For example, a packet can be retransmitted because of an error that caused the packet to be lost, or because of bad network conditions (low bandwidth or high delay) that caused the packet not to arrive on time. It can also be because of a non-responsive server or client. The expert info system will give you the symptom. How to solve the problem? We will learn later in this book.

See also

- Chapter 8, *Ethernet and LAN Switching* and the protocols chapters

Ethernet and LAN Switching

8

In this chapter, we will cover the following topics:

- Discovering broadcast and error storms
- Analyzing spanning tree protocols
- Analyzing VLANs and VLAN tagging issues

Introduction

In this chapter, we will focus on how to find and resolve layer 2-based problems with a focus on Ethernet-based issues, such as broadcast/multicast events, errors, and how to find the source. We will also focus on LAN protocols such as spanning tree and VLANs.

These issues need to be resolved before we go up to layer 3, layer 4, and application layers, since layer 2 problems will be reflected in the upper layer protocols. For example, packet losses in layer 2 will cause retransmissions in TCP (a layer 4 protocol), and result in application slowness.

Discovering broadcast and error storms

One of the most commonly seen and troublesome problems in communication networks is broadcast/multicast and error storms. These problems can happen because of layer 2 loops, layer 2-based attacks, a problematic network adapter, or an application or service that sends packets to the network. In this chapter, we will provide some basic recipes to find, isolate, and solve these types of problems.

 A broadcast/multicast storm is when you get thousands and even tens of thousands of such packets per second. In most cases, it will exhaust the bandwidth and lock out the network completely.

Getting ready

When these problems occur, the network you usually call on to solve problems will be very slow or it has stopped working.?

Some important facts to remember:

- Broadcasts are not forwarded by routers.
- Broadcasts are not forwarded between VLANs (this is why VLANs are called broadcast domains), so every VLAN is a broadcast domain by itself.
- Error packets are not forwarded by LAN switches, such as packets with the wrong CRC, packets smaller than the minimum size of 64 bytes, and so on.
- Multicasts are forwarded through switches unless configured otherwise.
- Multicasts are forwarded through routers only if the routers are configured to do so.
- A reasonable number of broadcasts are transmitted in every network. This is how networks work, but a high rate of broadcasts/multicasts could be a problem.
- Broadcasts/multicasts are forwarded to the control plane/CPU of the switch or router, if it is configured to do so or enabled with layer 3 capabilities. This may result in control plane instability (for example, OSPF adjacency flaps).

There is a difference between too many broadcasts and a broadcast storm. Too many broadcasts (for example, a few hundred per second) can load the network, but still, in most cases, users will not notice. Broadcast storms will lock out the network completely. It is very important to baseline the percentage of broadcast packets in a network, so that it can be used as a data point during troubleshooting.

How to do it...

To find out where the problem comes from, go through the following steps:

1. Since slow network is a problem sensed by the users, start by asking the following questions:
    - Is this problem in the HQ or at a specific branch(es)?
    - Is this over the network or in a specific VLAN?
    - Is this over the building or in a specific floor?

Don't ask the users about VLANs, of course; users are not networking experts. Ask them about the applications running on their group, in their department, and so on to understand the scope of the issue.

In an organization network, VLAN will usually be configured per department (or several departments) and per geographical area (or several areas) or even per organization functionality; for example, HR VLAN, finance VLAN, users of a specific software VLAN, and so on. By asking if the problem is as per one of these characters, you will be able to narrow down to the area in which you need to look for the problem.

2. The next question should be a trivial one: is the network still working? In a broadcast/multicast storm, the network will become very slow; in most cases to the point that applications will stop functioning. In this case, you have the following typical problems:
   - Spanning tree problems
   - A device that generates broadcasts
   - Routing loops (discussed in `Chapter 10`, *Network Layer Protocols and Operations*)

The question I'm always asked is: how many broadcasts are too many?

Well, there are of course several answers for this. It depends on what the network devices are doing and the protocols that are running on them.

A reasonable number of broadcasts should be from 1-2 up to 4-5 per device per minute. For example, if your network is built from 100 devices on a single VLAN, you should expect no more than 5-10 broadcasts per second (5 broadcasts x 100 devices gives 500 broadcasts per minute, that is, around 9-10 per second). More than that is also reasonable as long as they are not coming in thousands and from an unknown source.

Spanning tree problems

In spanning tree problems, you will get thousands and even tens of thousands of broadcasts per second (refer to the *How it works...* section in this recipe to know why). In this case, your Wireshark, and probably your laptop, will freeze. Close Wireshark, start to disconnect redundant cables to isolate the problem (pretty much making the network layer 2 loop free), and check the STP configuration in the switches.

A device that generates broadcasts

A typical broadcast storm generated from a specific device will have the following characteristics:

- A significant number of broadcasts per second (thousands and more)
- In most cases, the broadcasts will be from a single source; but in the case of attacks, they can be from multiple sources
- Usually in constant packet/second rate, that is, with intervals between frames that are nearly equal

Let us see how we can find a broadcast storm according to the parameters mentioned in the preceding list in the next three screenshots.

In the following screenshot, we see a large number of broadcast packets sent from a source MAC (HP network adapter) to ff:ff:ff:ff:ff:ff:

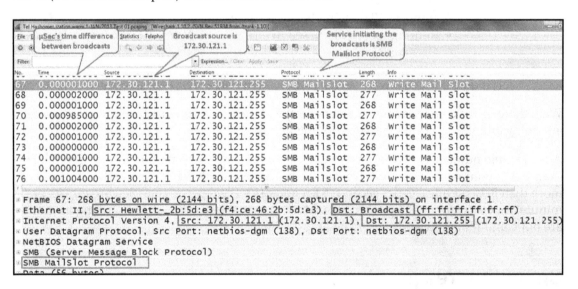

Figure 8.1: Broadcast flooding

As seen in the preceding screenshot, the time column is configured in seconds (which means the delta between the timestamps of two successive packets will be reported in seconds). You can configure it by navigating to **View | Time Display Format**.

The rate of packets can be viewed by navigating to **Statistics | IO Graph**. The following screenshot shows the rate of the broadcast packets is 5,000 packets/second:

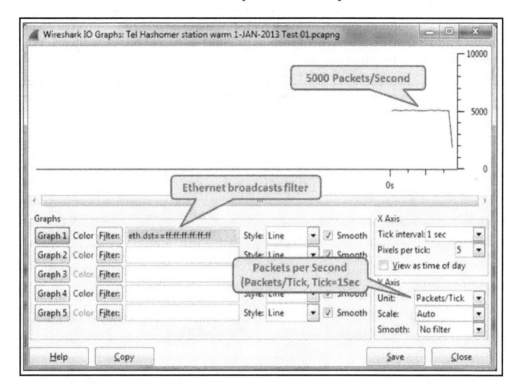

Figure 8.2: Broadcast flooding: I/O graph

By navigating to **Statistics | Conversations** option, we can see conversations between the devices from the perspective of Ethernet, IPv4, TCP/UDP. In the top portion of the following screenshot, we can see an enormous number of broadcasts between two MAC addresses, while the bottom portion of the screenshot reports the same conversions but from the IPv4 addresses' perspective. In summary, this has 87,142 broadcast packets captured in the time duration of 18 seconds.

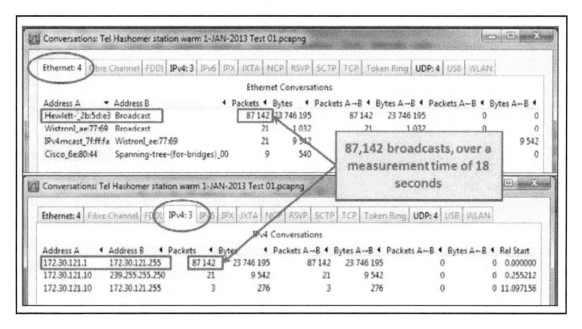

Figure 8.3: Broadcast flooding: conversations

In the preceding case, the problem was due to a service called SMB mailslot protocol. Simple trial and error to find out what this service is and disabling it on the station solved the broadcast storm problem.

 It is important to note this: when you disable a service (especially one that belongs to the operating system), make sure that the system keeps functioning and stays stable over time. Don't leave the site before you have verified it!

Also, I would recommend that you run Wireshark again to confirm that no broadcast flooding is seen.

Fixed pattern broadcasts

You can also have broadcasts in fixed patterns, for example, every fixed amount of time, as shown in this screenshot:

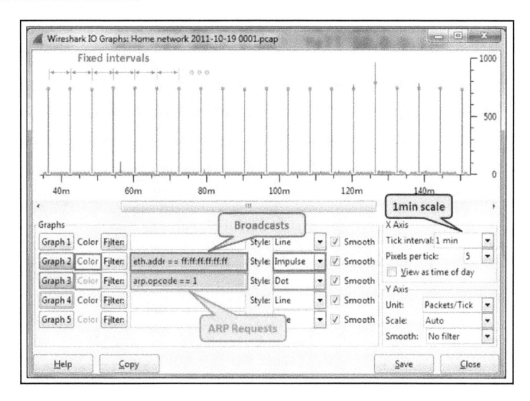

Figure 8.4: fixed pattern broadcasts

The graph is configured for a **Tick interval** (under **X Axis**) of **1 min**, and for the following filters:

- The red filter for all broadcasts in the network (`eth.addr ==ff:ff:ff:ff:ff:ff`)
- The green filter for broadcasts that are ARP requests (`arp.opcode ==1`)

What we see here is that around every 5 minutes, there is a burst of ARP requests (the green dots). If we click on one of the dots in the graph, it will take us to the packet in the capture pane.

In the following screenshot, we see the scan pattern that happens every 5 minutes:

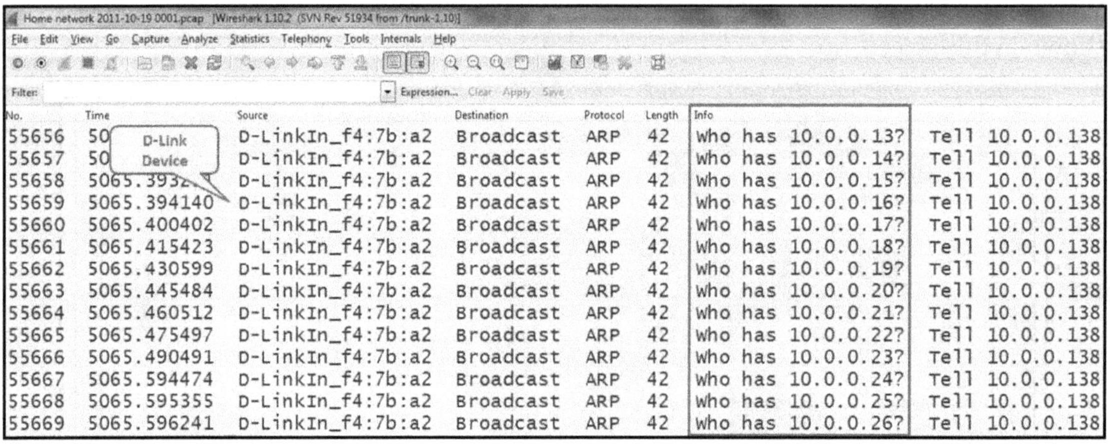

Figure 8.5: ARP scan

We can see that it is the d-link router (based on the source MAC address) that scans the internal network. This can be good or bad, but it's good to check what is running in our network.

How it works...

Broadcasts in IPv4 networks are quite common, and these layer 3 broadcasts will be sent over layer 2 broadcasts. Every time a layer 3 device sends a broadcast to the network (destined to the subnet's broadcast address; refer to `Chapter 10`, *Network Layer Protocols and Operations*, for more information), it will be converted to all fs destination MAC addresses.

There are several families of broadcasts that you will see in IP-based networks. Some of them are as follows:

- TCP/IP-based network protocols, such as ARP requests, DHCP requests, and others
- Network protocols, such as **NetBIOS Name Service (NBNS)** queries, **NetBIOS Server Message Block (SMB)** announcements, **Network Time Protocol (NTP)**, and others
- Applications that send broadcasts, such as Dropbox, Microsoft network load balancing, and others

In IPv6, we don't have broadcasts, but we have unicasts, multicasts, and anycasts. Since the protocol works with multicasts for discovery mechanisms, announcements, and other mechanisms, we will see a lot of them.

There's more...

One problem I come across in many cases is how to use the broadcast and multicast storm control definitions in LAN switches (the storm-control broadcast level **[high level] [lower level]** command in Cisco devices). The problem is that in many cases I see configurations that limit the number of broadcasts to 50, 100, or 200 broadcasts per second, and this is not enough. In a network, you might install a piece of software that sends broadcasts or multicasts to the network that cross these values. Then, according to what you have configured in the switch, it will start sending traps to the management system, generating syslog messages, or even disconnecting ports (the storm-control action **{shutdown | trap}** command in Cisco devices).

The solution for this is simply to configure high levels of broadcasts as the threshold. When a broadcast storm happens, you will get thousands of broadcasts; so configuring a threshold level of 1,000 to 2,000 broadcasts or multicasts per second provides you with the same protection level without any disturbances to the regular network operation.

If you are not comfortable with having a high threshold level for storm control, then you should audit the network traffic with a goal of determining the rate of broadcasts sent by end stations during peak working hours and use that data to set an appropriate threshold.

See also

- For more information about IPv4, refer to `Chapter 10`, *Network Layer Protocols and Operations*

Analyzing spanning tree problems

All of us have worked with, or at least heard about, **Spanning Tree Protocol** (**STP**). The reason I call this recipe *Analyzing spanning tree problems* is that there are three major versions of it, as follows:

- **STP**: This is an IEEE 802.1D standard from 1998, called 802.1D-1998
- **Rapid Spanning Tree Protocol (RSTP)**: This is an IEEE 802.1W standard from 2001, later added to 802.1D, called 802.1D-2004
- **Multiple Spanning Tree (MST)**: This was originally defined in IEEE 802.1S and later merged into IEEE 802.1Q

There are also some proprietary versions from Cisco and other vendors. In this recipe, we will focus on the standard versions and learn how to troubleshoot problems that might occur during STP/RSTP/MST operations.

Getting ready

The best way to find STP problems is to log in to the LAN switches and use the vendor's commands (for example, Cisco IOS or Juniper JUNOS CLI) to find and fix the problem. If you have properly configured SNMP on your network device, you will get all the messages on the management console, unless STP problems somehow cause issues for the switches to communicate with the management system.

The purpose of this recipe is to show how to use Wireshark for this purpose, even though we still recommend using it as a second-line tool for this purpose. So just open your laptop, start Wireshark, and start capturing data on the LAN.

How to do it...

There are several things to notice in a network regarding STP:

- Which STP version is running on the network?
- Are there any topology changes?

Which STP version is running on the network?

Wireshark will provide you with the version of the STP type (STP, RSTP, or MST) running on the network by looking at the **Bridge Protocol Data Units** (**BPDUs**). BPDUs are the update frames that are multicast between switches.

The protocol versions are:

- For STP, the protocol version ID equals 0
- For RSTP/MST, the protocol version ID equals 3

> In the standards, you will not find the word switch; it will always be bridge or multiport bridge. In this book, we will use the terms bridge and switch.

Are there too many topology changes?

When you monitor STP operations, you may be concerned by many topology changes. Topology changes are normal in STP, but too many of them can have an impact on the network's performance as it may cause MAC address aging, which results in unknown unicast flooding.

A topology change happens when a new device is connected to or disconnected from the network. You can see a topology change in the following screenshot:

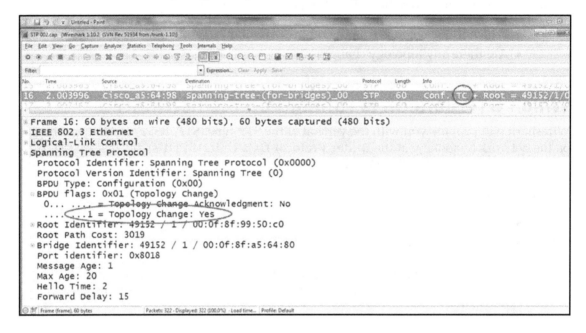

Figure 8.6: STP: topology change

When you see too many topology changes, the LAN switch ports that are connected to hosts that do not support STP (typically, end stations that users frequently power on and off) should be configured with the port fast feature (applied for Cisco switches; for other vendors, check out the vendor's manual).

In the old STP (IEEE 802.1d), after connecting a device to a switch port, it takes the switch around a minute to start and forward packets. This can be a problem when a client tries to log in to the network servers during this period of time, or requests an IP address via DHCP. The port fast feature forces the port to start forwarding within a few seconds (usually 8 to 10), in order to prevent these kinds of problems.

If topology changes continue, check what could be the problem and who is causing it. Please be aware that even though most of the topology changes originate at the ports connected to the end stations, it can also be due to a link flap between two switches.

How it works...

The STP prevents a loop in the local area networks. A loop can happen if you connect two or more switches with multiple connections, as shown in the following diagram:

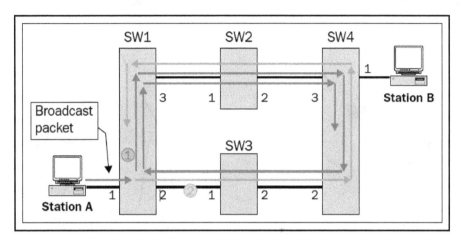

Figure 8.7: Spanning tree: how a loop is created

Let's see how a loop is created:

- **Station A** sends a broadcast to the network. A broadcast can be an ARP, NetBIOS, or any other packet with all fs in the destination MAC address.
- Since broadcasts are forwarded to all ports of the switch, **SW1** receives the broadcast from port **1** and forwards it to ports **2** and **3**.
- **SW2** and **SW3** will forward the packets to their other ports, which will get them to ports **2** and **3** of **SW4**.
- **SW4** will forward the packet from port **2** to port **3**, and the packet coming from port **3** to port **2**.
- We will get two packets circling endlessly—the one that has been forwarded to port **3** (the red arrows) and the one that has been forwarded to port **2** (the green arrows) of **SW1**.
- Depending on the switch forwarding speed, we will get up to tens of thousands of packets, which will block the network completely.

The STP prevents this from happening by simply building a tree topology, that is, by defining a loop-free topology. Links are disconnected and brought back to service in case of a failure.

In the following diagram, we see how we initially connect all switches with multiple connections between them, and how STP creates the tree:

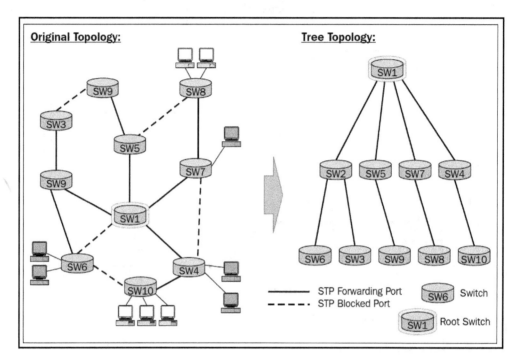

Figure 8.8: Spanning tree: original versus tree topology

BPDUs are update frames that are exchanged between the LAN switches using layer 2 multicast. First, on the Ethernet level, as we see in the following screenshot, the packet will be multicast from the source MAC of the switch sending the update:

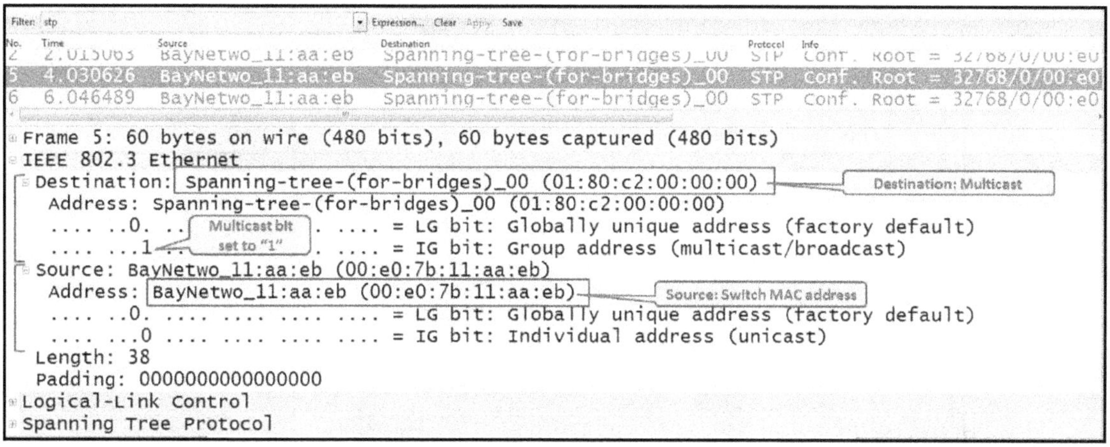

Figure 8.9: Spanning tree source and destination MAC address

The BPDU is carried by Ethernet 802.3 frame, which has the format as shown in the next diagram:

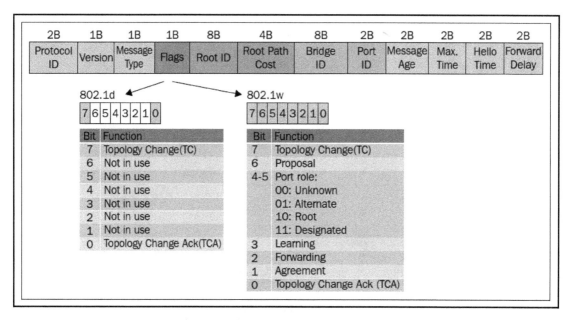

Figure 8.10: Spanning tree BPDU Ethernet frame format

In the following table, you can see the fields in the STP frame:

Field	Bytes	What is it?	Values	Display filter
Protocol ID	2	The protocol identifier	Always 0	`stp.protocol`
Version	1	The protocol version	For STP = 0 For RSTP = 2 For MST = 3	`stp.version`
Message type	1	The BPDU type	For STP = 0 For RSTP = 2 For MST = 2	`stp.type`
Flags	1	The protocol flags	In the previous illustration	`stp.flags`
Root ID	8	The root identifier (root ID), that is, the bridge priority concatenated with the bridge hardware address (MAC)	The MAC address of the root bridge	`stp.root.prio`, `stp.root.ext`, and `stp.root.hw`
Root path cost	4	The path cost to the root switch	Path cost as calculated by spanning tree. If this is the root, path cost will be zero.	`stp.root.cost`
Bridge ID	8	The bridge identifier (bridge ID), that is, the bridge priority concatenated with the bridge hardware address (MAC)	The bridge MAC address	`stp.bridge.prio`, `stp.bridge.ext`, and `stp.bridge.hw`
Port ID 2	2	The port identifier	The identifier of the port from which the update was sent	`stp.port`
Message age	2	The message age field indicates the amount of time that has elapsed since a bridge sent the configuration message on which the current configuration message is based	For every BPDU, the bridge that sends the frame sends a value of 0, incremented by 1 for every bridge that forwards it	`stp.msg_age`
Max. time	2	The maximum age, which is the maximum time (practically the number of bridges) that the frame can stay in the network	Usually 20 seconds	`stp.max_age`
Hello time	2	Time between BPDUs	Usually 2 seconds	`stp.hello`

Forward delay	2	The forward delay field indicates the length of time that bridges should wait before transitioning to a new state after a topology change	Usually 15 seconds	`stp.forward`

Note that in the case of MST, an additional header will be added for the MST parameters.

Port states

In STP, the port states are as follows:

- **Disabled**: In this state, no frames are forwarded and no BPDUs are heard
- **Blocking**: In this state, no frames are forwarded but BPDUs are heard
- **Listening**: In this state, no frames are forwarded, but the port listens for frames
- **Learning**: In this state, no frames are forwarded but MAC addresses are learned by the switch
- **Forwarding**: In this state, frames are forwarded and MAC addresses are learned by the switch

The moment you connect a device to the LAN switch, the port goes through these stages, and the time it takes is as follows:

- From blocking to listening takes 20 seconds
- From listening to learning takes 15 seconds
- From learning to forwarding takes 15 seconds

In RSTP and MST, the port states are as follows:

- **Discarding**: In this state, frames are discarded
- **Learning**: In this frame, no frames are forwarded and MAC addresses are captured
- **Forwarding**: Frames are forwarded and MAC addresses are captured

The entire port state transition from discarding to forwarding should take a few seconds depending on the network topology and complexity.

There's more...

For spanning tree debugging, the best thing is to get the data from a direct connection to the LAN switches. A well-configured SNMP trap to a management system can also assist in this task.

Some examples of STP packets are as follows:

In the following screenshot, you can see an STP frame. You can see that the source MAC address is a Nortel address, and in the BPDU itself, the root and the bridge identifiers are equal; this is because the bridge that sends the packet is the root. The port ID is 8003, which in Nortel switches indicates port number 3.

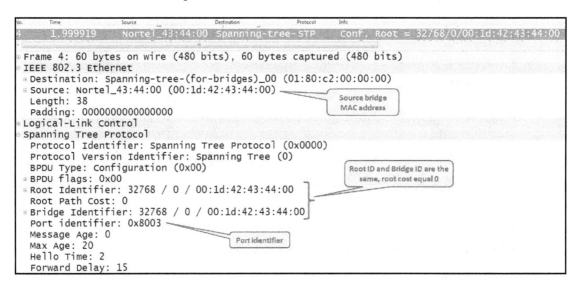

Figure 8.11: Spanning tree BPDU from a root switch

In the following screenshot, you can see a rapid STP BPDU. You can see here that the protocol identifier equals 2 and the port state that is designated.

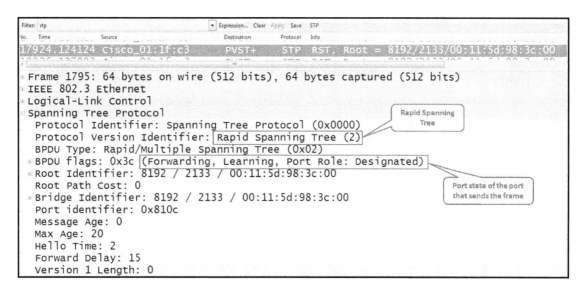

Figure 8.12: Spanning tree BPDU parameters

In the previous screenshot, you can see an example for MST. Here we see the MST extension right after the standard STP frame.

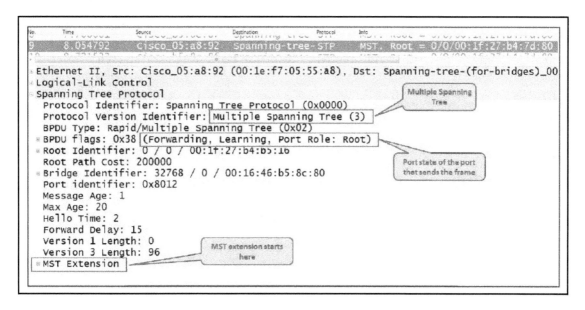

Figure 8.13: MST BPDU and extension

Analyzing VLANs and VLAN tagging issues

VLAN, or Virtual LAN, is a mechanism that divides a LAN into separate LANs without any direct communication between them even though they co-exist in the same physical infrastructure, and this is where the name virtual comes from. In this section, we will have a look at recipes to monitor VLAN traffic.

The purpose of this recipe is to give the reader a general description of how to use Wireshark for VLAN issues. An easier way to solve related problems is to use the vendor's CLI (Cisco IOS, Juniper JUNOS, and so on) for this purpose.

Getting ready

We will discuss two issues in this recipe:

- How to monitor traffic inside a VLAN?
- How to view tagged frames going through a VLAN-tagged port?

In the first case, a simple configuration is required. In the second case, there are some points to take care of.

While capturing on a VLAN, you won't necessarily see the VLAN tags in packets. The question of whether you will see the VLAN tags actually depends on the operating system you are running, and whether your **Network Interface Card** (**NIC**) and the NIC driver support this feature.

 The question of whether your OS and NIC supports VLAN tagging entirely depends on the OS and the NIC vendor. Go to the vendor's manuals or Google to find out.

In the following diagram, you can see a typical topology with VLANs. The upper switch is connected by two trunks (these are ports that tag the Ethernet frames) to the lower switches. On this network, you have VLANs 10, 20, and 30, while PCs connected to each of the VLANs will not be able to see PCs from other VLANs.

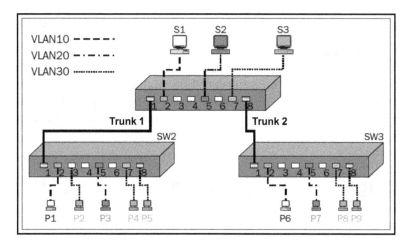

Figure 8.14: VLAN tagging

How to do it...

Connect Wireshark to the switch you want to monitor. Let's look at the preceding configuration (shown in the preceding diagram).

Monitoring traffic inside a VLAN

In order to monitor traffic on an entire VLAN:

1. Connect your laptop to the central switch and to one of the ports.
2. Configure the port mirror from the monitored VLAN to the port you are connected to. For example, if you connect your laptop to **SW1** port **4** and you want to monitor traffic from **VLAN10**, the commands will be (in Cisco):
   - `Switch(config)#monitor session 1 source vlan 10`
   - `Switch(config)#monitor session 1 destination interface fastethernet0/4`

This will show you traffic from **VLAN10** that is forwarded through the central switch, **SW1**.

 For further information on how to configure port mirroring on various vendor websites, search for SPAN (in Cisco), port mirror, or mirroring (HP, Dell, Juniper, and others). While monitoring traffic in a blade center, usually you can only monitor traffic on a physical port; however, there are applications that enable you to monitor traffic on a specific server on a blade (for example, Cisco Nexus 1000V).

Viewing tagged frames going through a VLAN tagged port

Monitoring tagged traffic is not a straightforward mission. The issues of whether you see VLAN tags while capturing data with Wireshark or not will depend on the network adapter you have, the driver that runs over it, and what they do with VLAN tags.

The simplest way to verify that your laptop can capture tagged frames is as follows:

1. Start capturing the tagged port with the port mirror. If you see tags, continue with your work.
2. If you don't see any tags, go to the adapter configuration. In Windows 7, you get there by clicking on **Start** and then navigating to **Control Panel | Network and Internet | View Network Status and Tasks | Change Adapter Settings | Local Area Connection**. Next, perform the steps as shown in the following screenshot:

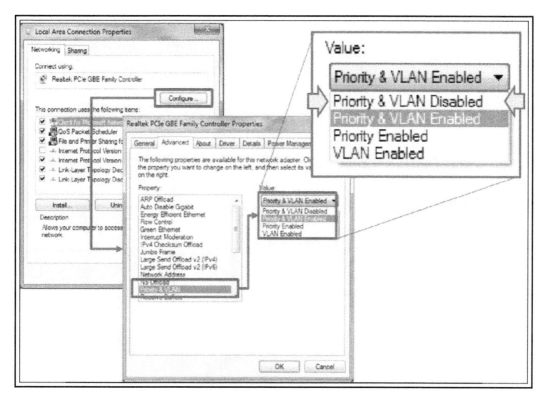

Figure 8.15: Enabling priority and VLAN

Configure the adapter with priority and VLAN disabled. This will move the tags for the WinPcap driver and for the Wireshark

> In the previous screenshot, we see an example of a Lenovo laptop with Realtek NIC. The illustration gives an example on a popular device, but it can be different on other laptops or servers. The principle should be the same: disable the adapter by extracting the VLAN tag so that it will be forwarded to the WinPcap driver and presented on Wireshark.

How it works...

Tags are small pieces of data added to a packet in order to add VLAN information to it. The tag is a 4 bytes long string (32-bits), as presented in one of the following diagrams. Most network adapters and their drivers will simply pass VLAN tags to the upper layer to handle them. In these cases, Wireshark will see VLAN tags and present them. In more sophisticated adapters and drivers, the VLAN tag will be handled by the adapter itself. This includes some of the most common adapters with Intel and Broadcom Gigabit chipsets. In these cases, you will have to disable the VLAN feature.

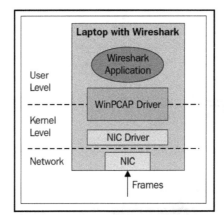

Figure 8.16: VLAN tagging and network adapters

When configuring the NIC driver, in order to ensure that it will not handle VLAN tags, the packets will simply be forwarded to the WinPcap driver and presented by Wireshark.

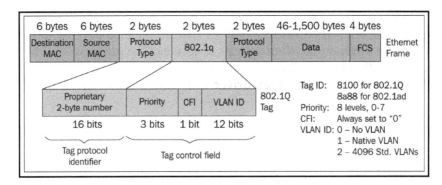

Figure 8.17: VLAN tagging

In the following screenshot, you see an example for a tagged frame; the frame is tagged with VLAN `ID = 20`:

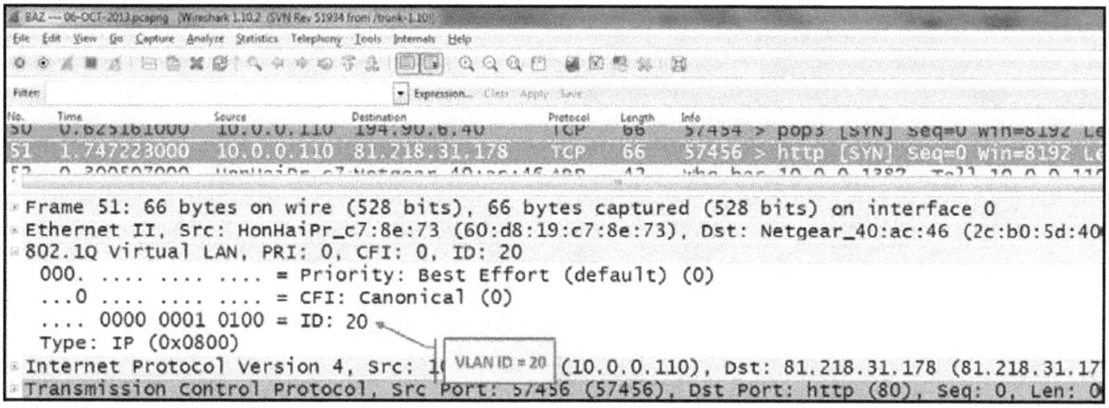

Figure 8.18: Packet with a VLAN tag

There's more...

Wireshark will also capture double tags, just like the 802.1ad standard. These tags are what's called service tags and are added at the service provider edge in order to divide between the provider and the customer tags. The provider tag is called S-tag (802.1ad), and the customer tag is called C-tag (802.1Q). It is also referred to as a QinQ mechanism.

See also

- For more information about WinPcap, go to the WinPcap home page at `http://www.winpcap.org/`
- For more information on the UNIX/Linux library, refer to the tcpdump home page at `http://www.tcpdump.org/`

Wireless LAN 9

In this chapter, we will learn about:

- Introduction to wireless networks and standards
- Wireless radio issues, analysis, and troubleshooting
- Capturing wireless LAN traffic

Skills learned

By the end of this chapter, the reader will be able to analyze Wireless LAN traffic and diagnose connectivity and performance problems reported by users.

Introduction to wireless networks and standards

Wireless networks have become very popular in the last decade, and it is now one of the most essential connectivities we need for our gadgets to stay connected. At a high level, a wireless network can be of the following types:

- **Wireless Personal Area Networks (WPAN)**: Wireless devices stay within 5-10 meters of each other and can be built ad-hoc-based
- **Wireless Local Area Network (WLAN)**: Wireless devices stay within 100 meters of each other

- **Wireless Metropolitan Area Network (WMAN)**: Wireless devices stay less than 100 meters away from each other and within ~5 kilometers (3.1 miles), and usually provide coverage for a suburb or town

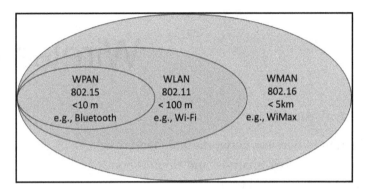

Figure 9.1: Types of Wireless Networks

Let's have a quick look at various WLAN standards. The IEEE 802.11 committee has been developing wireless LAN standards since the mid-1990s and has published several, from 802.11b to 802.11ac, as given here:

Standard	802.11b	802.11a	802.11g	802.11n	802.11ac
Year	1999	1999	2003	2009	2013
Frequency	2.4 GHz	5 GHz	2.4 GHz	2.4 / 5 GHz	5 GHz
Number of channels	3	<=24	3	Dynamic	Dynamic
Transmission technology	DSSS	OFDM	DSSS / OFDM	OFDM	OFDM
Data rate (Mbps)	1, 2, 5.5, 11	6, 9, 12, 18, 24, 36, 48, 54	6, 9, 12, 18, 24, 36, 48, 54 - OFDM	<= 450	1300 (Wave1), 6930 (Wave2)

Understanding WLAN devices, protocols, and terminologies

It is important to know the wireless radio fundamentals and various WLAN devices so that it will be helpful to understand user-reported problems and troubleshoot them.

Access point (AP)

Wireless LAN networks are based on **access points** (**AP**)—hardware that allows wireless stations/devices (referred to as STA) to connect to it and in turn to a wired network. An AP usually connects to an upstream switch/router.

Wireless LAN controller (WLC)

A **Wireless LAN Controller** (**WLC**) is a piece of hardware that communicates with and manages a large number of lightweight APs using the IEEE CAPWAP (Control and Provisioning of Wireless Access Points) protocol, which is based on Cisco's **Lightweight Access Point Protocol** (**LWAPP**). CAPWAP carries both control traffic (DTLS-encrypted) as well as data traffic (DTLS encryption optional) between the APs and Controller.

APs can be deployed in standalone or centralized mode.

- **Standalone**: As the name suggests, in this mode, APs are deployed and maintained individually. This is the most commonly seen type of deployment in small/medium businesses, where only a few APs are needed.

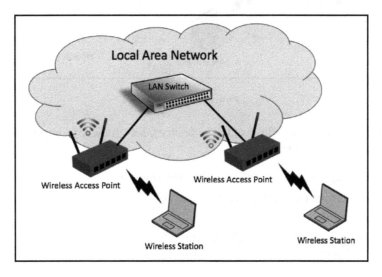

Figure 9.3: Wireless APs in standalone mode

- **Centralized**: In this mode, large number of APs are managed by wireless LAN controller(s) for their device configurations, security/policy settings, software/firmware updates and so on. The connectivity between the APs and Controller can be either via a layer 2/3 network. As mentioned earlier, APs are managed by wireless controller using CAPWAP protocol, which handles both data as well as control traffic.

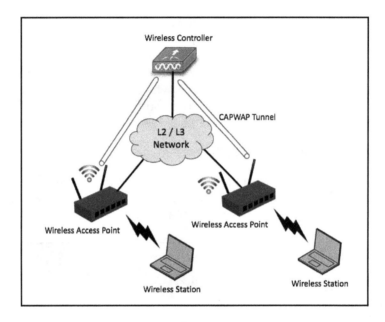

Figure 9.4: Wireless APs in centralized mode

With a basic understanding of wireless LAN devices, let's look into a few more terminologies used in wireless:

- **STA:** Wireless station or client using the service
- **AP:** The device providing wireless service to the clients
- **DS**: Distribution, the LAN that connects the APs
- **BSS**: **Basic Service Set** (**BSS**), or units of wireless devices operating with the same media characteristics (for example, radio frequency and modulation scheme)
- **ESS**: **Extended Service Set** (**ESS**), or logical units of basic service set(s) in the same logical network segment (for example, IP subnet and VLAN)

Refer to the following diagram for a better understanding of these terminologies:

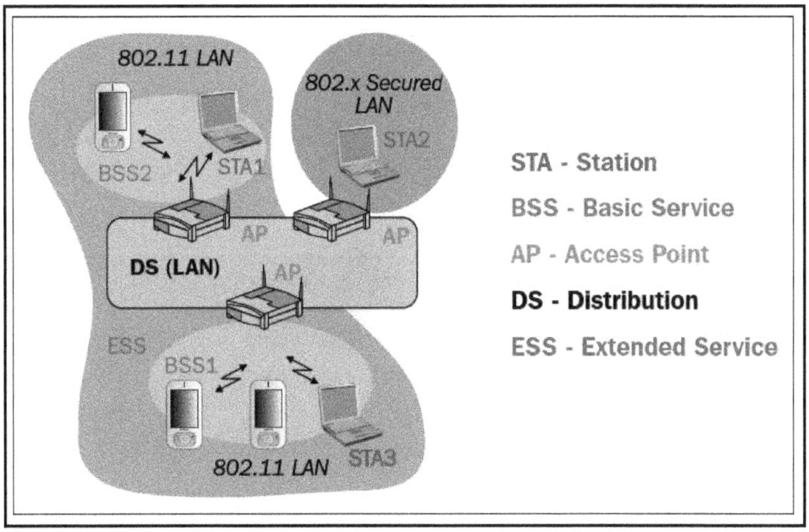

Figure 9.5: Wireless LAN distribution and service sets

Wireless radio issues, analysis, and troubleshooting

Getting ready

When users complain about no or poor connectivity through a Wi-Fi network, go as close as you can to the users' location with your laptop and verify that you are getting the Wi-Fi network.

How to do it...

To find out where the problem comes from, go through the following steps:

1. Do the users have poor wireless connectivity or absolutely no connectivity?
2. Is the poor wireless connectivity issue seen in different parts of the floor/building or only in a specific section of the floor/building?

Zero wireless connectivity

If the users have zero connectivity, then access and check the status and health of the access points (operating in standalone mode) providing coverage in the area affected.

If the APs are centrally managed by a controller, then their user interface (GUI) should provide ways to check the status of the APs, their health, and specifically the SSIDs they provide services for. From the following screenshot, we can see that a Cisco Wireless Controller reports the number of APs, their uptime, and so on.

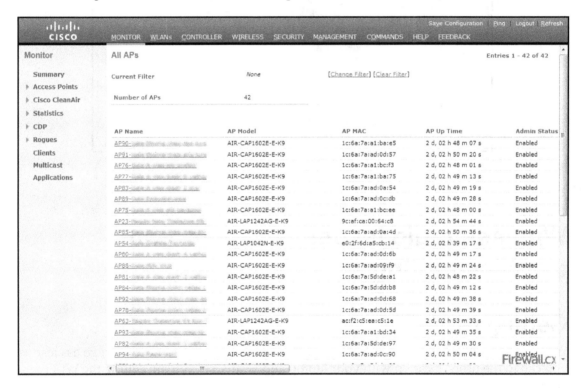

Figure 9.6: Cisco wireless controller APs list and status

Please be aware that there is a process for APs to discover the controller, join the wireless domain, and download the configurations/policies. I recommend referring to specific vendors' troubleshooting documents to diagnose and resolve the issues.

If the APs are missing from the controller's user interface, then there could be a connectivity issue between them. Troubleshooting connectivity issues between APs and the controller with packet captures is the same as between two PCs in a network.

Please be aware that not all the SSIDs are broadcast by the APs. So, if a user complains of not seeing a specific SSID, it could be due to APs not broadcasting them. If it is so, then try joining the specific SSID manually, with username/password credentials.

Poor or intermittent wireless connectivity

If the users report intermittent connectivity and poor performance, carry out the following steps.

The basic tool is right in the laptop (as we can see in the following screenshot), where you have the first indication for:

- The signal strength, which is also referred to as **Received Signal Strength Indicator (RSSI)**
- The access point ID, that is, the **Service Set Identification (SSID)**
- The security protocol used
- Radio type (802.11n, as shown in the screenshot)

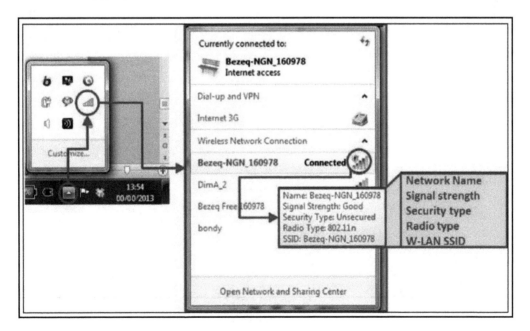

Figure 9.7: Wi-Fi network and details in a PC

Once you have confirmed that the proper Wi-Fi network is available at the user's location, use dedicated software (for example, the free version of Acrylic Wi-Fi, Homedale for Windows, the free version of NetSpot for Apple Mac, or the macOS wireless diagnostics tool). Thus, you discover the available networks, signal strength, channels, link quality, and many more details. This will provide an overview of the Wi-Fi networks available at the location and also possible frequency disturbances, interference, and radio problems. Some pieces of software also provide options to monitor signal quality for a specific duration.

RSSI levels indicate that the higher the number, the lower the strength:

- **-60 dBm and better**: This indicates a good signal level
- **-80 dBm to -60 dBm**: This indicates a reasonable signal level
- **-80 dBm to -90 dBm**: This indicates a weak signal level
- **-90 dBm and lower**: This indicates a very weak signal

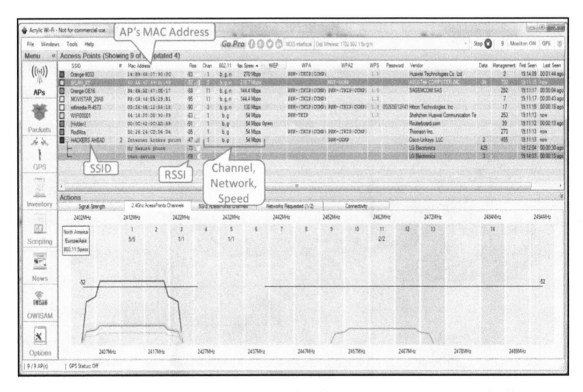

Figure 9.8: Wi-Fi networks, RSSI levels and speed from acrylic

If you have RSSI in the reasonable range and above, the received level is usually enough and you should look for frequency disturbances and other radio problems. **Signal-to-Noise Ratio (SNR)** is one of the important parameters; it provides the ratio between the signal power and noise power in the environment.

 A rule of thumb that I usually apply for wireless network design is that, for standard enterprise applications, I require 75 dBm and better; and for wireless networks that should also be used for VoIP, I require -65 dBm or better.

If you want to check whether there are any disturbances, you can use software that will discover RSSI over time, and it will give you a more accurate picture of your network. In the following screenshot, you see one such piece of software called **inSSIDer**; it gives you a more accurate picture of which access points are working and their details.

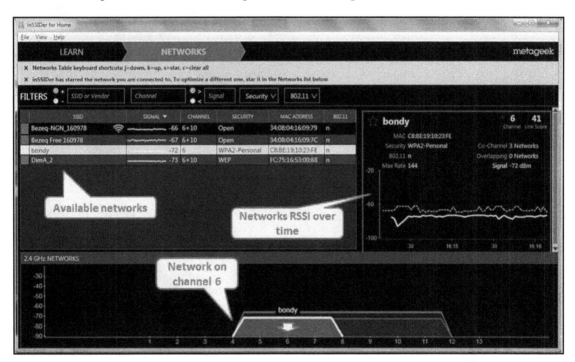

Figure 9.9: RSSI over time from inSSIDer

Try to find out the following problems:

- Different APs working on the same channel in the same area
- Low SNR, seen when RSSI is low (normally lower than -90 dBm) and/or noise is high

802.11 networks operate in the 2.4 GHz ISM (industrial, scientific, and medical) band, which is unlicensed. As a result, it is crowded due to transmissions from all kinds of devices such as wireless video cameras, microwave ovens, cordless phones/headsets, wireless gaming consoles/controllers, motion detectors, and even fluorescent lights.

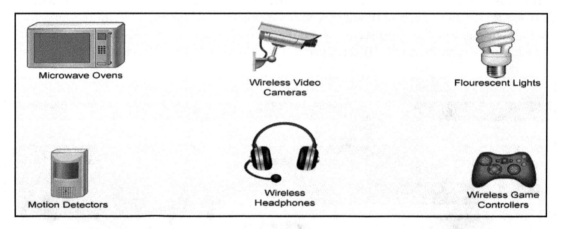

Figure 9.10: 802.11 interferers

You can expect frequency disturbances in areas such as airports, seaports, and military zones. The next step is to use spectrum analyzers to check which frequencies are used in your area. Spectrum analyzers are available from various vendors such as Fluke Networks, Agilent, and Anritsu.

Wireshark can be used to analyze Wi-Fi control frames. The first thing to look for is whether the APs are sending beacon frames and they are also received at the wireless station. In the following screenshot, you can see these frames:

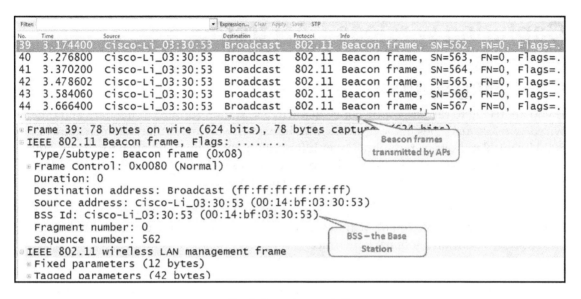

Figure 9.11: Beacon frames sent by APs

The APs periodically send beacon frames to announce its presence, SSID, security method used, and so on, along with timestamps.

Wireless stations/devices continuously scan all 802.11 radio signals and listen to beacons to determine the best access point and wireless network to associate with. The stations acknowledge the beacon in order to register to an AP and specific SSID.

Wireless stations can also send Probe Request frames to discover nearby access points, which will respond with probe response frames to provide further information.

After identifying the preferred wireless network and acknowledging the beacon frame, a standard DHCP process will start, as described in Chapter 10, *Network Layer Protocols and Operations*.

Capturing wireless LAN traffic

Capturing options

If you are trying to capture traffic between a wireless station running Wireshark and other wired/wireless machines in the network, and interested only in regular network data, not in 802.11 control packets or radio/link-layer information, then you don't have to do anything special. Just open Wireshark, choose the specific wireless interface you are interested in, apply the necessary filters and run it in promiscuous mode.

> Using Wireshark, if you want to capture traffic between different processes running within the wireless station, then the capture should be done on a loopback interface.

If you are trying to capture traffic that is not only sent to or from the wireless station running Wireshark but also between different wireless devices in the network—and if you are interested in 802.11 control packets or radio/link-layer information—then you have to do it by enabling monitor mode, highlighted as follows (Wireshark version 10.6, running on Apple macOS Sierra 10.12.6). This type of capture is often referred to as **Over-the-Air (OTA)** packet capture.

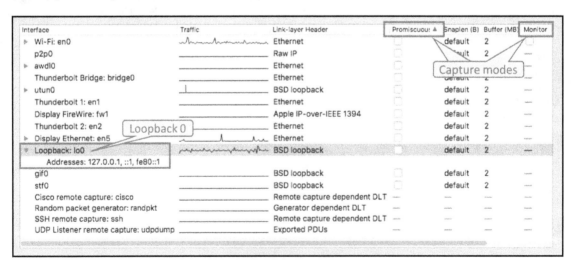

Figure 9.12: Wireshark interface capture options

Please be aware that Wireshark provides limited capabilities to perform OTA packet captures; several commercial tools and applications are available to provide more comprehensive monitoring and troubleshooting capabilities and features.

In Unix-based operating systems and Apple macOS (10.6 or above), there are a few built-in tools such as `airportd`, airport utility, Wireless Diagnostics, and tcpdump that can be leveraged for capturing and analyzing wireless packets.

Getting ready

With a basic understanding of the available options to capture traffic, let's discuss the steps seen during a successful association of a station to the wireless network and also access to network services/data:

- Wireless stations receive beacon frames from AP and/or exchange Probe Request and Responses with AP to get associated.
- On successful association, the stations go through the authentication process and get permission.
- Wireless clients provided with IPv4/v6 address based on the network policy.
- In the web authentication process, users agree to terms and conditions from the wireless service provider. This step may be optional, depending on the provider.

With the aforementioned steps, numerous issues can occur in the network; they may stop a station from getting successfully associated with wireless networks and accessing data. Here, we are going to look into some very commonly seen issues:

- Wireless station not joining a specific SSID
- After a successful association to an SSID, users are not able to authenticate

How to do it...

Please review the previous section—wireless radio issues, analysis, and troubleshooting—and make sure there are no radio/link-layer issues.

Wireless station not joining a specific SSID

Run Wireshark in monitor mode and filter the traffic sent and received by a wireless station (device under troubleshooting), with applicable filters.

As discussed in previous chapters, locate the field of interest in a given frame, right-click on it, and select **Apply as Column** to add the field as a column. For example, you can add data rate, strength, and so on, which will be very helpful during troubleshooting.

Consider a scenario where an Apple wireless device just got activated and joining is an SSID. As you see next, the wireless device sends a probe request and gets a probe response from the AP. Filter used: (wlan.fc == 0x4000) or (wlan.fc == 0x5008):

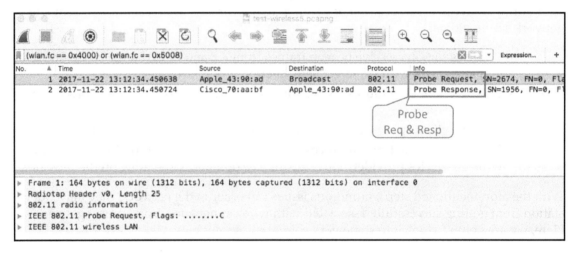

Figure 9.13: Probe request and response

Please note that the probe request is a broadcast, which is destined to all Fs mac-addresses.

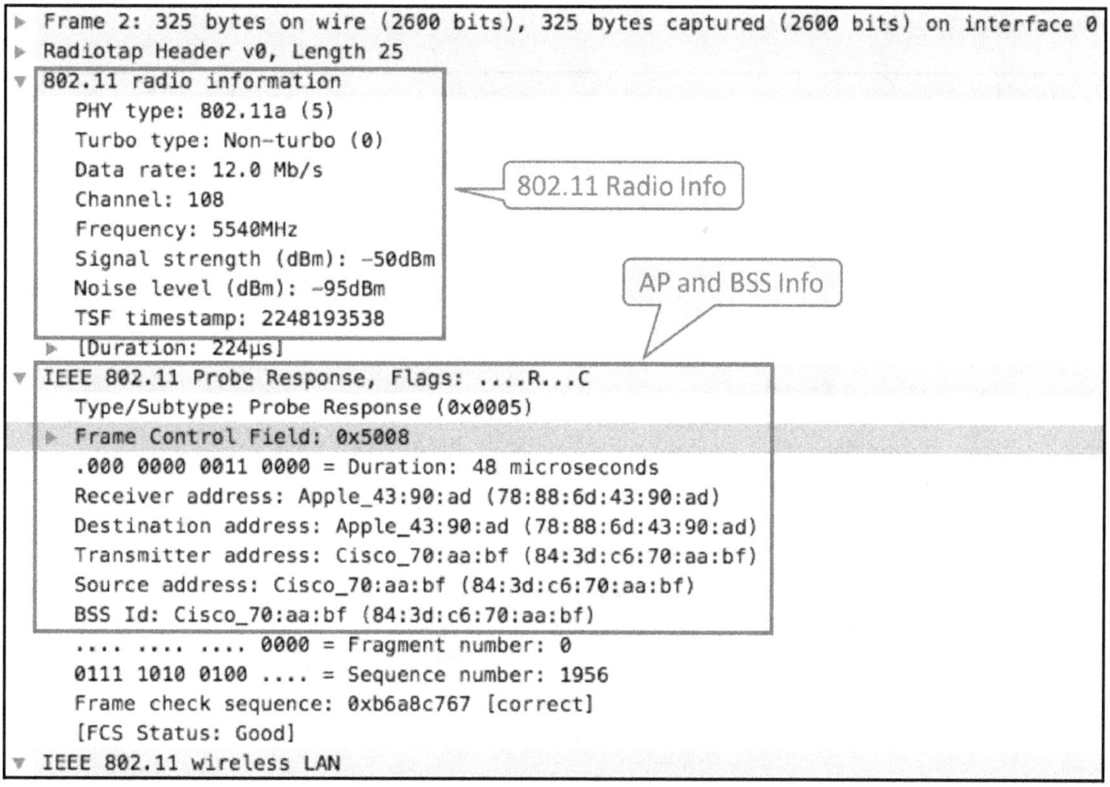

```
▶ Frame 2: 325 bytes on wire (2600 bits), 325 bytes captured (2600 bits) on interface 0
▶ Radiotap Header v0, Length 25
▼ 802.11 radio information
    PHY type: 802.11a (5)
    Turbo type: Non-turbo (0)
    Data rate: 12.0 Mb/s
    Channel: 108
    Frequency: 5540MHz
    Signal strength (dBm): -50dBm
    Noise level (dBm): -95dBm
    TSF timestamp: 2248193538
  ▶ [Duration: 224µs]
▼ IEEE 802.11 Probe Response, Flags: ....R...C
    Type/Subtype: Probe Response (0x0005)
  ▶ Frame Control Field: 0x5008
    .000 0000 0011 0000 = Duration: 48 microseconds
    Receiver address: Apple_43:90:ad (78:88:6d:43:90:ad)
    Destination address: Apple_43:90:ad (78:88:6d:43:90:ad)
    Transmitter address: Cisco_70:aa:bf (84:3d:c6:70:aa:bf)
    Source address: Cisco_70:aa:bf (84:3d:c6:70:aa:bf)
    BSS Id: Cisco_70:aa:bf (84:3d:c6:70:aa:bf)
    .... .... .... 0000 = Fragment number: 0
    0111 1010 0100 .... = Sequence number: 1956
    Frame check sequence: 0xb6a8c767 [correct]
    [FCS Status: Good]
▼ IEEE 802.11 wireless LAN
```

802.11 Radio Info

AP and BSS Info

Figure 9.14: Probe response header details: radio, AP, and BSS

As you see here, a valid probe response will have radio/link-layer information such as frequency, channel, SNR, and so on in the 802.11 radio information header, and transmitter and BSS information in the 802.11 probe response header.

The next image shows SSID, supported rates in Mbps, and other capabilities in the 802.11 wireless LAN header. Make sure that all of the information looks valid and compatible to the wireless adapter.

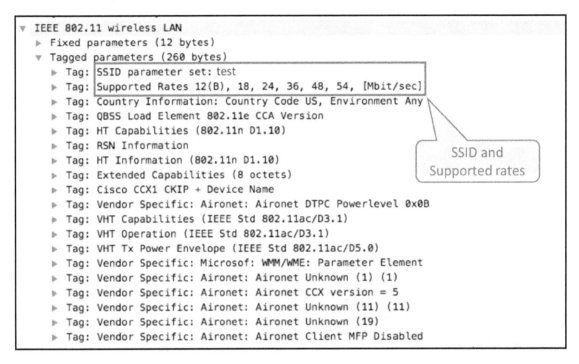

Figure 9.15: Probe response header details: SSID and rates

After getting a response, the wireless client gets associated with a specific SSID serviced by the AP. As shown next, after the probe request and response, the client and AP exchange a few more messages to complete the association process.

Source	Destination	Protocol	Info
Apple_43:90:ad	Broadcast	802.11	Probe Request, SN=2674, FN=0, Flags=........C, SSID=...
Cisco_70:aa:bf	Apple_43:90:ad	802.11	Probe Response, SN=1956, FN=0, Flags=....R...C, BI=1...
Apple_43:90:ad	Cisco_70:aa:bf	802.11	Authentication, SN=2675, FN=0, Flags=........C
	Apple_43:90:ad (78:8...	802.11	Acknowledgement, Flags=........C
Cisco_70:aa:bf	Apple_43:90:ad	802.11	Authentication, SN=2967, FN=0, Flags=........C
Apple_43:90:ad	Cisco_70:aa:bf	802.11	Association Request, SN=2676, FN=0, Flags=....R...C,...
	Apple_43:90:ad (78:8...	802.11	Acknowledgement, Flags=........C
Cisco_70:aa:bf	Apple_43:90:ad	802.11	Association Response, SN=2968, FN=0, Flags=........C

Figure 9.16: Wireless client and AP association process

If you look at the 802.11 Wireless LAN header in the final Association Response frame sent by the AP, you should see the **Status Code** field as Successful. This indicates successful association of the client with the specific AP and SSID.

```
▶ Frame 8: 181 bytes on wire (1448 bits), 181 bytes captured (1448 bits) on interface 0
▶ Radiotap Header v0, Length 25
▶ 802.11 radio information
▶ IEEE 802.11 Association Response, Flags: ........C
▼ IEEE 802.11 wireless LAN
  ▼ Fixed parameters (6 bytes)
    ▶ Capabilities Information: 0x0111
      Status code: Successful (0x0000)
      ..00 0000 0101 1111 = Association ID: 0x005f
▶ Tagged parameters (122 bytes)
```

Figure 9.17: Wireless client and AP association: status code

Users not able to authenticate after successful association

After successful association, if you see user data exchanged between the client and the AP, then most probably there is no security policy implemented. This is commonly seen in department stores or hotels, where guests are allowed to access wireless networks with no device-level authentication. Remember, an application-level authentication may occur when users open the browser, where they are requested to provide username/password credentials and/or accept terms and conditions to continue to use wireless services.

Before troubleshooting authentication issues, let's understand the authentication framework and various methods.

Extensible Authentication Protocol (**EAP**) is one of the most prevalent authentication frameworks seen in today's deployments, and widely supported by various vendors and wireless clients. This framework, which itself is not an authentication mechanism, provides common authentication functions and negotiation, referred to as EAP methods. There are currently 40 or more methods that are used to secure the communication between devices, for example, LEAP, EAP-TLS, EAP-MD5, EAP-FAST, EAP-IKEv2, and so on.

Note:

- EAP is defined in RFC5274. Earlier it was defined in RFC3748.
- The requirements for methods used specifically in Wireless LAN are described in RFC4017.

- Refer to the IANA EAP Registry for types and codes used in EAP packets, at the following link: `https://www.iana.org/assignments/eap-numbers/eap-numbers.xhtml`.
- IEEE 802.1X defines the encapsulation of EAP over LAN, which is also referred to as EAPoL.

Please refer to the following screenshot to follow the events that occur after successful association.

Filter used: `(wlan.da == 78:88:6d:43:90:ad or wlan.sa == 78:88:6d:43:90:ad) && (eapol.type == 0)`. Here, `78:88:6d:43:90:ad` is the wireless client's MAC address:

- Frame #9: AP sends a request to the wireless client to identify itself.
- Frame #10: The Apple wireless client identifies itself.
- Frame #12: The AP wants to set up a secure tunnel to protect all the EAP communication (referred, as Protected EAP—PEAP) using the EAP-TLS method.</li>
- Frame #13: The client starts to send TLS ver1.2 frames to the AP.
- Frames #15-46: The AP and wireless device exchange a few more packets to complete the authentication process and encapsulation method.

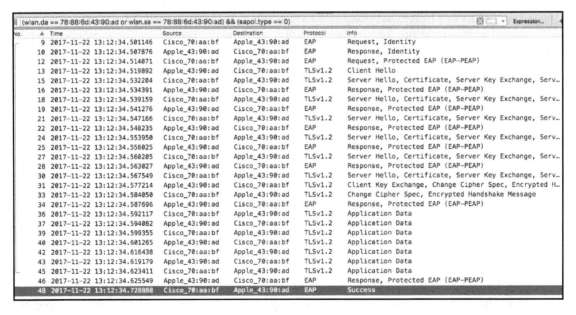

Figure 9.18: EAP process

- Frame #48: The EAP process completes with code *Success* in the EAP header. The details are as follows:

```
▶ Frame 48: 71 bytes on wire (568 bits), 71 bytes captured (568 bits) on interface 0
▶ Radiotap Header v0, Length 25
▶ 802.11 radio information
▶ IEEE 802.11 QoS Data, Flags: ......F.C
▶ Logical-Link Control
▼ 802.1X Authentication
    Version: 802.1X-2004 (2)
    Type: EAP Packet (0)
    Length: 4
  ▼ Extensible Authentication Protocol
      Code: Success (3)
    Id: 197
    Length: 4
```

Figure 9.19: – EAP process - final status code

After a successful EAP process, the wireless client and AP have to complete a four-way handshake, which is designed for the AP and wireless client to prove their legitimacy to each other independently without disclosing the key shared earlier. This is very critical to protect the network from any kind of malicious APs. Make sure the four-way handshake completes so that the wireless client can access the data.

eapol.keydes.type == 2					Expression...

No.	Time	Source	Destination	Protocol	Info
49	2017-11-22 13:12:34.729182	Cisco_70:aa:bf	Apple_43:90:ad	EAPOL	Key (Message 1 of 4)
50	2017-11-22 13:12:34.729886	Apple_43:90:ad	Cisco_70:aa:bf	EAPOL	Key (Message 2 of 4)
52	2017-11-22 13:12:34.731210	Cisco_70:aa:bf	Apple_43:90:ad	EAPOL	Key (Message 3 of 4)
53	2017-11-22 13:12:34.731904	Apple_43:90:ad	Cisco_70:aa:bf	EAPOL	Key (Message 4 of 4)

Figure 9.20: Four-way handshake

There's more...

AirPcap from Riverbed

In the scenarios discussed earlier, a very specific authentication and encapsulation method was considered and performed from an Apple Mac laptop. You can use various commercial tools available in the market, such as the AirPcap wireless adapter from Riverbed, which is fully integrated with Wireshark, and SteelCentral packet analyzer. This product bundle provides a comprehensive report and visualization. Please refer to the following link for further details: `https://www.riverbed.com/products/steelcentral/steelcentral-riverbed-airpcap.html`.

More ways to capture traffic between Wireless Clients, APs, and Controller

In earlier sections, we discussed only the interaction between the wireless client and AP, and the relevant packet captures. Vendors such as Cisco Systems and Aruba/HPE provide ways to run the AP and/or Wireless Controller in a sniffer mode. In this mode, the AP/WLC sends traffic destined to a specific UDP port (for example, `5555`); it can be captured in a wireless client using Wireshark with the UDP port `5555` filter and decoded as peekremote (it is airopeek in older versions). This option helps to confirm the traffic from AP to client reach with no loss, and also to verify various radio/link layer parameters.

In normal conditions, all the control/data payloads between wireless clients and APs are encrypted, and cannot be decrypted using Wireshark. I would recommend that you talk to the specific vendor to see if it is possible to decrypt these packets at AP/WLC.

Also, in centralized deployment mode, data/control traffic between APs and WLC is CAPWAP-tunneled. CAPWAP traffic can be captured (just like we do it for traffic between two PCs in a network) and decoded using Wireshark.

> Make sure you check the **Cisco Wireless Controller Support** option under **Wireshark** | **Preferences** | **Protocols** | **CAPWAP-CONTROL** in order to decode CAPWAP control packets. If not selected, the packets may be labeled as *malformed* packets in the Wireshark display.

10
Network Layer Protocols and Operations

In this chapter, you will learn about the following:

- The IPv4 principles of operations
- IPv4 address resolution protocol operation and troubleshooting
- ICMP – protocol operation, analysis, and troubleshooting
- Analyzing IPv4 unicast routing operations
- Analyzing IP fragmentation failures
- IPv4 multicast routing operations
- The IPv6 principles of operations
- IPv6 extension headers
- ICMPv6 – protocol operations, analysis, and troubleshooting
- IPv6 auto configuration
- DHCPv6-based address configuration
- IPv6 neighbor discovery protocol operation and analysis

Introduction

In this chapter, we will primarily focus on layer 3 of the OSI reference model and learn how to analyze the layer 3 protocols (IPv4/IPv6) operations, as well as unicast and multicast traffic flow analysis. We will also look at the **Address Resolution Protocol** (**ARP**)/ND, dynamic and stateless IPv6 address configuration, and more. We will discuss the basic issues that you might face while troubleshooting these protocols.

We will learn how to analyze end-to-end IPv4 and IPv6 connectivity failures for unicast and multicast traffic using Wireshark.

While there are variously structured troubleshooting approaches available, the bottom-up troubleshooting approach is the most efficient and effective approach. It starts from the bottom layer (physical) of the OSI reference model. When there is an end-to-end connectivity failure between end points, this approach starts inspecting the elements at bottom layer and moves toward the top layer until the cause of the failure is identified. The approach is as follows:

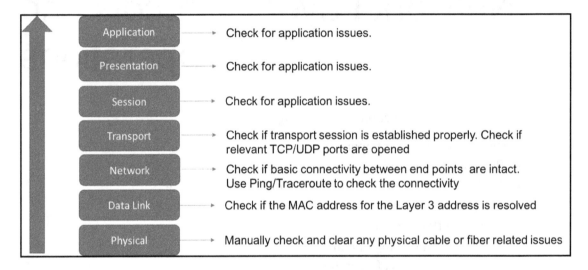

ISO bottom-up troubleshooting model

The IPv4 principles of operations

In the OSI reference model, the network layer is responsible for providing globally unique device identification using network layer addressing and providing connectivity between end systems residing in different networks for data transfer. The basic functionality of the network layer is to receive the segment from upper (transport) layer, encapsulate it with network layer header that carries the source and destination identifiers, and forward the packet to the remote end system.

IP is the network layer protocol and is the most commonly deployed network layer protocol of the internet and other network is IPv4. The format of the IPv4 header is as follows:

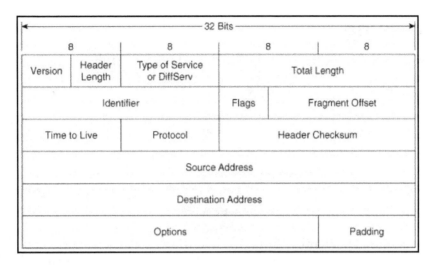

IPv4 packet header

The following is a sample Wireshark capture of an IP packet:

```
▽ Internet Protocol Version 4, Src: 10.0.0.1 (10.0.0.1), Dst: 10.0.0.101 (10.0.0.101)
    Version: 4
    Header Length: 20 bytes
  ▽ Differentiated Services Field: 0x00 (DSCP 0x00: Default; ECN: 0x00: Not-ECT (Not ECN-Capable Transport))
      0000 00.. = Differentiated Services Codepoint: Default (0x00)
      .... ..00 = Explicit Congestion Notification: Not-ECT (Not ECN-Capable Transport) (0x00)
    Total Length: 100
    Identification: 0x002e (46)
  ▽ Flags: 0x00
      0... .... = Reserved bit: Not set
      .0.. .... = Don't fragment: Not set
      ..0. .... = More fragments: Not set
    Fragment offset: 0
    Time to live: 255
    Protocol: ICMP (1)
  ▽ Header checksum: 0xa705 [validation disabled]
      [Good: False]
      [Bad: False]
    Source: 10.0.0.1 (10.0.0.1)
    Destination: 10.0.0.101 (10.0.0.101)
    [Source GeoIP: Unknown]
    [Destination GeoIP: Unknown]
```

Sample IP packet

IP addressing

An IPv4 address is a unique and logical network layer identifier that is assigned to each device on an IP network. It is a 32-bit identifier that consists of a network portion and host portion. The address format is as follows:

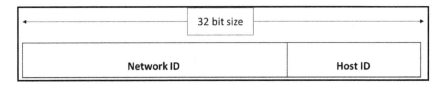

IPv4 address format

The network ID is used to identify the network in which the host resides. All nodes within the same network will share the same network ID. The host ID is used to identify the host within the network. Each node within the network will have a unique host ID. An IP address is always assigned with a subnet mask that identifies the network ID portion of the address. For example, the IP address 10.0.0.1 with a subnet mask of 255.255.255.0 denotes that the first three octets are the network ID and the last octet is the host ID.

While the size of the IPv4 address is 32-bits, the syntax used to represent the address is based on dotted decimal. The 32-bits are split into four octets and each octet is represented as a decimal value with a dot as demarcation.

There are three types of IPv4 addresses, outlined as follows:

- **Unicast address**: Used for point-to-point communication where data is sent from one node to one receiver in the same or different network. The address range for unicast is from 1.0.0.0 to 223.255.255.255.
- **Multicast address**: Used for point-to-multipoint communication where data is sent from one node to multiple receivers in the same or different network. The address range for multicast is from 224.0.0.0 to 239.255.255.255.
- **Broadcast address**: Used for point-to-multipoint communication where the data is sent from one node to all receivers in the same network. The last IP address in each subnet is the broadcast address. The address 255.255.255.255 is known as the limited broadcast address.

IPv4 address resolution protocol operation and troubleshooting

Ethernet is the popular and predominantly deployed **Local Area Network (LAN)** technology, spanning a transmission speed rate of 10 Mbps to 400 Gbps. This data link layer protocol uses a 48-bit MAC address as a data link layer identifier. In this recipe, we will discuss the IPv4 ARP and its related issues.

Getting ready

In the bottom-up troubleshooting approach, the first step for any connectivity issue is to ensure that the ARP resolution is successful for the respective IP address.

How to do it...

Consider the following screenshot of LAN topology:

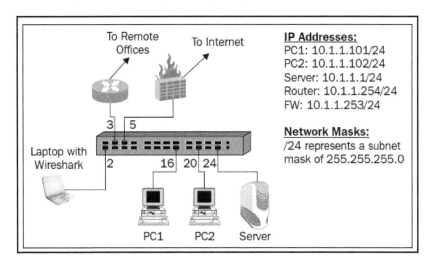

LAN topology

In the preceding scenario, assume **PC1** is trying to reach **PC2**:

1. Trigger ping probes from **PC1** (10.1.1.101) to **PC2** (10.1.1.102). This will trigger an ARP request from **PC1** to **PC2**.
2. Check the ARP table on **PC1** using arp-a, to see whether the MAC address for 10.1.1.102 is populated in the local table.
3. If you see the MAC address for 10.1.1.102 in the **PC1** local table, that confirms that **PC1** sent the ARP request and received the ARP response from **PC2**.
4. If you don't see the MAC address for 10.1.1.102 in **PC1**, connect Wireshark to one of the free ports on Switch and capture the packet (with port mirroring). It will be useful to perform the capture on both the ingress and egress directions of the ports connecting **PC1** and **PC2**:

```
▷ Frame 1: 48 bytes on wire (480 bits), 48 bytes captured (480 bits)
▽ Ethernet II, Src: fa:16:3e:7a:ee:a6 (fa:16:3e:7a:ee:a6), Dst: Broadcast (ff:ff:ff:ff:ff:ff)
  ▷ Destination: Broadcast (ff:ff:ff:ff:ff:ff) ──────────→ ARP packet sent to Broadcast MAC destination address
  ▷ Source: fa:16:3e:7a:ee:a6 (fa:16:3e:7a:ee:a6)
    Type: ARP (0x0806)
    Padding: 000000000000000000000000000000000000
▽ Address Resolution Protocol (request) ──────────→ ARP Request
    Hardware type: Ethernet (1)
    Protocol type: IP (0x0800)
    Hardware size: 6
    Protocol size: 4
    Opcode: request (1)
    Sender MAC address: fa:16:3e:7a:ee:a6 (fa:16:3e:7a:ee:a6) ──────→ PC1 MAC address
    Sender IP address: 10.1.1.101 (10.1.1.101)
    Target MAC address: 00:00:00_00:00:00 (00:00:00:00:00:00) ──────→ Querying MAC address for 10.1.1.102
    Target IP address: 10.1.1.102 (10.1.1.102)
```

ARP packet capture

5. Check whether the ARP request from **PC1** is seen in the capture. The preceding screenshot shows the ARP request from **PC1**. As you may notice, the ARP packet was destined to broadcast the MAC address ff.ff.ff.ff.ff.ff:
   • If the ARP request packet is seen in the capture on the port connecting **PC1** (ingress direction) but not in the capture on the port connecting **PC2** (egress direction), the switch might have dropped the ARP packet.
   • If the ARP request packet is not seen in the capture on the port connecting PC1 (ingress direction), check the physical cable connecting **PC1** to Switch.

- If the ARP request packet is seen in the capture on both the ports connecting **PC1** and **PC2**, but there is no ARP response, check **PC2**:

```
▷ Frame 5: 60 bytes on wire (480 bits), 60 bytes captured (480 bits)
▽ Ethernet II, Src: fa:16:3e:ce:50:b0 (fa:16:3e:ce:50:b0), Dst: fa:16:3e:7a:ee:a6 (fa:16:3e:7a:ee:a6)
  ▷ Destination: fa:16:3e:7a:ee:a6 (fa:16:3e:7a:ee:a6) ──────────→ ARP Response Unicasted to PC1
  ▷ Source: fa:16:3e:ce:50:b0 (fa:16:3e:ce:50:b0)
    Type: ARP (0x0806)
    Padding: 000000000000000000000000000000000000
▽ Address Resolution Protocol (reply) ─────────────────→ ARP Reply
    Hardware type: Ethernet (1)
    Protocol type: IP (0x0800)
    Hardware size: 6
    Protocol size: 4
    Opcode: reply (2)
    Sender MAC address: fa:16:3e:ce:50:b0 (fa:16:3e:ce:50:b0) ───────→ PC2 MAC address
    Sender IP address: 10.1.1.102 (10.1.1.102)
    Target MAC address: fa:16:3e:7a:ee:a6 (fa:16:3e:7a:ee:a6) ───────→ PC1 MAC address
    Target IP address: 10.1.1.101 (10.1.1.101)
```

ARP reply capture

6. Check whether the ARP reply packet is seen in the capture. The preceding screenshot shows the ARP reply from **PC2** to **PC1**. As can be seen, the ARP reply is unicasted to the **PC1** MAC address:
   - If the ARP reply packet is seen in the capture on the port connecting **PC2** (ingress direction) but not in the capture on the port connecting **PC1** (egress direction), the switch might have dropped the ARP reply packet.
   - If the ARP reply packet is not seen in the capture on the port connecting **PC2** (ingress direction), check the physical cable connecting **PC2** to Switch.
   - If the ARP reply packet is seen in the captures on both ports connecting **PC1** and **PC2**, but there is no entry in the **PC1** ARP table, check **PC1**.

The following are a few useful display filters:

Filter	Description	Example
arp	Filters all ARP packets	arp
arp.opcode == <opcode>	ARP Operation code based filter. Opcode of 1 will filter all ARP Request packets and Opcode 2 will filter all ARP Reply packets	arp.opcode == 1 arp.opcode == 2
arp.src.hw_mac == <mac>	Filter the ARP packet that MAC address defined in *Sender MAC address* field	arp.src.hw_mac == fa:16:3e:ce:50:b0
arp.dst.hw_mac == <mac>	Filter the ARP packet that MAC address defined in *Target MAC address* field	arp.dst.hw_mac == fa:16:3e:ce:50:b0
arp.isgratuitous == <>	Filter all Gratuitous ARP packets	arp.isgratuitous == true

Wireshark ARP display filters

ARP attacks and mitigations

ARP is a very simple protocol without any authentication or other inbuilt security mechanisms, and so it is vulnerable to attack. A malicious user within the network can use ARP as a means of ARP poisoning to eavesdrop, or can use ARP sweeping for **denial-of-service** (**DoS**) attacks. In this section, we will discuss different ARP-based attacks and how to use Wireshark to detect them.

ARP poisoning and man-in-the-middle attacks

One of type of man-in-the-middle attack is when an attacker poisons the ARP cache of the devices that they want to listen to with the MAC address of their Ethernet NIC. Once the ARP cache has been successfully poisoned, each of the victim devices sends all their packets to the attacker while communicating with the other device. The attacker, of course, will resend it to them after reading the data.

This is called a **man-in-the-middle** attack since it puts the attacker in the middle of the communication path between the victim devices. It is also called **ARP poisoning** since the attacker actually poisons the victim's ARP cache with wrong information.

In the following diagram, we see an example of a man-in-the-middle attack:

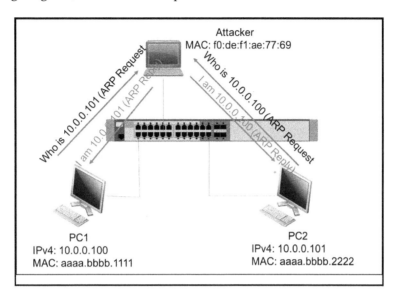

ARP poisoning attack

The following is the Wireshark capture:

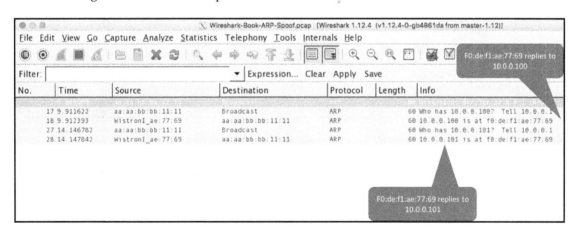

ARP spoofing capture

It should be noted that the attacker is responding to ARP requests for both `10.0.0.100` and `10.0.0.101` with a MAC address of `f0:de:f1:ae:77:69`. In a production network, it is likely that you will see hundreds of thousands of packets captured within a few seconds. The Wireshark display filters would be helpful in narrowing down the packets of interest to us.

Gratuitous ARP

Gratuitous ARP (**GARP**) can be used by any node to advertise its own MAC address with the respective IP address as the ARP reply, even when there is no ARP request. The primary purpose for such advanced notification is to ensure that the neighbors' ARP caches are updated on any changes in the local MAC address. GARP will always be destined to broadcast the MAC address:

```
▷ Frame 1: 60 bytes on wire (480 bits), 60 bytes captured (480 bits)
▽ Ethernet II, Src: aa:aa:bb:bb:11:11 (aa:aa:bb:bb:11:11), Dst: Broadcast (ff:ff:ff:ff:ff:ff)
    ▷ Destination: Broadcast (ff:ff:ff:ff:ff:ff)
    ▷ Source: aa:aa:bb:bb:11:11 (aa:aa:bb:bb:11:11)
      Type: ARP (0x0806)
      Padding: 000000000000000000000000000000000000
▽ Address Resolution Protocol (reply/gratuitous ARP)
      Hardware type: Ethernet (1)
      Protocol type: IP (0x0800)
      Hardware size: 6
      Protocol size: 4
      Opcode: reply (2)
      [Is gratuitous: True]
      Sender MAC address: aa:aa:bb:bb:11:11 (aa:aa:bb:bb:11:11)
      Sender IP address: 10.0.0.1 (10.0.0.1)
      Target MAC address: Broadcast (ff:ff:ff:ff:ff:ff)
      Target IP address: 10.0.0.1 (10.0.0.1)
```

GARP packet

While it is expected to see GARP in a production environment, it could also be used by any malicious attacker to eavesdrop by sending GARP with its own MAC address for any IP address:

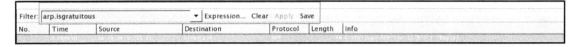

GARP filter

`arp.isgratuitous` is a Wireshark display filter that helps to list the GARP packets from a swarm of captured packets.

ARP sweep-based DoS attacks

For network inventory, it is a common practice to use a management system and send a sweep of ARP requests to all IP addresses within the subnet. In such an approach, the target IP address will keep changing, but the sender IP address and sender MAC address will remain the same and be set to the management system address. For efficient communication, the default behavior of the end host is to learn the sender IP and MAC address from the ARP request and populate the local ARP cache. The ARP sweep, along with this behavior, can also be used by any malicious attacker to deplete the ARP cache of all end hosts within the LAN network by changing the sender's IP and MAC addresses.

ARP requests and replies are a part of the regular network operation. Here are some rules of thumb to make sure they are actually so:

- For ARP requests from a diverse set of sources:
    - If the sources are legitimate, it is a normal operation
    - If the sources are malicious, it could be an attack
- For ARP requests originating from a single source:
    - If the source is a management system, it is a normal operation
    - If the source is a router, it could be a network scan
    - If the source is not legitimate, it could be an attack

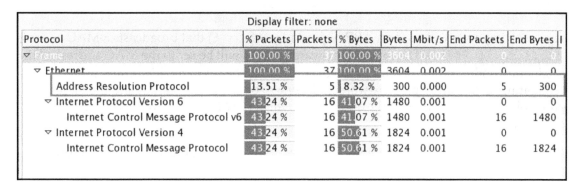

Protocol	% Packets	Packets	% Bytes	Bytes	Mbit/s	End Packets	End Bytes	I
▽ Frame	100.00 %	37	100.00 %	3604	0.002	0	0	
▽ Ethernet	100.00 %	37	100.00 %	3604	0.002	0	0	
Address Resolution Protocol	13.51 %	5	8.32 %	300	0.000	5	300	
▽ Internet Protocol Version 6	43.24 %	16	41.07 %	1480	0.001	0	0	
Internet Control Message Protocol v6	43.24 %	16	41.07 %	1480	0.001	16	1480	
▽ Internet Protocol Version 4	43.24 %	16	50.61 %	1824	0.001	0	0	
Internet Control Message Protocol	43.24 %	16	50.61 %	1824	0.001	16	1824	

Display filter: none

IP statistics

Wireshark statistics can be used to identify whether there is any ARP sweep. This can be viewed through **Statistics | Protocol Hierarchy** in Wireshark header field. As shown in the preceding example, the number of ARP packets can be viewed through this option, which will help us understand whether there is any sweep of ARP packets in the network.

How it works...

For end-to-end communication, any node is required to resolve the 48-bit Ethernet MAC address associated to the layer 3 IPv4 or IPv6 network address.

When the layer 3 network is IPv4, ARP is used to resolve the MAC address associated with the IPv4 address. The ARP packet format is as follows:

Hardware Type		Protocol Type	
Hardware Length	Protocol Length	OpCode (1 = Request, 2 = Reply)	
Sender Hardware Address (0-3 Octets)			
Sender Hardware Address (4-5 Octets)		Sender Protocol Address (0 – 1 Octets)	
Sender Protocol Address (2 – 3 Octets)		Target Hardware Address (0-1 Octets)	
Target Hardware Address (2-5 Octets)			
Target Protocol Address			

ARP packet format

The resolving node will send an ARP request (OpCode = 1) that broadcasts a MAC address (ff.ff.ff.ff.ff.ff). The sender hardware address will be set to the MAC address of the originating node, and the sender protocol address will be set to the IP address of the originating node. The target hardware address will be set to zero values and the target protocol address will be set to the address for which the MAC resolution is being performed.

The responding node will reply with ARP reply (Opcode = 2) unicasted to the resolving node.

ARP operation is only local, that means the ARP request, which is a broadcast, will be sent only on the LAN. When the source address *S* and destination address *D* belong to same LAN (same IP network and mask), the ARP will try to resolve the MAC address of *D* by sending ARP request carrying target protocol address as *D*. But when the source address *S* and destination address *D* are in different LANs (different IP network and mask), the resolution will be done for the default gateway address.

ICMP – protocol operation, analysis, and troubleshooting

Internet Control Message Protocol (**ICMP**) is a network layer protocol that serves the purpose of error reporting and network path diagnostic functions. The Ping and Traceroute utility tools leverage ICMP messages for fault detection and isolation. ICMP messages are sent using basic IP header. The protocol field in IP header will be set to ICMP followed by the ICMP payload. The ICMP packet has the following format:

Type	Code	Checksum
ICMP Message Dependant Variable		

ICMP header format

The ICMP message types used for network connectivity verification are echo request (`Type = 8`) and echo reply (`Type = 0`).

Getting ready

When there are any issues with an end application such as a web service or mail service, the first troubleshooting step using the bottom-up approach is to verify the data-link layer. Once we have verified the data-link layer using the steps defined in the previous section, the next step is to verify the network connectivity between the end points. Network connectivity between end points can be verified by commonly used fault detection and isolation utility tools, such as Ping and Traceroute.

How to do it...

Consider the following screenshot of IPv4 topology and closely observe the Ping probe:

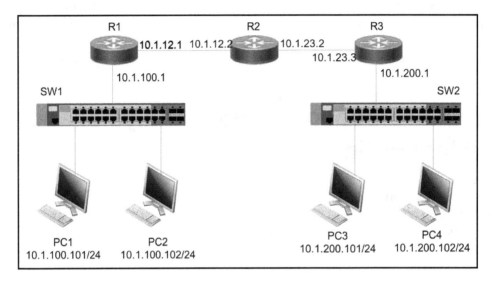

IPv4 topology

In the preceding diagram, when a Ping probe is triggered from **PC1** to **PC2**, there will not be any change in IP or Ethernet header from **PC1** to **PC2** as they both are in same LAN:

1. Trigger a Ping probe from **PC1** (`10.1.100.101`) to **PC2** (`10.1.100.102`). This will generate an ICMP echo request message from **PC1** to **PC2**.
2. If there is no echo reply from **PC2**, make sure that the MAC address for **PC2** is populated in the local ARP cache table.
3. Connect Wireshark to one of the free ports on **SW1** and capture the packets (port mirroring):

```
▽ Internet Protocol Version 4, Src: 10.1.100.101 (10.1.100.101), Dst: 10.1.100.102 (10.1.100.102)
    Version: 4
    Header Length: 20 bytes
  ▷ Differentiated Services Field: 0x00 (DSCP 0x00: Default; ECN: 0x00: Not-ECT (Not ECN-Capable Transport))
    Total Length: 100
    Identification: 0x001d (29)
  ▷ Flags: 0x00
    Fragment offset: 0
    Time to live: 255
    Protocol: ICMP (1) ───────────────────→ Protocol is ICMP
  ▷ Header checksum: 0xdeae [validation disabled]
    Source: 10.1.100.101 (10.1.100.101)
    Destination: 10.1.100.102 (10.1.100.102)
    [Source GeoIP: Unknown]
    [Destination GeoIP: Unknown]
▽ Internet Control Message Protocol
    Type: 8 (Echo (ping) request) ───────────→ ICMP Echo Message
    Code: 0
    Checksum: 0x6d4a [correct]
    Identifier (BE): 6 (0x0006)
    Identifier (LE): 1536 (0x0600)
    Sequence number (BE): 0 (0x0000)
    Sequence number (LE): 0 (0x0000)
    [Response frame: 14]
  ▷ Data (72 bytes)
```

ICMP packet

4. Check whether the ICMP echo request from **PC1** is seen in the capture. The preceding screenshot shows the ICMP Echo Message from **PC1** to **PC2**:
  - If the echo message is seen in port connecting **PC1** and **PC2**, but there is no response yet, check the Firewall and other settings on **PC2**.
  - If the echo message is seen in port connecting **PC1** but not in port connecting **PC2**, check whether the switch is dropping the packet.

- If the echo message is not seen in port connecting **PC1**, check the physical cable connecting **PC1** to **SW1**:

```
▽ Internet Protocol Version 4, Src: 10.1.100.102 (10.1.100.102), Dst: 10.1.100.101 (10.1.100.101)
    Version: 4
    Header Length: 20 bytes
  ▷ Differentiated Services Field: 0x00 (DSCP 0x00: Default; ECN: 0x00: Not-ECT (Not ECN-Capable Transport))
    Total Length: 100
    Identification: 0x001d (29)
  ▷ Flags: 0x00
    Fragment offset: 0
    Time to live: 255
    Protocol: ICMP (1)
  ▷ Header checksum: 0xdeae [validation disabled]
    Source: 10.1.100.102 (10.1.100.102)
    Destination: 10.1.100.101 (10.1.100.101)
    [Source GeoIP: Unknown]
    [Destination GeoIP: Unknown]
▽ Internet Control Message Protocol
    Type: 0 (Echo (ping) reply)  ─────────────▶ ICMP Echo Reply
    Code: 0
    Checksum: 0x754a [correct]
    Identifier (BE): 6 (0x0006)
    Identifier (LE): 1536 (0x0600)
    Sequence number (BE): 0 (0x0000)
    Sequence number (LE): 0 (0x0000)
    [Request frame: 13]
    [Response time: 1.158 ms]
  ▷ Data (72 bytes)
```

5. Check whether the ICMP reply from **PC2** is seen in the capture. The preceding figure shows the ICMP reply from **PC2** to **PC1**:
   - If the echo reply is seen in port connecting **PC1** and **PC2**, then everything is working fine.
   - If the echo reply is seen in port connecting **PC2** but not in port connecting **PC1**, check whether the switch is dropping the packet.
   - If the echo reply is not seen in port connecting **PC2**, check the physical cable connecting **PC2** to **SW1**.

The following are few useful display filters for ICMP:

Filter	Description	Example
icmp	Filters all ICMP packets	icmp
icmp.type == <type>	ICMP type based filter. Type 8will filter all ICMP Echo messages and Type 0 will filter all ICMP Echo replies	icmp.type == 0 icmp.type == 8
icmp.code == <code>	ICMP Code based filter.	icmp.code == 0

ICMP attacks and mitigations

While ICMP is a wonderful error-reporting and diagnostic utility tool, it has also been used as a source for DoS attacks in many networks.

ICMP flood attack

ICMP flood attack is one of the common DoS attacks, where a malicious user within the network will trigger a swarm of ICMP packets to a target host (such as a server):

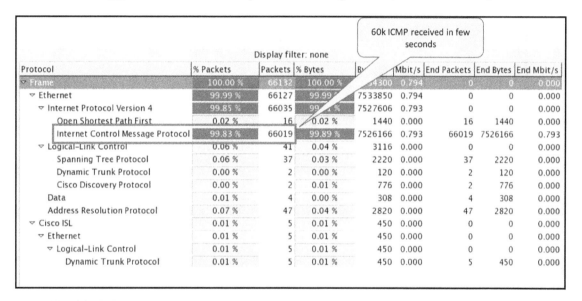

Wireshark statistics can be used to identify whether there is any ICMP attack. The statistics can be viewed through **Statistics | Protocol Hierarchy** in the Wireshark header field. As shown in the preceding screenshot, there are 60,000 ICMP packets in a few seconds.

ICMP smurf attack

ICMP smurf attack is another distributed DoS attack where a malicious attacker will trigger a large number of ICMP echo messages to one or more destinations with the target (victim) host's spoofed address as the source IP address of the ICMP echo messages. This will result in the victim host receiving a large volume of echo reply messages, causing its buffer to overrun and deplete:

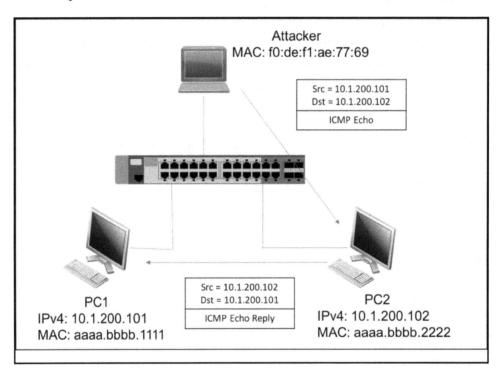

Single network topology

In the preceding diagram, the attacker generates an ICMP echo message with the spoofed address of **PC1**. This attack results in **PC1** receiving an ICMP echo reply from unintended responders, causing buffer depletion issues.

When layer 2 security features are enabled, the source MAC address cannot be spoofed. So, capturing the packet and using the source MAC address may help identify the attacker to shut down the attack.

How it works...

In order to validate the reachability between **PC1** and **PC3**, the Ping utility tool will be used to trigger ICMP messages from **PC1** to **PC3** as shown in the following diagram:

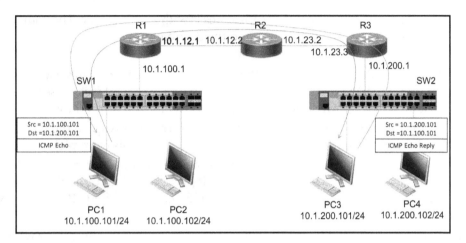

An ICMP echo request (type 8) will be generated with the source address as `10.1.100.101` destined to `10.1.200.101` and forwarded to the default gateway. Each router along the path will forward it based on the forwarding table. **PC3**, upon receiving the ICMP echo request message, will reply with an ICMP echo reply (type 0) to figure. Ping failure will indicate a connectivity issue between **PC1** and **PC3**.

Analyzing IPv4 unicast routing operations

IPv4 unicast routing is the process of forwarding unicast data packets from a host in one network to a receiver in the same or another network. The data packet may traverse one or more routers along the path that will perform a lookup in the IP header to take a forwarding decision.

Getting ready

Just open Wireshark, connect it to the network, configure port mirroring to the device that you want to test, and start it. Fragmentation will mostly influence interactive applications such as databases, and these are the places where we should look for problems.

How it works...

If **PC1** in the 10.1.100.0/24 network wants to communicate to **PC4** in 10.1.200.0/24, it performs the following:

1. **PC1** generates the data and encapsulates it with an IP header. The source IP address is set to 10.1.100.101 and the destination IP address is set to 10.1.200.102.

2. **PC1** encapsulates the packet with an Ethernet header. The source MAC address is set to the **PC1** MAC address and the destination MAC address is set to the R1 (default gateway) MAC address. The frame will be forwarded towards SW1.

3. SW1 is a simple Layer 2 switch and so it performs a lookup on the Ethernet header and forwards to the destination MAC (R1 in this example).

4. R1 receives the packet and decapsulates the Ethernet header, as the destination MAC address matches its own address. It performs a lookup in the local routing table for the destination IP address in the IP header and finds R2 as the next hop to reach 10.1.200.0/24.

5. R1 decrements the TTL in the IP header and encapsulates the packet with the Ethernet header. The source MAC address is set to R1 and the destination MAC address is set to R2. The frame will be forwarded to R2.

6. R2 performs the same forwarding behavior. It decapsulates the Ethernet header, decrements the TTL of the IP header, and forwards it to R3 with the new Ethernet header encapsulated.

7. R3, upon receiving the frame, will decapsulate the Ethernet header, decrement the TTL of the IP header, and encapsulate it with the Ethernet header. The source MAC is set to R3 and the destination MAC address will be set to the MAC address of **PC4**.

8. **PC4** will receive the frame, decapsulate the Ethernet and IP headers, and consume it to the appropriate application.

As can be seen, routers along the path modify some fields in the IP header (TTL for example) and the Ethernet encapsulation changes along the path. Any connectivity failure between **PC1** and **PC4** may be due to various reasons involving wrong Ethernet encapsulation, TTL handling, and packets being too big to handle. We will see how Wireshark can be used to analyze such packet routing issues.

IP TTL failures and attacks

As we saw in the previous sections, whenever a transit router is performing a lookup in the IP header, it will decrement the IP TTL by 1 before forwarding the packet out to the next hop router. If a router receives a packet with a TTL of 1 and if the destination IP address is not its own address, the default behavior is to drop the packet and generate an ICMP error message of type 11 (time to live exceeded). This behavior ensures that a packet in a routing loop does not bounce between nodes forever, but will be dropped after 255 iterations (the maximum value of TTL that can be set is 255):

1145 Warn	Sequence	ICMP	No response seen to ICMP request in frame 1145
1146 Note	Sequence	IPv4	"Time To Live" only 4
1146 Warn	Sequence	ICMP	No response seen to ICMP request in frame 1146
1147 Note	Sequence	IPv4	"Time To Live" only 3
1147 Warn	Sequence	ICMP	No response seen to ICMP request in frame 1147
1148 Note	Sequence	IPv4	"Time To Live" only 2
1148 Warn	Sequence	ICMP	No response seen to ICMP request in frame 1148
1149 Note	Sequence	IPv4	"Time To Live" only 1
1149 Warn	Sequence	ICMP	No response seen to ICMP request in frame 1149
1150 Warn	Sequence	ICMP	No response seen to ICMP request in frame 1150
1151 Warn	Sequence	ICMP	No response seen to ICMP request in frame 1151

The **Expert Info** option of Wireshark provides a warning that there are packets received with a TTL less than 5 and highlights those packets, as shown the preceding screenshot. This can be viewed by doing the following:

1. Go to **Analyze** and click the **Expert Info** option
2. Click the **Warning or Notes** section to see more details

IP TTL can be used by malicious attackers to trigger a DoS attack by sending a large volume of packets with a low TTL value (less than 5). Transit nodes will keep punting the packet to the CPU to generate ICMP error messages, which may result in hogging the CPU. There are various options available, such as a CPU protection mechanism or limiting the traffic rate for the CPU, that can help mitigate such attacks.

Duplicate IP addresses

We'll start with the phenomena, such as slow access to a server or to another device, slow access to the internet, and all the pings that you don't get replies to.

- When you have slow access to a network device, one of the problems may be that the IP address of your device collides with another address. To verify this, ping the IP address.

> In some devices, when their address collides with an identical address, the driver will simply be turned off (the little symbol at the bottom-left corner of the screen in the Windows operating system). In other devices, you will not get any notification of a conflict, and this is the place where problems will arise.

- Type arp -a in the **command-line interface** (**CLI**). Use the command cmd in Windows (or any shell in Linux). If you get two lines for the IP address you've pinged with different MAC addresses, there is a duplicate.
- Google the MAC addresses of the two devices, and the first part of the address will tell you who the vendor is. This will lead you to the troublemaker.
- If you need the location of the device, log in to your LAN switch (when you have a managed switch, of course), and from the switch MAC address table, you will see the switch port that you are connected to. There is a software that shows you the list of devices that are connected to every switch along with their MAC address, IP address, DNS names, and more. Google for switch port mapper or switch port mapping tools and you will find lots of them.
- If you don't get anything with Ping and ARP, simply start Wireshark and port mirror the network VLANs. Wireshark will show you a duplicate address error with the relevant details.
- The error message that you will get will be as shown in the following screenshot:

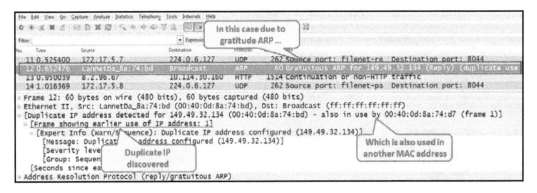

When you ping an IP address that appears twice on your local network, the two devices (or more) that have the same IP address will answer to the ARP request that you sent, and your ARP cache will have two entries for the same IP address.

In many cases, your device will indicate it by closing its IP driver and notify you by a pop-up window or any other type of notification that you will be aware of.

In other cases, the colliding devices will not notify you of the conflict, and then you will find a problem only with Ping and ARP, as described before.

In any case, when you connect Wireshark to the network and see duplicate IP messages, don't ignore them.

Analyzing IP fragmentation failures

Fragmentation is a common mechanism in IP that takes a large IP packet and divides it into smaller packets that will fit in the Layer-2 Ethernet frames. When any router receives a packet that is larger than the **Maximum Transmission Unit** (**MTU**) of the outgoing interface, the packet will be fragmented. In most cases, there shouldn't be any problems with the mechanism, but there might be performance issues due to this mechanism. IP fragmentation may also be used as a source for a DoS attack.

TCP path MTU discovery

While the forwarding semantic associated with the IP header allows any transit node to fragment the packet, it may create performance issues (as mentioned in the previous section) as the receiver is required to re-assemble the packets before processing. We could force the transit node to not fragment the packet but instead signal the presence of a lower MTU in the path and let the originator adjust the MSS. This process is known as **Path MTU Discovery (PMTUD)** and is an efficient way of detecting the lowest MTU along the path and using the value to adjust the MSS for efficient data transmission.

How to do it...

When fragmentation takes place, you will see UDP or TCP packets along with fragmented IP protocol packets, as shown in the following screenshot:

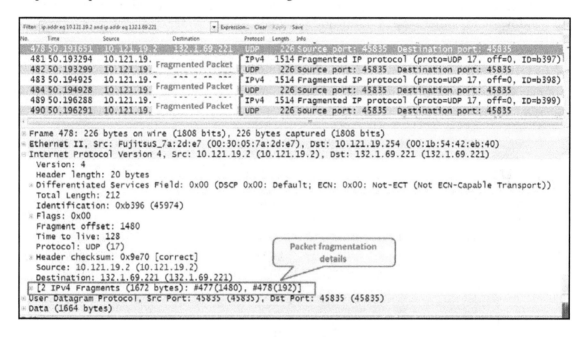

Packet fragmentation details

If suspecting performance problems, for example, a database client that experiences slow connectivity with the server, follow these steps to see whether the problem is due to fragmentation:

1. Test the connectivity between clients and the server to verify that there are no other problems.

2. Look for fragmentation between the client and the server. Fragments will be shown as in the previous screenshot (IPv4 fragments).

3. In the case that you suspect fragmentation to be the reason for the problem, it can be rectified either by fixing the MTU of the transit path or by tweaking the application to send smaller packets that do not cause fragmentation to the network.

4. The recommended packet size in Ethernet is not greater than 1460 bytes minus the TCP header size. Thus, the segments coming out of the interface should have a size of 1420-1440 bytes.

In cases where we need more bytes for the header, for example, when we use tunneling mechanisms and TCP options, the DBA will have to reduce this size even more. The best way will be simply to reduce it to such a size that you will not see any fragments.

Fragmentation-based attack

While it is normal to see IP fragments in the network, a malicious attacker can also use the fragmentation for DoS attacks. This attack is known as a Tiny Fragment Attack, where the attacker will send a large volume of tiny fragmented packets to the target host. Such tiny fragments need to be re-assembled by the target host, causing it to hit performance issues or other buffer overrun issues:

			Packet fragments of size 100 bytes		
100 3.410610	10.1.234.2	10.1.200.102	IPv4	118 Fragmented IP protocol (proto=ICMP 1, off=80, ID=002a)
101 3.410622	10.1.234.2	10.1.200.102	IPv4	118 Fragmented IP protocol (proto=ICMP 1, off=160, ID=002a)
102 3.410634	10.1.234.2	10.1.200.102	IPv4	118 Fragmented IP protocol (proto=ICMP 1, off=240, ID=002a)
103 3.410638	10.1.234.2	10.1.200.102	IPv4	118 Fragmented IP protocol (proto=ICMP 1, off=320, ID=002a)
108 3.412428	10.1.234.2	10.1.200.102	ICMP	116 Echo (ping) request id=0x0008, seq=3/768, ttl=254 (no response f
109 3.412435	10.1.234.2	10.1.200.102	IPv4	118 Fragmented IP protocol (proto=ICMP 1, off=80, ID=002b)
110 3.412439	10.1.234.2	10.1.200.102	IPv4	118 Fragmented IP protocol (proto=ICMP 1, off=160, ID=002b)

In the preceding screenshot, it can be seen that the capture fragments are of size 100 bytes; the attacker could use an even smaller size to trigger a DoS attack on the target host.

By default, Wireshark will reassemble any fragmented packets in the capture and display them as one reassembled packet. This may give an impression that there is no fragmentation in the network. By changing the preference settings, we will be able to display the real fragmented packet in Wireshark.

This can be done by the following steps:

1. Go to **Edit** and click **Preference**
2. Click **Protocols** and then select **IPv4**
3. Unset the **Reassemble fragmented IPv4 datagrams** field

How it works...

It is important to understand the two terms that define the size of the data units that are sent over the network, as you see in the following diagram:

- **Maximum Transfer (or Transmission) Unit (MTU):** This is the size of the IP packet, including the header and the data
- **Maximum Segment Size (MSS):** This is the maximum size of the TCP segments:

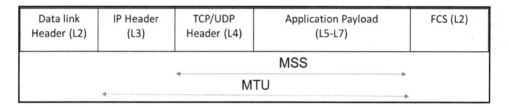

The fragmentation mechanism that is used in IPv4 works as shown in the following diagram:

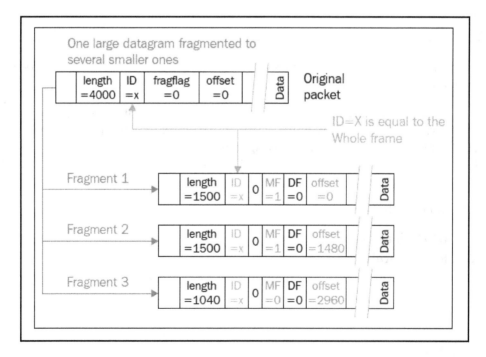

An original large packet enters the NIC or the router with a packet size that needs to be fragmented. The packet is fragmented into several parts depending on the original size.

For the fragmentation, we have these fields:

- `ID`: This is identical to the ID of the original IP Packet
- `Bit 0`: Always 0
- `Bit 1 (DF bit)`: 0 = may fragment, 1 = don't fragment
- `Bit 2 (MF bit)`: 0 = last fragment, 1 = more fragments
- `Fragment Offset`: This indicates the number of bytes from the beginning of the original packet

In IPv4, the NIC itself can fragment the packet along with every router on the way to the destination.

PMTUD leverages the **Don't Fragment** (`DF`) flag in IP header. When any transit router receives an IP packet of a size bigger than the outgoing interface's IP MTU, and if the `DF` flag in the packet header is set to 1, the router will drop the packet and generate an ICMP error message of type 3 (`Destination unreachable`) with code 4 (fragmentation needed and DF was set). This message will be sent to the originator of the packet and will carry the MTU size of the outgoing interface:

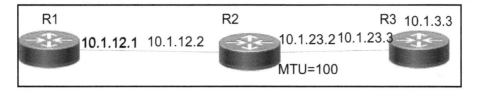

Path MTU discovery topology

In the preceding diagram, the **MTU** value of the outgoing interface on **R2** to reach **R3** is **100**. When **R2** receives any IP packet of a size more than 100, it drops the packet and generates the ICMP error message:

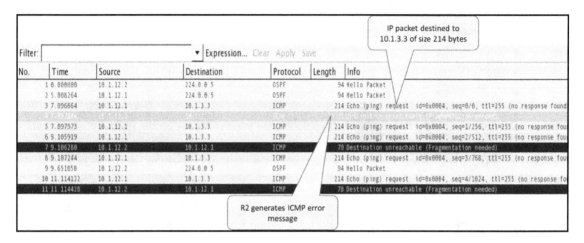

R2 drops the packet and generates the ICMP error message, as shown in the preceding screenshot. The originating host will use the MTU value in the received message to tweak the MSS of the session for efficient data transmission.

```
▽ Internet Protocol Version 4, Src: 10.1.12.2 (10.1.12.2), Dst: 10.1.12.1 (10.1.12.1)
    Version: 4
    Header Length: 20 bytes
  ▷ Differentiated Services Field: 0x00 (DSCP 0x00: Default; ECN: 0x00: Not-ECT (Not ECN-Capable Transport))
    Total Length: 56
    Identification: 0x0000 (0)
  ▷ Flags: 0x00
    Fragment offset: 0
    Time to live: 255
    Protocol: ICMP (1)
  ▷ Header checksum: 0x8fc0 [validation disabled]
    Source: 10.1.12.2 (10.1.12.2)
    Destination: 10.1.12.1 (10.1.12.1)
    [Source GeoIP: Unknown]
    [Destination GeoIP: Unknown]
▽ Internet Control Message Protocol
    Type: 3 (Destination unreachable)              Destination unreachable
    Code: 4 (Fragmentation needed)                 error message generated
    Checksum: 0x63b4 [correct]                      with outgoing interface
    MTU of next hop: 100                            MTU as 100
  ▷ Internet Protocol Version 4, Src: 10.1.12.1 (10.1.12.1), Dst: 10.1.3.3 (10.1.3.3)
  ▷ Internet Control Message Protocol
```

The following are a few useful filters for IP fragments:

Filter	Description	Example
ip.flags.mf == <flag>	Filters all fragmented packets with MF flag set to 1	ip.flags.mf == 1
ip.fragment	Filter all fragmented packets	ip.fragment
ip.flags.df == <flag>	Filters all packets with DF flag set	ip.flags.df == 1

IPv4 multicast routing operations

IPv4 multicast routing is the process of forwarding data packets from the source to one or more receivers residing in same or different networks. The source address of the multicast packet will be a unicast address, while the destination address will be a multicast address (224.0.0.0 to 239.255.255.255). The end applications that are using multicast to receive the traffic will resolve the multicast address using an out-of-band mechanism and will use a multicast group membership protocol like IGMP to join the respective multicast group. The host will send IGMP join towards the connected router.

The multicast-enabled router connecting the receivers is known as the **Last Hop Router (LHR)**, and the multicast-enabled router connecting the source is known as the **First Hop Router (FHR)**. The LHR will use a multicast routing protocol such as PIM to build a multicast tree toward the FHR using the shortest path. The FHR will forward multicast data traffic over the multicast tree. Multicast can be deployed in different modes. Below are the two most commonly deployed multicast modes:

- **Sparse mode**: In this mode, a common node will be positioned as a **Rendezvous Point (RP)** and each LHR will build the multicast tree towards the RP. This tree is known as a shared tree. The FHR, on receiving multicast traffic from a connected source, will unicast the packet to the RP, which in turn will forward it to the receivers over at the shared tree.
- **Source-specific multicast**: In this mode, each LHR will build the multicast tree towards the FHR connected to the source itself. There is no need for an RP in this mode.

How it works...

In the following diagram, assume that the receivers are joining a stream using `239.1.1.1` as multicast address from the source connected to **R1**:

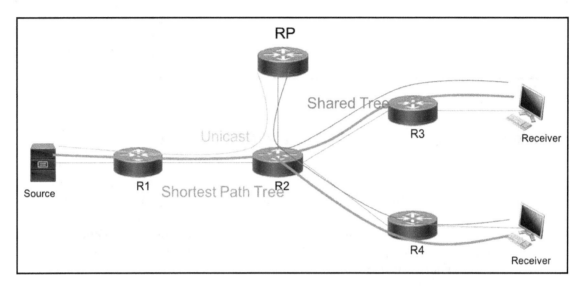

In our example, `10.1.8.8` is acting as the **RP**, and this **RP** is connected to **R2**:

- Receivers will send an IGMP join request for `239.1.1.1` to the connected multicast routers. The LHR routers (**R3** and **R4**), upon receiving the IGMP joins from the receivers, will build a shared tree towards the RP. In our example, **R3** and **R4** will use **R2** as an upstream router to build the tree towards RP.
- The FHR connected to source, upon receiving the first multicast traffic, will encapsulate it with a PIM register message and unicast the packet towards the **RP**:

```
▽ Internet Protocol Version 4, Src: 10.1.12.1 (10.1.12.1), Dst: 10.1.8.8 (10.1.8.8)
    Version: 4
    Header Length: 20 bytes
  ▷ Differentiated Services Field: 0x00 (DSCP 0x00: Default; ECN: 0x00: Not-ECT (Not ECN-Capable Transport))
    Total Length: 108
    Identification: 0x0000 (0)
  ▷ Flags: 0x00
    Fragment offset: 0
    Time to live: 253
    Protocol: PIM (103)
  ▷ Header checksum: 0x9520 [validation disabled]
    Source: 10.1.12.1 (10.1.12.1)
    Destination: 10.1.8.8 (10.1.8.8)
    [Source GeoIP: Unknown]
    [Destination GeoIP: Unknown]
▽ Protocol Independent Multicast
    0010 .... = Version: 2
    .... 0001 = Type: Register (1)
    Reserved byte(s): 00
    Checksum: 0xdeff [correct]
  ▷ PIM options
▽ Internet Protocol Version 4, Src: 10.1.17.7 (10.1.17.7), Dst: 239.1.1.1 (239.1.1.1)
    Version: 4
    Header Length: 20 bytes
  ▷ Differentiated Services Field: 0x00 (DSCP 0x00: Default; ECN: 0x00: Not-ECT (Not ECN-Capable Transport))
    Total Length: 80
    Identification: 0x0001 (1)
  ▷ Flags: 0x00
    Fragment offset: 0
    Time to live: 254
    Protocol: UDP (17)
  ▷ Header checksum: 0xb191 [validation disabled]
    Source: 10.1.17.7 (10.1.17.7)
    Destination: 239.1.1.1 (239.1.1.1)
    [Source GeoIP: Unknown]
    [Destination GeoIP: Unknown]
▷ User Datagram Protocol, Src Port: 51468 (51468), Dst Port: 1967 (1967)
▷ Data (52 bytes)
```

IP Unicast Header

Multicast Data

- As shown in the preceding screenshot, **R1** will encapsulate the multicast data packet (with the source as `10.1.17.7`, and the destination as `239.1.1.1`) with a PIM register encapsulation header. It further encapsulates it using an IP unicast header with the source as the FHR router (`10.1.12.1`) and destination as the **RP** (`10.1.8.8`).

- The **RP** will decapsulate the header and forward the multicast traffic over to the shared tree.

- By default, the LHR routers, upon receiving the multicast traffic, will build another tree toward the source. This tree is called the **Shortest Path Tree**.

While the forwarding behavior for multicast traffic is different from unicast traffic, there is not much difference in how the IP header is treated along the path. For example, any router will decrement the TTL for both unicast and multicast traffic. So, all the troubleshooting analysis procedure we defined for IPv4 unicast is applicable for IPv4 multicast capture as well.

There's more...

End applications using multicast traffic are mostly audio or video applications, and the traffic rate at which the multicast stream is received is one of the criteria to be considered for troubleshooting. Wireshark allows us to list all the UDP multicast streams with a simple analysis in terms of PPS, average BW used, and more. This statistic will be very useful while troubleshooting multicast traffic. The statistics can be viewed by following these steps:

1. Go to **Statistics** and click **UDP Multicast Streams**
2. Check the available fields for multicast information

IPv6 principle of operations

With the dawn of the dot-com bubble in early 1990s, more businesses started relying on IP networks, which meant a drastic depletion of IPv4 address space. Soon the industry realized that there was a need for a new network layer protocol that could accommodate and gratify the growing network requirements. This made the industry start working on next-gen IP (IPng).

While the initial efforts were performed to extend the Stream Protocol (ST2) as a quick fix for the network address depletion, features such as **Network Address Translation** (**NAT**) and Dynamic Address Allocation (such as DHCP) addressed the exhaustion to a certain extent, allowing the industry enough time to work on IPng. IPng was developed to not only tackle the address space challenge but also consider the other limitations and challenges that were facing IPv4. ST2 was officially designated as IPv5 and IPng was officially designated as IPv6.

IPv6 is of 128-bit size and therefore provides a very large address space. While the size of an IPv6 address is four times larger than IPv4, the header size is simplified for efficient packet processing. The format of an IPv6 header is as follows:

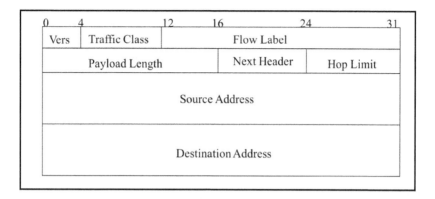

The following is a sample Wireshark capture of an IPv6 packet:

```
▽ Internet Protocol Version 6, Src: 2001:db8:12::1 (2001:db8:12::1), Dst: 2001:db8:12::2 (2001:db8:12::2)
  ▽ 0110 .... = Version: 6
    [0110 .... = This field makes the filter "ip.version == 6" possible: 6]
  ▽ .... 0000 0000 .... .... .... .... .... = Traffic class: 0x00000000
    .... 0000 00.. .... .... .... .... .... = Differentiated Services Field: Default (0x00000000)
    .... .... ..0. .... .... .... .... .... = ECN-Capable Transport (ECT): Not set
    .... .... ...0 .... .... .... .... .... = ECN-CE: Not set
    .... .... .... 0000 0000 0000 0000 0000 = Flowlabel: 0x00000000
    Payload length: 60
    Next header: ICMPv6 (58)
    Hop limit: 64
    Source: 2001:db8:12::1 (2001:db8:12::1)
    Destination: 2001:db8:12::2 (2001:db8:12::2)
    [Source GeoIP: Unknown]
    [Destination GeoIP: Unknown]
```

IPv6 addressing

As with IPv4, an IPv6 address is a unique and logical network layer identifier assigned to each device connected to the network. An IPv6 address is of 128-bit size and comprises a Network Prefix and Interface ID. While IPv4 is represented as four octets of decimals, an IPv6 address is represented as eight blocks of 16-bit hex values with colons as demarcation. The format of an IPv6 address is as follows:

Network Prefix				Interface ID			
←16→	←16→	←16→	←16→	←16→	←16→	←16→	←16→

The Network Prefix is used to identify the network in which the host resides, while the Interface ID is used to identify the host within the network. While the 128-bit representation is made efficient by referring the address in hex values, here are a few good practices to further simplify the representation:

- All leading zeros in an IPv6 address can be omitted
- Contiguous zeros can be represented as ::
- :: can occur only once within the address

There are a number of different types of IPv6 address; here are details of some of them:

- **Link-local address**: This is a non-routable unicast address with a link-specific scope and is used for link local communication where the packet will not be sent more than one hop. All control plane communications (such as OSPF hello messages) belong to this category. Any interface enabled with IPv6 will be assigned with a link-local address. The address range is fe80::/10.
- **Global unicast address**: This is the public routable unicast address with a global scope. Most internet devices will be assigned from this range. The address range is 2000::/3.
- **Unique local address**: This is a private range unicast address and is not routable in public internet. The address ranges are fc00::/8 and fd00::/8.
- **Multicast address**: Just like IPv4, this address is used for point-to-multipoint communication. The address range is ff00::/8.

There are also few other types of address, such as IPv4 embedded address and solicited node multicast address, which are not explained here for the sake of brevity.

It can be noted that IPv6 does not have any broadcast address, as all types of broadcast communication can be addressed by the IPv6 multicast address. As mentioned previously, the address range for multicast is ff00::/8 and the last 4 bits of the first block defines the scope of the multicast address. For example, 1 has a node-local scope, 2 has a link-local scope, 5 has a site-local scope, and E has a global scope. The following table gives clear information about different addresses and scopes:

Address	Scope	Meaning
FF01::1	Node-Local	All Nodes
FF01::2	Node-Local	All Routers
FF02::1	Link-Local	All Nodes
FF02::2	Link-Local	All Routers
FF02::5	Link-Local	OSPFv3 Routers
FF02::6	Link-Local	OSPFv3 DR Routers
FF02::1:FFXX:XXXX	Link-Local	Solicited-Node

IPv6 extension headers

The IP options defined for IPv4 headers are primarily intended to carry additional network layer information. But the presence of IP options in IPv4 will end up punting the packet to CPU and thereby introducing performance issues due to the slow path packet forwarding. In IPv6, extension headers are proposed to encode such control plane information as a separate flexible header without increasing the sizing of the IPv6 header. The IPv6 extension header is positioned between the IPv6 header and the transport layer header in a packet, and the presence of an IPv6 extension header is identified by setting the next header to the relevant value.

Here are a few commonly used IPv6 extension headers:

Protocol number (IPv6 NH Value)	Extension header name	Description	Reference
0	IPv6 hop-by-hop option	Optional extension header used to carry additional information that may be processed by every node along the path. This may require the packet to be punted to CPU on all nodes.	RFC 8200
44	Fragment header for IPv6	Used by source to send packet larger than Path MTU.	RFC 8200

| 50 | Encapsulation security payload | Used to carry security information to provide confidentiality, authentication, integrity, and more. | RFC 4303 |
| 60 | Destination header | Used by source to carry information intended only for the ultimate destination. | RFC 8200 |

Here is the IPv6 packet format with extension headers:

IPv6 Header Next Header = TCP	TCP Header + Data	

IPv6 Header Next Header = Fragment	Fragment Header Next Header = TCP	TCP Header + Data

IPv6 Header Next Header = Hop-by-Hop	HbH Header Next Header = Fragment	Fragment Header Next Header = TCP	TCP Header + Data

The following is a sample capture:

```
▽ Internet Protocol Version 6, Src: 2001:db8:12::1 (2001:db8:12::1), Dst: 2001::2 (2001::2)
   ▷ 0110 .... = Version: 6
   ▷ .... 0000 0000 .... .... .... .... .... = Traffic class: 0x00000000
     .... .... .... 0000 0000 0000 0000 0000 = Flowlabel: 0x00000000
     Payload length: 60
     Next header: IPv6 hop-by-hop option (0)
     Hop limit: 64
     Source: 2001:db8:12::1 (2001:db8:12::1)
     Destination: 2001::2 (2001::2)
     [Destination Teredo Server IPv4: 0.0.0.0 (0.0.0.0)]
     [Destination Teredo Port: 65535]
     [Destination Teredo Client IPv4: 255.255.255.253 (255.255.255.253)]
     [Source GeoIP: Unknown]
     [Destination GeoIP: Unknown]
   ▽ Hop-by-Hop Option
        Next header: IPv6 destination option (60)          ──────► Hop-by-Hop
        Length: 0 (8 bytes)                                         Extension Header
      ▷ IPv6 Option (PadN)
   ▽ Destination Option
        Next header: ICMPv6 (58)                            ──────► Destination
        Length: 0 (8 bytes)                                         Extension Header
      ▷ IPv6 Option (PadN)
   ▷ Internet Control Message Protocol v6
```

IPv6 extension headers and attacks

While IPv6 is designed with security in mind, the extension header may still be used as a source for DoS attacks. As mentioned previously, the presence of a Hop-by-Hop extension header will require all transit nodes along the path to process the header, consuming a lot of CPU. Similarly, when a large volume of packets with IPv6 destination extension header is forwarded to a specific host or server, it may consume a lot of resources on the server.

Getting ready

Just open Wireshark, connect it to the network, configure port mirroring to the device, and start the capture. The presence of an IPv6 extension header can be verified through the Wireshark capture.

How to do it...

The IPv6 packets carrying the IPv6 extension header is shown in the following screenshot:

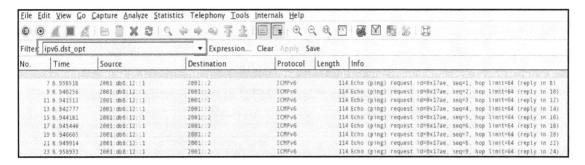

In the preceding screenshot, filtering the packets using `ipv6.dst_opt` will list all the IPv6 packets carrying an IPv6 destination option extension header. Alternately, we could use an `ipv6.hop_opt` filter to list all the IPv6 packets with IPv6 Hop-by-Hop options.

While the preceding task will help to narrow down the packets or the count of packets received with the extension header, it may require additional manual analysis to understand whether it is an expected behavior or an attack.

IPv6 fragmentation

As mentioned in an earlier section, fragmentation is the process of dividing the packet into smaller fragments to fit the lowest MTU along the path. The way packet fragmentation is handled by IPv6 is completely different from IPv4. The following are a couple of the primary differences in how IPv6 handles the fragmentation:

- While in IPv4 any router is allowed to fragment the packet (assuming DF bit is not set), IPv6 only allows the source of the IPv6 packet to fragment and none of the transit nodes can fragment an IPv6 packet.
- In IPv4, the fragment details are carried as part of IPv4 header, but in IPv6 a new extension header is defined and this header will be included only in fragmented packets.

How it works...

In the following diagram, the **MTU** value of the outgoing interface on **R2** is set to **1280**, which is the minimum **MTU** required for IPv6 packet forwarding:

If a router receives an IPv6 packet larger than the **MTU** of the outgoing interface, the default behavior is to drop the packet and generate an ICMPv6 error message:

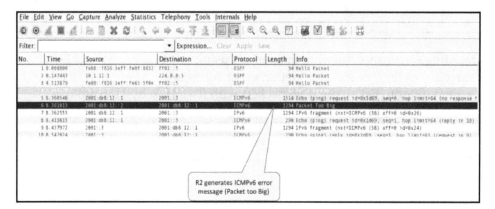

In the preceding screenshot, **R2** drops the packet and generates an ICMPv6 error message with the outgoing **MTU** interface to the actual source of the packet (**R1** in our example).

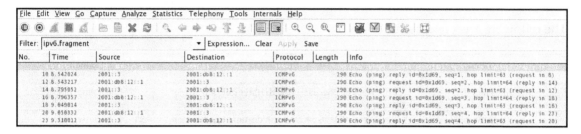

R1 will cache this information and fragment the packet based on the received **MTU** size, as shown in the preceding screenshot.

```
▽ Internet Protocol Version 6, Src: 2001:db8:12::1 (2001:db8:12::1), Dst: 2001::3 (2001::3)
    ▷ 0110 .... = Version: 6
    ▷ .... 0000 0000 .... .... .... .... = Traffic class: 0x00000000
      .... .... .... 0000 0000 0000 0000 0000 = Flowlabel: 0x00000000
      Payload length: 1240
      Next header: IPv6 fragment (44)                  ──────▶  Next Header is set
      Hop limit: 64                                              to Fragment
      Source: 2001:db8:12::1 (2001:db8:12::1)                    Extension Header
      Destination: 2001::3 (2001::3)
      [Destination Teredo Server IPv4: 0.0.0.0 (0.0.0.0)]
      [Destination Teredo Port: 65535]
      [Destination Teredo Client IPv4: 255.255.255.252 (255.255.255.252)]
      [Source GeoIP: Unknown]
      [Destination GeoIP: Unknown]
    ▽ Fragmentation Header
         Next header: ICMPv6 (58)
         Reserved octet: 0x0000                          ──────▶  Fragment EH carries
         0000 0000 0000 0... = Offset: 0 (0x0000)                  all fragmentation
         .... .... .... .00. = Reserved bits: 0 (0x0000)          related details
         .... .... .... ...1 = More Fragment: Yes
         Identification: 0x00000026                      Wireshark also point the frame
      Reassembled IPv6 in frame: 8 ───────────────────   number of the fragmented
                                                          packet in the capture for ease of
                                                          analysis
```

As shown in the preceding screenshot, the IPv6 fragment extension header will carry all the fragmentation-related details. In IPv4, all this information is carried as part of the IPv4 header itself. But with IPv6, it is included as part of the extension header.

IPv6 fragmentation can also be used by a malicious attacker for DoS attacks. An attacker may send a large volume of packets with an IPv6 fragment extension header, causing the target host to consume resources in reassembling the fragmented packets.

The following are a few useful filters:

Filter	Description	Example
ipv6.hop_opt	Filters all IPv6 packets with HbH extension header	ipv6.hop_opt
ipv6.dst_opt	Filters all IPv6 packets with destination extension header	ipv6.dst_opt
ipv6.fragment	Filters all IPv6 packets with fragment extension header	ipv6.fragment

ICMPv6 – protocol operations, analysis, and troubleshooting

ICMPv6 is an enhanced version of ICMP for IPv6 that not only performs error reporting and path diagnostics functionalities, but is extended further for other network layer functions. ICMPv6 plays a key role in:

- IPv6 router and neighbor discovery
- IPv6 stateless auto configuration
- Path MTU discovery
- Fault detection and isolation

ICMPv6 is an integral part of IPv6, and the next header field of IPv6 will be set to 58. The ICMPv6 packet has the following format:

Type	Code	Checksum
Message Body		

There are different types of ICMPv6 message available for error reporting, informational, or discovery purposes. In this section, we will see how ICMPv6 can be used for fault detection and isolation, and in the forthcoming sections, we will see more applications of ICMPv6.

Getting ready

When the end application using IPv6 faces connectivity issues, fault detection and isolation utility tools such as Ping and Traceroute can be used to detect or isolate the failure. When the Ping tool is used for an IPv6 address, it uses ICMPv6 messages for path diagnostics. Wireshark on one or more devices along the path can be used to capture the packets at different points for analysis.

How to do it...

1. In the following diagram, **R1** is performing path diagnostics towards **R3**'s address, 2001::3. When a ping is triggered on **R1**, it generates an ICMPv6 echo message and forwards it to **R2**:

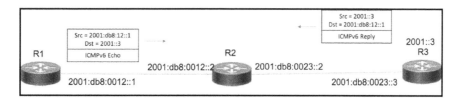

2. As shown in the following screenshot, **R1** sends an ICMPv6 echo request message (ICMPv6 type = 128) towards **R3**.

```
▽ Internet Protocol Version 6, Src: 2001:db8:12::1 (2001:db8:12::1), Dst: 2001::3 (2001::3)
  ▷ 0110 .... = Version: 6
  ▷ .... 0000 0000 .... .... .... .... .... = Traffic class: 0x00000000
    .... .... .... 0000 0000 0000 0000 0000 = Flowlabel: 0x00000000
    Payload length: 1240
    Next header: IPv6 fragment (44)
    Hop limit: 63
    Source: 2001:db8:12::1 (2001:db8:12::1)
    Destination: 2001::3 (2001::3)
    [Destination Teredo Server IPv4: 0.0.0.0 (0.0.0.0)]
    [Destination Teredo Port: 65535]
    [Destination Teredo Client IPv4: 255.255.255.252 (255.255.255.252)]
    [Source GeoIP: Unknown]
    [Destination GeoIP: Unknown]
  ▷ Fragmentation Header
▽ Internet Control Message Protocol v6
    Type: Echo (ping) request (128)
    Code: 0
    Checksum: 0xcf47
    Identifier: 0x1ce0
    Sequence: 1
    [Response In: 12]
  ▷ Data (1224 bytes)
```

ICMPv6 Echo
Request message

3. **R3**, upon receiving the ICMPv6 echo request, will reply with an ICMPv6 echo reply.

```
▽ Internet Protocol Version 6, Src: 2001::3 (2001::3), Dst: 2001:db8:12::1 (2001:db8:12::1)
  ▷ 0110 .... = Version: 6
  ▷ .... 0000 0000 .... .... .... .... .... = Traffic class: 0x00000000
    .... .... .... 0000 0000 0000 0000 0000 = Flowlabel: 0x00000000
    Payload length: 1240
    Next header: IPv6 fragment (44)
    Hop limit: 64
    Source: 2001::3 (2001::3)
    [Source Teredo Server IPv4: 0.0.0.0 (0.0.0.0)]
    [Source Teredo Port: 65535]
    [Source Teredo Client IPv4: 255.255.255.252 (255.255.255.252)]
    Destination: 2001:db8:12::1 (2001:db8:12::1)
    [Source GeoIP: Unknown]
    [Destination GeoIP: Unknown]
  ▷ Fragmentation Header
▽ Internet Control Message Protocol v6
    Type: Echo (ping) reply (129)
    Code: 0
    Checksum: 0xce47
    Identifier: 0x1ce0
    Sequence: 1
    [Response To: 10]                      ──────────→  ICMPv6 Echo Reply
    [Response Time: 103.977 ms]                         message
```

As shown in the preceding screenshot, **R3** replies with an ICMPv6 echo reply to **R1**.

During some failure scenarios, we might notice some intermittent packet drops. In a large `pcap` file, it might be hard to narrow down the list of ICMPv6 messages for which we didn't get response. The **Expert Info** option will be helpful here:

1. Go to **Analyze** and click on **Expert Info**
2. Check **Warnings:**

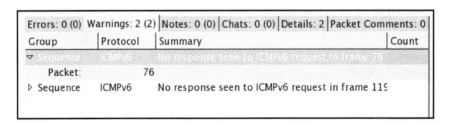

This lists all the ICMPv6 echo messages for which there is no ICMPv6 response in the capture.

IPv6 auto configuration

One of the primary benefits associated with IPv6 is its ability to autoconfigure the interface address. This ability allows IPv6 enabled devices to act in plug-and-play mode.

Getting ready

When the end host using IPv6 auto configuration is not working properly, the first thing to do is to ensure that the link-local address is auto configured properly. This can be verified by checking the interface address configuration. In Unix/Linux devices, `ifconfig -a` will list the IPv6 addresses configured on the interface. If you don't see anything, the IPv6 stack on the host might have some issues. If you see an IPv6 link-local address, the next step is to capture the packet using Wireshark and see whether the router solicitation and advertisement messages are exchanged.

How to do it...

1. When IPv6 auto configuration is enabled on the end host, it is expected to send a router solicitation message to all router multicast addresses.

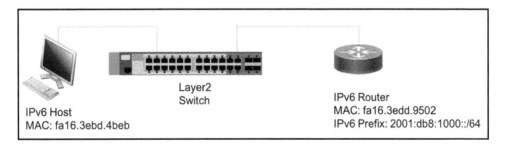

2. Check whether the message is sent by the host in the Wireshark capture:

```
▷ Ethernet II, Src: fa:16:3e:bd:4b:eb (fa:16:3e:bd:4b:eb), Dst: IPv6mcast_02 (33:33:00:00:00:02)
▽ Internet Protocol Version 6, Src: fe80::f816:3eff:febd:4beb (fe80::f816:3eff:febd:4beb), Dst: ff02::2 (ff02::2)
   ▷ 0110 .... = Version: 6
   ▷ .... 1110 0000 .... .... .... .... .... = Traffic class: 0x000000e0
     .... .... .... 0000 0000 0000 0000 0000 = Flowlabel: 0x00000000
     Payload length: 16
     Next header: ICMPv6 (58)
     Hop limit: 255
     Source: fe80::f816:3eff:febd:4beb (fe80::f816:3eff:febd:4beb)
     Destination: ff02::2 (ff02::2)
     [Source GeoIP: Unknown]
     [Destination GeoIP: Unknown]
▽ Internet Control Message Protocol v6
     Type: Router Solicitation (133)
     Code: 0
     Checksum: 0x75af [correct]
     Reserved: 00000000
   ▽ ICMPv6 Option (Source link-layer address : fa:16:3e:bd:4b:eb)
        Type: Source link-layer address (1)
        Length: 1 (8 bytes)
        Link-layer address: fa:16:3e:bd:4b:eb (fa:16:3e:bd:4b:eb)
```

RS message is sent with link local source address and destinated to All-Router Multicast address

ICMPv6 message type

ICMPv6 Option proactively carries the local MAC address that can be used for address resolution

3. As shown in the preceding screenshot, the IPv6 host sends an ICMPv6 router solicitation message. It can be observed that the ICMPv6 options carry the MAC address of the end host in the router solicitation message. Any router that is receiving this message will cache the MAC address for the address resolution.

4. The next step is to check whether the router is sending a router advertisement message with the relevant details that can be used by the end host for auto configuration:

```
▽ Internet Protocol Version 6, Src: fe80::f816:3eff:fedd:9502 (fe80::f816:3eff:fedd:9502), Dst: ff02::1 (ff02::1)
  ▷ 0110 .... = Version: 6
  ▷ .... 1110 0000 .... .... .... .... = Traffic class: 0x000000e0
      .... .... .... 0000 0000 0000 0000 0000 = Flowlabel: 0x00000000
    Payload length: 64
    Next header: ICMPv6 (58)
    Hop limit: 255
    Source: fe80::f816:3eff:fedd:9502 (fe80::f816:3eff:fedd:9502)
    Destination: ff02::1 (ff02::1)
    [Source GeoIP: Unknown]
    [Destination GeoIP: Unknown]
▽ Internet Control Message Protocol v6
    Type: Router Advertisement (134)
    Code: 0
    Checksum: 0x0eaf [correct]
    Cur hop limit: 64
  ▽ Flags: 0x00
      0... .... = Managed address configuration: Not set
      .0.. .... = Other configuration: Not set
      ..0. .... = Home Agent: Not set
      ...0 0... = Prf (Default Router Preference): Medium (0)
      .... .0.. = Proxy: Not set
      .... ..0. = Reserved: 0
    Router lifetime (s): 1800
    Reachable time (ms): 0
    Retrans timer (ms): 0
  ▽ ICMPv6 Option (Source link-layer address : fa:16:3e:dd:95:02)
      Type: Source link-layer address (1)
      Length: 1 (8 bytes)
      Link-layer address: fa:16:3e:dd:95:02 (fa:16:3e:dd:95:02)
  ▷ ICMPv6 Option (MTU : 1500)
  ▽ ICMPv6 Option (Prefix information : 2001:db8:1000::/64)
      Type: Prefix information (3)
      Length: 4 (32 bytes)
      Prefix Length: 64
    ▷ Flag: 0xc0
      Valid Lifetime: 4294967295 (Infinity)
      Preferred Lifetime: 4294967295 (Infinity)
      Reserved
      Prefix: 2001:db8:1000:: (2001:db8:1000::)
```

RA message is sent with link local source address and destinated to All-Node Multicast address

ICMPv6 Option proactively carries the local MAC address that can be used for address resolution

Global Unique Prefix with validity and lifetime details.

5. As shown in the preceding screenshot, the router sends a router advertisement message to the all-node multicast address, `ff02::1`. All nodes in the LAN will be listening to this multicast, and so will process the information in the message.

6. The ICMPv6 router advertisement message carries the IPv6 prefix details with a minimum size of 64 bits. In the preceding screenshot, prefix `2001:db8:1000::/64` is advertised. This prefix will be advertised with a two-timer variable. The **Valid lifetime** is the length of the time this prefix can be used on the link as a valid address. The **Preferred lifetime** is the length of the time this address generated from the received prefix prefers.

If the preceding router advertisement is not seen in the capture, the router configuration needs to be verified to ensure that relevant IPv6 auto configuration is enabled to advertise the prefix.

How it works...

The process of auto configuring the IPv6 address is known as **Stateless Address Auto Configuration (SLAAC)**. As we saw earlier, when IPv6 is enabled on any device, a link-local address from the `fe80::/10` range is assigned by default. As mandated by the IPv6 address format, the interface ID (last 64 bits) of an IPv6 address *must* be unique for each host within the network. So how can we assure that the auto configured IPv6 address is unique for each host within the network? In an LAN, the MAC address is a data-link layer identifier assigned to each host and is expected to be unique within the network. This is to ensure that the frame is delivered to the right host. IPv6 auto configuration leverages the uniqueness of the MAC address for IPv6 auto configuration. But there is one challenge – the MAC address is of a 48-bit size while the interface ID is of a 64-bit size. The MAC address comprises a 24-bit Organizational Unique Identifier (OUI) followed by 24-bit Vendor-assigned Identifier. This MAC address is converted to a 64-bit EUI-64 addressing format using the following procedure:

- A 16-bit hex value `FFFE` is inserted between the OUI and Vendor-assigned identifier
- The U/L flag (bit 7) in the OUI is set to `1`

The following is an illustration of the preceding steps:

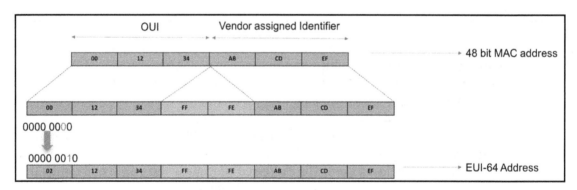

The resulting 64-bit value is concatenated to the 64-bit network prefix {`fe80::/10` + 54 `bits all-zero value`} to auto configure a 128-bit unique IPv6 link-local address. As the name suggests, this address is link-local scoped and so cannot be used for communicating with nodes outside the LAN network.

IPv6 SLAAC signals a global unique prefix from the router and leverages the end host capability of generating the EUI-64 address to auto configure a globally unique IPv6 address. ICMPv6 plays the role of signaling protocol for the router to advertise the global unique prefix to the end hosts within the LAN network. The following are the two ICMPv6 message types used for this purpose:

- Router solicitation message
- Router advertisement message

Any end host that is enabled with IPv6 auto configuration will send an ICMPv6 router solicitation message. The source address of this ICMPv6 message is normally set to the link-local address of the interface and the destination address is set to an all-router link-local multicast address (ff02::2). The message has the following format:

Type=133	Code=0	Checksum
Reserved		
Options		

The router connected to the LAN network will periodically send ICMPv6 router advertisement messages carrying the prefix and other related details that can be used by the end host for address autoconfiguration. The source address of this ICMPv6 message will be set to the link-local address of the router interface and the destination address will be set to all-node link-local multicast address (ff02::1). The message has the following format:

Type=133	Code=0			Checksum
Hop Limit	M	O	Rsvd	Router Lifetime
Reachable Time				
Retransmission Timer				
Options				

DHCPv6-based address assignment

While IPv6 SLAAC is simpler and easier as it works as plug-and-play, it is not the only option for autoconfiguring the IPv6 address. DHCPv6 is another centralized address assignment option that can be used for address assignment and management. In this recipe, we will see how to analyze some of the most common DHCPv6 issues.

Getting ready

Ensure that you have a DHCPv6 server configured to assign an IPv6 address for the requesting clients. In Unix/Linux devices, `ifconfig -a` will list the IPv6 address configured on the interfaces. If you don't see the DHCPv6 assigned address, capture the packets using Wireshark in the LAN.

How to do it...

1. Check whether the end host sends a DHCPv6 solicit message. This is the first message that will be sent by the client to identify the list of available DHCPv6 servers offering a IPv6 address. The message will be sent with the source address as link-local address and the destination address will be a link-local scoped multicast address known as an all-DHCP-relay address (`ff02::1:2`).

2. If you don't see a solicit message in the capture, it is possible that the end host is not properly configured or is not functioning properly:
   - Check whether the relevant interface is enabled with IPv6.
   - Check whether a link-local address is assigned for the interface.
   - Check whether the interface is enabled to receive an IPv6 address from DHCPv6:

```
▷ Ethernet II, Src: fa:16:3e:bd:4b:eb (fa:16:3e:bd:4b:eb), Dst: IPv6mcast_01:00:02 (33:33:00:01:00:02)
▽ Internet Protocol Version 6, Src: fe80::f816:3eff:febd:4beb (fe80::f816:3eff:febd:4beb), Dst: ff02::1:2 (ff02::1:2)
    ▷ 0110 .... = Version: 6
    ▷ .... 1110 0000 .... .... .... .... .... .... = Traffic class: 0x000000e0
      .... .... .... 0000 0000 0000 0000 0000 = Flowlabel: 0x00000000
      Payload length: 56
      Next header: UDP (17)
      Hop limit: 255
      Source: fe80::f816:3eff:febd:4beb (fe80::f816:3eff:febd:4beb)
      Destination: ff02::1:2 (ff02::1:2)
      [Source GeoIP: Unknown]
      [Destination GeoIP: Unknown]
▷ User Datagram Protocol, Src Port: 546 (546), Dst Port: 547 (547)
▽ DHCPv6
      Message type: Solicit (1)
      Transaction ID: 0xb7f78f
    ▽ Elapsed time
        Option: Elapsed time (8)
        Length: 2
        Value: 0000
        Elapsed time: 0 ms
    ▽ Client Identifier
        Option: Client Identifier (1)
        Length: 10
        Value: 00030001fa163ed3a6b0
        DUID: 00030001fa163ed3a6b0
        DUID Type: link-layer address (3)
        Hardware type: Ethernet (1)
        Link-layer address: fa:16:3e:d3:a6:b0
    ▷ Option Request
    ▷ Identity Association for Non-temporary Address
```

Solicit message is sent with link local source address and destinated to All-DHCP-Relay-Address

Any Solicit message with a missing Client ID will be ignored.

3. If the solicit message is seen, ensure that the client identifier is included in the message. This is the ID used by the DHCPv6 server to uniquely identify the client that helps with client management and reassigning the same address to the client. Any solicit message without a client ID will be ignored by the server. So if you see this message without a client ID, it is expected that the server will not assign an IPv6 address to the client.

4. Next, check whether the advertise message is seen in the capture. If the server successfully received the solicit message with a client ID, it will unicast with a DHCPv6 advertise message. If there are more multiple servers in the network, all the servers will reply with an advertise message.

5. If you don't see a DHCPv6 advertise message, it is possible that the server is not configured properly or is not functioning properly:
    - Check whether there are any servers listening to ff02::1:2. This can be verified by simply triggering an ICMPv6 ping from the client to ff02::1:2. If we get a response, it verifies that there is a server listening to solicit messages.
    - Check whether the server is configured with the DHCPv6 pool.

- Check whether there is any issue in the IPv6 or DHCPv6 stack on the server side. This may vary depending on the type of server being used for this purpose:

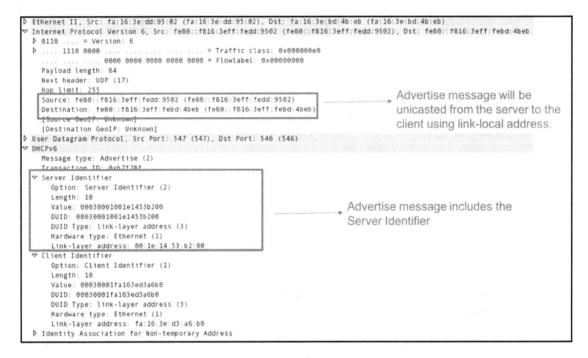

> Ethernet II, Src: fa:16:3e:dd:95:02 (fa:16:3e:dd:95:02), Dst: fa:16:3e:bd:4b:eb (fa:16:3e:bd:4b:eb)
▽ Internet Protocol Version 6, Src: fe80::f816:3eff:fedd:9502 (fe80::f816:3eff:fedd:9502), Dst: fe80::f816:3eff:febd:4beb
  ▷ 0110 .... = Version: 6
  ▷ .... 1110 0000 .... = Traffic class: 0x000000e0
    .... 0000 0000 0000 0000 0000 = Flowlabel: 0x00000000
    Payload length: 84
    Next header: UDP (17)
    Hop limit: 255
    Source: fe80::f816:3eff:fedd:9502 (fe80::f816:3eff:fedd:9502)
    Destination: fe80::f816:3eff:febd:4beb (fe80::f816:3eff:febd:4beb)
    [Source GeoIP: Unknown]
    [Destination GeoIP: Unknown]
▷ User Datagram Protocol, Src Port: 547 (547), Dst Port: 546 (546)
▽ DHCPv6
    Message type: Advertise (2)
    Transaction ID: 0xb7f78f
  ▽ Server Identifier
      Option: Server Identifier (2)
      Length: 10
      Value: 00030001001e1453b200
      DUID: 00030001001e1453b200
      DUID Type: link-layer address (3)
      Hardware type: Ethernet (1)
      Link-layer address: 00:1e:14:53:b2:00
  ▽ Client Identifier
      Option: Client Identifier (1)
      Length: 10
      Value: 00030001fa163ed3a6b0
      DUID: 00030001fa163ed3a6b0
      DUID Type: link-layer address (3)
      Hardware type: Ethernet (1)
      Link-layer address: fa:16:3e:d3:a6:b0
  ▷ Identity Association for Non-temporary Address

Advertise message will be unicasted from the server to the client using link-local address.

Advertise message includes the Server Identifier

6. The preceding screenshot shows the DHCPv6 advertise message from the server. As can be noted, this message will be unicasted to the client requesting an address. The advertise message carries a server identifier that uniquely identifies the server from other available servers in the network..

7. The next step is to check whether the client is sending a DHCPv6 request message. If the advertise message does not carry the client identifier (from the solicit message), the client will ignore the message:

```
▷ Ethernet II, Src: fa:16:3e:bd:4b:eb (fa:16:3e:bd:4b:eb), Dst: IPv6mcast_01:00:02 (33:33:00:01:00:02)
▽ Internet Protocol Version 6, Src: fe80::f816:3eff:febd:4beb (fe80::f816:3eff:febd:4beb), Dst: ff02::1:2 (ff02::1:2)
   ▷ 0110 .... = Version: 6
   ▷ .... 1110 0000 .... .... .... .... .... = Traffic class: 0x000000e0
     .... .... .... 0000 0000 0000 0000 0000 = Flowlabel: 0x00000000
     Payload length: 98
     Next header: UDP (17)
     Hop limit: 255
     Source: fe80::f816:3eff:febd:4beb (fe80::f816:3eff:febd:4beb)
     Destination: ff02::1:2 (ff02::1:2)
     [Source GeoIP: Unknown]
     [Destination GeoIP: Unknown]
▷ User Datagram Protocol, Src Port: 546 (546), Dst Port: 547 (547)
▽ DHCPv6
     Message type: Request (3)
     Transaction ID: 0xb7ffbd
   ▷ Elapsed time
   ▽ Client Identifier
        Option: Client Identifier (1)
        Length: 10
        Value: 00030001fa163ed3a6b0
        DUID: 00030001fa163ed3a6b0
        DUID Type: link-layer address (3)
        Hardware type: Ethernet (1)
        Link-layer address: fa:16:3e:d3:a6:b0
   ▽ Option Request
        Option: Option Request (6)
        Length: 4
        Value: 00170018
        Requested Option code: DNS recursive name server (23)
        Requested Option code: Domain Search List (24)
   ▽ Server Identifier
        Option: Server Identifier (2)
        Length: 10
        Value: 00030001001e1453b200
        DUID: 00030001001e1453b200
        DUID Type: link-layer address (3)
        Hardware type: Ethernet (1)
        Link-layer address: 00:1e:14:53:b2:00
▷ Identity Association for Non-temporary Address
```

Request message is sent with link local source address and destinated to All-DHCP-Relay-Address

Request message carries both Client and Server Identifier

8. If you see the request message, check whether the message is carrying the relevant client and server identifiers. This message will be sent to the all-DHCP-relay address and so it will be delivered to all servers in the network.

9. The last message to check is the DHCPv6 reply message. The server, upon receiving the DHCPv6 request message from the client, will assign an IPv6 address from the local pool. If there is more than one server in the network, the server identifier will be used to identify which server will assign the address:

```
▷ Ethernet II, Src: fa:16:3e:dd:95:02 (fa:16:3e:dd:95:02), Dst: fa:16:3e:bd:4b:eb (fa:16:3e:bd:4b:eb)
▽ Internet Protocol Version 6, Src: fe80::f816:3eff:fedd:9502 (fe80::f816:3eff:fedd:9502), Dst: fe80::f816:
   ▷ 0110 .... = Version: 6
   ▷ .... 1110 0000 .... .... .... .... .... = Traffic class: 0x000000e0
     .... .... .... 0000 0000 0000 0000 0000 = Flowlabel: 0x00000000
     Payload length: 84
     Next header: UDP (17)
     Hop limit: 255
     Source: fe80::f816:3eff:fedd:9502 (fe80::f816:3eff:fedd:9502)          Reply message will be unicasted
     Destination: fe80::f816:3eff:febd:4beb (fe80::f816:3eff:febd:4beb)     from the server to the client
     [Source GeoIP: Unknown]                                                using link-local address.
     [Destination GeoIP: Unknown]
▷ User Datagram Protocol, Src Port: 547 (547), Dst Port: 546 (546)
▽ DHCPv6
     Message type: Reply (7)
     Transaction ID: 0xb7ffbd
   ▷ Server Identifier
   ▷ Client Identifier
   ▽ Identity Association for Non-temporary Address
        Option: Identity Association for Non-temporary Address (3)
        Length: 40
        Value: 00030001000a8c000010e000005001820010db802000000...
        IAID: 00030001
        T1: 43200
        T2: 69120
     ▽ IA Address
        Option: IA Address (5)
        Length: 24                                                         ─────────▶ Assigned Address
        Value: 20010db802000000adf8c97f60492ffafffffffffffffff
        IPv6 address: 2001:db8:200:0:adf8:c97f:6049:2ffa (2001:db8:200:0:adf8:c97f:6049:2ffa)
        Preferred lifetime: infinity
        Preferred lifetime: infinity
```

10. As shown in the preceding screenshot, the DHCPv6 reply message is the actual message that carries the IPv6 address. This message will be unicasted from the server to the client.

How it works...

Consider the following diagram where a DHCPv6 client that is enabled to receive an IPv6 address from DHCPv6 server will send a DHCPv6 solicit message:

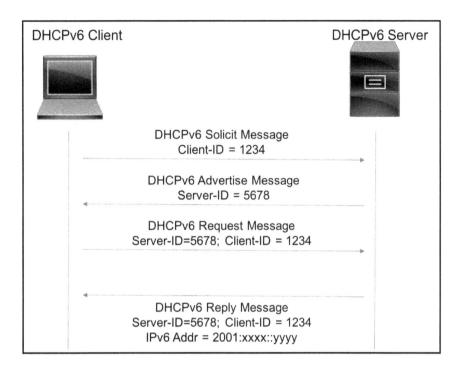

This message is a UDP packet with the destination port as 547. A DHCPv6 solicit message will be flooded to all-DHCPv6 multicast address ff02::1:2. The source address will be set to the link-local IPv6 address of the client.

The DHCPv6 server, upon receiving the solicit message, will send a DHCPv6 advertise message. This message will be unicasted back to the link-local address of the DHCPv6 client. One or more DHCPv6 servers may be present in the network and all servers will be sending DHCPv6 advertise messages. Each server will include its own server ID in the advertise message.

The DHCPv6 client, upon receiving the advertise message will send a DHCPv6 request message. This message will carry a server ID to identify the server from which it is requesting the address assignment.

The DHCPv6 server will assign an IPv6 address from the local pool and send a DHCPv6 reply message with the prefix and associated details, such as the lifetime of the prefix.

The following are a few useful filters:

Filter	Description	Example
dhcpv6	Filters all DHCPv6 packets	dhcpv6
dhcpv6.msgtype ==<>	Filters all DHCPv6 packets based on the message type	dhcpv6.msgtype == solicit dhcpv6.msgtype == advertise
dhcpv6.iaaddr.ip == <>	Filters all DHCPv6 packets with the specific IA address	dhcpv6.iaaddr.ip == <addr>

IPv6 neighbor discovery protocol operation and analysis

When the Layer 3 network is IPv6 addressed, IPv6 **Neighbor Discovery (ND)** protocol is used to resolve the MAC address associated to the IPv6 address. Unlike ARP, IPv6 ND uses ICMPv6 for address resolution by defining different ICMPv6 packet types.

ICMPv6 neighbor solicitation is an ICMPv6 message type used by a resolving node to query the link layer address for an IPv6 address. This is analogous to an ARP request for IPv4. This message will be designated to the IPv6 solicited node multicast address as there is no broadcast address in IPv6. The neighbor solicitation message format is as follows:

Type = 135	Code = 0	Checksum
Reserved		
Target Address (8 Octets)		
Options (Variable)		

ICMPv6 neighbor advertisement is an ICMPv6 message type used by a responding node to reply with the link layer address for the associated IPv6 address. This message is analogous to an ARP reply for IPv4. This message will be unicasted to the resolving node.

The neighbor advertisement message format is as follows:

Type = 136	Code = 0			Checksum
R	S	O		Reserved
Target Address (8 Octets)				
Options (Variable)				

How to do it...

1. In the following diagram, assume **PC1** (2001:DB8::1) is trying to reach **PC2** (2001:DB8::2):

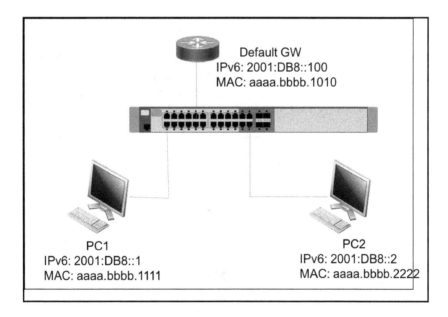

IPv6 Topology

2. Trigger IPv6 ping probes from **PC1** to **PC2**. This will trigger IPv6 ND neighbor solicitation from **PC1** to **PC2**.

3. Check the local IPv6 neighbor table on **PC1** to see whether the MAC address for `2001:DB8::2` is populated in the local table. Different vendors uses different show commands to query the local table:

   - In macOS, use `ndp -na` to list the IPv6 neighbor details.
   - In Windows, use `netsh interface ipv6 show neighbor`.

4. If the MAC address for `2001:DB8::2` is seen in **PC1**, it ensures that the IPv6 neighbor solicitation from **PC1** is received by **PC2** and replied with a neighbor advertisement

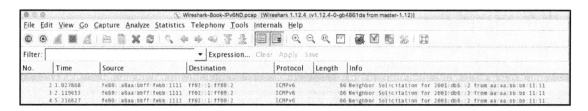

5. If you don't see the MAC address for `2001:DB8::2` in **PC1**, connect Wireshark to one of the free ports on switch and capture the packet (with port mirroring). It will be useful to perform the capture on both the ingress and egress directions of the ports connecting **PC1** and **PC2**:

6. Check whether the ICMPv6 neighbor solicitation message from **PC1** is seen in the capture. The preceding screenshot shows the message from **PC1**. The MAC address of PC1 will be carried in the IPv6 options:

   - If the ICMPv6 NS packet is seen in the capture on port connecting **PC1** (ingress direction) but not in the capture on port connecting **PC2** (egress direction), the switch might have dropped the packet.
   - If the ICMPv6 NS packet is not seen in the capture on port connecting **PC1**, check the physical cable connecting **PC1** to the switch or the NIC port of **PC1**.
   - If the ICMPv6 NS packet is seen in both ingress and egress captures, but there is no ICMPv6 NA, check **PC2**.

7. Similarly, check whether the ICMPv6 neighbor advertisement packet is seen in the capture from **PC2**:

   - If the IPv6 NA packet is seen in the capture on port connecting **PC2** (ingress direction) but not in the capture on port connecting **PC1** (egress direction), the switch might have dropped the reply packet.
   - If the IPv6 NA packet is not seen in the capture on port connecting **PC2** (ingress direction), check the physical cable connecting **PC2** to Switch.
   - If the IPv6 NA packet is seen in both captures on ports connecting **PC1** and **PC2**, but there is yet no entry in the **PC1** IPv6 neighbor table, check **PC1**.

The following are a few useful filters:

Filter	Description	Example
icmpv6.type == <type>	ICMPv6 type based filter. Type 135 will filter all IPv6 neighbor solicitation packets and type 136 will filter all IPv6 neighbor advertisement packets	icmpv6.type == 135 icmpv6.type == 136
icmpv6.nd.ns.target_address == <ipv6_addr>	Filter the NS packet with target IPv6 address	icmpv6.nd.ns.target_address == 2001:DB8::2
icmpv6.nd.ns.target_address == <ipv6_addr>	Filter the NA packet with target IPv6 address	icmpv6.nd.na.target_address == 2001:db8::1

IPv6 duplicate address detection

Duplicate addresses have always been a challenge in IPv4 networks. There is no inbuilt duplicate address detection mechanism with IPv4, which causes issues in the production network. Considering these challenges, IPv6 is designed with an inbuilt **Duplicate Address Detection (DAD)** mechanism.

How it works...

When a host is configured with an IPv6 address using a static or other dynamic mechanism (like SLAAC or DHCPv6), the host will send an ICMPv6 NS message to the new IPv6 address before assigning the address to the interface. If the address that is being validated for DAD is the only IPv6 address available for the host, the NS message will be sent with an all-zero IPv6 address, as shown in the following screenshot:

```
▷ Ethernet II, Src: fa:16:3e:bd:4b:eb (fa:16:3e:bd:4b:eb), Dst: IPv6mcast_ff:49:2f:fa (33:33:ff:49:2f:fa)
▽ Internet Protocol Version 6, Src: :: (::), Dst: ff02::1:ff49:2ffa (ff02::1:ff49:2ffa)
   ▷ 0110 .... = Version: 6
   ▷ .... 1110 0000 .... .... .... .... .... = Traffic class: 0x000000e0
     .... .... .... 0000 0000 0000 0000 0000 = Flowlabel: 0x00000000
     Payload length: 32
     Next header: ICMPv6 (58)
     Hop limit: 255
     Source: :: (::)
     Destination: ff02::1:ff49:2ffa (ff02::1:ff49:2ffa)
     [Source GeoIP: Unknown]
     [Destination GeoIP: Unknown]
▽ Internet Control Message Protocol v6
     Type: Neighbor Solicitation (135)
     Code: 0
     Checksum: 0x82ec [correct]
     Reserved: 00000000
     Target Address: 2001:db8:200:0:adf8:c97f:6049:2ffa (2001:db8:200:0:adf8:c97f:6049:2ffa)
   ▽ ICMPv6 Option (Nonce)
       Type: Nonce (14)
       Length: 1 (8 bytes)
       Nonce: 798925f7e279
```

As mentioned in the ND section, an NS message will be sent to the solicited node multicast address. If it gets a response from any node, the host will detect the presence of another host with the same address and so it will not assign this duplicate address. If it does not receive any NA from any host, it is safe to assign and use the IPv6 address.

11

Transport Layer Protocol Analysis

In this chapter, you will learn about:

- UDP principle of operation
- UDP protocol analysis and troubleshooting
- TCP principle of operation
- Troubleshooting TCP connectivity problems
- Troubleshooting TCP retransmission issues
- TCP sliding window mechanism
- TCP enhancements – selective ACK and timestamps
- Troubleshooting TCP throughput

Introduction

In this chapter, we will primarily focus on the transport layer of the OSI reference model and learn how to analyze various layer 4 protocol (TCP/UDP/SCTP) operations. The transport layer protocol is a host-to-host communication protocol that is responsible for data exchange between end applications running on different hosts. The **User Datagram Protocol** (**UDP**) is a simple connectionless protocol that simply delivers the datagram to the intended recipient without any reliability mechanism. On the other hand, **Transport Control Protocol** (**TCP**) is a connection-oriented protocol and its primary purpose is to provide reliable, congestion-aware data delivery between end applications.

More than 80% of the total internet traffic leverages TCP as the transport layer protocol. Any end application that is sensitive to packet loss requires reliability and such applications use TCP as the transport layer protocol. For example, a web server using HTTP uses TCP port 80. While TCP provides reliability, it requires retransmission of the lost data; that may introduce jitter and delay. Some end applications such as voice/video over IP are less sensitive to packet loss but more sensitive to jitter/delay. Such applications use UDP instead TCP as the transport layer protocol.

In this chapter, we will discuss the basic principles of different transport layer protocols, commonly faced issues, and the use of Wireshark to analyze and troubleshoot the protocol.

UDP principle of operation

UDP is a lightweight transport layer protocol that works on a best effort basis. UDP is a good choice of transport layer protocol for end applications that can tolerate packet loss or if the reliability can be taken care of at the application layer. For example, **Trivial File Transfer Protocol** (TFTP), which is a simple file transfer protocol, leverages UDP as the transport layer protocol. TFTP sends acknowledgement for each block of datagrams received at the application layer. So, even though UDP does not have an inbuilt reliability mechanism, such applications can still use UDP as the transport layer protocol.

The protocol field of the IP header will be set to 17 for UDP. The format of the UDP header is as follows:

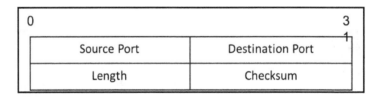

Figure 11.1: UDP header format

The host that originates the UDP stream will use any local unused port from range 1024 to 65535. The destination port will be used to identify the end application within the destination host. The destination port usually be from the well-known range 1 to 1023.

This table lists some of the well-known UDP application ports:

Application	UDP Port
Domain Name System	53
BOOTP Server	67
BOOTP Client	68

Table 11.2: Well-known UDP applications

Here is a sample Wireshark capture of a UDP packet:

```
▶ Frame 14: 331 bytes on wire (2648 bits), 331 bytes captured (2648 bits)
▶ Ethernet II, Src: aa:bb:cc:03:f3:30 (aa:bb:cc:03:f3:30), Dst: Broadcast (ff:ff:ff:ff:ff:ff)
▼ Internet Protocol Version 4, Src: 0.0.0.0, Dst: 255.255.255.255
     0100 .... = Version: 4
     .... 0101 = Header Length: 20 bytes (5)
   ▶ Differentiated Services Field: 0x00 (DSCP: CS0, ECN: Not-ECT)
     Total Length: 317
     Identification: 0x1e26 (7718)
   ▶ Flags: 0x00
     Fragment offset: 0
     Time to live: 255
     Protocol: UDP (17)
     Header checksum: 0x9c8a [validation disabled]
     [Header checksum status: Unverified]
     Source: 0.0.0.0
     Destination: 255.255.255.255
     [Source GeoIP: Unknown]
     [Destination GeoIP: Unknown]
▼ User Datagram Protocol, Src Port: 68, Dst Port: 67
     Source Port: 68
     Destination Port: 67
     Length: 297
     Checksum: 0xf189 [unverified]
     [Checksum Status: Unverified]
     [Stream index: 2]
▶ Bootstrap Protocol (Discover)
```

Figure 11.3: UDP packet Wireshark capture

UDP protocol analysis and troubleshooting

While most of the applications using UDP are tolerant to packet loss, a substantial packet loss for any UDP stream may result in a very frustrating end user experience. In this section, we will discuss some of the common causes for UDP stream failure and how Wireshark can be used to analyze and troubleshoot such failures.

Getting ready

When the UDP stream is not functioning properly, the very first step is to ensure that the network connectivity to the remote host is working fine. This is verified by using a utility tool such as Ping or Traceroute. Troubleshooting of any failure in network connectivity can be performed as defined in `Chapter 10`, *Network Layer Protocols and Operations*. If the network connectivity is fine, we do the following procedure.

How to do it...

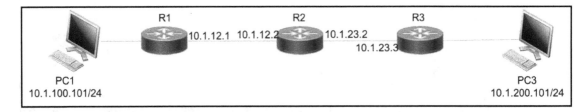

Figure 11.4: UDP topology

In the preceding diagram, the end application using the UDP stream between **PC1** (`10.1.100.101`) and **PC3** (`10.1.200.101`) is not functioning properly:

1. Ensure that the UDP ports are allowed on Firewalls or other security settings. A firewall in the transit path or on the endpoint that is not allowing the UDP port may drop the packets.
2. Get the UDP destination port to which **PC1** is sending the data and check whether the relevant UDP port is opened on **PC3** to receive data. This can be done by checking the process on **PC3** or by performing a port scan.

3. When **PC3** can be accessed, `netstat` can be used on the host directly and can check whether the destination port is opened.

4. When **PC3** cannot be accessed, the port scanning mechanism can be used to do the check. There are various port scanning tools available that can be used for this purpose. If the port is not opened on **PC3**, it will drop the packet and send an ICMP error message (Destination Port Unreachable).

5. If the port is opened, the next step is to perform Wireshark capture and packet analysis. Since UDP is connection-less, it is recommended to simultaneously capture the packet as close as possible to both the endpoints.

```
▶ Frame 7: 94 bytes on wire (752 bits), 94 bytes captured (752 bits)
▼ Ethernet II, Src: fa:16:3e:65:5f:0e (fa:16:3e:65:5f:0e), Dst: fa:16:3e:0f:88:52 (fa:16:3e:0f:88:52)
  ▼ Destination: fa:16:3e:0f:88:52 (fa:16:3e:0f:88:52)
      Address: fa:16:3e:0f:88:52 (fa:16:3e:0f:88:52)
      .... ..1. .... .... .... .... = LG bit: Locally administered address (this is NOT the factory default)
      .... ...0 .... .... .... .... = IG bit: Individual address (unicast)
  ▼ Source: fa:16:3e:65:5f:0e (fa:16:3e:65:5f:0e)
      Address: fa:16:3e:65:5f:0e (fa:16:3e:65:5f:0e)
      .... ..1. .... .... .... .... = LG bit: Locally administered address (this is NOT the factory default)
      .... ...0 .... .... .... .... = IG bit: Individual address (unicast)
    Type: IPv4 (0x0800)
▶ Internet Protocol Version 4, Src: 10.1.12.1, Dst: 10.1.3.3
▼ User Datagram Protocol, Src Port: 50238, Dst Port: 1967
    Source Port: 50238
    Destination Port: 1967
    Length: 60
  ▶ Checksum: 0x0378 [correct]
    [Checksum Status: Good]
    [Stream index: 2]
▶ Data (52 bytes)
```

Figure 11.5 UDP checksum

In the preceding screenshot, check whether the UDP checksum is right. If the checksum is not verified, the destination host will drop the packet. Since UDP is connection-less, there will not be any error message or acknowledgment sent about the checksum error. By default, Wireshark may not validate the checksum in the capture. This needs to be enabled in the tool as follows:

1. Go to **Edit** and click on **Preference**.

2. Click on **Protocols** and then select **UDP**.

3. Set **Validate the UDP checksum if possible**.

4. If the UDP checksum is fine, compare the UDP streams from both the captures to ensure that the packets are making it towards the destination:

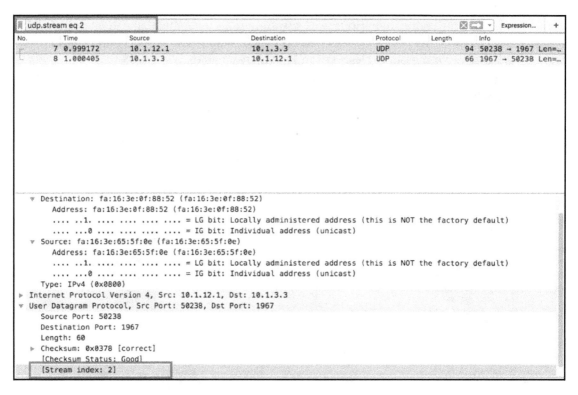

Figure 11.6: UDP Stream index

5. Wireshark allows us to follow a specific UDP stream that can be used to compare between captures. Each capture will have a UDP stream index number, as shown in the preceding screenshot. This can be applied as a filter to follow the UDP stream. It basically lists all the packets with the same source/destination IP and source/destination UDP ports in the received order.

6. If there are no issues observed in the capture compared, it could be an issue in the host stack.

The following are a few useful UDP filters:

Filter	Description	Example
udp	Filters all UDP packets	udp
udp.stream eq <>	Filters all UDP packet matching the stram index	udp.stream eq 2
udp.port == <>	Filters all UDP port matching the value in source or destination port field	udp.port == 65000
udp.srcport == <>	Filters all UDP port matching the value in source port field	udp.srcport == 65000
udp.dstport == <>	Filters all UDP port matching the value in destination port field	udp.dstport == 65000

TCP principle of operation

TCP is a highly reliable transport layer protocol used for connection-oriented host-to-host communication. End applications that are very sensitive to data loss can leverage TCP as the transport layer protocol. Majority of the internet traffic is dominated by TCP. It is extensively used by many applications, including email, peer-to-peer file sharing, and the famous WWW applications. TCP receives data from the application layer and segments it into data units, which will be encapsulated with the TCP header. The protocol data unit with the TCP header encapsulated is known as a **segments**. As mentioned earlier, TCP is connection oriented so that a connection will be established between the endpoints using a three-way handshake. Reliability is achieved by acknowledging the recipient of each segments and any missing segment will be retransmitted.

The protocol field of the IP header will be set to 6 for TCP. The format of the TCP header is as follows:

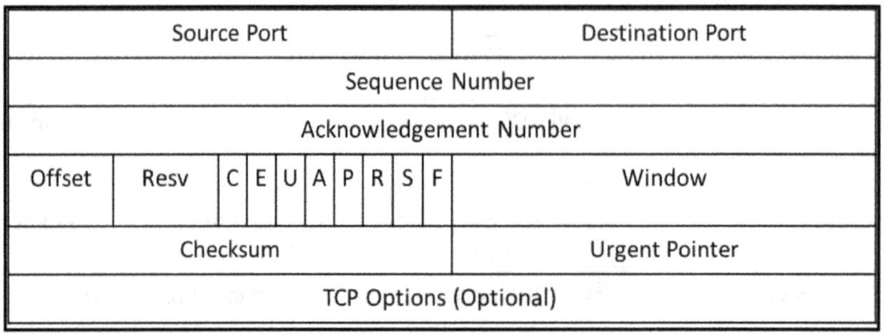

Source Port									Destination Port
Sequence Number									
Acknowledgement Number									
Offset	Resv	C	E	U	A	P	R	S	F	Window
Checksum									Urgent Pointer
TCP Options (Optional)									

Figure 11.7: TCP header format

While comparing to UDP header which is a fixed 8 byte header, TCP is of 20 bytes in size. The size may vary depending on the presence of TCP options. The **Sequence Number** and **Acknowledgement Number** play a key role in providing reliability to end application data transmission. More details are covered in the forthcoming recipe sections.

The following table lists some of the well-known UDP application ports:

Application	TCP Port
WWW/HTTP	80
Simple Mail Transfer Protocol(SMTP)	25
Secure Shell (SSH)	22

Table 11.8: Well-known UDP applications

The following is a sample Wireshark capture of a TCP packet:

```
▶ Frame 2: 58 bytes on wire (464 bits), 58 bytes captured (464 bits)
▶ Ethernet II, Src: fa:16:3e:6e:ee:87 (fa:16:3e:6e:ee:87), Dst: fa:16:3e:d6:12:52 (fa:16:3e:d6:12:52)
▼ Internet Protocol Version 4, Src: 10.0.128.1, Dst: 10.1.3.3
      0100 .... = Version: 4
      .... 0101 = Header Length: 20 bytes (5)
  ▶ Differentiated Services Field: 0xc0 (DSCP: CS6, ECN: Not-ECT)
      Total Length: 44
      Identification: 0x2f77 (12151)
  ▶ Flags: 0x00
      Fragment offset: 0
      Time to live: 254
      Protocol: TCP (6)
      Header checksum: 0xf58f [correct]
      [Header checksum status: Good]
      [Calculated Checksum: 0xf58f]
      Source: 10.0.128.1
      Destination: 10.1.3.3
      [Source GeoIP: Unknown]
      [Destination GeoIP: Unknown]
▼ Transmission Control Protocol, Src Port: 31245, Dst Port: 23, Seq: 0, Len: 0
      Source Port: 31245
      Destination Port: 23
      [Stream index: 0]
      [TCP Segment Len: 0]
      Sequence number: 0    (relative sequence number)
      Acknowledgment number: 0
      0110 .... = Header Length: 24 bytes (6)
  ▼ Flags: 0x002 (SYN)
          000. .... .... = Reserved: Not set
          ...0 .... .... = Nonce: Not set
          .... 0... .... = Congestion Window Reduced (CWR): Not set
          .... .0.. .... = ECN-Echo: Not set
          .... ..0. .... = Urgent: Not set
          .... ...0 .... = Acknowledgment: Not set
          .... .... 0... = Push: Not set
          .... .... .0.. = Reset: Not set
      ▶ .... .... ..1. = Syn: Set
          .... .... ...0 = Fin: Not set
          [TCP Flags: ··········S·]
      Window size value: 4128
      [Calculated window size: 4128]
      Checksum: 0xbf83 [unverified]
      [Checksum Status: Unverified]
      Urgent pointer: 0
  ▶ Options: (4 bytes), Maximum segment size
  ▶ [Timestamps]
```

Figure 11.9: TCP packet capture

Troubleshooting TCP connectivity problems

When two TCP processes wish to communicate, they open the connection, send the data, and then close the connection. This happens when you open a browser to the internet and connect from your mail client to the mail server, or with Telnet to your router or any other application that works over TCP.

When TCP opens the connection, it sends a request for open connection from the source port to the destination port. Some problems can occur during the establishment or closing of the application. Using Wireshark to locate and solve these problems is the goal of this recipe.

Getting ready

If you experience one of the following problems, use Wireshark in order to find out what the reason for it is. These problems can be of many types, which are as follows:

- You try to run an application and it does not work. You try to browse the internet and you don't get any response.
- You try to use your mail but you don't get a connection to the mail server.
- Problems can be due to simple reasons, such as the server is down, the application is not running on the server, or the network is down somewhere on the way to the server.
- Problems can also be due to more complicated reasons, such as DNS problems, insufficient memory on the server that does not enable you to connect (due to high memory consumption by an application, for example), duplicate IPs, and many others.

In this recipe, we focus on these GO/NO-GO problems; they are usually quite easy to solve.

How to do it...

Here, you will learn some indicators and what you can see when you use Wireshark for debugging TCP connectivity problems. Usually, these problems result in you trying to run an application and getting no results.

When you try to run an application (for example, a database client, a mail client, watching cameras servers, and so on) and don't get any output, follow these steps:

1. Verify that the server and applications are running.
2. Verify that your client is running, you have an IP address configured (manually or by DHCP), and that you are connected to the network.
3. Ping the server and verify that you have connectivity to it.
4. In the capture file, look for one of the following patterns:
   - Triple SYN messages with no response
   - **SYN messages with a reset** (RST) response

In both cases, it could be that a firewall is blocking the specific application or the application is not running.

In the following screenshot, we see a simple case in which we simply don't get access to web server 81.218.31.171 (packets 61, 62, and 63). It can be because it is not permitted by a firewall, or simply because there is a problem with the server. We can also see that we have a connection to another website (108.160.163.43; packets 65, 66, and 67), so the connection problem is only with 81.218.31.171.

In the next illustration, we see a slightly more complex case of the same situation. In this case, we've had a cameras server that the customer wanted to log in to and watched the cameras on a remote site. The camera's server had the IP address 135.82.12.1 and the problem was that the customer was able to get the main web page of the server with the login window but couldn't log in to the system. In the following screenshot, we can see that we open a connection to the IP address 135.82.12.1. We can see that a TCP connection is opened to the HTTP server, and at first, it looks as if there are no connectivity problems:

No.	Time	Source	Destination	Protocol	Length	Info
2113	17.665372	10.0.0.3	135.82.12.1	TCP	66	62423 > http [SYN] Seq=0 Win=8
2120	17.746627	135.82.12.1	10.0.0.3	TCP	66	http > 62423 [SYN, ACK] Seq=0
2121	17.746693	10.0.0.3	135.82.12.1	TCP	54	62423 > http [ACK] Seq=1 Ack=1
2122	17.747085	10.0.0.3	135.82.12.1	H?	316	GET / HTTP/1.1
2130	17.862143	135.82.12.1	10.0.0.3		54	http > 62423 [ACK] Seq=1 Ack=2(
2189	18.736301	135.82.12.1	10.0.0.		145	[TCP segment of a reassembled]
2191	18.767301	135.82.12.1	10.0.0.		1466	[TCP segment of a reassembled]

Filter: ip.addr==135.82.12.1 — Expression... Clear Apply Save

Connection opened to IP Address 135.82.12.1 TCP Port 80 (http)

The problems arise when we filter all traffic to IP address 135.82.12.1, that is, the cameras server.

Here, we can see that when we try to connect to TCP port 6036, we get an RST/ACK response, which can be for the following reasons:

- A firewall that blocks port 6036 (that was the case here)
- When the **port address translation (PAT)** is configured and we translate only port 80 and not 6036
- The authentication of the username and password were done on TCP port 6036, the firewall allowed only port 80, the authentication was blocked, and the application didn't work

No.	Time	Source	Destination	Protocol	Length	Info
2620	36.423135	10.0.0.3	135.82.12.1	TCP	54	62438 > http [ACK] Seq=915
		10.0.0.3	135.82.12.1	TCP	66	62442 > 6036 [SYN] Seq=0 W
		135.82.12.1	10.0.0.3	TCP	54	6036 > 62442 [RST, ACK] Se
		fe80::c067:2c23:335:ff02::c		SSDP	208	M-SEARCH * HTTP/1.1
		10.0.0.3	194.90.1.5	ICMP	74	Echo (ping) request id=0x(
		194.90.1.5	10.0.0.3	ICMP	74	Echo (ping) reply id=0x(
2626	37.329129	10.0.0.3	135.82.12.1	TCP	62	62442 > 6036 [SYN] Seq=0 W
2627	37.369547	135.82.12.1	10.0.0.3	TCP	54	6036 > 62442 [RST, ACK] Se
2628	38.023274	10.0.0.3	194.90.1.5	ICMP	74	Echo (ping) request id=0x(

Connection Trials to TCP port 6036:
- SYN request
- RST/ACK response

To summarize, when you don't have connectivity to a server, check the server and the client to see whether all TCP/UDP ports are forwarded throughout the network and whether you have any ports that you don't know about.

In some cases, when you install new applications in your network, it is good to connect Wireshark on the client and the server and check what is actually running between them. The software house will not always tell you what they are actually transferring over the network (sometimes this is because they are not aware of it!) and firewalls can block information that you are not aware of.

How it works...

Starting a TCP connection, as seen in the following illustration:

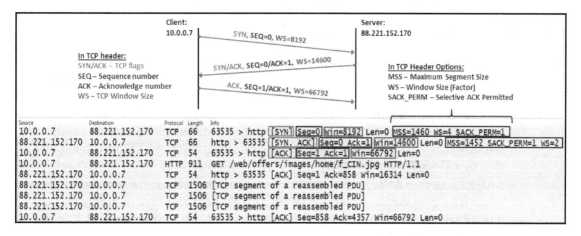

It happens in three steps:

1. The TCP process on the client side sends an SYN packet. This is a packet with the SYN flag set to 1. In this packet, the client:
    - Specifies its initial sequence number. This is the number of the first byte that the client sends to the server.
    - Specifies its window size. This is the buffer the clients allocate to the process (the place in the client's RAM).
    - Sets the options that will be used by it: MSS, Selective ACK, and so on.

2. When the server receives the request to establish a connection, the server:
    - Sends an SYN/ACK packet to the client, confirming the acceptance of the SYN request.
    - Specifies the server's initial sequence number. This is the number of the first byte that the server sends to the client.

- Specifies the server's window size. This is the buffer size that the server allocates to the process (the place in the server's RAM).
- Responds to the options requested and sets the options on the server side.

2. When receiving the server's SYN/ACK, the client:
   - Sends an ACK packet to the server, confirming the acceptance of the SYN/ACK packet from the server.
   - Specifies the client's window size. This is the buffer size that the client allocates to the process. Although this parameter was defined in the first packet (the SYN packet), the server will refer to this one since it is the latest window size received by the server.

In the options field of the TCP header, we have the following main options:

- **Maximum segment size** (**MSS**): This is the maximum size of the TCP datagram, that is, the number of bytes from the beginning of the TCP header to the end of the entire packet.
- **Windows size** (**WSopt**): This factor is multiplied with the window size field in the TCP header to notify the receiver on a larger size buffer. Since the maximum window size in the header is 64 KB, a factor of 4 gives us 64 KB multiplied by 4, that is, a 256 KB window size.
- **SACK**: Selective ACK is an option that enables the two parties of a connection to acknowledge specific packets, so when a single packet is lost, only this packet will be sent again. Both parties of the connection have to agree on SACK in the connection establishment.
- **Timestamps options** (**TSopt**): This parameter was explained earlier in this chapter, and refers to measurement of the delay between the client and the server.

By this stage, both sides:

- Agree to establish a connection
- Know the other side's initial sequence number
- Know the other side's window size

Anything but a full three-way handshake while establishing a connection should be considered as a problem. This includes SYN without a response, SYN and then SYN/ACK and no last ACK, SYN which is answered with a reset (RST flag equal to 1), and so on.

Wireshark allows the user to view the complete flow in a pictorial representation of the TCP segment exchanges. A sample is as follows:

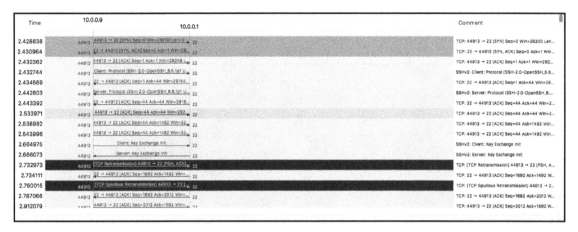

In order to view the TCP flow in the preceding format, click one of the packets that belong to the TCP flow and perform the following:

1. Go to **Statistics**
2. Click on **Flow Graph**

There's more...

Some rules of thumb are as follows:

- In case an SYN packet is answered with RST, look for the firewall that blocks the port numbers.
- Triple SYN without any answer occurs either due to an application that didn't respond, or a firewall that blocks the request on a specific port.
- Always verify that you have **Network Address Translation** (**NAT**), port forwarding, and mechanisms that play with TCP or UDP ports. These mechanisms can interfere with the standard operation of TCP.

When the TCP endpoints establish a new TCP connection, the sequence number in the SYN packet will start with an arbitrary number and will be sequentially incremented by 1 for every 1 byte. For ease of analysis, Wireshark replaces the sequence number with a relative sequence number in such a way that the SYN packet will start with a sequence number of 0 and increment sequentially.

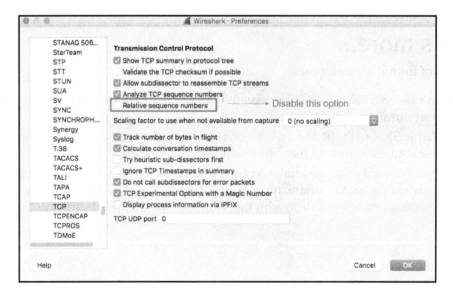

In the preceding screenshot, it can be observed that the sequence number is set to 0 and marked as (**relative sequence number**). This is not the real sequence number exchanged by the TCP endpoints. The original sequence number can be retained by disabling the **Relative Sequence number** option in **Protocol Preferences**.

Follow these steps to disable the option:

1. Go to **Preference**
2. Click on **Protocols** and then select **TCP**
3. Disable relative sequence numbers

Troubleshooting TCP retransmission issues

When TCP sends a packet or a group of packets (refer to the *How it works...* section at the end of this recipe), it waits for an acknowledgment to confirm the acceptance of these packets. Retransmissions obviously happen due to a packet that has not arrived, or an acknowledgment that has not arrived on time. There can be various reasons for this, and finding the correct reason is the goal of this recipe.

Getting ready

When you see that the network becomes slow, one of the reasons for this can be retransmissions. Connect Wireshark in the port mirror to the suspicious client or server, and watch the results.

In this recipe, we will see some common problems that we may encounter with Wireshark and what they indicate.

How to do it...

Let's get started:

1. Start capturing data on the relevant interface.
2. Go to the **Analyze** | **Expert Info** menu.
3. Under **Notes**, look for **Retransmissions.**
4. You can click on the (+) sign and a list of retransmissions will open. A single mouse click on every line will bring you the retransmission in the packet capture pane.
5. Now comes the important question: how do you locate the problem?

When you capture packets over a communication line, server interface, link to the internet, or any other line, you can have traffic from many IP addresses, many applications, and even specific procedures on every application. An example is accessing a specific table in a database application. The important thing here is to locate the TCP connections on which the retransmissions happen.

You can see where the retransmissions come from in these ways:

- Moving packet by packet in the **Expert Info** window and finding out for which packets it takes you into the packet capture pane (good for experienced users)
- In the packet pane, you can configure the display filter `expert.message == "Retransmission (suspected)"`, and you will get all retransmissions in the capture file
- Applying the filter and then checking the **Limit to display filter** section in the bottom-right corner of the window in the **Statistics à Conversations** window

Case 1 – retransmissions to many destinations

In the following screenshot, you can see that we've got many retransmissions spread between many servers, with destination ports `80` (HTTP). What we can also see from here is that the `10.0.0.5` port sends the retransmission; so packets were lost on the way to the internet, or an acknowledgement was not sent back on time from the web servers.

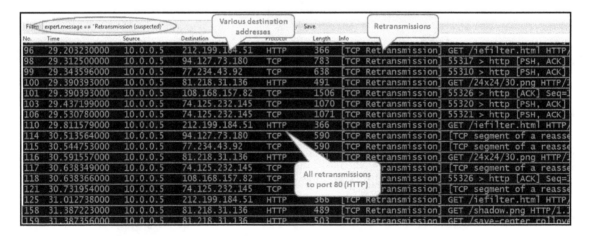

Well, obviously something is wrong on the line to the internet. How can we know what it is?

1. From the **Statistics** menu, open **IO Graph**.
2. In this case (case 1), we can see that the line is nearly empty. It is probably an error or another loaded line on the way to the internet.
3. You can check the packet losses and errors that cause them by logging in to the communications equipment or by any SNMP browser (when the SNMP agent is configured on the equipment). Check out the following screenshot for reference:

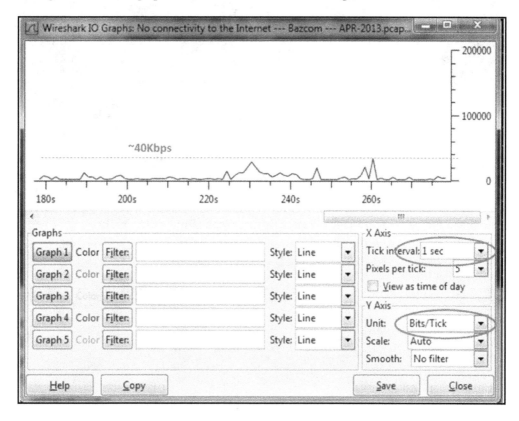

Case 2 – retransmissions on a single connection

If all retransmissions are on a single IP, with a single TCP port number, it will be a slow application. We can see this in the following screenshot:

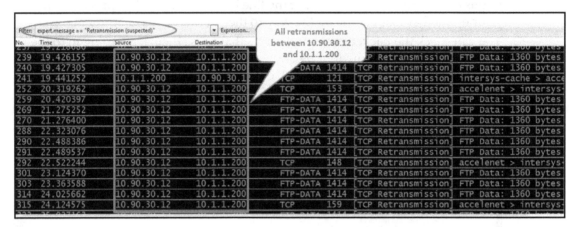

For retransmissions on a single connection, perform the following steps:

1. We can also verify this by opening **Conversations** from the **Statistics** menu and selecting the **Limit to display filter** checkbox. We will get all the conversations that have retransmissions, in this case, a single conversation.

2. By choosing the **IPv4:1** tab as shown in the following screenshot, we will see from which IP addresses we get the retransmissions:

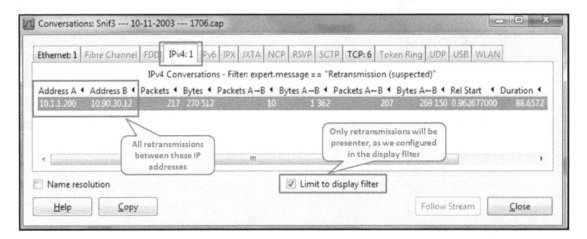

3. By choosing the **TCP:6** tab as shown in the following screenshot, we will see from which port numbers (or applications) we get the retransmissions:

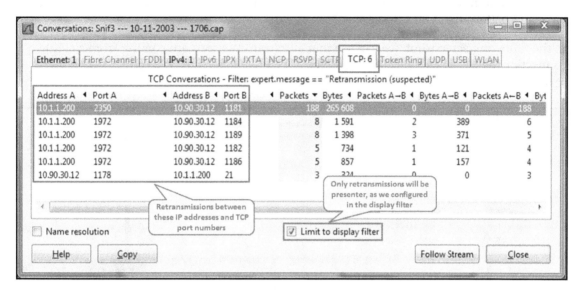

To isolate the problem, perform the following steps:

1. Look at the IO graph, and make sure that the line is not busy.

An indication of a busy communication line will be a straight line very close to the maximum bandwidth of the line. For example, if you have a 10 Mbps communication line, you port-mirror it and see in the IO graph a straight line that is close to the 10 Mbps. This is a good indication of a loaded line. A non-busy communication line will have many ups and downs, peaks, and empty intervals.

2. If the line is not busy, it can be a problem on the server for IP address 10.1.1.200 (10.90.30.12 is sending most of the retransmissions, so it could be that 10.1.1.200 responds slowly).

3. From the packet pane we can see that the application is FTP-DATA. It is possible that the FTP server works in an active mode. Hence we've opened a connection on one port (2350) and the server changed the port to 1972, so that it can be a slow non-responsive FTP software (that was the problem here eventually).

Case 3 – retransmission patterns

An important thing to watch out for in TCP retransmissions is whether the retransmissions have any pattern that you can see.

In the following screenshot, we can see that all retransmissions are coming from a single connection, between a single client and NetBIOS Session Service (TCP port 139) on the server.

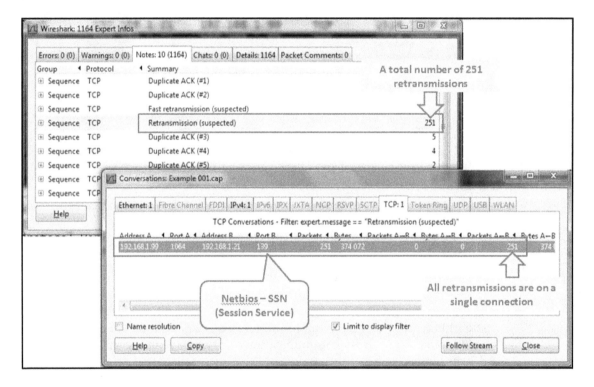

Looks like a simple server/application problem, but when we look at the packet capture pane, we can see something interesting (refer to the following screenshot):

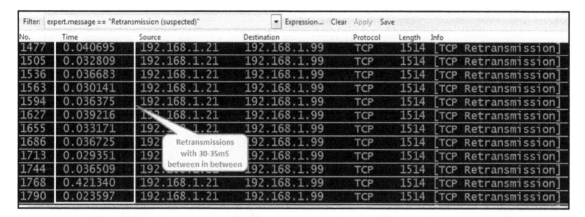

The interesting thing is that when we look at the pattern of retransmissions, we can see that they occur cyclically every 30 milliseconds. The time format here is seconds, since the previously displayed packet and the time scale are in seconds.

The problem in this case was a client that performed a financial procedure in the software that caused the software to slow down every 30-36 milliseconds.

Case 4 – retransmission due to a non-responsive application

Another reason for retransmissions can be when a client or a server does not answer to requests. In this case, you will see five retransmissions, with an increasing time difference. After these five consecutive retransmissions, the connection is considered to be lost by the sending side (in some cases, reset will be sent to close the connection depending on the software implementation). After the disconnection, two things may happen:

- An SYN request will be sent by the client in order to open a new connection. What the user will see in this case is a freeze in the application, and after 15-20 seconds, it will start to work again.
- No SYN will be sent, and the user will have to run the application (or a specific part of it) again.

In the following screenshot, we can see a case in which a new connection is opened:

No.	Time	Source				Length	Info
			Time intervals increases with every retransmission		Five consecutive retransmissions		
1159	0.000406	192.1.. ..50	192.168.201.93	TCP	60	http > tscchat [ACK] Seq=220556 Ack=29209
1160	0.220322	192.168.201.93	192.168.3.50	TCP	590	[TCP Retransmission] [TCP segment of a re
1161	0.656270	192.168.201.93	192.168.3.50	TCP	590	[TCP Retransmission] [TCP segment of a re
1162	1.203085	192.168.201.93	192.168.3.50	TCP	590	[TCP Retransmission] [TCP segment of a re
1163	2.406248	192.168.201.93	192.168.3.50	TCP	590	[TCP Retransmission] [TCP segment of a re
1164	4.812443	192.168.201.93	192.168.3.50	TCP	590	[TCP Retransmission] [TCP segment of a re
1165	9.625596	192.168.201.93	192.168.3.50	TCP	62	agentview > http [SYN] Seq=0 Win=65535 Le
1166	0.004414	192.168.3.50	192.168.201.93	TCP	60	http > agentview [SYN, ACK] Seq=0 Ack=1 W
1167	0.000033	192.168.201.93	192.168.3.50	TCP	54	agentview > http [ACK] Seq=1 Ack=1 Win=65
1168	0.000164	192.168.201.93	192.168.3..		590	[TCP segment of a reassembled PDU]
1169	0.000020	192.168.201.93	192.168.3..		53	[TCP segment of a reassembled PDU]

A new connection established

Case 5 - retransmission due to delayed variations

TCP is a protocol that is quite tolerant to delays as long as the delay does not vary. When you have variations in a delay, you can expect retransmissions. The way to find out whether this is the problem is as follows:

1. The first thing to do is, of course, ping the destination and get the first piece of information of the communications line delay. Look at the *How it works...* section to see how it should be done.

2. Check for the delay variations, which can happen due to the following reasons:

   - A non-stable or busy communication line. In this case, you will see delay variations using the `ping` command. It will usually happen on lines with a narrow bandwidth, and in some cases on cellular lines.

   - A loaded or inefficient application. In this case, you will see many retransmissions on this specific application only.

   - Loaded communication equipment (CPU load, buffer load, and so on). You can check this by accessing the communication equipment directly.

3. Use the Wireshark tools as explained in `Chapter 18`, *Troubleshooting Bandwidth and Delay Issues*.

The bottom line with TCP retransmissions is that retransmissions are a natural behavior of TCP as long as we don't have too many of them. Degradation in performance will start when the retransmissions are around 0.5 percent, and disconnections will start at around 5 percent. It also depends on the application and its sensitivity to retransmissions.

Finding out what it is

When you see retransmissions on a communication link (to the internet, on a server, between sites, or any other link), perform the following steps:

1. Locate the problem. Is it a specific IP address, specific connection, specific application, or some other problem?
2. Check whether the problem is because of the communication link, packet loss, or a slow server or PC. Check whether the application is slow.
3. If it is not due to any of the preceding reasons, check for delay variations.

How it works...

Let's see the regular operation of TCP and the causes of the problems that may occur.

Regular operation of the TCP sequence/acknowledge mechanism

One of the mechanisms that is built into TCP is the retransmission mechanism. This mechanism enables the recovery of data that is damaged, lost, duplicated, or delivered out of order.

This is achieved by assigning a sequence number to every transmitted byte, and expecting an **acknowledgment** (**ACK**) from the receiving party. If the ACK is not received within a timeout interval, the data is retransmitted.

At the receiver end, the sequence numbers are used to verify that the information comes in the order that it was sent in. If not, rearrange it to its previous state.

This mechanism works as follows:

1. At the connection establishment, both sides tell each other what their initial sequence number will be.
2. When data is sent, every packet has a sequence number. The sequence number indicates the number of the first byte in the TCP payload. The next packet that is sent will have the sequence number of the previous one plus the number of bytes in the previous packet plus 1 (in the next screenshot).

3. When a packet is sent, the **retransmission timeout** (RTO) counter starts to count the time from the moment it was sent.

> The retransmission timeout timer is based on the Van Jacobson congestion avoidance and control algorithm, which basically says the TCP is tolerant to high delays but not to fast delay variations.

4. When the receiver receives the packet, it answers with an ACK packet that tells the sender to send the next packet. In the following screenshot you will see how it works:

You can see from here that `10.0.0.7` is downloading a file from `62.219.24.171`. The file is downloaded via HTTP (the Wireshark window was configured to show `tcp.seq` and `tcp.ack` from the **Edit | Preferences** columns configuration, as described in `Chapter 1`, *Introduction to Wireshark Version 2*).

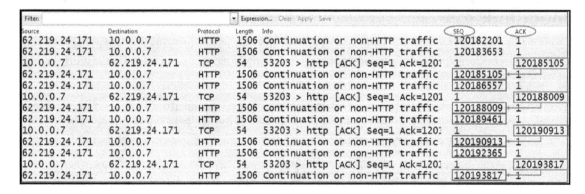

From here, 62.219.24.171 sends packets with sequence numbers that end with 85101, 86557, after which 10.0.0.7 sends an ACK back telling the sender to send the packet that ends with 88009. The sender then sends it. And so on.

You can see an illustration of this here:

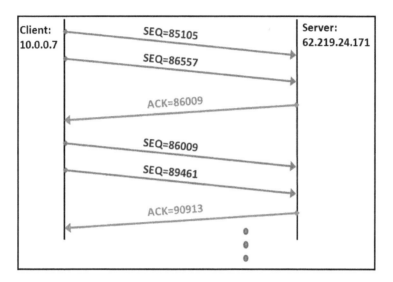

What are TCP retransmissions and what do they cause?

When a packet acknowledgment is lost or when an ACK does not arrive on time, the sender will perform two things:

- Send the packet again, as described earlier in this recipe
- Decrease the throughput

In the next screenshot, we see an example of retransmissions that reduces the sender throughput (thin red lines added for clarity):

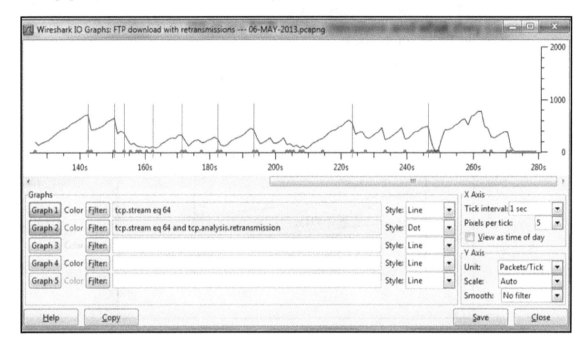

There's more...

TCP is tolerant to high delays as long as they are reasonably stable. The algorithm that defines the TCP behavior under delay variations (among other things) is called the **Van Jacobson** algorithm, after its inventor. The Van Jacobson algorithm enables tolerance of up to 3-4 times the average delay; so if, for example, you have a delay of 100 milliseconds, then TCP will be tolerant to delays of up to 300-400 milliseconds as long as they are not changed frequently.

See also

- You can check out the Van Jacobson algorithm at
  http://ee.lbl.gov/papers/congavoid.pdf

TCP sliding window mechanism

When the endpoints establish a TCP session, the Window size field in the TCP header will be used to signal the receiving buffer capacity and govern the amount of data that can be received and processed. Each endpoint will maintain a local **receive window** (**RWND**). This is the maximum amount of data the receiver can receive for buffering and processing. The endpoint will include this RWND value in the TCP header. The sender uses RWND as input to decide the Sliding window size. It can send TCP segments to a peer of size defined in the window size before waiting for an acknowledgment.

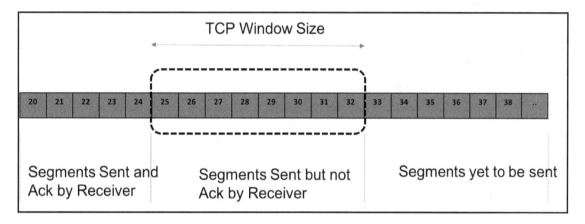

The sender endpoint maintains the sliding window by managing the number of outstanding TCP segments waiting for an acknowledgement. The sender slides the window towards the right as and when it receives the ACK for the segments it has sent and are waiting for acknowledgement.

Without the sliding window mechanism, the TCP sender will end up sending one segment at a time and wait for acknowledgement before sending the next segment causing a significant impact on the overall TCP throughput.

Getting ready

Connect the Wireshark on the server and capture the packets. It is lot easier to analyze the sliding window behavior by filtering the specific TCP stream. In order to follow a specific stream, choose the first TCP packet (SYN packet) of the stream to be analyzed, and perform the following:

1. Go to **Analyze**
2. Choose **Follow**
3. Choose **TCP Stream**

How to do it...

In the following topology, **PC1** is establishing a TCP session with **PC3** for data transfer.

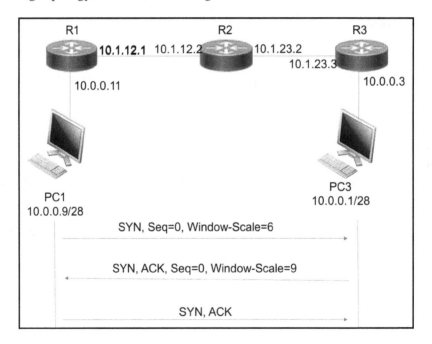

Check whether the TCP endpoints are exchanging the TCP window size with a value more than **0**. If the window size is set to **0**, the receiver is not capable of receiving any traffic and the data transfer will fail.

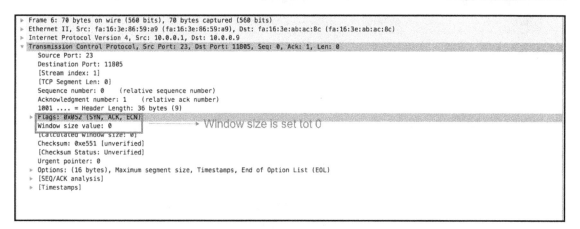

The preceding is an example of TCP zero window. The receiving node (10.0.0.9) is not capable of accepting any new sessions or data and so when it receives the SYN segment from any peer for a new TCP session, it replies with SYN, ACK segment and set the window size as 0. Normally, this condition will be rectified by itself once the receiver is ready to take additional data. When the receiver sends zero window message, it is normal to see the sender sending **TCP zero window probe**. This is a message sent by the sender to see whether the receiver's zero window condition is still true. For each response received from receiver for TCP zero window message, it exponentially increment the timer before sending the next probe message.

If the packet capture continuously shows that the receiver is sending with window size as 0, it may be an indication that the end server is not functioning properly, or that the incoming port buffer is full or stuck and may need additional analysis on the server side to fix any issue.

```
▶ Internet Protocol Version 4, Src: 10.0.0.1, Dst: 10.0.0.9
▼ Transmission Control Protocol, Src Port: 22, Dst Port: 44913, Seq: 0, Ack: 1, Len: 0
    Source Port: 22
    Destination Port: 44913
    [Stream index: 0]
    [TCP Segment Len: 0]
    Sequence number: 0    (relative sequence number)
    Acknowledgment number: 1    (relative ack number)
    1010 .... = Header Length: 40 bytes (10)
  ▶ Flags: 0x012 (SYN, ACK)
    Window size value: 28960
    [Calculated window size: 28960]    ──────────► Initial window size exchanged is 28960
    Checksum: 0x8bd1 [unverified]
    [Checksum Status: Unverified]
    Urgent pointer: 0
  ▼ Options: (20 bytes), Maximum segment size, SACK permitted, Timestamps, No-Operation (NOP), Window scale
    ▶ TCP Option — Maximum segment size: 1460 bytes
    ▶ TCP Option — SACK permitted
    ▶ TCP Option — Timestamps: TSval 1313603, TSecr 1316161
    ▶ TCP Option — No-Operation (NOP)
    ▼ TCP Option — Window scale: 9 (multiply by 512)    ──────────► Window scale is 9
        Kind: Window Scale (3)
        Length: 3
        Shift count: 9
        [Multiplier: 512]
  ▶ [SEQ/ACK analysis]
  ▶ [Timestamps]
```

Once the issue on the server is fixed, it should be able to negotiate the right window size. In the preceding example, 10.0.0.1 replies with a non-zero window size in the SYN, ACK segment. It could be noted that the server also included a TCP option carrying window scale of value 9. The TCP peer will use a combination of window size and window scale to identify the sliding window size. More details about the window scaling is in the *How it works...* section.

In all the subsequent packets, each peer will include the window size that will be used the peer to scale up or scale down the sliding window size.

How it works...

The TCP sliding window mechanism works as follows:

1. After the connection is established, the sender sends data to the receiver, filling the receiver window.
2. After several packets, the receiver sends an ACK to the sender, confirming the acceptance of the bytes sent by it. Sending the ACK empties the receiver window.
3. This process is continuous when the sender is filling the window, and the receiving party empties them and sends confirmation of the information.
4. Increasing the receiver window size tells the sender to increase the throughput, and decreasing it tells them to decrease the throughput. It works according to the following WS/RTT rule (with some changes according to the TCP version):

$$\text{Throughput [Bytes/Sec]} = \frac{\text{Window Size [Bytes]}}{\text{RTT [Sec]}}$$

✓ Throughput – the effective Bytes/Sec send by an application on a TCP connection
✓ Window Size – the TCP receiver window size
✓ RTT – the Round Trip Time between the sender and the receiver

The window size field in TCP header is represented in bytes and this field is a 16-bit field that allows carrying a maximum value of 65,535. With most of the hardware, it is possible to handle more than 65,535 bytes of TCP segments. In order to signal a window size of more than 65,535, the TCP Window scale is included during the initial TCP three-way handshake. TCP peer uses the Window size value and Scale value to derive the window size.

$$\text{Sliding Window [Bytes]} = \text{Window} * (2**\text{Scale})$$

For example, when the Window size is set to 457 and the scale value is set to 6, the Sliding window will be calculated as 29,248 bytes.

```
▶ Frame 5: 66 bytes on wire (528 bits), 66 bytes captured (528 bits)
▶ Ethernet II, Src: fa:16:3e:09:27:cf (fa:16:3e:09:27:cf), Dst: fa:16:3e:ef:a9:bb (fa:16:3e:ef:a9:bb)
▶ Internet Protocol Version 4, Src: 10.0.0.9, Dst: 10.0.0.1
▼ Transmission Control Protocol, Src Port: 44913, Dst Port: 22, Seq: 1, Ack: 1, Len: 0
     Source Port: 44913
     Destination Port: 22
     [Stream index: 0]
     [TCP Segment Len: 0]
     Sequence number: 1    (relative sequence number)
     Acknowledgment number: 1    (relative ack number)
     1000 .... = Header Length: 32 bytes (8)
   ▶ Flags: 0x010 (ACK)
     Window size value: 457
     [Calculated window size: 29248]
     [Window size scaling factor: 64]
     Checksum: 0x29f6 [unverified]
     [Checksum Status: Unverified]
     Urgent pointer: 0
   ▼ Options: (12 bytes), No-Operation (NOP), No-Operation (NOP), Timestamps
     ▶ TCP Option – No-Operation (NOP)
     ▶ TCP Option – No-Operation (NOP)
     ▶ TCP Option – Timestamps: TSval 1316162, TSecr 1313603
   ▶ [SEQ/ACK analysis]
   ▼ [Timestamps]
       [Time since first frame in this TCP stream: 0.003524000 seconds]
       [Time since previous frame in this TCP stream: 0.001398000 seconds]
```

Wireshark calculates the sliding window and displays it as highlighted in the preceding example.

TCP enhancements – selective ACK and timestamps

Various TCP enhancements have been introduced over a period of time to augment the TCP performance. In this section, we will discuss a couple of these important enhancements and see how Wireshark can be used to analyze the same.

Getting ready

When you observe that the TCP flow performance is degraded and is not working as expected, connect Wireshark to capture the TCP flow for analysis.

How to do it...

For backward compatibility, a feature enhancement like **selective ACK** (**SACK**) or TCP timestamp will be negotiated during the initial three-way handshake. The TCP endpoints will include the relevant TCP options in the SYN and SYN/ACK packets.

TCP selective acknowledgement option

TCP SACK is a TCP option that will be included in the SYN and SYN/ACK segments. When the TCP endpoints are enabled with TCP SACK feature, the endpoint signal the capability to peer by including the same in SYN packet.

```
▶ Frame 7: 74 bytes on wire (592 bits), 74 bytes captured (592 bits)
▶ Ethernet II, Src: fa:16:3e:ab:ac:8c (fa:16:3e:ab:ac:8c), Dst: fa:16:3e:86:59:a9 (fa:16:3e:86:59:a9)
▶ Internet Protocol Version 4, Src: 10.0.128.1, Dst: 192.168.0.7
▼ Transmission Control Protocol, Src Port: 25617, Dst Port: 23, Seq: 0, Len: 0
    Source Port: 25617
    Destination Port: 23
    [Stream index: 2]
    [TCP Segment Len: 0]
    Sequence number: 0    (relative sequence number)
    Acknowledgment number: 0
    1010 .... = Header Length: 40 bytes (10)
  ▶ Flags: 0x0c2 (SYN, ECN, CWR)
    Window size value: 4128
    [Calculated window size: 4128]
    Checksum: 0x2358 [unverified]
    [Checksum Status: Unverified]
    Urgent pointer: 0
  ▼ Options: (20 bytes), Maximum segment size, SACK permitted, No-Operation (NOP), No-Operation (NOP), Timestamps, End of Option List (EOL)
    ▶ TCP Option - Maximum segment size: 536 bytes
    ▼ TCP Option - SACK permitted
        Kind: SACK Permitted (4)
        Length: 2
    ▶ TCP Option - No-Operation (NOP)
    ▶ TCP Option - No-Operation (NOP)
    ▼ TCP Option - Timestamps: TSval 112797030, TSecr 0
        Kind: Time Stamp Option (8)
        Length: 10
        Timestamp value: 112797030
        Timestamp echo reply: 0
    ▶ TCP Option - End of Option List (EOL)
  ▼ [Timestamps]
      [Time since first frame in this TCP stream: 0.000000000 seconds]
      [Time since previous frame in this TCP stream: 0.000000000 seconds]
```

As seen in the preceding example, TCP SACK option will be seen in SYN and SYN/ACK segments. If this TCP option is not seen in the capture, ensure that the feature is enabled on the TCP endpoints. Depending on the vendor and platform, this feature may be enabled by default.

```
▶ Frame 101: 78 bytes on wire (624 bits), 78 bytes captured (624 bits)
▶ Ethernet II, Src: fa:16:3e:ab:ac:8c (fa:16:3e:ab:ac:8c), Dst: fa:16:3e:86:59:a9 (fa:16:3e:86:59:a9)
▶ Internet Protocol Version 4, Src: 10.0.128.1, Dst: 192.168.0.7
▼ Transmission Control Protocol, Src Port: 25617, Dst Port: 23, Seq: 57, Ack: 3321, Len: 0
      Source Port: 25617
      Destination Port: 23
      [Stream index: 2]
      [TCP Segment Len: 0]
      Sequence number: 57      (relative sequence number)
      Acknowledgment number: 3321    (relative ack number)
      1011 .... = Header Length: 44 bytes (11)
   ▶ Flags: 0x010 (ACK)
      Window size value: 4128
      [Calculated window size: 66048]
      [Window size scaling factor: -2 (no window scaling used)]
      Checksum: 0x1a8f [unverified]
      [Checksum Status: Unverified]
      Urgent pointer: 0
   ▼ Options: (24 bytes), SACK, No-Operation (NOP), No-Operation (NOP), Timestamps, End of Option List (EOL)
      ┌─────────────────────────────────────────┐
      │▼ TCP Option - SACK 3845-4369            │
      │    Kind: SACK (5)                       │
      │    Length: 10                           │
      │    left edge = 3845 (relative)          │
      │    right edge = 4369 (relative)         │
      │    [TCP SACK Count: 1]                   │
      └─────────────────────────────────────────┘
      ▶ TCP Option - No-Operation (NOP)
      ▶ TCP Option - No-Operation (NOP)
      ▶ TCP Option - Timestamps: TSval 112808766, TSecr 0
      ▶ TCP Option - End of Option List (EOL)
   ▶ [SEQ/ACK analysis]
   ▶ [Timestamps]
```

When the receiver wants to selectively acknowledge some of the segments, it includes the relevant sequence number in the SACK option. In the preceding example, the receiver acknowledges that it is expecting the segment with sequence number 3321. But it also includes SACK with sequence number 3845 to 4369 in the same segment. For more details on how SACK works, please check out the *How it works...* section.

TCP timestamp option

As like TCP SACK, TCP timestamp is a TCP option that will be included in the SYN and SYN/ACK segments. When the TCP endpoints are enabled with RTT measurement feature, the endpoints signal the capability of including TCP timestamp to peer by in SYN packet. When both the endpoints support this feature, the sender will include the TCP timestamp option in all the segments forwarded to peer.

```
▶ Frame 7: 74 bytes on wire (592 bits), 74 bytes captured (592 bits)
▶ Ethernet II, Src: fa:16:3e:ab:ac:8c (fa:16:3e:ab:ac:8c), Dst: fa:16:3e:86:59:a9 (fa:16:3e:86:59:a9)
▶ Internet Protocol Version 4, Src: 10.0.128.1, Dst: 192.168.0.7
▼ Transmission Control Protocol, Src Port: 25617, Dst Port: 23, Seq: 0, Len: 0
    Source Port: 25617
    Destination Port: 23
    [Stream index: 2]
    [TCP Segment Len: 0]
    Sequence number: 0    (relative sequence number)
    Acknowledgment number: 0
    1010 .... = Header Length: 40 bytes (10)
  ▶ Flags: 0x0c2 (SYN, ECN, CWR)
    Window size value: 4128
    [Calculated window size: 4128]
    Checksum: 0x2350 [unverified]
    [Checksum Status: Unverified]
    Urgent pointer: 0
  ▼ Options: (20 bytes), Maximum segment size, SACK permitted, No-Operation (NOP), No-Operation (NOP), Timestamps, End of Option List (EOL)
    ▶ TCP Option - Maximum segment size: 536 bytes
    ▼ TCP Option - SACK permitted
        Kind: SACK Permitted (4)
        Length: 2
    ▶ TCP Option - No-Operation (NOP)
    ▶ TCP Option - No-Operation (NOP)
    ▼ TCP Option - Timestamps: TSval 112797030, TSecr 0
        Kind: Time Stamp Option (8)
        Length: 10
        Timestamp value: 112797030
        Timestamp echo reply: 0
    ▶ TCP Option - End of Option List (EOL)
  ▼ [Timestamps]
      [Time since first frame in this TCP stream: 0.000000000 seconds]
      [Time since previous frame in this TCP stream: 0.000000000 seconds]
```

As seen in the preceding example, the TCP timestamp option will be seen in SYN and SYN/ACK segments. If this TCP option is not seen in the capture, ensure that the feature is enabled on the TCP endpoints. Depending on the vendor and platform, this feature may be enabled by default.

As shown in the preceding screenshot, the sender will include the local time in **TSval** field while sending the segment out. The sender will include a zero value in **timestamp echo reply (TSecr)**.

```
▶ Frame 144: 78 bytes on wire (624 bits), 78 bytes captured (624 bits)
▶ Ethernet II, Src: fa:16:3e:ab:ac:8c (fa:16:3e:ab:ac:8c), Dst: fa:16:3e:86:59:a9 (fa:16:3e:86:59:a9)
▶ Internet Protocol Version 4, Src: 10.0.128.1, Dst: 192.168.0.7
▼ Transmission Control Protocol, Src Port: 25617, Dst Port: 23, Seq: 57, Ack: 7498, Len: 0
    Source Port: 25617
    Destination Port: 23
    [Stream index: 2]
    [TCP Segment Len: 0]
    Sequence number: 57    (relative sequence number)
    Acknowledgment number: 7498    (relative ack number)
    1011 .... = Header Length: 44 bytes (11)
  ▶ Flags: 0x010 (ACK)
    Window size value: 3966
    [Calculated window size: 63456]
    [Window size scaling factor: -2 (no window scaling used)]
    Checksum: 0x8880 [unverified]
    [Checksum Status: Unverified]
    Urgent pointer: 0
  ▼ Options: (24 bytes), SACK, No-Operation (NOP), No-Operation (NOP), Timestamps, End of Option List (EOL)
    ▶ TCP Option - SACK 7528-7536
    ▶ TCP Option - No-Operation (NOP)
    ▶ TCP Option - No-Operation (NOP)
    ▼ TCP Option - Timestamps: TSval 112816072, TSecr 112804954
        Kind: Time Stamp Option (8)
        Length: 10
        Timestamp value: 112816072
        Timestamp echo reply: 112804954
    ▶ TCP Option - End of Option List (EOL)
  ▶ [SEQ/ACK analysis]
  ▶ [Timestamps]
```

The receiver should include TSecr only in the Ack packet. As shown in the preceding example, the receiver is replying with TSecr and TSval included. The sender will use the combination of these two to derive the RTT value. More details about the feature are available in *How it works...* section.

How it works...

TCP selective acknowledgement

In the previous sections, we discussed how the TCP sequence number and acknowledgment number help provide reliability to the end application. But the default acknowledgement and the retransmission behavior are not throughput efficient due to the nature of TCP requiring to retransmit all the segments from the missing segment within the sliding window. The following is an illustration that helps us understand the default behavior better.

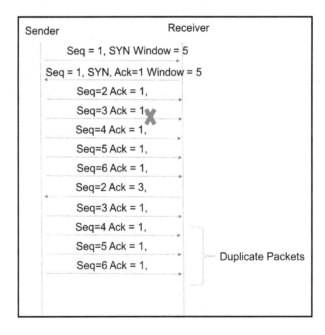

For illustration, we are using a TCP session with window size of five segments. Based on the window size, the Sender can send five segments before waiting for the acknowledgement. Accordingly, it sends five segments with *seq=2,3,4,5,6*. Receiver had received the segments with *seq=2,4,5,6*, but it didn't receive the segment with *seq=3*. While sending the ACK, the receiver sends with *ack=3*. As noted before, the ender will not only retransmit segment with *seq=3*, but also the remaining segments in the window.

This leads to retransmitting duplicate segments, causing throughput issues.

Selective acknowledgement solves this issue by allowing the receiver to selectively acknowledge non-contiguous segments. TCP SACK is a TCP option that will be negotiated during the initial TCP three-way handshake.

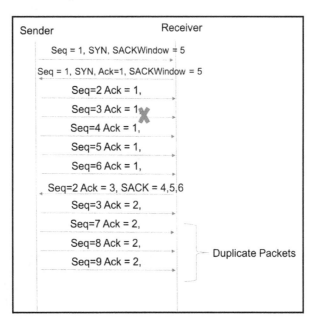

In the same example, the sender and receiver are enabled with TCP SACK. Please note that, TCP SACK will be included in the SYN segment to signal the capability to peer. Using the same example, when the receiver didn't receive segment with *seq=3*, it sends ACK segment with *ack=3*, but it also includes selective ACK for 4,5,6. This instructs the sender to just send the missing segments and not to retransmit other received segments. This avoids duplication and helps provide efficient throughput.

TCP timestamp

There are certain end applications that benefits from continuous **round trip time (RTT)** measurement. RTT measurement is performed by leveraging the TCP timestamp options. A TCP timestamp option will be included in all the segments. This option carries two fields as TSval and TSecr. The the sender will include local time when the segment is sent out in TSval field and TSecr will be set to 0. The receiver upon acknowledging a segment will include local time in the TSval and include the TSval from the last received segment from the sender.

The sender will use the combination of TSval and TSecr in the ACK segment to compute the RTT. For efficiency, most implementation will perform RTT measurement in one or two segments in each window instead of performing it on a per segment basis.

There's more...

While the preceding section discusses about a couple of TCP options, there are more such options serving different purpose. The following are few of the options:

- TCP authentication
- Maximum segment size
- TCP compression filter
- Multipath TCP

Troubleshooting TCP throughput

There are various tools available in the industry to perform network throughput measurement that are more out-of-band in nature. Such tools establish test TCP sessions and the monitor performs. While such tools are useful, the performance calculation is done on the production traffic. SLA constrained end applications using TCP as transport protocol requires a mechanism to ensure that the TCP stream achieves the desired throughput. In order to confirm the same, we need a simple and efficient mechanism to measure the throughput on a per TCP stream basis. This can be used for various purposes including performance benchmarking, SLA based service assurance, and so on.

There are numerous reasons that might impact the performance of TCP throughput some of which are discussed in the previous sections such as retransmission, session reset. In this section, we will discuss about how to use Wireshark to perform TCP throughput measurement and analysis.

Getting ready

In order to perform throughput measurement, the first thing you must do is capture the stream. You can perform the capture on the end server (if it supports) or on the transit path. As mentioned in the previous sections, use the relevant filter to display only the TCP stream to be measured.

How to do it...

1. Check the throughput of the TCP flow that is being measured. This is done by filtering the respective TCP stream and then check the IO graph for throughput. The following are the steps to view the throughput graph.
2. Go to **Statistics** and select **IO Graph.**
3. Now create a new graph with `tcp.stream == <stream number>` filter.
4. A sample is shown as follows:

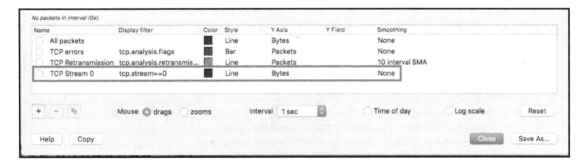

5. If the throughput shown in the output is as expected, we can conclude that the stream is working fine. If the throughput is not as expected, we need additional analysis as follows.
6. Check whether the window size is negotiated to a larger size. If the RWND is less, it might result in lower throughput as sender will wait for acknowledgment for segments within the sliding window.

7. Get the expert information for the TCP stream and check the count of different errors and warnings. This helps understand the possible reason for the throughput. For more details about Expert Info, please read `Chapter 6`, *Using Advanced Statistics Tools*.

Severity	Summary	Group	Protocol	Cour
▶ Error	Malformed Packet (Exception occurred)	Malformed	SSH	4
▶ Warning	Previous segment(s) not captured (common at capture start)	Sequence	TCP	173
▶ Note	This frame is a (suspected) retransmission	Sequence	TCP	209
▶ Note	This frame is a (suspected) spurious retransmission	Sequence	TCP	1
▶ Note	Duplicate ACK (#1)	Sequence	TCP	143
▶ Note	Duplicate ACK (#2)	Sequence	TCP	101
▶ Note	Duplicate ACK (#3)	Sequence	TCP	66
▶ Note	Duplicate ACK (#4)	Sequence	TCP	32
▶ Note	Duplicate ACK (#5)	Sequence	TCP	24
▶ Note	Duplicate ACK (#6)	Sequence	TCP	20
▶ Note	Duplicate ACK (#7)	Sequence	TCP	19
▶ Note	Duplicate ACK (#8)	Sequence	TCP	16
▶ Note	Duplicate ACK (#9)	Sequence	TCP	13
▶ Note	Duplicate ACK (#10)	Sequence	TCP	12
▶ Note	Duplicate ACK (#11)	Sequence	TCP	12
▶ Note	Duplicate ACK (#12)	Sequence	TCP	12
▶ Note	Duplicate ACK (#13)	Sequence	TCP	12
▶ Note	Duplicate ACK (#14)	Sequence	TCP	12
▶ Note	Duplicate ACK (#15)	Sequence	TCP	12
▶ Note	Duplicate ACK (#16)	Sequence	TCP	12
▶ Note	Duplicate ACK (#17)	Sequence	TCP	12
▶ Note	Duplicate ACK (#18)	Sequence	TCP	12
▶ Note	Duplicate ACK (#19)	Sequence	TCP	12
▶ Note	Duplicate ACK (#20)	Sequence	TCP	12
▶ Note	Duplicate ACK (#21)	Sequence	TCP	12
▶ Note	Duplicate ACK (#22)	Sequence	TCP	12
▶ Note	Duplicate ACK (#23)	Sequence	TCP	12
▶ Note	Duplicate ACK (#24)	Sequence	TCP	12
▶ Note	Duplicate ACK (#25)	Sequence	TCP	12
▶ Note	Duplicate ACK (#26)	Sequence	TCP	12
▼ Note	Duplicate ACK (#27)	Sequence	TCP	12

```
425   [TCP Dup ACK 363#27] 44913 → 22 [ACK] Seq=2724 Ack=22...
871   [TCP Dup ACK 772#27] 44913 → 22 [ACK] Seq=2832 Ack=50...
1204  [TCP Dup ACK 1146#27] 44913 → 22 [ACK] Seq=2904 Ack=7...
```

8. In the preceding figure, it could be noted that there are 173 instances of missing segments and multiple instances of duplicates. Expert Information will help us provide with errors such as out-of-order segments, connection reset, zero window.

9. If there are numerous instances of [TCP Retransmission] missing segments, there might be some packet loss in the network. Use the network connectivity check tools such as ping to validate the health of the underlay network. Alternately, capturing the stream on multiple capturing point in the network will help narrow down the dropping node.

```
 99 12.475560    192.168.0.5      192.168.0.7       TCP     590 [TCP Out-Of-Order] 23 → 24090 [ACK] Seq=3289 Ack=57 Win=999936 Len=524
100 12.476192    192.168.0.7      192.168.0.5       TCP      66 [TCP Dup ACK 97#1] 24090 → 23 [ACK] Seq=57 Ack=3289 Win=999472 Len=0
102 14.807786    192.168.0.5      192.168.0.7       TCP     590 [TCP Retransmission] 23 → 24090 [ACK] Seq=3289 Ack=57 Win=999936 Len=524
103 14.809273    192.168.0.7      192.168.0.5       TCP      66 24090 → 23 [ACK] Seq=57 Ack=4337 Win=999472 Len=0
```

10. If there are numerous instances of out-of-order packet, the packets belonging to the same stream might be taking different path with different delay/jitter. Ideally, all nodes along the path will perform load balancing at a flow level so that all packets that belong to same flow will always follow the same path. In scenarios involving link flap (intermittent or continuous) or any legacy node performing per-packet load balancing may result in such out-of-order packets.

11. If there are numerous instances of TCP window full errors, the receiving node is not capable of handling the packet at rate sent by the sender. If the issue is seen consistently, careful tweaking of RWND on the receiving side might be required.

12. Some of the TCP enhancements like higher RWND size, selective ACK, fast retransmission can be enabled on the endpoints to improve the overall throughput.

How it works...

There is no specific working mechanism for TCP throughput. TCP throughput is an outcome of various TCP features enabled on the endpoints. How such different features work is already covered in different *How it works...* sections under the TCP topic.

12
FTP, HTTP/1, and HTTP/2

In this chapter, we'll cover the following topics:

- Analyzing FTP problems
- Filtering HTTP traffic
- Configuring HTTP preferences
- Analyzing HTTP problems
- Exporting HTTP objects
- HTTP flow analysis
- Analyzing HTTPS traffic – SSL/TLS basics

Introduction

FTP is a protocol created for transferring files over TCP/IP across a network. It is a protocol that runs over TCP ports 20 and 21 for the data and control connections respectively.

HTTP and HTTPS are both used for browsing the internet, or connecting to other software that are hosted inside your organization or in the cloud. HTTPS is used when we secure HTTP with SSL/TLS in order to protect the clear text data exchange from intrusion and hacking. It is used when connecting to your bank, mail account (for example, Gmail), or any other secured application.

Starting from 1991, HTTP has gone through different revisions, such as versions 0.9, 1.0, 1.1, and the latest, 2.0, published in 2015.

In this chapter, we will discuss these protocols, how they work, and how to use Wireshark to find common errors and problems in the network.

Analyzing FTP problems

FTP has two modes of operation:

- **Active mode (ACTV)**: In this mode, the client initiates a control connection to the server, and the server initiates a data connection to the client
- **Passive mode (PASV)**: In this mode, the client initiates both the control and data connections to the server

Both types of connections can be implemented, and they will be explained later in this recipe, in the *How it works...* section.

Getting ready

When working with FTP, if you suspect any connectivity or slow response problems, configure port mirror to one of the following:

- The FTP server port
- The client port
- A link that the traffic crosses

If required, configure a capture or display filter.

How to do it...

To check FTP performance problems, follow these steps:

1. First, check for any Ethernet, IP, or TCP problems as described in previous chapters. In many cases, slow responses happen due to networking problems and not necessarily due to application problems. Perform simple ICMP ping (with a larger packet size, say 1,500 bytes) between the client and server, as it helps to find if there is any delay or failures along the path.
2. Check for TCP retransmissions and duplicate ACKs. Check whether they are on the entire traffic or only on the FTP connection:
    - If you get it on various connections, it is probably due to a slow network that influences the entire traffic
    - If you get it only on FTP connections to the same server or client, it can be due to a slow server or client

3. When you are copying a single file in an FTP file transfer, you should get a straight line in the I/O graph and a straight gradient in the TCP stream graph (time sequence).

4. In this screenshot, we can see what a bad FTP looks like in the TCP stream graph (time sequence):

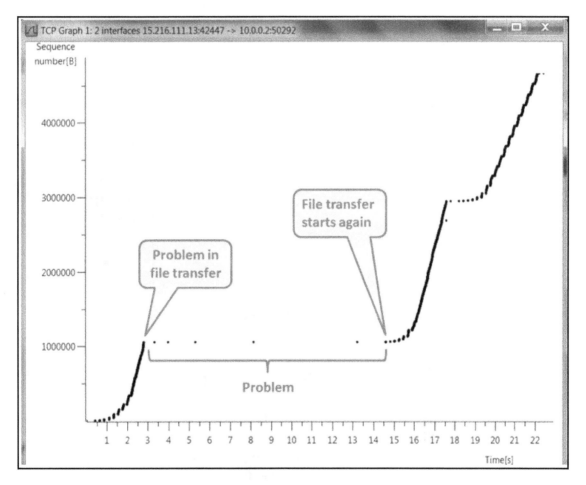

Figure 12.1: Failing FTP—TCP stream graph

5. In the following screenshot, we can see what it looks like in the I/O graph (configured with filters):

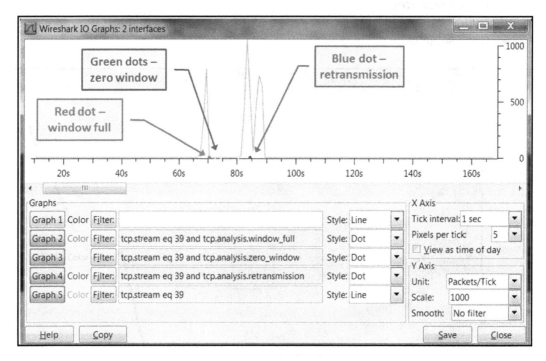

Figure 12.2: Failing FTP—I/O graphs

6. In the capture file shown in the following screenshot, we can see TCP window problems. These are listed as follows:

- The server 15.216.111.13 sends a **TCP Window Full** message to the client, indicating that the server send window is full (packet 5763).

- The client 10.0.0.2 sends a **TCP Zero Window** message to the server, telling the server to stop sending data (packet 5778).

- The server keeps sending **TCP Zero Window Probe** messages to the client, asking the client whether the condition is still zero window (this tells the server not to send any more data). The client answers these messages with **TCP Zero Window Probe Ack**, indicating that this is still the case (packets 5793 to 5931).

- After a while, the client sends the message **TCP Window Update** to the server, telling it to start increasing the FTP throughput (packet 5939).

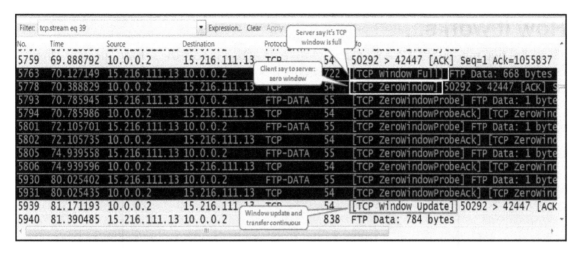

Figure 12.3: Failing FTP—slow client

7. In the preceding case, it was simply a slow client. We solved the problem by working over it and deleting some unnecessary processes.

If you are facing connectivity problems, it could be due to a non-functioning server, a firewall that blocks the connection on the way, or software installed on the server or client that blocks it. In this case, go through the following steps:

1. Was the TCP connection opened properly with the SYN/SYN-ACK/ACK packets? If not, it could be due to the following:
   - The firewall that blocks communications. Check with the system administrator.
   - The server that is not running. Check this on the server in the process table, FTP server management, and so on.
   - A software of the server blocks connectivity. It can be an antivirus that has an additional firewall that blocks connections, VPN client, or any other security or protection software.
   - Check the connectivity on the client, too. It could be that it is blocked by a VPN client, a firewall on the client, and so on.

2. In the active mode, the client opens connection to the server that opens another connection. Make sure that the firewalls on the way support it, or use passive mode.

How it works...

There are two modes of FTP: active and passive. In active mode, the server opens another connection to the client, while in passive mode, it is the client that opens the second connection to the server. Let's see how it works.

In passive mode, the operations are as shown in the following diagram:

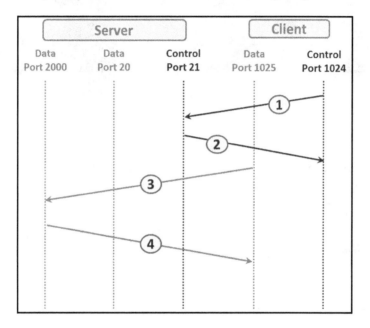

Figure 12.4: FTP passive mode steps

These are described here:

1. The client opens a control connection from a random port *P* (1024 in the example) to server port 21

2. The server answers back from port 21 to the client port 1024

3. Now, the client opens a data connection from the port *P+1* (1025 in the example) to a data port that the server has opened and notified the client about (port 2000 in the example)

4. The server answers from the data port (2000 in the example) to the client port that initiated the connection, that is, the data port *P+1* (1025 in the example)

In active mode, the operation is slightly different:

1. The client opens a control connection from a random port *P* (1024 in the example) to server port 21
2. The server answers from port 21 to client port 1024
3. The server opens the data connection from port 20 to the client port *P+1* (1025 in the example)
4. The client answers from the data port *P+1* (1025 in the example) to server port 20

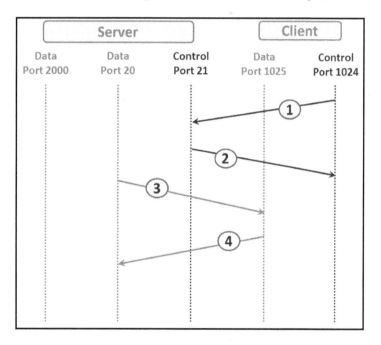

Figure 12.5: FTP active mode steps

There's more...

FTP is a very simple application, and in most of the cases, FTP problems have very simple solutions. Some examples are as follows:

- **Problem 1**: I've monitored an international connection with FTP clients on one side of the network and an FTP server on the other side. The customer complained about slow performance and blamed the international service provider. When I checking with the service provider, they said the connection is nearly not loaded (usage of only 20 percent of a 10 Mbps line), a fact that I confirmed when I checked the line. When I looked at the TCP issues (retransmissions, window problems, and so on), there were none. Just to check, I removed the FTP server and install another one (there are many free ones), and it started to work. It was a simple problem of an inefficient FTP server.
- **Problem 2**: A customer complained that when connecting to an FTP server, the connection was refused after every five or six attempt. When I checked it with Wireshark, I saw that the FTP connection refused messages (and I already knew about this from the customer's complaint), so it looked like a dead end. Just to check, I started to stop the services running on the server, and the problem came out. It was an antivirus software that was interfering with this specific FTP server.

> The bottom line is: even with Wireshark (and other software), sometimes common sense will help you more.

Filtering HTTP traffic

There are many filters that can be configured for HTTP. In this recipe, let's concentrate on the display filters that are mostly used in this context.

Getting ready

Configure port mirror as described in previous recipes, and take a quick look at Chapter 3, *Using Capture Filters*.

How to do it...

To configure HTTP filters, you can write the filter expression directly in the display window bar; open the expression window and choose the HTTP parameters by right-clicking on the required parameter in the packet pane (as described in `Chapter 4`, *Using Display Filters*).

There are various filters that can be configured on HTTP.

Name-based filters are as follows:

- **Requests to a specific website**: `http.host == "www.packtpub.com"`
- **Requests to websites containing the word PacktPub**: `http.host contains "packt.pub"`
- **Requests that were forwarded from PacktPub**: `http.referer == http://www.packtpub.com/`

Request methods filters are as follows:

- **All GET requests**: `http.request.method == GET`
- **All HTTP requests**: `http.request`
- **All HTTP responses**: `http.response`
- **All HTTP requests that are not GET**: `http.request and not http.request.method == GET`

Error codes filters:

- **HTTP error responses (code 4xx for client errors, code 5xx for server errors)**: `http.response.code >= 400`
- **HTTP client error responses**: `http.response.code >= 400` and `http.response.code <= 499`
- **HTTP server error responses**: `http.response.code >= 500` and `http.response.code <= 599`
- **HTTP response code 404 (not found)**: `http.response.code == 404`

When you configure a simple filter such as `http.host == packtpub`, you don't need to close it in the `""` characters. If you need a more complex string such as `packtpubrn` or a string of several words, then you will need to close it in `""`, for example, `"http.host == packtpubrn"`.

How it works...

Let's see some details on HTTP.

HTTP methods

The main HTTP requests methods were published in RFCs 2616. There are additional HTTP methods that were standardized over the years. Additional methods were added later by updates to RFC 2616 (2817, 5785, 6266, and 6585) and additional standards (RFC 2518, 3252, 5789).

These are the basic methods as described in RFC 2616:

- OPTIONS: This is used for client request to determine the capabilities of a web server.
- GET: This is used when we request a URL.
- HEAD: This is like GET, but the server should not return a message body in the response.
- POST: This is used to send data to the server. For example, when using webmail, it will be used to send email commands.
- DELETE: This is used to request the server to delete a resource identified by the request URI.
- PUT: This is used to request that the enclosed entity be stored under the request URI attached to the request.
- TRACE: This is used to request a remote, application layer loopback of the request message.
- CONNECT: This is used to connect to a proxy device.

Status codes

These are the categories of message codes that are standardized by HTTP:

Category	Name	Reason
1xx	Informational	Provides general information, without any indication of failure or success
2xx	Success	Indicates that the action requested by the client was received, accepted, and processed successfully

3xx	Redirection	Indicates that further action should be taken by the user agent to fulfill the request
4xx	Client error	Indicates an error on the client side
5xx	Server error	Indicates an error on the server side

Table 12.6: HTTP status codes

A full list of HTTP status codes can be found at `http://www.iana.org/assignments/http-status-codes/http-status-codes.xhtml`.

There's more...

In some cases, you will see a line called `Line-based text data: text/html` under the HTTP line in the packet details pane. It is shown in the following screenshot:

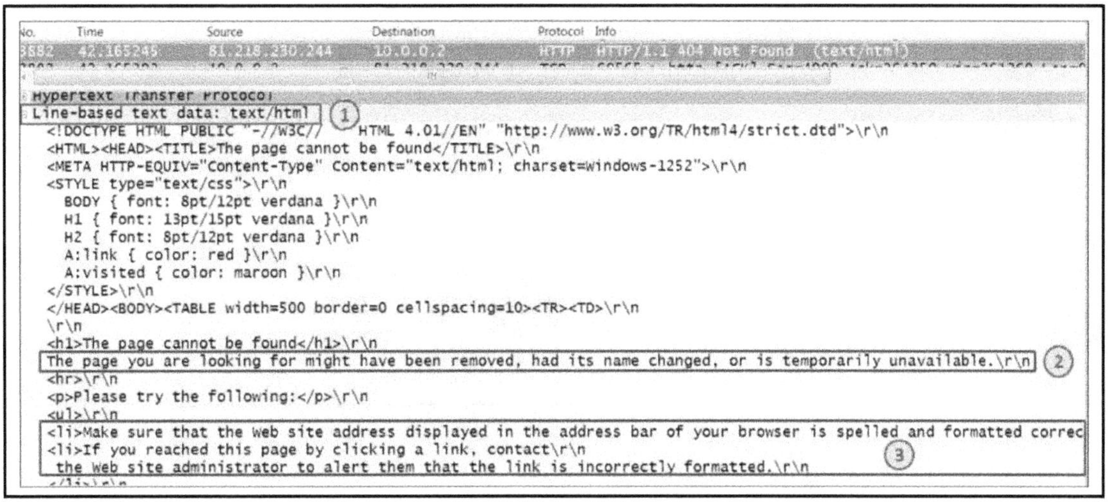

Figure 12.7: HTTP error and explanation

You will see the line-based text data right beneath to the HTTP line in the packet details pane (marked as **1** in the preceding screenshot). Below this, you will see some explanations (marked as **2** and **3** in the preceding screenshot) for what could be the reason for the error.

Configuring HTTP preferences

There are some preferences that you can change when working with HTTP. Let's see what they are.

Getting ready

Start Wireshark and go to the next section.

How to do it...

1. Choose **Edit | Preferences**.
2. Under **Protocols**, select **HTTP**. You will see the following window:

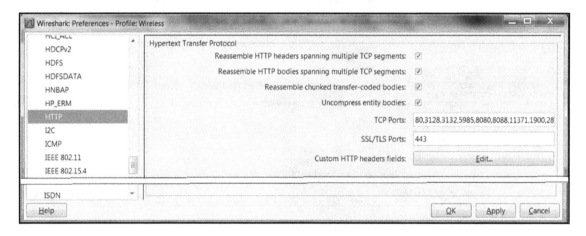

Figure 12.8: HTTP preferences

By default, all the four options are checked. These are options that reassemble the HTTP headers and bodies when fragmentation is performed on the lower layers. In the **TCP Ports** field, you will get a list of the port numbers that Wireshark will dissect as HTTP. In this list, you see the default port 80, ports 8080 and 8088 (usually used for proxies), and others. If you have an application working with HTTP with a port that is not listed, add it here. Do the same with HTTPS **SSL/TLS Ports**—the default is 443. If you use another port, add it here. Port 80 is listed as the port for **Stream Control Transmission Protocol (SCTP)**

Custom HTTP headers fields

Custom HTTP headers fields enable us to create a new HTTP display filters under the `http.header` filter.

Let's look at the example in the following screenshot:

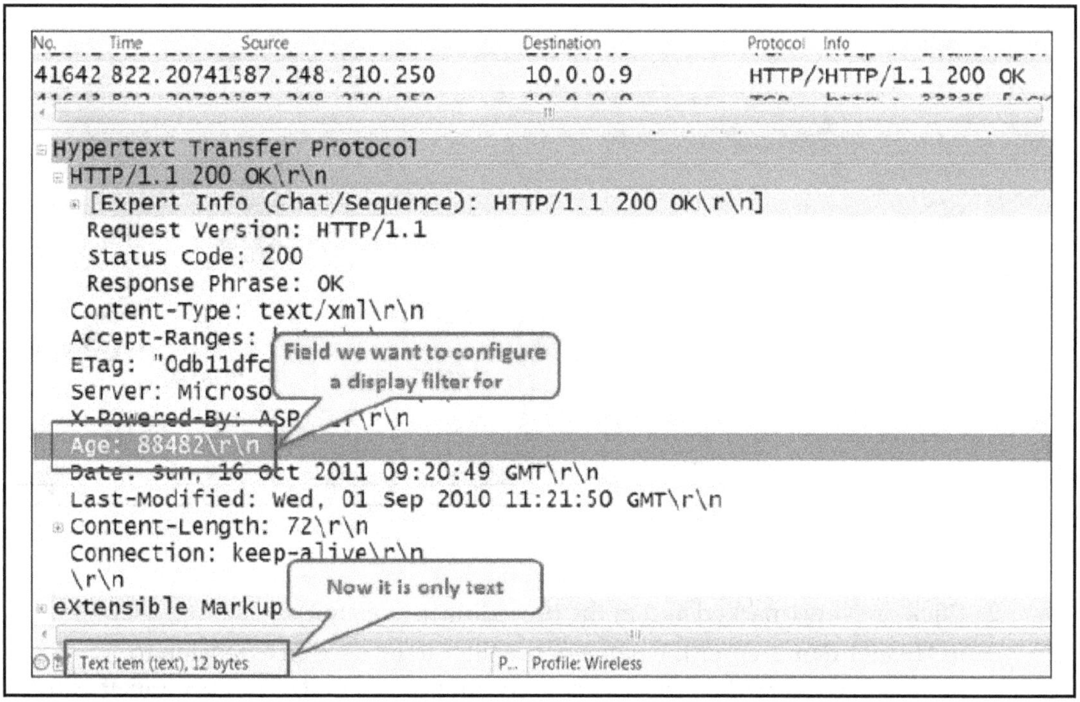

Figure 12.9: HTTP headers—age

To create a new HTTP display filter under the http.header filter, perform the following steps:

1. In the HTTP preferences window (marked as **1** in the following screenshot), click on the **Edit...** button in **Custom HTTP headers fields**.

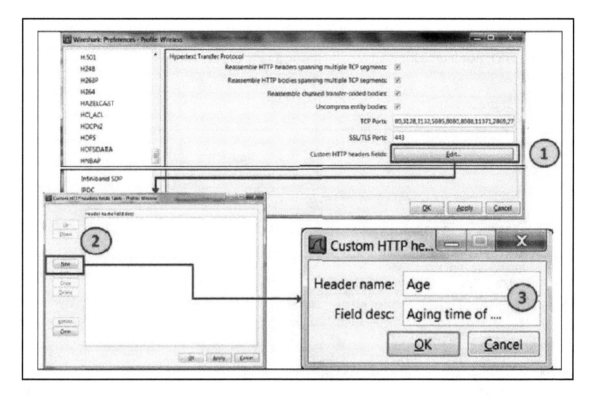

Figure 12.10: HTTP customer headers fields

2. Click on **New** (marked as **2** in the preceding screenshot).

3. In **Header name**, enter the name of the filter to be used in extension to `http.header` (marked as **3** in the preceding screenshot). For example, if you want to configure a filter on the age parameter, type the name `Age` in the **Header name** field (case sensitive!).

4. In the **Field desc** field, type any description that will remind you what you have configured. For example, type `Aging time of ....` (any description will do, it is just a note).

5. Click on **OK**.

6. In the **Display Filter** textbox, you will be able to use the `http.header.Age` filter. For example, you will be able to configure the display filter `http.header.Age` that contains 88482 that will give you all the packets with the `Age` field that contains the requested number

7. You can configure many additional filters with this option.

This filter configuration is mostly used when you are using proprietary parameters in the HTTP header, and you want to filter accordingly.

How it works...

The reassembly feature is important because there are some cases in which IP fragmentation is used, and therefore the TCP message is also segmented. Marking the reassembly options simply tells Wireshark to reassemble the monitored packets (what the receiver side is doing and is therefore able to understand it).

There's more...

Usually Wireshark shows dissected packets with port 80 as HTTP only if it sees a valid HTTP header. If you want to see all packets with TCP port 80 as HTTP, perform the following steps:

1. Go to **Preferences** and choose **TCP** in **Protocols**
2. Uncheck/disable **Allow dissector to reassemble TCP streams**

Analyzing HTTP problems

The bottom line is, of course, how to analyze the HTTP problems. This is what this recipe is all about. HTTP problems can happen because of a slow server and/or client, TCP performance issues, and some other reasons that we will see in this recipe.

Getting ready

When you experience bad performance while browsing the Internet, connect the Wireshark with port mirror to the PC that experiences the problem. When it is the whole network that suffers from bad performance, port-mirror the main connection to the Internet or the web server infrastructure.

How to do it...

There can be various reasons for a slow browsing problem, and we'll try to figure it out step-by-step.

The steps are given as follows:

1. First, check that you don't simply have a loaded line to the Internet or core connections in the network, high error rate on the communications line, or any of these obvious issues that cause most of the problems (see `Chapter 5`, *Using Basic Statistics Tools* chapter and `Chapter 6`, *Using Advanced Statistics Tools* for further details).

2. To negate a TCP issue (as explained in detail in `Chapter 11`, *Transport Layer Protocol Analysis*), check the following details:
   - In the expert info window, you don't get too many retransmissions and duplicate ACKs (< 1% is still tolerable).
   - Make sure that you don't get resets on the HTTP connections. It might be due to firewalls or site restrictions.

3. Make sure that you don't get the following DNS problems:
   - Slow response time
   - Names are not found, not correct, and so on

4. If none of these apply, well! Let's dig in to HTTP.

 Don't forget to look at the network and IT environment as a whole. You cannot separate TCP from HTTP, or DNS problems from the slow browsing of applications. It could be that you have a very slow HTTP server; and because of its slow responses, you will get TCP retransmissions. Or, because of the slow DNS server, you will get a web page that opens after many seconds. Just go step by step and isolate the problems.

When you open a web page for the first time, it can take a few seconds. In this case, you should check the following conditions:

- Check whether the line is not loaded.
- Check the delay on the line (a ping to the website will do the job).
- Look for error codes. Usually you will see the reason for the error on the browser, but not always.

- Configure the filter `http.response >= 400` and see how many errors you get. In the following sections, we see several examples of what you should pay attention to.

Code	Status	Explanation
100	Continue	Request completed successfully and the session can continue.
101	Switching protocols	The server is changing to a different HTTP version. It will be followed by an upgrade header.

Table 12.1: HTTP informational codes

Code	Status	Explanation
200	OK	Standard OK response
201	Created	The request has been fulfilled and a new resource has been created
202	Accepted	The request was accepted and is still in process
203	Non-authoritative information	The request was received with content from another server, and it was understood
204	No content	The request was received and understood, and the answer that is sent back has no content
205	Reset content	This is a server request to the client to reset the data that was sent to it
206	Partial content	Response for a partial document request

Table 12.2: HTTP success codes

Code	Status	Explanation	What to do
300	Multiple choices	The requested address refers to more than one file. It can happen, for example, when the resource has been removed, and the response provides a list of potential locations for it.	-

301	Moved permanently	The requested resource has been moved permanently. Future requests should be forwarded to the attached URI.	-
302	Moved temporarily (found)	Page has been moved temporarily, and the new URL is available. Usually, you will be automatically forwarded.	Usually, you will see a found code, and then another GET to the URL indicated
303	See other	The response to the request can be found in a different URI. It should be retrieved using an HTTP GET to that resource.	-
304	Not modified	When a request header includes an if modified since parameter, this code will be returned if the file has not changed since that date.	-
305	Use proxy	The requested resource must be accessed through a proxy.	Check what proxy is required

Table 12.3: HTTP redirect codes

Code	Status	Explanation	What to do
400	Bad request	The request could not be understood by the server due to a syntax problem. The request should be modified by the client before resending to it.	Check the website address. This can also happen due to a site error.
401	Authorization required	The client is denied access due to the lack of authentication codes.	Check your username and password.
402	Payment required	Reserved for future use.	

403	Forbidden	The client is not allowed to see a specific file. This can be due to the server access limit.	Check the credentials. Also, there are fewer chances that the server is loaded.
404	Not found	The requested resource could not be found.	This can be because the resource was deleted, or it never existed. It can also be due to URL misspellings.
405	Method not allowed	The method you are using to access the file is not supported or not allowed by the resource.	
406	Not acceptable	Content generated by the resource is not acceptable according to the client request.	Check/update your browser.
407	Proxy authentication required	Request authentication is required before it can be performed.	The client must first authenticate itself with the proxy.
408	Request timed out	It took the server longer than the allowed time to process the request.	Check the response time and load on the network.
409	Conflict	The request submitted by the client cannot be completed because it conflicts with some established rules.	Can be because you try to upload a file that is older that the existing one or problems alike. Check what the client is trying to do.
410	Gone	The URL requested by the client is no longer available from that system.	Usually, this is a server problem. It can be due to a file that was deleted or location was forwarded to a new location.
411	Content length required	The request is missing its content length header.	Compatibility issue on a website. Change/update your browser.

412	Precondition failed	The client has not set up a configuration that is required for the file to be delivered.	Compatibility issue on a website. Change/update your browser.
413	Request entity too long	The requested file was too big to process.	Server limitation.
414	Request URI too long	The address you entered was overly long for the server.	Server limitation.
415	Unsupported media type	The file type of the request is not supported.	Server limitation.

Table 12.4: HTTP client error codes

A simple example for a client error is presented in following screenshot. To get to this window, perform the following steps:

1. Right-click on the packet with the error code.
2. Choose **Follow TCP stream**. You should get the following window:

```
}
GET /poker-client/broadcast.htm HTTP/1.1   (1)
Accept: image/gif, image/jpeg, image/pjpeg, image/pjpeg, application/x-shockwave-flash, application/
x-ms-application, application/x-ms-xbap, application/vnd.ms-xpsdocument, application/xaml+xml,
application/vnd.ms-excel, application/vnd.ms-powerpoint, application/msword, */*
Referer: http://www.888poker.com/poker-client/promotions.htm   (2)
Accept-Language: en-us
Accept-Encoding: gzip, deflate
User-Agent: Mozilla/4.0 (compatible; MSIE 7.0; Windows NT 5.1; Trident/4.0; GTB7.1; Mozilla/4.0
(compatible; MSIE 6.0; Windows NT 5.1; SV1) ; .NET CLR 1.1.4322; .NET CLR 2.0.50727;
OfficeLiveConnector.1.3; OfficeLivePatch.0.0; .NET CLR 3.0.4506.2152; .NET CLR 3.5.30729;
InfoPath.1)
Host: www.888poker.com   (3)

HTTP/1.1 404 Not Found   (4)
Date: Sun, 16 Oct 2011 09:11:58 GMT
Server: Microsoft-IIS/6.0
srv: 2344432
```

Figure 12.11: Sample client error

You can see the following conditions:

- I tried to browse the URI `/poker-client/broadcast.htm`(marked as **1** and **3** in the preceding screenshot)
- The URI was forwarded by the referrer: `http://www.888poker.com/poker-client/promotions.htm` (marked as **2** in the preceding screenshot)
- The status code was **404 Not Found** (marked as **4** in the preceding screenshot)

Just to clear things, I was not playing poker. I was working on a networking problem.

Code	Status	Explanation	What to do
500	`Internal server error`	The web server encountered an unexpected condition that prevented it from carrying out the client request for access to the requested URL.	Response that is usually caused by a problem in your Perl code when a CGI program is run.
501	`Not implemented`	The request cannot be executed by the server.	A server problem.
502	`Bad gateway`	The server you're trying to reach is sending back errors.	A server problem.
503	`Service unavailable`	The service or file that is being requested is not currently available.	A server problem.
504	`Gateway timeout`	The gateway has timed out. This message is like the `408` timeout error, but this one occurs at the gateway of the server.	Server is down or non-responsive.
505	`HTTP version not supported`	The HTTP protocol version that you want to use for communicating with the server is not supported by it.	Server does not support the HTTP version.

Table 12.5: HTTP server error codes

You can get the service unavailable status (code 503) due to various reasons. In the following example, there is a small office that has the following complaint: they can browse Facebook, but the moment they click on a link on this site, they get the new page as blocked. In the following screenshot, you can see that the problem was simply a firewall that blocked it (obviously):

Figure 12.12: HTTP service unavailable: firewall blocks

How it works...

In standard HTTP browsing, you should see a very simple pattern, as follows:

- TCP opens the connection (three-way handshake)
- HTTP sends a GET command
- Data is downloaded to your browser

In most of the cases, opening a web page will open multiple connections, and in many cases, tens of them. For example, when you open a news page (www.cnn.com, www.foxnews.com, and www.bbc.co.uk), it opens the main page, bar rolling breaking news, commercials, window reporting local weather, connections to other sites, and so on. Don't be surprised if a single page will open nearly hundred connections, or even more.

In the case of a web page that opens multiple connections (as most web pages do), each connection requires a DNS query, response, TCP SYN-SYN/ACK-ACK, and HTTP GET; only then will the data start to appear on your screen.

There's more...

When you don't see anything in the packet details pane, right-click on a packet and choose **Follow TCP stream**. This will give you a detailed window (as shown in the preceding screenshot), which provides you with a lot of data for the connection.

Another tool that is widely used for HTTP is Fiddler. It can be found at `http://fiddler2.com/`. Fiddler is a free tool that is intended for HTTP debugging. It is not in the scope of this book.

Exporting HTTP objects

Exporting HTTP objects is a simple feature for exporting HTTP statistics, websites and files accessed by HTTP.

Getting ready

To export HTTP objects, choose **File** | **Export Objects** | **HTTP**.

How to do it...

To export HTTP objects, follow these steps:

1. You can use this feature when capture is running, or you can save the captured file. You will get the following window:

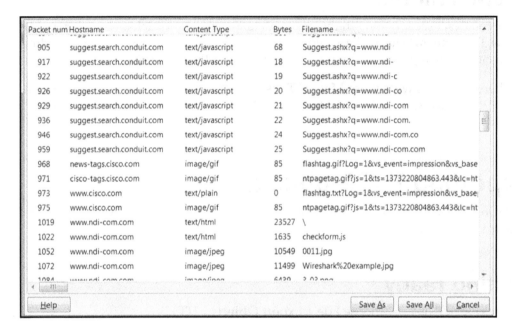

Packet num	Hostname	Content Type	Bytes	Filename
905	suggest.search.conduit.com	text/javascript	68	Suggest.ashx?q=www.ndi
917	suggest.search.conduit.com	text/javascript	18	Suggest.ashx?q=www.ndi-
922	suggest.search.conduit.com	text/javascript	19	Suggest.ashx?q=www.ndi-c
926	suggest.search.conduit.com	text/javascript	20	Suggest.ashx?q=www.ndi-co
929	suggest.search.conduit.com	text/javascript	21	Suggest.ashx?q=www.ndi-com
936	suggest.search.conduit.com	text/javascript	22	Suggest.ashx?q=www.ndi-com.
946	suggest.search.conduit.com	text/javascript	24	Suggest.ashx?q=www.ndi-com.co
959	suggest.search.conduit.com	text/javascript	25	Suggest.ashx?q=www.ndi-com.com
968	news-tags.cisco.com	image/gif	85	flashtag.gif?Log=1&vs_event=impression&vs_base
971	cisco-tags.cisco.com	image/gif	85	ntpagetag.gif?js=1&ts=1373220804863.443&lc=ht
973	www.cisco.com	text/plain	0	flashtag.txt?Log=1&vs_event=impression&vs_base
975	www.cisco.com	image/gif	85	ntpagetag.gif?js=1&ts=1373220804863.443&lc=ht
1019	www.ndi-com.com	text/html	23527	\
1022	www.ndi-com.com	text/html	1635	checkform.js
1052	www.ndi-com.com	image/jpeg	10549	0011.jpg
1072	www.ndi-com.com	image/jpeg	11499	Wireshark%20example.jpg
1084	www.ndi-com.com	image/jpeg	6420	2_02.png

Help   Save As   Save All   Cancel

Figure 12.13: HTTP object export

2. From here you can get a list of the websites that were accessed, including the files that were accessed in each one of them. You can see the website, file types, size, and names.
3. You can use the **Save As** or **Save All** buttons for saving the data in a file.
4. In the **Content Type** column, you will see the following contents:
   - Text: **text/plain**, **text/html**, **text/javascript**. If it's a JavaScript, check what is it; it might be a security risk.
   - Images: **image/jpeg**, **image/gif**, and other types of images. You can open it with a viewer.
   - Applications: **application/json**, **application/javascript**, and other types of applications.
   - Any other file of text discovered by Wireshark.

For the export HTTP objects feature to work, first go to TCP preferences and enable TCP packets reassembly (allow subdissector to reassemble TCP streams).

You will get a directory with all the objects captured in the capture file. Objects can be pictures (for example, packet `1052` and `1057` in the preceding screenshot), text (packets `1019`, `1022`, and others in the preceding screenshot), and others.

How it works...

This feature scans HTTP streams in the currently opened capture file or the running capture; takes reassembled objects such as HTML documents, image files, executable files, and other readable formats; and lets you save them to a disk. The saved objects can then be opened with the proper viewer, or they can be executed in the case of executable files just by clicking on them. This feature can be helpful for various purposes, including eavesdropping and saving objects for backup (for example, files that were sent through e-mails).

There's more...

You have several pieces of software that perform the same things graphically and provide visualization of statistics; some of them are as follows:

- Xplico: `http://www.xplico.org/`
- NetworkMiner: `http://www.netresec.com/?page=NetworkMiner`

When you see an unknown website with an application that you don't know and a filename that looks suspicious, Google it; it might be a risk (we will get back to this in the security chapter).

HTTP flow analysis

The follow TCP stream feature, discussed in brief earlier in the book, is a very helpful feature that can help you with an in-depth understanding of the TCP flows that are captured when you monitor the network. In this recipe, we will see some of its advantages.

Getting ready

Port-mirror the device or link you want to monitor and start packet capture.

How to do it...

To open the **Follow TCP Stream** window, perform the following steps:

1. Right-click on one of the packets in the stream you want to view.
2. The stream you choose is filtered by the Wireshark. You will see this in the display filter bar that will show you the number of stream in the capture. You will see the following window:

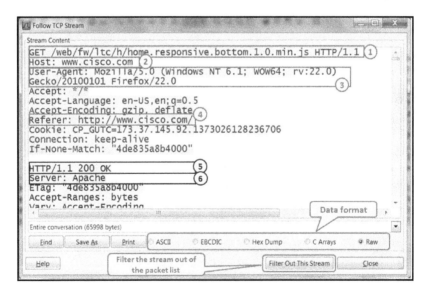

Figure 12.14: Follow TCP stream

3. You can see the stream details, for example:
    - The GET method (marked as **1** in the preceding screenshot)
    - The requested HOST(marked as **2** in the preceding screenshot)
    - The client type, Mozilla Firefox in this case (marked as **3** in the preceding screenshot)
    - The referrer, Cisco in this case (**4** in the screenshot)
    - The HTTP **OK** response (**5** in the screenshot)
    - The server type (**6** in the screenshot)

4. These are obvious examples. When having problems, or just issues to investigate, you will be able to see many types of parameters here that will indicate the following cases:
    - A user is using a Kazza client (as shown in the following screenshot) for file sharing (is it allowed in your organization?).

Figure 12.15: Follow TCP stream—parameters

- In the following screenshot, you can see a software bug. A quick Google search shows that it is an historical one, but other bugs can also be found in this way.

Figure 12.16: Follow TCP stream—more info

5. You can also check for the following:
   - Error and bugs messages
     - Viruses and worms. Names such as blast, probe, and Xprobe, especially when you see them with a `.exe` extension, should ring a big warning bell (more details about this issue will be provided in `Chapter 19`, *Security and Network Forensics*)

How it works...

The follow TCP stream feature simply analyzes the TCP data from the first SYN-SYN/ACK/ACK handshake to the end of the connection, which is indicated by RST of the FIN packets. It also isolates the specific stream, helping us to follow the errors and problems in it.

There's more...

There are many problems that can be found and allocated using the follow TCP stream feature, and it will be discussed further in the next chapters. Use this feature to isolate a TCP stream.

Analyzing HTTPS traffic – SSL/TLS basics

HTTPS is a secure version of the HTTP. The *S* means that it is secured by Secure Socket Layer (SSL)/Transport Layer Security (TLS). It is used when you connect to your bank account, Webmail service, or any other service that runs over HTTP and requires security.

In this recipe, we will see how it works and what can fail when we are using HTTPS communications.

Getting ready

Port-mirror to the suspected device or link that forwards traffic from several devices, and start the capture. HTTPS works with TCP port 443, and this is what you should watch, unless you have a custom application that uses different ports, as discussed in the *Configuring HTTP preferences* recipe.

How to do it...

To monitor HTTPS sessions, perform the following steps:

1. HTTPS session establishment can be done in four or five steps. It is described in the *How it works...* section of this recipe.

2. Watch the order of the packet in the session establishment, and make sure the messages you get are according to the order shown in the following diagram (in brackets, you'll see what should be shown in the packet):

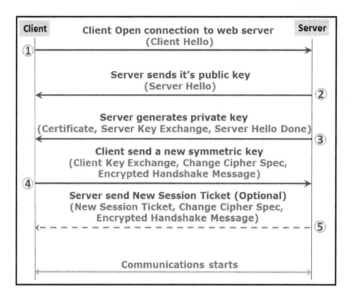

Figure 12.17: HTTPS secure connection establishment

3. Followings are the common alerts (and their levels) described in RFC 2246. Alert levels indicate the severity of the messages, and messages with a level of fatal result in termination of the session.

- `close_notify (Alert level = 0)`: This message notifies the recipient that the sender has finished sending messages on this connection. The session can be resumed later.

- `unexpected_message (10)`: This alert is returned if an inappropriate message was received. This is a critical error that can indicate a bad implementation on one of the sides.

- `bad_record_mac (20)`: This alert is returned if a record is received with incorrect **Message Authentication Code** (**MAC**). This is a critical error that can indicate a bad implementation on one of the sides.

- `decryption_failed (21)`: This alert is returned if a TLS ciphertext was decrypted in a wrong way. This is a critical message that can indicate a bad implementation on one of the sides.

- record_overflow (22): This alert is returned if a TLS ciphertext record was received with a length longer than allowed length. This is a fatal error, and it usually indicates a bad implementation on one of the sides.
- decompression_failure (30): This message indicates that a decompression function received a wrong input. This is a critical error that can indicate a bad implementation on one of the sides.
- handshake_failure (40): Reception of this alert message indicates a negotiation error that occurred when the sender was unable to negotiate the set of security parameters, given the options available. This is a critical error that can indicate a bad implementation on one of the sides.
- bad_certificate (42): This is a certificate error. It occurs when a certificate is corrupt, contains signatures that were not verified correctly, or any other error.
- unsupported_certificate (43): This indicates that the received certificate was not of the supported type.
- certificate_revoked (44): This indicates that a certificate was canceled by its signer.
- certificate_expired (45): This indicates an invalid certificate or a certificate that has expired.
- certificate_unknown (46): This indicates that a certificate was not accepted due to unspecified reason.
- illegal_parameter (47): This tells that a field in the handshake process was out of range or inconsistent with other fields. This is a critical error that can indicate a bad implementation on one of the sides.
- unknown_ca (48): This indicates that a valid certificate was received, but was not accepted because it couldn't be matched with a known, trusted CA. This is a critical error and should be checked with the certificate issuer.
- access_denied (49): This tells that a valid certificate was received, but it was not approved by the access control of the receiver, and the sender decided not to proceed with negotiation.
- decode_error (50): This tells that a message was too long and, therefore, could not be decoded. This is a critical error that can indicate a bad implementation on one of the sides.

- `decrypt_error` (51): This indicates that a handshake cryptographic operation failed, including the ones that failed due to signature verification, key exchange, or validation of a finished message.
- `export_restriction` (60): This tells that a negotiation which is not compliance with export restrictions was detected.
- `protocol_version` (70): Tells that the protocol version which the client has attempted to negotiate is not supported.
- `insufficient_security` (71): This is returned when a negotiation has failed because the server required ciphers with higher security than those supported by the client.
- `internal_error` (80): This is an internal error not related to the peer of the connection.
- `user_canceled` (90): This tells that the handshake was canceled for a reason other than a protocol failure.
- `no_renegotiation` (100): This is sent by the client or the server in response to a hello request after the initial handshaking.

In each one of the failures mentioned, the connection will not be established.

How it works...

SSL and TLS are protocols that secure a specific application, for example, HTTP, SMTP, Telnet, and others. SSL Versions 1, 2, and 3 were developed by Netscape in the mid 1990s for their Navigator browser, while TLS is a standard from the IETF (RFC 2246, RFC 4492, RFC 5246, RFC 6176, and others). TLS 1.0 was first introduced in RFC 2246 in January 1999 as an upgrade of the SSL Version 3.0 (third paragraph at `http://tools.ietf.org/html/rfc2246`).

The TLS handshake protocol involves the following procedures for establishing a TLS connection:

1. Exchange hello messages to agree on the algorithms to work with, and exchange random values for the key generation
2. Exchange the necessary cryptographic parameters to allow the client and the server to agree on a pre-master secret key
3. Exchange certificates and cryptographic information to allow the client and server to authenticate each other

4. Generate a master secret key from the pre-master secret and exchanged random values

5. Allow the client and server to verify that their peer has calculated the same security parameters and that the handshake occurred without being tampered by an attacker

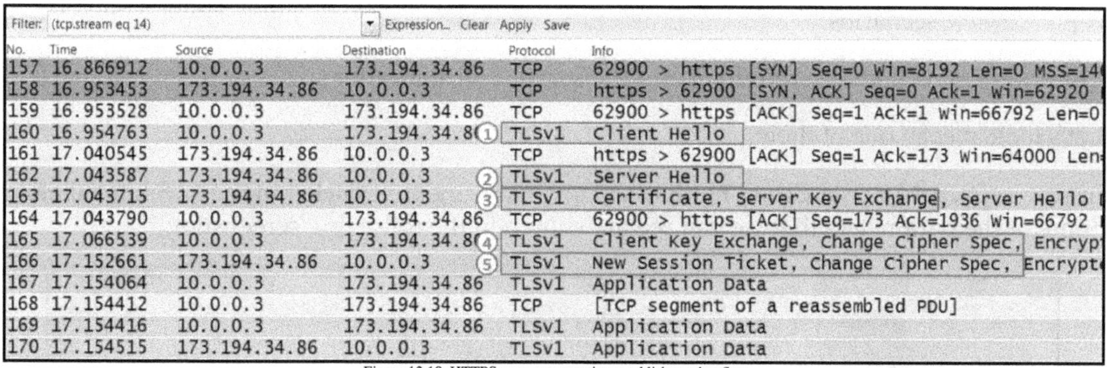

Figure 12.18: HTTPS secure connection establish: packet flow

Let's see how it works. In the preceding screenshot, we see how TCP SSL/TLS establishes a connection (packets 157-158-159) and packet 160 starts the TLS handshake. Let's see the details:

1. Select cryptographic algorithms:
   - As seen in packet 160, the client sends a **Client Hello** message that starts the negotiation (**1**)
   - The server responds with a **Server Hello** message (**2**), as seen in packet 162

2. As seen in packet 163, the server sends a certificate to the client (**3**)

3. With this certificate, the client authenticates the server, takes the certificate, and generates the pre-master key (**4**), as in packet 165

4. The server generates master key (**5**), as in packet 166

5. The handshake between the server and client completes and the transactions begin, as you can see in packet 167 onward

This refers to a mechanism (defined in RFC 4507) that enables the TLS server to resume sessions and avoid keeping the per-client session state. The TLS server encapsulates the session state into a ticket and forwards it to the client. The client can subsequently resume a session using the obtained ticket. This happens, for example, when you reopen a connection to your Webmail account (Gmail and so on) and is common to these scenarios.

Communication between the client and the server will start after step 4 or 5.

Let's look at each one of them:

In step 1, packet 160 is a **Client Hello** message that is the first packet in the TLS handshake. Some of the parameters that we can see are shown in the following screenshot:

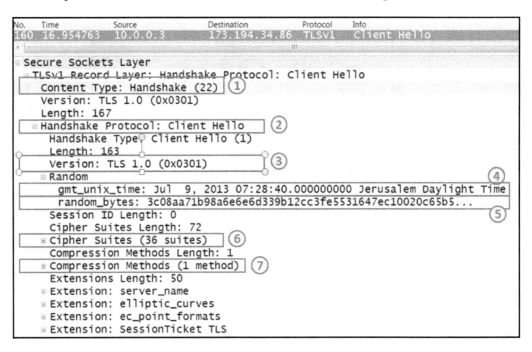

Figure 12.19: HTTPS client hello

These parameters are explained here:

- The area highlighted as **1** shows that the content of the packet is a handshake (ssl.record.content_type == 22).
- The area highlighted as **2** shows that the packet is a **Client Hello** message sent from the client to the web server. This message starts the handshake.
- The area highlighted as **3** shows the highest SSL and TLS version supported by the client.
- Area **4** shows the client time that will be used in the key generation process.
- The area highlighted as **5** shows the random data that is generated by the client for use in the key generation process.
- Area **6** shows the ciphers supported by the client. The ciphers are listed in order of preference.
- The area highlighted as **7** shows the data compression methods that are supported by the client.

As shown in the following screenshot, packet 162 is a **Server Hello** message, which includes the following details:

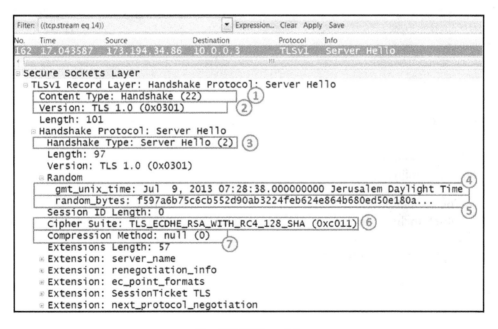

Figure 12.20: HTTPS server hello

These details are explained here:

- The area highlighted as **1** shows that the content of the packet is a handshake (`ssl.record.content_type == 22`).
- The area highlighted as **2** shows the TLS version that will be used in this session.
- Area **3** shows that the packet is a **Server Hello** message sent from the server to the client.
- Area **4** shows the server time used in the key generation process.
- The area highlighted as **5** shows the random data that is generated by the server for use in the key generation process.
- The area highlighted as **6** shows the cipher suite to be used in this conversation. It is chosen from the list of ciphers sent by the client.
- The area highlighted as **7** shows the data compression method that will be used for the session.

The next packet is the response from the server issuing a certificate:

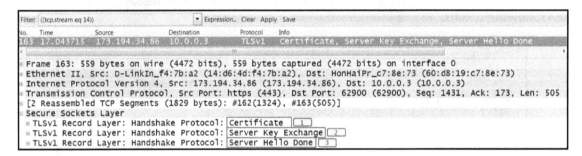

Figure 12.21: HTTPS server certificate

It is explained as follows:

- The area highlighted as **1** shows that the server sends the **Certificate** command, which includes the server's certificate. By clicking on the (+) sign on the left of this line and digging in to the details, you will see the certificate issuer, validity time, algorithm, and other data.

- Area **2** shows that the server sends the **Server Key Exchange** command (usually Diffie-Hellman), including the required parameters (public key, signature, and so on).
- The area highlighted as **3** shows that the server sends the **Server Hello Done** command. This command indicates that the server has completed this phase of the SSL handshake. The next step is the client authentication.

The next packet (packet 165 in this example) is the response from the client, accepting the certificate and generating a pre-master key.

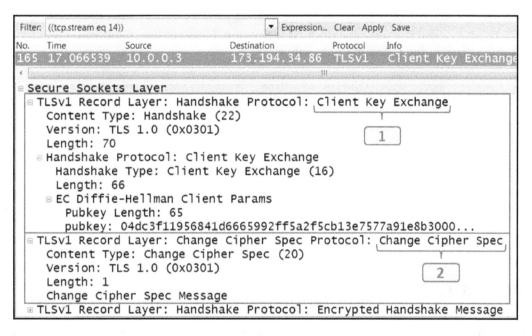

Figure 12.22: HTTPS client pre-master key

It is explained as follows:

- The area marked as **1** shows that the client sends the **Client Key Exchange** command. This command contains the pre-master secret that was created by the client and was then encrypted using the server's public key. The symmetric encryption keys are generated by the client and the server, based on the data exchanged in the client and server hello messages.
- The area marked as **2** shows that the client sends the **Change Cipher Spec** notification to the server. This is done in order to indicate that the client will start using the new session keys for hashing and encryption.

The last step is when the server sends a **New Session Ticket** to the client, and it will look like the example in the following screenshot:

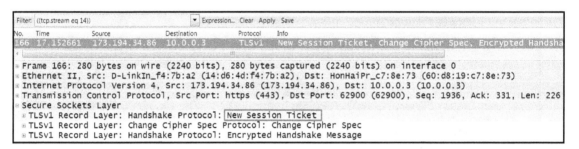

Figure 12.23: HTTPS server new session ticket

There's more...

I've been asked several times whether it is possible to decrypt sessions that are encrypted with SSL/TLS. Well, it's possible if you have the private key, which is provided to you by the server you connect to; and to get it is not an easy thing to do.

There are methods to hijack this key, and in some cases they will work. It is not an obvious thing to do, and in any case it is not the goal of this book. If you get the private key, you simply add it in the protocol list in the preferences window and continue from there. Additional details about this feature can be obtained from `http://wiki.wireshark.org/SSL`, as well as from many other websites and blogs.

13
DNS Protocol Analysis

This chapter covers the following topics:

- Analyzing DNS record types
- Analyzing regular DNS operations
- Analyzing DNSSEC regular operations
- Troubleshooting DNS performance

Introduction

DNS is a name resolution protocol that is used to resolve domain names to IP addresses. The internet is nothing more than a collection of network domains connected together with unique IP addresses as the identifier. It is not practically possible to remember each domain or the device based on an IP address. Instead, it is lot easier to remember the domains using names, and use some dynamic way of converting the names to an IP address.

DNS is a distributed client/server-based communication model. DNS is an application layer protocol where the client will send a DNS query carrying the domain name to the server, which in turn will respond with a DNS response for the respective IP address associated with the domain name. DNS runs on UDP port number 53. The server will maintain a database with a unique domain name and the associated IP addresses. The database can maintain the domain name or the hostnames within the domain. The functionality of converting the domain names to an IP address is known as DNS lookup.

The DNS domain name space is hierarchical in nature, that is, it is subdivided into different domains that makes it flexible and scalable. The DNS hierarchy comprises the following components:

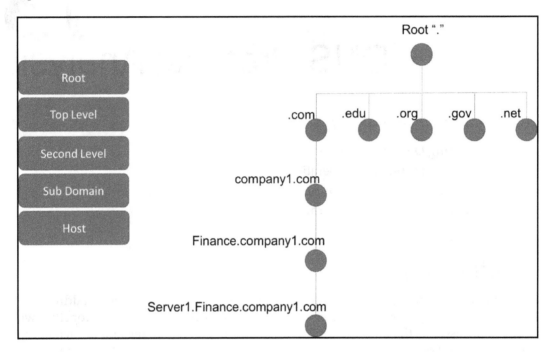

Figure 13.1: DNS hierarchy

In this chapter, we will discuss the basic principles of the DNS protocol, the functionality, commonly faced issues, and the use of Wireshark to analyze and troubleshoot the protocol.

Analyzing DNS record types

The DNS database is a collective set of DNS records, where each record is an entry in the database comprising a label, class, type, and data with instructions about how to handle the request for the respective record. While there are a lot of record types available for solving different purposes, a few of the commonly encountered record types are A record, AAAA record, and CNAME.

In this recipe, we will discuss various common DNS record types and see how Wireshark can be used to analyze the associated behavior and issues.

Getting ready

To analyze the types of DNS records, we need to capture the DNS query and response packets. In order to do so, connect Wireshark to the path between the client and the DNS server and capture the packets.

How to do it...

In the previous diagram, trigger a DNS query from the client to the name server and capture the DNS query packet for record type analysis. The DNS query can be triggered from the client using different mechanisms, which may vary depending on the configuration, software version, vendor platform, and so on of the client. The following are few examples that we could use to trigger the query from the client:

- Open a web browser on the client and type a URL, such as `www.packtpub.com`.
- Open a terminal and trigger a ping to a known domain name. In Ubuntu and other Linux distributions, `ping xyz.com` will trigger a DNS query to resolve an IPv4 address while `ping6 xyz.com` will trigger a DNS query to resolve an IPv6 address of the domain.

- Use a tool such as dig, a CLI-based tool that can be used to trigger a DNS query for different types of DNS records.

```
▶ Frame 30: 90 bytes on wire (720 bits), 90 bytes captured (720 bits)
▶ Ethernet II, Src: fa:16:3e:cd:a9:38 (fa:16:3e:cd:a9:38), Dst: fa:16:3e:08:9d:85 (fa:16:3e:08:9d:85)
▶ Internet Protocol Version 4, Src: 10.0.128.1, Dst: 192.168.0.7
▶ User Datagram Protocol, Src Port: 28629, Dst Port: 53
▼ Domain Name System (query)
    [Response In: 31]
    Transaction ID: 0x5288
  ▼ Flags: 0x0100 Standard query
      0... .... .... .... = Response: Message is a query
      .000 0... .... .... = Opcode: Standard query (0)
      .... ..0. .... .... = Truncated: Message is not truncated       ──────────▶DNS Query
      .... ...1 .... .... = Recursion desired: Do query recursively                Packet
      .... .... .0.. .... = Z: reserved (0)
      .... .... ...0 .... = Non-authenticated data: Unacceptable
    Questions: 1
    Answer RRs: 0
    Authority RRs: 0
    Additional RRs: 1
  ▼ Queries
    ▼ csr2v6.company1.com: type AAAA, class IN
        Name: csr2v6.company1.com
        [Name Length: 19]                                            ──────────▶Record type is AAAA
        [Label Count: 3]
        Type: AAAA (IPv6 Address) (28)
        Class: IN (0x0001)
  ▼ Additional records
    ▼ <Root>: type OPT
        Name: <Root>
        Type: OPT (41)
        UDP payload size: 4096
        Higher bits in extended RCODE: 0x00
        EDNS0 version: 0
      ▼ Z: 0x0000
          0... .... .... .... = DO bit: Cannot handle DNSSEC security RRs
          .000 0000 0000 0000 = Reserved: 0x0000
        Data length: 0
```

Figure 13.2: DNS query

The preceding screenshot is a sample capture of a DNS query that was triggered for an AAAA record type. The query type will be set to DNS standard query. Any query must carry the domain name for which the record should be resolved and the type of record requested.

```
▶ Frame 31: 118 bytes on wire (944 bits), 118 bytes captured (944 bits)
▶ Ethernet II, Src: fa:16:3e:08:9d:85 (fa:16:3e:08:9d:85), Dst: fa:16:3e:cd:a9:38 (fa:16:3e:cd:a9:38)
▶ Internet Protocol Version 4, Src: 192.168.0.7, Dst: 10.0.128.1
▼ User Datagram Protocol, Src Port: 53, Dst Port: 28629
      Source Port: 53
      Destination Port: 28629
      Length: 84
      Checksum: 0xd5af [unverified]
      [Checksum Status: Unverified]
      [Stream index: 0]
▼ Domain Name System (response)
      [Request In: 30]
      [Time: 0.001555000 seconds]
      Transaction ID: 0x5288
   ▶ Flags: 0x8580 Standard query response, No error    ────────▶ DNS Response
      Questions: 1
      Answer RRs: 1
      Authority RRs: 0
      Additional RRs: 1
   ▼ Queries
      ▼ csr2v6.company1.com: type AAAA, class IN
            Name: csr2v6.company1.com
            [Name Length: 19]
            [Label Count: 3]
            Type: AAAA (IPv6 Address) (28)
            Class: IN (0x0001)
   ▼ Answers
      ▼ csr2v6.company1.com: type AAAA, class IN, addr 2001:2222::2
            Name: csr2v6.company1.com
            Type: AAAA (IPv6 Address) (28)
            Class: IN (0x0001)
            Time to live: 10
            Data length: 16
            AAAA Address: 2001:2222::2
   ▶ Additional records
```

Figure 13.3: DNS response

The preceding screenshot is the sample capture of the DNS response for the query in *Figure 13.2*. For ease of analysis, Wireshark highlights the packet number of the DNS query in the DNS response packet. The preceding is the response that carries AAAA record response for the domain name that was requested by the client.

For each DNS query requesting any record type, there must be a response for the respective record from the server. If we don't see any such response or get a negative response, it indicates some issue that needs additional analysis. For example, a missing record in the server database for the queried record type might result in responding with an error message.

How it works...

There are different DNS record types serving different purposes. We will discuss some of the commonly seen record types and their purpose.

SOA record

Start of authority (**SOA**) is a resource record type that contains administrative information, such as global parameters and configuration of each DNS zone that is part of the domain for which the DNS server is responsible for name resolution. The definition and record format for SOA is defined in RFC 1035.

```
▼ Queries
    ▼ kernel.org: type SOA, class IN
        Name: kernel.org
        [Name Length: 10]
        [Label Count: 2]
        Type: SOA (Start Of a zone of Authority) (6)
        Class: IN (0x0001)
▼ Answers
    ▼ kernel.org: type SOA, class IN, mname ns11.constellix.com
        Name: kernel.org
        Type: SOA (Start Of a zone of Authority) (6)
        Class: IN (0x0001)
        Time to live: 86400
        Data length: 47
        Primary name server: ns11.constellix.com
        Responsible authority's mailbox: dns.constellix.com
        Serial Number: 2015010376
        Refresh Interval: 43200 (12 hours)
        Retry Interval: 3600 (1 hour)
        Expire limit: 1209600 (14 days)
        Minimum TTL: 180 (3 minutes)
▼ Authoritative nameservers
    ▶ <Root>: type NS, class IN, ns m.root-servers.net
    ▶ <Root>: type NS, class IN, ns k.root-servers.net
    ▶ <Root>: type NS, class IN, ns j.root-servers.net
    ▶ <Root>: type NS, class IN, ns a.root-servers.net
    ▶ <Root>: type NS, class IN, ns c.root-servers.net
    ▶ <Root>: type NS, class IN, ns l.root-servers.net
    ▶ <Root>: type NS, class IN, ns g.root-servers.net
    ▶ <Root>: type NS, class IN, ns d.root-servers.net
    ▶ <Root>: type NS, class IN, ns h.root-servers.net
    ▶ <Root>: type NS, class IN, ns e.root-servers.net
    ▶ <Root>: type NS, class IN, ns i.root-servers.net
    ▶ <Root>: type NS, class IN, ns f.root-servers.net
    ▶ <Root>: type NS, class IN, ns b.root-servers.net
▶ Additional records
```

Figure 13.4: SOA resource record

The preceding screenshot is a sample capture of an SOA resource record. Each zone will have just one SOA record with the following details:

- **Name of the zone**: Defines the name of the zone within the domain.
- **Primary nameserver**: DNS master for the domain. This acts as the primary source of data records for this zone.
- **Responsible authority**: Mailbox info of the authority responsible for this zone.
- **Serial number**: This value is sequentially incremented for each zone transfer. It can be considered the current version of the DNS database.
- **Time intervals**: Different refresh and retry intervals.

A resource record

An A resource, also known as address record, is the resource record that stores the IPv4 address associated to the domain name. This is one of the most commonly seen records on the internet. More than one IP address may be associated with the same domain name for load balancing purposes. So it is common to see multiple A records in the DNS response packet.

```
▶ Frame 38: 120 bytes on wire (960 bits), 120 bytes captured (960 bits)
▶ Ethernet II, Src: fa:16:3e:08:9d:85 (fa:16:3e:08:9d:85), Dst: fa:16:3e:cd:a9:38 (fa:16:3e:cd:a9:38)
▶ Internet Protocol Version 4, Src: 192.168.0.7, Dst: 10.0.128.1
▶ User Datagram Protocol, Src Port: 53, Dst Port: 35280
▼ Domain Name System (response)
    [Request In: 37]
    [Time: 0.001240000 seconds]
    Transaction ID: 0xcc3c
  ▶ Flags: 0x8580 Standard query response, No error
    Questions: 1
    Answer RRs: 2
    Authority RRs: 0
    Additional RRs: 1
  ▼ Queries
    ▶ csr2.company1.com: type A, class IN
  ▼ Answers
    ▼ csr2.company1.com: type A, class IN, addr 192.168.2.2
        Name: csr2.company1.com
        Type: A (Host Address) (1)
        Class: IN (0x0001)
        Time to live: 10
        Data length: 4
        Address: 192.168.2.2
    ▼ csr2.company1.com: type A, class IN, addr 192.168.0.6
        Name: csr2.company1.com
        Type: A (Host Address) (1)
        Class: IN (0x0001)
        Time to live: 10
        Data length: 4
        Address: 192.168.0.6
  ▶ Additional records
```

Figure 13.5: A resource record

The preceding screenshot is a sample capture of an A record response with multiple IP addresses associated with the same domain name. In the preceding screenshot, `192.168.2.2` and `192.168.0.6` are associated with the hostname `csr2.company1.com`. The DNS server, upon receiving the DNS query for `csr2.company1.com`, will respond with multiple answer objects, with each object carrying one IP address and the associated details. How or what IP address is used by the client is a local matter and it is implementation-specific.

AAAA resource record

An AAAA resource record, also known as IPv6 address record, is a resource record that stores the IPv6 address associated with the domain name. More than one IPv6 address may be associated with the same domain name for load balancing purposes. So it is common to see multiple AAAA records in the DNS response packet.

The sample capture shown in preceding is an AAAA record. As with an A record, the DNS response may carry more than one AAAA record in the response if there are more than one IPv6 address is associated with the domain name.

CNAME resource record

A CNAME resource record, also known as a canonical name record, is the resource record used to specify that a domain name is an alias for another domain name. A CNAME record will always point to another domain name and it will not point to any IP address. This record helps with seamless domain name change from one to another without impacting the end users.

CNAME record		
Foo.example.com	Bar.example.com	CNAME
Bar.example.com	10.1.1.1	IP

Figure 13.6: CNAME record

In the previous example, we see `foo.example.com` is the alias name created for `bar.example.com`. When the server receives a request for `foo.example.com`, it replies with a CNAME carrying the new domain name `bar.example.com`. The client will in turn send a request for `bar.example.com` to resolve the IP address. It will be transparent to the client and therefore allow a smooth domain name transition.

There's more...

In the previous section, we saw some of the most commonly seen resource records and the associated semantics. There are more such resource records that are available in the industry. Details about other resource records and explanations for each record are available at the IANA: `https://www.iana.org/assignments/dns-parameters/dns-parameters.xhtml#dns-parameters-4`.

Analyzing regular DNS operations

In this recipe, we will see how to find out if DNS is working properly or not. We will see some scenarios of DNS operations, and what can go wrong.

Getting ready

Open Wireshark and start capturing data. You should mirror a device that is using DNS, or the DNS server itself.

How to do it...

Connect Wireshark to the LAN switch attached to the monitored device, and configure a port mirror to the device from which you suspect the problem is coming. Go through the following steps:

1. In case of user complaints, configure the port mirror for monitoring the user device.
2. In case of a general problem in the network, configure the port mirror to the DNS server:
   - When the DNS server is configured on the internal server, configure a port mirror on the server
   - When the DNS server is configured on the external server, configure a port mirror to the link that connects you to the internet

How it works...

DNS is the major protocol used for name resolution, and it is used when browsing the internet. It is also used for working in an organization's network. The DNS standards describe three functionalities:

- Namespace, which is how the DNS name looks and how it is allocated
- The name registration process, that is, how we register DNS names and how they are forwarded through the DNS server's network
- The resolving process, that is, how names are resolved to the IP addresses

In this recipe, we will focus on the third subject, that is, what happens when we browse the internet, send or receive emails, or access internal servers in our organization.

DNS server assignment

The first step involved in troubleshooting DNS related issues is to ensure that the right DNS server settings are configured on the clients. This is critical to ensure that the IP address resolved as part of a DNS query is legitimate and is not spoofed. There are two different types of DNS client configuration, as follows:

- Manually setting the DNS server on the client
- Dynamic DNS

With manual configuration, we need to statically define the DNS server information on the client. Depending on the client, the configuration may vary. For example, in Linux distributions, the DNS server should be configured in the `/etc/resolv.conf` file.

With **Dynamic DNS** (**DDNS**), we leverage the dynamic configuration protocols to advertise the DNS server information. In a large network, it is very common to see DHCP as the address assignment protocol. DHCP can be leveraged to dynamically advertise one or more DNS servers.

```
▶ User Datagram Protocol, Src Port: 67, Dst Port: 68
▼ Bootstrap Protocol (Offer)
    Message type: Boot Reply (2)
    Hardware type: Ethernet (0x01)
    Hardware address length: 6
    Hops: 0
    Transaction ID: 0x00000134
    Seconds elapsed: 0
  ▶ Bootp flags: 0x8000, Broadcast flag (Broadcast)
    Client IP address: 0.0.0.0
    Your (client) IP address: 10.2.0.3
    Next server IP address: 0.0.0.0
    Relay agent IP address: 0.0.0.0
    Client MAC address: fa:16:3e:08:9d:85 (fa:16:3e:08:9d:85)
    Client hardware address padding: 00000000000000000000
    Server host name not given
    Boot file name not given
    Magic cookie: DHCP
  ▶ Option: (53) DHCP Message Type (Offer)
  ▶ Option: (61) Client identifier
  ▶ Option: (54) DHCP Server Identifier
  ▶ Option: (51) IP Address Lease Time
  ▶ Option: (58) Renewal Time Value
  ▶ Option: (59) Rebinding Time Value
  ▶ Option: (1) Subnet Mask
  ▶ Option: (3) Router
  ▼ Option: (6) Domain Name Server
      Length: 4
      Domain Name Server: 192.168.0.7
  ▼ Option: (255) End
      Option End: 255
```

Figure 13.7: DNS info in DHCP response

As shown in the preceding screenshot, DNS server information is one of the DHCP options that will be included while assigning the IP address.

In an IPv6 environment, it is possible to advertise the DNS server information as part of the IPv6 router advertisement. Any client that is enabled with IPv6 auto configuration will use the DNS server received as part of an IPv6 RA message.

DNS operation

User programs (web browser, mail client, and many others) interact with the DNS server through a resolver, which is also part of the operating system. The resolver interacts with external name servers that provide it with the required IPs (the name server can be local or remote; it is external to the resolver). The way the user queries the DNS server is OS specific. DNS queries and responses are sent and received between the resolver and the name server. It is shown in the following diagram:

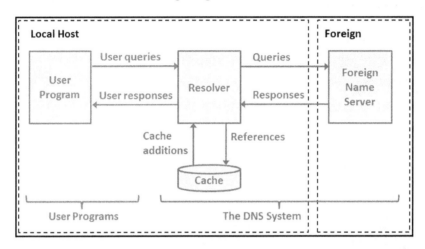

The local name server is usually located in the organization network, and interacts with the DNS server of your ISP. In the case of a home or small office network, your DNS server can be configured on the router that connects you to the internet, or directly to the DNS server of your ISP:

- When the DNS server is on the router, you query the DNS on the router that queries your ISP DNS
- When your DNS is located on the ISP network, you query the DNS server directly

DNS namespace

The DNS namespace is based on a hierarchical tree structure, as presented in the following diagram. The structure is as follows:

- The network of root servers (http://www.iana.org/domains/root/servers).
- The network of **Top-Level Domain** (**TLD**) servers (http://www.iana.org/domains/root/db).

- Each top-level domain has name servers similar to that of IANA administers. Top-level domains contain second-level domains. TLDs are the highest-level servers, for example, country servers, as illustrated in the following diagram.
- **Second-Level Domain** (**SLD**) contains the domains and names for organizations and countries. The names in second-level domains are administered by the organization or country specified:

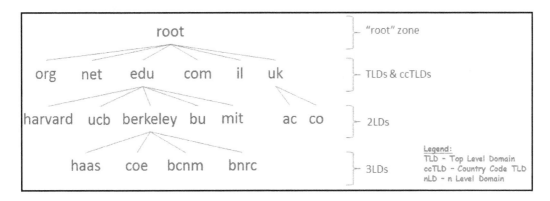

There are some important definitions, as shown in the following diagram:

- **Domain**: Constitutes all branches under `ndi-com.com`, in this case an SLD
- **Zone**: A contiguous portion of a DNS domain in the DNS namespace, whose database records exist and are managed in a particular DNS database file stored on one or multiple DNS servers:

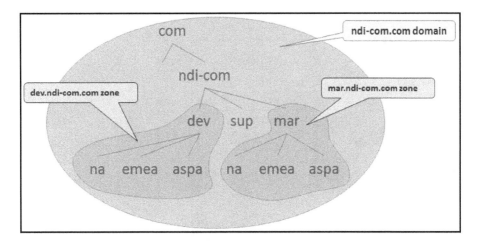

The resolving process

There are two reasons for using DNS servers:

- The first reason is that it is used for internal communication in your organization. In this case, you have a DNS server in your organization that resolves the IP addresses to names in your organization.
- It is used for connecting to the internet, browsing, sending emails, and so on.

When both services are used, you will send the DNS query to your organization server, which will send the query to the internet. For example, when you want to get to a local server in your organization, you will send a DNS query to the local DNS and you will get the server IP. When you browse a website on the internet, your local DNS server forwards the request to the external DNS, for example, the ISP DNS.

Have you configured the correct DNS server? Theoretically, when you connect to the internet, you can configure any DNS server in the world. Usually, the best DNS server to use is the nearest one. In your organization, you should configure your local DNS as first priority, and then the DNS servers of your ISP.

There are various utilities to check the DNS response. Some of them are as follows:

- Namebench (goo.gl/86yjKU)
- DNS Benchmark from GRC (https://www.grc.com/dns/benchmark.htm)

In the test results, you should get a good response time for your configured DNS servers. If not, change them.

There's more...

When a process on the end device is looking for the IP address of a specific name, it interacts with the local resolver that goes out to the DNS servers. When the DNS server does not find the entry you are looking for in its database, it can respond in two ways; recursive or iterative:

- **Recursive mode**: In this mode, when the application (for example, a web browser) wants to resolve the name of a website, `www.packtpub.com`, it sends a DNS request to the local DNS server (marked as **1** in the following diagram). The local DNS server sends the request to a root server (marked as **2** and **3** in the following diagram), then to the TLD (marked as **3** and **4** in the following diagram), and finally to the authoritative server of `www.packtpub.com`, which gives us the required address (marked as **6** and **7** in the following diagram). Then, the local DNS server sends us the required address (marked as **8** in the following diagram). In each one of the responses, the resolver gets the DNS to query in the next step:

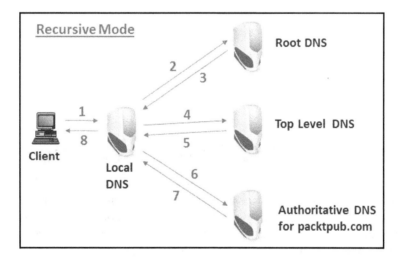

- **Iterative mode**: In this mode, a DNS client can receive a response from the DNS server that will tell the client where to look for the requested name. When the application (for example, a web browser) wants to browse the website `www.packtpub.com`, it sends a DNS request to the local DNS server (marked as **1** in the following diagram). The local server forwards the request to a root DNS server (marked as **2** in the following diagram). If it doesn't know the answer, it forwards the request to the TLD (marked as **3** in the following diagram) and the authoritative DNS (marked as **4** in the following diagram). Then, the answer is sent all the way back to the client (marked as **5**, **6**, **7**, and **8** in the following diagram):

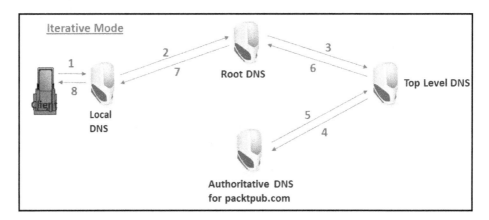

Analyzing DNSSEC regular operations

DNS plays a key role on the internet by performing the resolution of the domain name to a respective IP address. While it performs a very essential service, it does not provide any data integrity or origin authority. Such a lack of security can be manipulated to spoof the domain name with a malicious IP address and forward all the data toward the malicious server. DNS cache poisoning is one such known attack that leverages this security hole for data leaks.

DNS Security Extension (**DNSSEC**) is a suite of security extensions to the DNS protocol that introduces the concept of zone signing, thereby helping to provide data integrity and origin authority to the DNS resource records.

Getting ready

DNSSEC is an extension to the existing DNS packet format and so does not need any encryption or related consideration from a packet capture point of view. As with traditional DNS packets, Wireshark will be able to capture DNSSEC packets using the same port mirroring concept.

How to do it...

On the captured packet, perform the following simple verification:

1. Check if the DNS query sent from the client is set with the DNSSEC option. This will be included in the additional records field of the DNS query packet:

```
▶ Frame 71: 93 bytes on wire (744 bits), 93 bytes captured (744 bits)
▶ Ethernet II, Src: Apple_96:f7:dd (ac:bc:32:96:f7:dd), Dst: BelkinIn_62:62:ff (c0:56:27:62:62:ff)
▶ Internet Protocol Version 4, Src: 10.83.218.91, Dst: 194.150.168.168
▶ Transmission Control Protocol, Src Port: 49697, Dst Port: 53, Seq: 1, Ack: 1, Len: 39
▼ Domain Name System (query)
    [Response In: 73]
    Length: 37
    Transaction ID: 0x443c
  ▶ Flags: 0x0100 Standard query
    Questions: 1
    Answer RRs: 0
    Authority RRs: 0
    Additional RRs: 1
  ▼ Queries
    ▼ isoc.org: type A, class IN
        Name: isoc.org
        [Name Length: 8]
        [Label Count: 2]
        Type: A (Host Address) (1)
        Class: IN (0x0001)
  ▼ Additional records
    ▼ <Root>: type OPT
        Name: <Root>
        Type: OPT (41)
        UDP payload size: 4096
        Higher bits in extended RCODE: 0x00
        EDNS0 version: 0
      ▼ Z: 0x8000
          1... .... .... .... = DO bit: Accepts DNSSEC security RRs
          .000 0000 0000 0000 = Reserved: 0x0000
        Data length: 0
```

In the preceding screenshot, it can be seen that the additional record field is set with a flag that indicates that the client accepts DNSSEC security resource records.

2. The DNS server, upon receiving the request, will reply with a DNS response that carries the relevant details of the requested record (for example, an IP address for an A record) carrying a **Resource Record Signature** (**RRSIG**). These are digital signatures associated with the resource record:

```
▶ Frame 73: 566 bytes on wire (4528 bits), 566 bytes captured (4528 bits)
▶ Ethernet II, Src: BelkinIn_62:62:ff (c0:56:27:62:62:ff), Dst: Apple_96:f7:dd (ac:bc:32:96:f7:dd)
▶ Internet Protocol Version 4, Src: 194.150.168.168, Dst: 10.83.218.91
▶ Transmission Control Protocol, Src Port: 53, Dst Port: 49697, Seq: 1, Ack: 40, Len: 512
▼ Domain Name System (response)
    [Request In: 71]
    [Time: 0.128259000 seconds]
    Length: 510
    Transaction ID: 0x443c
  ▶ Flags: 0x81a0 Standard query response, No error
    Questions: 1
    Answer RRs: 2
    Authority RRs: 6
    Additional RRs: 1
  ▶ Queries
  ▼ Answers
    ▼ isoc.org: type A, class IN, addr 212.110.167.157
        Name: isoc.org
        Type: A (Host Address) (1)
        Class: IN (0x0001)
        Time to live: 86326
        Data length: 4
        Address: 212.110.167.157
    ▼ isoc.org: type RRSIG, class IN
        Name: isoc.org
        Type: RRSIG (46)
        Class: IN (0x0001)
        Time to live: 86326
        Data length: 156
        Type Covered: A (Host Address) (1)
        Algorithm: RSA/SHA1 + NSEC3/SHA1 (7)
        Labels: 2
        Original TTL: 86400 (1 day)
        Signature Expiration: Feb  2, 2018 03:50:00.000000000 EST
        Signature Inception: Jan 19, 2018 03:50:00.000000000 EST
        Key Tag: 9959
        Signer's name: isoc.org
        Signature: 670006bd992d01371cbb06e1d051b4e3d65c2ae3a3476a84...
  ▶ Authoritative nameservers
  ▶ Additional records
```

In the preceding screenshot, it can be seen that the DNS response from the server will be replied with RRSIG.

3. The DNS client now requests DNSKEY for the domain name as follows:

```
▶ Frame 84: 93 bytes on wire (744 bits), 93 bytes captured (744 bits)
▶ Ethernet II, Src: Apple_96:f7:dd (ac:bc:32:96:f7:dd), Dst: BelkinIn_62:62:ff (c0:56:27:62:62:ff)
▶ Internet Protocol Version 4, Src: 10.83.218.91, Dst: 194.150.168.168
▶ Transmission Control Protocol, Src Port: 49698, Dst Port: 53, Seq: 1, Ack: 1, Len: 39
▼ Domain Name System (query)
    [Response In: 86]
    Length: 37
    Transaction ID: 0xdd86
  ▶ Flags: 0x0100 Standard query
    Questions: 1
    Answer RRs: 0
    Authority RRs: 0
    Additional RRs: 1
  ▼ Queries
    ▼ isoc.org: type DNSKEY, class IN
        Name: isoc.org
        [Name Length: 8]
        [Label Count: 2]
        Type: DNSKEY (48)
        Class: IN (0x0001)
  ▶ Additional records
```

4. The DNS server replies with the public key that is used to sign the resource record:

```
▶ Frame 86: 813 bytes on wire (6504 bits), 813 bytes captured (6504 bits)
▶ Ethernet II, Src: BelkinIn_62:62:ff (c0:56:27:62:62:ff), Dst: Apple_96:f7:dd (ac:bc:32:96:f7:dd)
▶ Internet Protocol Version 4, Src: 194.150.168.168, Dst: 10.83.218.91
▶ Transmission Control Protocol, Src Port: 53, Dst Port: 49698, Seq: 1, Ack: 40, Len: 759
▼ Domain Name System (response)
    [Request In: 84]
    [Time: 0.127825000 seconds]
    Length: 757
    Transaction ID: 0xdd86
  ▶ Flags: 0x81a0 Standard query response, No error
    Questions: 1
    Answer RRs: 3
    Authority RRs: 0
    Additional RRs: 1
  ▶ Queries
  ▼ Answers
    ▶ isoc.org: type DNSKEY, class IN
    ▼ isoc.org: type DNSKEY, class IN
        Name: isoc.org
        Type: DNSKEY (48)
        Class: IN (0x0001)
        Time to live: 13831
        Data length: 136
      ▶ Flags: 0x0100
        Protocol: 3
        Algorithm: RSA/SHA1 + NSEC3/SHA1 (7)
        [Key id: 9959]
        Public Key: 03010001aeeeb166fe5dda4762de2d5e551ebd9fe132639d...
    ▶ isoc.org: type RRSIG, class IN
  ▶ Additional records
```

5. The client uses the details to validate the integrity of the resource record received from the DNS server.

How it works...

DNSSEC is a technology that was developed to secure the DNS resource records by providing extended data integrity checks to the resource records. DNSSEC operates by digitally signing the resource records, starting from the root of the hierarchical DNS tree:

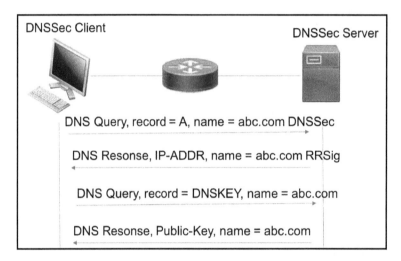

DNSKEY and RRSIG plays a key role in DNSSEC operations. The following is a simplified sequence of actions between the client and the server:

1. The DNS client sends a DNS query with the DNSSEC flag set in the additional record. This signals to the server that the client supports DNSSEC and expects the resource records to be digitally signed.
2. The DNS server, upon receiving the request, will reply with the response and include RRSIG. RRSIG are resource records that are digitally signed by a delegation signer.
3. The DNS client will send another request to the server for the same domain name but with the record type set to DNSKEY. This is the public key used to sign the resource record.
4. The DNS server will reply with the DNSKEY for the requested domain.
5. The DNS client uses the DNSKEY to compute the hashing and compare it with the RRSIG for data integrity.

6. If the hash does not match, the resource record is compromised and the client will not use it.

There's more...

The previous section is a simplified explanation of how DNSSEC works. More detailed information on DNSSEC, zone signature, and how it uses the signature chain is available in the following RFCs:

- **RFC 4033**: DNS security introduction and requirements
- **RFC 4034**: Resource records for the DNSSEC
- **RFC 4035**: Protocol modifications for the DNSSEC

Troubleshooting DNS performance

In this recipe, we will see how to troubleshoot DNS performance-related issues like slow responses. We will see how Wireshark can be used to analyze such issues.

Getting ready

DNS performance is measured by utilizing the timestamps on DNS request and response packets. In order to measure the performance, Wireshark should be connected and capture the DNS packets as close as possible to the client.

How to do it...

How will you know that this is the problem?

- When you are browsing the internet and getting very slow responses, perform the following steps:
    1. Port mirror the connection to the internet and check if you have any bottlenecks on the way to the internet. You can use I/O graphs for this purpose, as described in Chapter 6, *Using Advanced Statistics Tools*.
    2. Verify that you don't have a significant number of retransmissions or duplicate ACKs indicating a connection problem.

3. Verify that you don't have any window-related problems, such as zero window or window full.

- If answers are no for the preceding checks, it might be a DNS problem. You could have DNS problems in two cases:
  - When working in your organization
  - When connecting to the internet

- These issues can be resolved in two ways:
  - When facing problems in your organization, port mirror the switch port that is connected to the DNS server
  - When facing problems with the internet, port mirror the switch port that connects your organization to the internet

- Watch the DNS response time that you get. There are several ways to locate the problem, and they are given as follows:
  - The simplest way is to right-click on a packet from a DNS query stream, choose **Follow UDP Stream**, and then check the time between the query and response.
  - Another way is to use I/O graphs for this purpose. In the **IO Graphs** window, choose **Advanced...** in the **Y Axis** configuration and configure the filter dns.time with **AVG(*)** in the **Graphs** lines. Refer to the following screenshot:

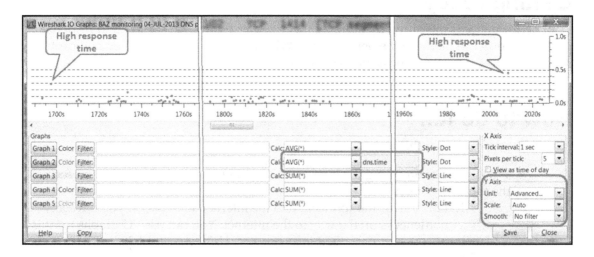

You will get a graph of the DNS response times throughout the capture time.

In this graph, you will see that most of the response times fall below 100 ms, which is quite reasonable. We have two peaks that indicate a probable problem, one at the beginning of the capture with 300 ms, and one at the end of the capture with 450 ms.

Reasonable times inside the organization (at a local site) should be no more than tens of ms. When browsing the internet, a good response time should be less than 100 ms, while up to 200 ms is still tolerable.

How it works...

As explained in the *Analyzing regular DNS operations* section, the mode of DNS operation may impact the overall resolution performance. For example, recursive mode may result in a DNS server recursively querying other servers, which introduces end-to-end delays that vary depending on various factors associated with the servers and the network path. In scenarios where multiple DNS servers are configured, iterative mode may help query the other servers if the first server does not have the resource record in the cache.

There's more...

While the use of Wireshark is one option to measure and troubleshoot the latency for name resolution, there are other tools available to perform similar testing. For example, dig is a CLI-based tool that is available in most Linux distributions. It allows you to trigger a DNS query of any record type and measure the time taken for the resolution.

The following is an example of how it can be used:

```
Ubuntu:~ naikumar$ dig www.packtpub.com

; <<>> DiG 9.8.3-P1 <<>> www.packtpub.com
;; global options: +cmd
;; Got answer:
;; ->>HEADER<<- opcode: QUERY, status: NOERROR, id: 4108
;; flags: qr rd ra; QUERY: 1, ANSWER: 2, AUTHORITY: 13, ADDITIONAL: 0

;; QUESTION SECTION:
;www.packtpub.com.        IN  A

;; ANSWER SECTION:
www.packtpub.com.     5    IN  CNAME   varnish.packtpub.com.
varnish.packtpub.com.  5   IN  A    83.166.169.231

;; AUTHORITY SECTION:
com.           172739  IN  NS  j.gtld-servers.net.

;; Query time: 60 msec
;; SERVER: 64.102.6.247#53(64.102.6.247)
;; WHEN: Fri Jan 19 16:48:54 2018
;; MSG SIZE  rcvd: 296

Ubuntu:~ naikumar$
```

14
Analyzing Mail Protocols

In this chapter, you will learn about:

- Normal operation of mail protocols
- Analyzing POP, IMAP, and SMTP problems
- Filtering and analyzing different error codes
- Malicious and spam email analysis

Introduction

One of the contributing factors in the evolution of digital marketing and business is email. Email allows users to exchange real-time messages and other digital information such as files and images over the internet in a very efficient manner. Each user is required to have a human-readable email address in the format of `username@domainname.com`. There are various email providers available on the internet, and any user can register to get a free email address.

There are different email application-layer protocols available for sending and receiving mails, and the combination of these protocols helps with end-to-end email exchange between users in the same or different mail domains. The three most commonly used application layer protocols are POP3, IMAP, and SMTP:

- **POP3**: **Post Office Protocol 3** (**POP3**) is an application layer protocol used by email systems to retrieve mail from email servers. The email client uses POP3 commands such as `LOGIN`, `LIST`, `RETR`, `DELE`, `QUIT` to access and manipulate (retrieve or delete) the email from the server. POP3 uses TCP port `110` and wipes the mail from the server once it is downloaded to the local client.

- **IMAP**: **Internet Mail Access Protocol** (**IMAP**) is another application layer protocol used to retrieve mail from the email server. Unlike POP3, IMAP allows the user to read and access the mail concurrently from more than one client device. With current trends, it is very common to see users with more than one device to access emails (laptop, smartphone, and so on), and the use of IMAP allows the user to access mail any time, from any device. The current version of IMAP is 4 and it uses TCP port 143.

- **SMTP**: **Simple Mail Transfer Protocol** (**SMTP**) is an application layer protocol that is used to send email from the client to the mail server. When the sender and receiver are in different email domains, SMTP helps to exchange the mail between servers in different domains. It uses TCP port 25:

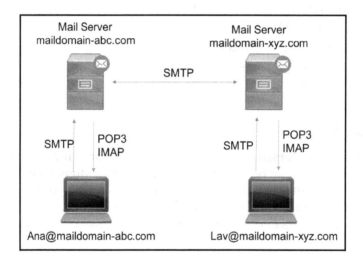

As shown in the preceding diagram, SMTP is the email client used to send the mail to the mail server, and POP3 or IMAP is used to retrieve the email from the server. The email server uses SMTP to exchange the mail between different domains.

In order to maintain the privacy of end users, most email servers use different encryption mechanisms at the transport layer. The transport layer port number will differ from the traditional email protocols if they are used over secured transport layer (TLS). For example, POP3 over TLS uses TCP port 995, IMAP4 over TLS uses TCP port 993, and SMTP over TLS uses port 465.

In this chapter, we will look at the normal operation of email protocols and how to use Wireshark for basic analysis and troubleshooting.

Normal operation of mail protocols

As we saw in the *Introduction*, the common mail protocols for mail client to server and server to server communication are POP3, SMTP, and IMAP4.

Another common method for accessing emails is web access to mail, where you have common mail servers such as Gmail, Yahoo!, and Hotmail. Examples include **Outlook Web Access** (**OWA**) and RPC over HTTPS for the Outlook web client from Microsoft.

In this recipe, we will talk about the most common client-server and server-server protocols, POP3 and SMTP, and the normal operation of each protocol.

Getting ready

Port mirroring to capture the packets can be done either on the email client side or on the server side.

How to do it...

POP3 is usually used for client to server communications, while SMTP is usually used for server to server communications.

POP3 communications

POP3 is usually used for mail client to mail server communications. The normal operation of POP3 is as follows:

1. Open the email client and enter the username and password for login access.
2. Use POP as a display filter to list all the POP packets. It should be noted that this display filter will only list packets that use TCP port 110. If TLS is used, the filter will not list the POP packets. We may need to use tcp.port == 995 to list the POP3 packets over TLS.
3. Check the authentication has been passed correctly. In the following screenshot, you can see a session opened with a username that starts with doronn@ (all IDs were deleted) and a password that starts with u6F.

4. To see the TCP stream shown in the following screenshot, right-click on one of the packets in the stream and choose **Follow TCP Stream** from the drop-down menu:

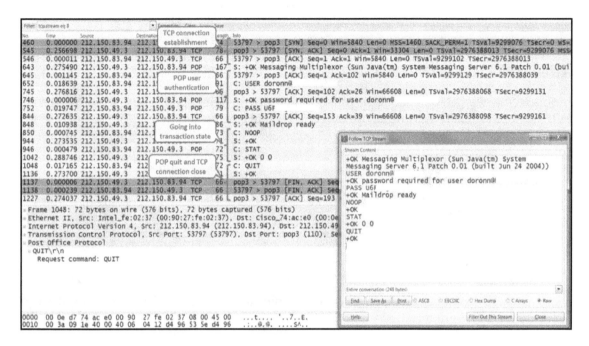

5. Any error messages in the authentication stage will prevent communications from being established. You can see an example of this in the following screenshot, where user authentication failed. In this case, we see that when the client gets a **Logon failure**, it closes the TCP connection:

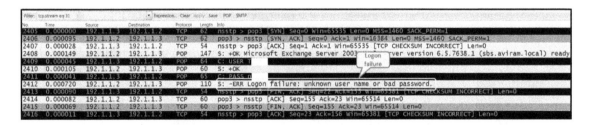

6. Use relevant display filters to list the specific packet. For example, `pop.request.command == "USER"` will list the POP request packet with the username and `pop.request.command == "PASS"` will list the POP packet carrying the password. A sample snapshot is as follows:

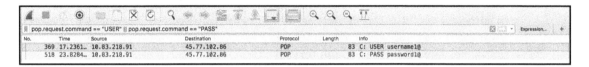

7. During the mail transfer, be aware that mail clients can easily fill a narrow-band communications line. You can check this by simply configuring the I/O graphs with a filter on POP.

8. Always check for common TCP indications: retransmissions, zero-window, window-full, and others. They can indicate a busy communication line, slow server, and other problems coming from the communication lines or end nodes and servers. These problems will mostly cause slow connectivity.

When the POP3 protocol uses TLS for encryption, the payload details are not visible. We explain how the SSL captures can be decrypted in the *There's more...* section.

IMAP communications

IMAP is similar to POP3 in that it is used to retrieve the mail from the server by the client. The normal behavior of IMAP communication is as follows:

1. Open the email client and enter the username and password for the relevant account.

2. Compose a new message and send it from any email account.

3. Retrieve the email on the client that is using IMAP. Different clients may have different ways of retrieving the email. Use the relevant button to trigger it.

4. Check you received the email on your local client.

SMTP communications

SMTP is commonly used for the following purposes:

- Server to server communications, in which SMTP is the mail protocol that runs between the servers
- In some clients, POP3 or IMAP4 are configured for incoming messages (messages from the server to the client), while SMTP is configured for outgoing messages (messages from the client to the server)

The normal behavior of SMTP communication is as follows:

- The local email client resolves the IP address of the configured SMTP server address.
- This triggers a TCP connection to port number 25 if SSL/TLS is not enabled. If SSL/TLS is enabled, a TCP connection is established over port 465.
- It exchanges SMTP messages to authenticate with the server. The client sends AUTH LOGIN to trigger the login authentication. Upon successful login, the client will be able to send mails.
- It sends SMTP message such as "MAIL FROM:<>", "RCPT TO:<>" carrying sender and receiver email addresses.
- Upon successful queuing, we get an OK response from the SMTP server.

The following is a sample SMTP message flow between client and server:

```
Trying 10.1.1.1...
Connected to smtp-server.
Escape character is '^]'.
220 smtp-server ESMTP ready
AUTH LOGIN
334 VXNlcm5hbWU6
<enter username>
334 UGFzc3dvcmQ6
<enter password>
235 2.0.0 OK
MAIL FROM:ana@domain-abc.co
250 2.1.0 Ok
RCPT TO:lav@domain-xyz.com
 250 2.1.0 Ok
DATA
354 Go ahead
test123.
250 2.0.0 Ok: queued
```

How it works...

In this section, let's look into the normal operation of different email protocols with the use of Wireshark.

Mail clients will mostly use POP3 for communication with the server. In some cases, they will use SMTP as well. IMAP4 is used when server manipulation is required, for example, when you need to see messages that exist on a remote server without downloading them to the client. Server to server communication is usually implemented by SMTP.

The difference between IMAP and POP is that in IMAP, the mail is always stored on the server. If you delete it, it will be unavailable from any other machine. In POP, deleting a downloaded email may or may not delete that email on the server.

In general, SMTP status codes are divided into three categories, which are structured in a way that helps you understand what exactly went wrong. The methods and details of SMTP status codes are discussed in the following section.

POP3

POP3 is an application layer protocol used by mail clients to retrieve email messages from the server. A typical POP3 session will look like the following screenshot:

File Edit View Go Capture Analyze Statistics Telephony Tools Internals Help

Filter: tcp.stream eq 8 ▾ Expression... Clear Apply Save IPv6

No.	Time	Source	Destination	Protocol	Info
460	0.000000	212.150.83.94	212.150.49.3	TCP	53797 > pop3 [SYN] Seq=0 Win=5840 Len=0 N
545	0.256698	212.150.49.3	212.150.83.94	T ①	pop3 > 53797 [SYN, ACK] Seq=0 Ack=1 Win=3
546	0.000011	212.150.83.94	212.150.49.3	TCP	53797 > pop3 [ACK] Seq=1 Ack=1 Win=5840 L
643	0.275490	212.150.49.3	212.150.83.94	P ②	S: +OK Messaging Multiplexor (Sun Java(tm
645	0.001145	212.150.83.94	212.150.49.3	T	53797 > pop3 [ACK] Seq=1 Ack=102 Win=5840
652	0.018639	212.150.83.94	212.150.49.3	POP	C: USER ddron@shtil.com
745	0.276816	212.150.49.3	212.150.83.94	TCP	pop3 > 53797 [ACK] Seq=102 Ack=26 Win=666
746	0.000006	212.150.49.3	212.150.83.94	P ③	S: +OK password required for user doronn@
752	0.019747	212.150.83.94	212.150.49.3	POP	C: PASS U6FU6F
844	0.272543	212.150.49.3	212.150.83.94	TCP	pop3 > 53797 [ACK] Seq=153 Ack=39 Win=666
848	0.010938	212.150.49.3	212.150.83.94	POP	S: +OK Maildrop ready
850	0.000745	212.150.83.94	212.150.49.3	POP	C: NOOP
944	0.273535	212.150.49.3	212.150.83.94	P ④	S: +OK
946	0.000479	212.150.83.94	212.150.49.3	POP	C: STAT
1042	0.288746	212.150.49.3	212.150.83.94	POP	S: +OK 0 0
1048	0.017165	212.150.83.94	212.150.49.3	POP	C: QUIT
1136	0.273700	212.150.49.3	212.150.83.94	POP	S: +OK
1137	0.000006	212.150.49.3	212.150.83.94	T ⑤	pop3 > 53797 [FIN, ACK] Seq=192 Ack=58 Wi
1138	0.000239	212.150.83.94	212.150.49.3	TCP	53797 > pop3 [FIN, ACK] Seq=58 Ack=193 Wi
1227	0.274037	212.150.49.3	212.150.83.94	TCP	pop3 > 53797 [ACK] Seq=193 Ack=59 Win=666

It has the following steps:

1. The client opens a TCP connection to the server.
2. The server sends an OK message to the client (**OK Messaging Multiplexor**).
3. The user sends the username and password.
4. The protocol operations begin. NOOP (no operation) is a message sent to keep the connection open, STAT (status) is sent from the client to the server to query the message status. The server answers with the number of messages and their total size (in packet 1042, OK 0 0 means no messages and it has a total size of zero)
5. When there are no mail messages on the server, the client send a QUIT message (1048), the server confirms it (packet 1136), and the TCP connection is closed (packets 1137, 1138, and 1227).
6. In an encrypted connection, the process will look nearly the same (see the following screenshot). After the establishment of a connection (**1**), there are several POP messages (**2**), TLS connection establishment (**3**), and then the encrypted application data:

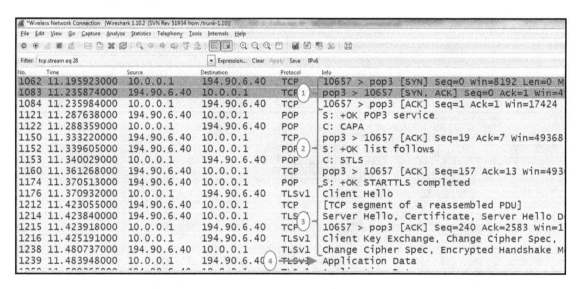

IMAP

The normal operation of IMAP is as follows:

1. The email client resolves the IP address of the IMAP server:

As shown in the preceding screenshot, the client establishes a TCP connection to port `143` when SSL/TSL is disabled. When SSL is enabled, the TCP session will be established over port `993`.

2. Once the session is established, the client sends an IMAP capability message requesting the server sends the capabilities supported by the server.

3. This is followed by authentication for access to the server. When the authentication is successful, the server replies with response code `3` stating the login was a success:

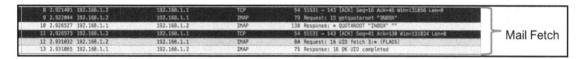

4. The client now sends the IMAP `FETCH` command to fetch any mails from the server.

5. When the client is closed, it sends a logout message and clears the TCP session.

SMTP

The normal operation of SMTP is as follows:

1. The email client resolves the IP address of the SMTP server:

```
▶ Frame 58: 78 bytes on wire (624 bits), 78 bytes captured (624 bits)
  Ethernet II, Src: Apple_96:f7:dd (ac:bc:32:96:f7:dd), Dst: BelkinIn_62:62:ff (c0:56:27:62:62:ff)
▶ Internet Protocol Version 4, Src: 10.83.218.91, Dst: 52.5.224.12
▼ Transmission Control Protocol, Src Port: 57988, Dst Port: 25, Seq: 0, Len: 0
    Source Port: 57988
    Destination Port: 25
    [Stream index: 9]
    [TCP Segment Len: 0]
    Sequence number: 0    (relative sequence number)
    [Next sequence number: 0    (relative sequence number)]
    Acknowledgment number: 0
    1011 .... = Header Length: 44 bytes (11)
  ▶ Flags: 0x002 (SYN)
    Window size value: 65535
    [Calculated window size: 65535]
    Checksum: 0x4eac [unverified]
    [Checksum Status: Unverified]
    Urgent pointer: 0
  ▶ Options: (24 bytes), Maximum segment size, No-Operation (NOP), Window scale, No-Operation (NOP), No-Operation (NOP), Timestamp
  ▶ [Timestamps]
```

2. The client opens a TCP connection to the SMTP server on port 25 when SSL/TSL is not enabled. If SSL is enabled, the client will open the session on port 465:

```
  61 2.948717  52.5.224.12    10.83.218.91    SMTP  95 S: 220 mailtrap.io ESMTP ready
  62 2.948825  10.83.218.91   52.5.224.12     TCP   66 57988 → 25 [ACK] Seq=1 Ack=30 Win=131712 Len=0
 156 7.979165  10.83.218.91   52.5.224.12     SMTP  78 C: AUTH LOGIN                        AUTH LOGIN request
 157 8.003876  52.5.224.12    10.83.218.91    TCP   66 25 → 57988 [ACK] Seq=30 Ack=13 Win=26880 Len=0
 158 8.005130  52.5.224.12    10.83.218.91    SMTP  84 S: 334 VXNlcm5hbWU6
 159 8.005185  10.83.218.91   52.5.224.12     TCP   66 57988 → 25 [ACK] Seq=13 Ack=48 Win=131712 Len=0
 254 13.0273.  10.83.218.91   52.5.224.12     SMTP  88 C: User: ZTN1OWU1MmNjNjg2NTE=
 259 13.0534.  52.5.224.12    10.83.218.91    SMTP  84 S: 334 UGFzc3dvcmQ6
 260 13.0535.  10.83.218.91   52.5.224.12     TCP   66 57988 → 25 [ACK] Seq=35 Ack=66 Win=131680 Len=0
 318 17.4058.  10.83.218.91   52.5.224.12     SMTP  87 C: Pass: NDY5OWI0OGI0OTQ1ZjY
 319 17.4334.  52.5.224.12    10.83.218.91    SMTP  80 S: 235 2.0.0 OK                     Success return
```

3. Upon successful TCP session establishment, the client will send an `AUTH LOGIN` message to prompt with the account username/password.
4. The username and password will be sent to the SMTP client for account verification.

5. SMTP will send a response code of `235` if authentication is successful:

319 17.4334...	52.5.224.12	10.83.218.91	SMTP	80 S: 235 2.0.0 OK	
320 17.4335...	10.83.218.91	52.5.224.12	TCP	66 57988 → 25 [ACK] Seq=56 Ack=80 Win=131680 Len=0	
397 21.9086...	10.83.218.91	52.5.224.12	SMTP	108 C: MAIL FROM:<ana-57e5e3@inbox.mailtrap.io> → Sender E-mail Address	
398 21.9370...	52.5.224.12	10.83.218.91	SMTP	80 S: 250 2.1.0 Ok	
399 21.9370...	10.83.218.91	52.5.224.12	TCP	66 57988 → 25 [ACK] Seq=98 Ack=94 Win=131648 Len=0	
498 26.6829...	10.83.218.91	52.5.224.12	SMTP	106 C: RCPT TO:<ana-57e5e3@inbox.mailtrap.io> → Receiver E-mail Address	
499 26.7088...	52.5.224.12	10.83.218.91	SMTP	80 S: 250 2.1.0 Ok	
500 26.7089...	10.83.218.91	52.5.224.12	TCP	66 57988 → 25 [ACK] Seq=138 Ack=108 Win=131648 Len=0	
604 31.1619...	10.83.218.91	52.5.224.12	SMTP	72 C: DATA	
605 31.1808...	52.5.224.12	10.83.218.91	SMTP	80 S: 354 Go ahead	
606 31.1808...	10.83.218.91	52.5.224.12	TCP	66 57988 → 25 [ACK] Seq=144 Ack=122 Win=131616 Len=0	
749 38.7780...	10.83.218.91	52.5.224.12	SMTP	88 C: DATA fragment, 22 bytes	
750 38.0312...	10.83.218.91	52.5.224.12	TCP	88 [TCP Retransmission] 57988 → 25 [PSH, ACK] Seq=144 Ack=122 ...	
751 38.8418...	52.5.224.12	10.83.218.91	TCP	66 25 → 57988 [ACK] Seq=122 Ack=166 Win=26880 Len=0	
752 38.8560...	52.5.224.12	10.83.218.91	TCP	78 [TCP Dup ACK 751#1] 25 → 57988 [ACK] Seq=122 Ack=166 Win=26...	
756 40.0975...	10.83.218.91	52.5.224.12	SMTP|IMF	69 Hi Ana, How are you? → E-mail Message	
757 40.1232...	52.5.224.12	10.83.218.91	TCP	66 25 → 57988 [ACK] Seq=122 Ack=169 Win=26880 Len=0	
758 40.1245...	52.5.224.12	10.83.218.91	SMTP	88 S: 250 2.0.0 Ok: queued → Successfully Queued	

6. The client now sends the sender's email address to the SMTP server. The SMTP server responds with a response code of `250` if the sender's address is valid.

7. Upon receiving an `OK` response from the server, the client will send the receiver's address. SMTP server will respond with a response code of `250` if the receiver's address is valid.

8. The client will now push the actual email message. SMTP will respond with a response code of `250` and the response parameter `OK: queued`.

9. The successfully queued message ensures that the mail is successfully sent and queued for delivery to the receiver address.

There's more...

Emails are sometimes referred to as one of the silent killers of networks, especially in small enterprises that use asymmetric lines to the internet. When sending text messages, they will not consume anything from the network; but when you send a large file of several megabytes or even tens of megabytes over a narrow-band uplink to the ISP, the rest of the users in your office will suffer from network slowdown for many seconds, even minutes. I've seen this problem in many small offices.

Another issue with mail clients is that in some cases (configurable), mail clients are configured to download all new data from the server when they start to work. If you have a customer that complains of a network slowdown at a time when all employees start their day in the office, it might be due to the tens or hundreds of clients who opened their mail clients simultaneously and the fact that the mail server is located over a WAN.

SSL decryption in Wireshark

As mentioned in the previous sections, all email protocols (SMTP, IMAP, and POP3) support SSL/TLS, where the transport layer information is encrypted and is not readable in Wireshark. In order to decrypt it, we need the SSL key used by the client.

These are the steps to follow:

1. Identify the SSL key used by the email client. Depending on the hardware and application, the procedure to get the SSL may vary:
   - In macOS, go to **Applications** and then to **Utilities**, and then open **Keychain Access**. This will list all the certificates and keys for different applications. Identify the right SSL key for the email client.
   - In Windows, go to **Microsoft Management Console (MMC)** and then to **Certificates**. This will list all the certificates for different applications. Identify the right certificate and export it.

2. Once the SSL key for the email client is identified, open **Preference** in Wireshark as follows:

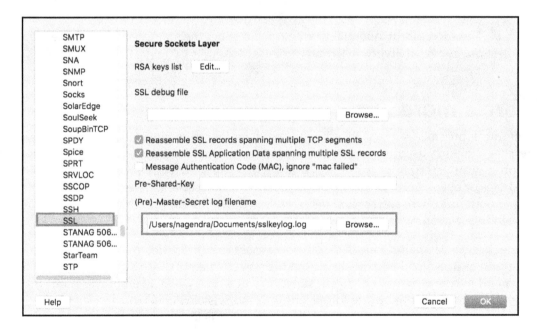

3. Select **SSL** from **Protocols**.
4. Choose the SSL key in the highlighted field and click **OK**.

5. The preceding process will let Wireshark use the SSL key to decrypt the message and display the decrypted version of the packet capture.

Analyzing POP, IMAP, and SMTP problems

In this recipe, we will discuss the use of Wireshark to analyze failures in email protocols.

Getting ready

When the failure is reported by a specific user while all other users are working fine, capture the packet as close as possible to the affected user. If the failure is reported for multiple users, capture the packet as close as possible to the server.

How to do it...

Depending on the direction of the failure, we may need to identify what email protocol we should be troubleshooting.

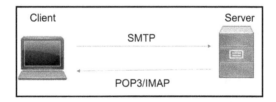

For example, if the user complains about a failure when sending email, we need to focus on SMTP, and if the failure is with receiving emails, we need to focus on IMAP or POP3 (depending on the protocol used by the client).

1. Once the direction of failure is identified, check that the TCP session for the relevant port is established:

No.	Time	Source	Destination	Protocol	Length	Info
320	23.3462…	192.168.1.2	192.168.1.1	TCP	78	51486 → 143 [SYN] Seq=0 Win=65535 Len=0 MSS=1460 WS=3…
329	24.3495…	192.168.1.2	192.168.1.1	TCP	78	[TCP Retransmission] 51486 → 143 [SYN] Seq=0 Win=6553…
334	25.3517…	192.168.1.2	192.168.1.1	TCP	78	[TCP Retransmission] 51486 → 143 [SYN] Seq=0 Win=6553…
337	26.3560…	192.168.1.2	192.168.1.1	TCP	78	[TCP Retransmission] 51486 → 143 [SYN] Seq=0 Win=6553…
342	27.3604…	192.168.1.2	192.168.1.1	TCP	78	[TCP Retransmission] 51486 → 143 [SYN] Seq=0 Win=6553…
344	28.3624…	192.168.1.2	192.168.1.1	TCP	78	[TCP Retransmission] 51486 → 143 [SYN] Seq=0 Win=6553…
361	30.3664…	192.168.1.2	192.168.1.1	TCP	78	[TCP Retransmission] 51486 → 143 [SYN] Seq=0 Win=6553…
375	34.3805…	192.168.1.2	192.168.1.1	TCP	78	[TCP Retransmission] 51486 → 143 [SYN] Seq=0 Win=6553…

tcp.port == 143

2. The preceding screenshot capture shows that the client is not able to establish the TCP session to the server on port 143. In this case, we should follow the traditional network troubleshooting behavior explained in Chapter 10, *Network Layer Protocols and Operations* and Chapter 11, *Transport Layer Protocol Analysis*.

3. If the session is established, the next step is to check if the application layer protocol is successfully authenticating with the server. A wrong username/password or malicious user attempt to access the server will be flagged with the following error messages:

```
▷ Frame 76: 135 bytes on wire (1080 bits), 135 bytes captured (1080 bits)
▽ Ethernet II, Src: QuantaCo_d2:be:29 (c4:54:44:d2:be:29), Dst: Apple_3b:34:fc (a8:20:66:3b:34:fc)
  ▽ Destination: Apple_3b:34:fc (a8:20:66:3b:34:fc)
      Address: Apple_3b:34:fc (a8:20:66:3b:34:fc)
      .... ..0. .... .... .... .... = LG bit: Globally unique address (factory default)
      .... ...0 .... .... .... .... = IG bit: Individual address (unicast)
  ▽ Source: QuantaCo_d2:be:29 (c4:54:44:d2:be:29)
      Address: QuantaCo_d2:be:29 (c4:54:44:d2:be:29)
      .... ..0. .... .... .... .... = LG bit: Globally unique address (factory default)
      .... ...0 .... .... .... .... = IG bit: Individual address (unicast)
    Type: IPv4 (0x0800)
▷ Internet Protocol Version 4, Src: 192.168.1.1, Dst: 192.168.1.2
▷ Transmission Control Protocol, Src Port: 143, Dst Port: 52605, Seq: 124, Ack: 36, Len: 81
▽ Internet Message Access Protocol
  ▽ Line: 3 NO Invalid user name or password. Please use full email address as user name.\r\n
      Response Tag: 3
      Response Status: NO
      Response: NO Invalid user name or password. Please use full email address as user name.
```

4. Check the username and password to ensure that the right one is used for authentication.

When you suspect slow server-to-server communications, follow these steps to resolve the problems:

1. Check if the servers are located on the same site:
   - If they are located on the same site, you probably have slow servers or another application problem. In most cases, the LAN will not cause any problems, especially when both servers are in the same data center.
   - If they are not located on the same site (when the servers are located in a remote site through WAN connections), check the load on the WAN connections. When sending large mails, they can easily block these lines, especially when they are narrow band (several Mbps).

2. First, look for TCP problems and check whether you see them only on SMTP, or on all other applications. For example, in the following screenshot, you can see many TCP retransmissions:

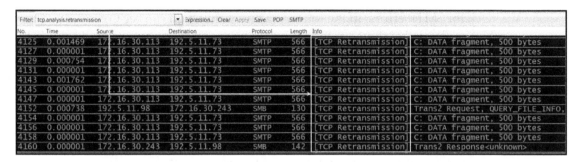

3. Check whether they are because of a slow SMTP server. Is it a mail problem? When you look at the following screenshot, you see that I've used the **TCP Conversation** statistics. After checking the **Limit to display filter** checkbox and clicking on **Packets** at the top of the window (to get the list from the higher amount of packets), we can see that only 793 packets are SMTP from the retransmitted packets. There were 9014 packets retransmitted between `172.16.30.247` and `172.16.30.2` on port `445` (Microsoft DS), 2319 packets were retransmitted between `172.16.30.180` and `192.5.11.198` on port `80` (HTTP), and so on:

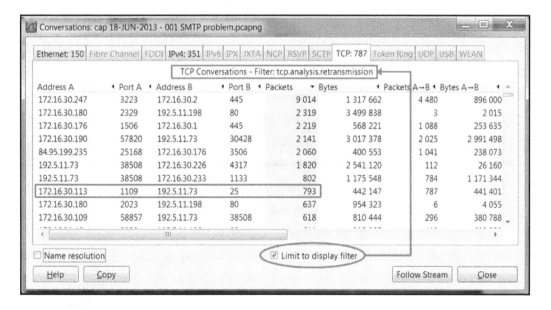

In this case, SMTP is influenced only from bad communications. It is not an SMTP problem.

4. Check for SMTP errors. In the following screenshot, you can see error code `451`, which is also called the `local error in processing` server error. Also, a list of errors is included.

> When something goes wrong, in most cases the server or the client will tell you about it. You just have to look at the messages and Google them. We will see many examples of this later.

You can also find a list of SMTP status codes in RFC 1893 at `http://www.ietf.org/rfc/rfc1893.txt`:

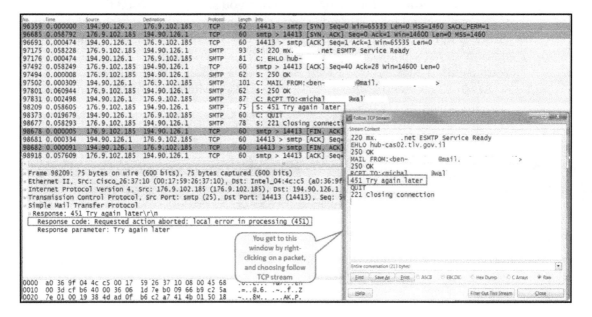

5. When you want to find out which errors have been sent by the two sides, configure a filter as shown in the following screenshot:

Here you can see various events (codes):

- `421`: This indicates that the mail service is probably unavailable (**1**).
- `452`: This indicates that the server cannot respond, and tells you to try again later. This happens due to load on the server or a server problem (**2**).
- `451`: (code `250` is shown in the screenshot, see the following note) This indicates the user over quota (**3**).
- `452`: This indicates that the mailbox size limit has been exceeded (**4**).
- `450`: (code `250` is shown in the screenshot, see the following note) This indicates that the host was not found (**5**).

> **TIP**
>
> In SMTP (like in many other protocols), you can get several error codes in the same message. What you see in the packet list in Wireshark may be the first one, or a partial list of it. To see the full list of errors in the SMTP message, go to the packet details and open the specific packet, as in the next screenshot.

When you see too many codes, it indicates the unavailability of the server. In this case, check with the server administrator:

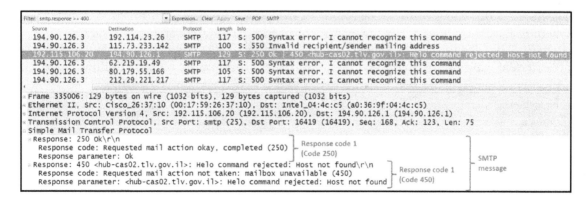

How it works...

The normal behavior of each email protocol (SMTP, IMAP, and POP3) is explained in the *Normal operation of mail protocols* recipe. Comparing the failure capture with the normal operation capture will help identify the issue causing the failure for the client.

Filtering and analyzing different error codes

In this recipe, we will discuss the use of Wireshark to filter certain messages, based on the error code, for analysis.

Getting ready

Capture the packets on the client or the server side, depending on the failure. To reiterate, when the protocols are using SSL/TLS to establish the session, we need the SSL key to decrypt the message before using the error code as a filter. Otherwise, the error code will be decrypted and it may not list in the filtered output.

How to do it...

Each of the email protocols uses different types of error codes to communicate any failure or issues between the client and the server. In this section, we will discuss on how to filter the error codes for each email protocol using Wireshark.

SMTP

The SMTP status codes from the server log or from the Wireshark capture are very useful when troubleshooting or analyzing email-related issues. Different status codes are exchanged between server and client to signal a working or failing condition. While there are different ways of filtering, we will see the common and useful filtering options:

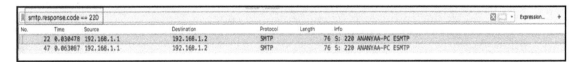

The use of `smtp.response` will filter all the SMTP messages with a response status code. If we know the status code, the filter can further be granulized using `smtp.response.code==<code>`.

Since the SMTP response status codes are defined in numeric values, Wireshark allows us to filter the status code based on range. For example, `smtp.response.code > 200` will list all the packets with a status code higher than `200`. The following is an example output:

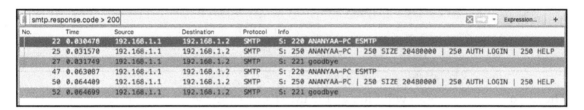

SMTP messages can also be filtered based on response parameters. The use of `smtp.rsp.parameters==<param>` will filter the packets based on the response parameters. The following is an example output that lists the SMTP packet with the `AUTH LOGIN` parameter:

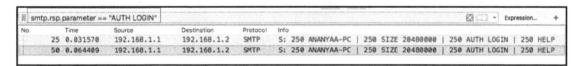

More details about the available SMTP status codes can be found in the *There's more...* section.

IMAP

Status responses such as `OK`, `NO`, `BAD`, `BYE`, and so on are used to signal why any IMAP command between the client and the server failed. Each IMAP command is associated with `OK`, `NO`, and `BAD` status responses, with additional details specific to the command. These status responses may be tagged or untagged, carrying additional details.

For example, the IMAP command DELETE is associated with response codes OK, NO, and BAD. The status response of OK indicates that the delete command is successful. The IMAP command LOGIN is associated with a response code of NO which will carry additional details such as an invalid username or password; this signals that the login attempt was a failure:

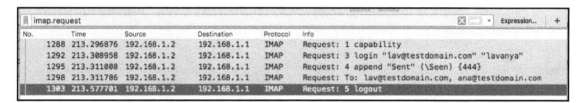

The use of imap.request will filter all the IMAP COMMAND messages from client to server. If we know the specific command, the filter can be further granulized using imap.request.command == "<>":

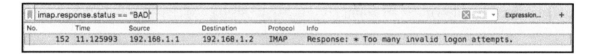

By using imap.response, we can filter all the IMAP response status messages from server to client. Imap.response.status ==<> can be used to filter by response status, such as OK, NO, or BAD.

POP3

As with IMAP, POP3 uses response messages to signal any failure between the client and server. POP3 primarily uses +OK and -ERR as response indicators, with additional details about the response:

```
▶ Frame 2371: 98 bytes on wire (784 bits), 98 bytes captured (784 bits)
▶ Ethernet II, Src: Cisco_ac:c3:0e (d4:8c:b5:ac:c3:0e), Dst: Apple_96:f7:dd (ac:bc:32:96:f7:dd)
▶ Internet Protocol Version 4, Src: 52.5.224.12, Dst: 10.118.20.8
▶ Transmission Control Protocol, Src Port: 1100, Dst Port: 63665, Seq: 58, Ack: 23, Len: 32
▼ Post Office Protocol
  ▼ -ERR Invalid login or password\r\n
      Response indicator: -ERR
      Response description: Invalid login or password
```

The preceding screenshot is an example where the Response indicator is -ERR and the description carries what type of ERR it is. In this case, ERR is related to login failure.

By using `pop.request` or `pop.response`, we can filter the packets based on POP3 request from client to server or the response from server to client, respectively. We can further use the indicator to filter based on specific response indicator:

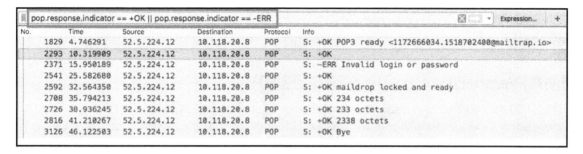

As shown here, the filter for the indicator should be `+OK` or `-ERR`.

How it works...

All email protocols use the same concept of sending a command and expecting a response or status code about the command. When the command or request from the client is executed successfully, the server sends a positive status code (such as `OK`). If there are any issues or a failure in executing the command, it sends a negative response code (such as `NO` or `BAD`). More details about the error codes are available in the *There's more...* section that follows:

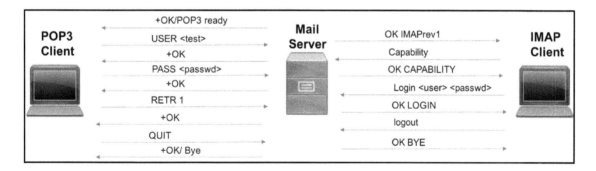

There's more...

The response code and the associated semantic for each response code is documented in different RFCs for each mail protocols. In this section, we will discuss about some of the common response codes and list the RFCs where additional details about the response codes are available.

IMAP response code (RFC 5530)

RFC 5530 lists all the response codes and the associated meaning for each response code. A consolidated view of the response codes for IMAP can also be retrieved from this IANA link: `https://www.iana.org/assignments/imap-response-codes/imap-response-codes.xhtml`.

POP3 response code (RFC 2449)

RFC 2449 lists the response code and the associated meaning for each POP3 response code. A consolidated view of POP3 response codes is also available at this IANA link: `https://www.iana.org/assignments/pop3-extension-mechanism/pop3-extension-mechanism.xhtml`.

SMTP and SMTP error codes (RFC 3463)

The structure of SMTP status codes is as follows:

```
class . subject . detail
```

For example, when you see status code `450`, it means the following:

- Class 4 indicates that it is a temporary problem
- Subject 5 indicates that it is a mail delivery status
- Detail 0 indicates an undefined error (RFC 3463)

The following table lists the various classes:

Status code	Meaning	Reason
2.x.xxx	Success	Operation succeeded.
4.x.xxx	Persistent transient failure	A temporary condition has prevented the server from sending the message. It may be due to server load or a network bottleneck. Usually, sending the message again will succeed.
5.x.xxx	Permanent failure	A permanent problem prevented the server from sending the message. Usually server or compatibility errors.

The following table lists the various subjects:

Status code	What is it?
x.0.xxx	Other or undefined status
x.1.xxx	Addressing status
x.2.xxx	Mailbox status
x.3.xxx	Mail system status
x.4.xxx	Network and routing status
x.5.xxx	Mail delivery protocol status
x.6.xxx	Message content or media status
x.7.xxx	Security or policy status

The following table lists the various details. A full list of status details is too long to be listed here, but can be found in the standard pages at `http://tools.ietf.org/html/rfc3463`.

Some common status codes are listed in the following table:

Status code	What is it?	What may be the reason?
220	Service is ready	Service is running and ready to perform mail operations.
221	Service closing transmission channel	Usually OK. This is how the server closes the service when it is not required.
250	Requested mail action is OK	Message was delivered successfully.
251	Not a local user, mail will be forwarded	Everything is OK.
252	Cannot verify the user	The user couldn't be verified by the server. The mail will be delivered.
421	Service not available	The mail transfer service is not available and cannot serve incoming mails due to a transient event. This may be due to a server problem (a service that is not running) or a server limitation.
422	Mail size problem	The recipient's mailbox has passed its quota or has a limit on incoming mail.
431	Out of memory or disk full	Server disk is either full or out of memory. Check the server.
432	Incoming mail queue has been stopped	This may be due to a server error (a service that stopped).
441	The receiving server is not responding	The server that sends the message indicates that the destination server did not response.
442	Bad connection	There is a problem with the connection to the destination server.
444	Unable to route	The server was unable to determine the next hop for the message.
445	Mail system congestion	The mail server is temporarily congested.

447	Delivery time has expired	The message was considered too old by the rejecting system. This is usually due to queuing or transmission problems.
450	Requested action not taken	Message could not be transmitted. This is usually due to a problem with the mail service on the remote server.
451	Invalid command	This indicates an unsupported or out of sequence command. The action was aborted by the receiving server. This was probably due to load on the sending or the receiving server.
452	Requested action was not taken	Insufficient storage on the receiving server.
500	Syntax error	The command sent by the server was not recognized as a valid SMTP or ESMTP command.
512	DNS error	The host server, which is the destination for the mail that was sent, could not be located.
530	Authentication problem	Authentication is required from the receiving server, or your server has been added to a blacklist by the receiving server.
542	Recipient address was rejected	A message indicating that your server address was rejected by the receiving server. This is usually due to anti-spam software, IDS/IPS systems, smart firewalls, or other security systems.

Malicious and spam email analysis

In this recipe, we will discuss the use of Wireshark to perform some basic analysis of malicious and spam emails, and use this to filter spam emails on the server itself.

Getting ready

In most cases, spam emails will be sent from outside the domain and targeted at clients within the enterprise. So, it is best to perform packet capture on the server side for analysis.

How to do it...

1. The first step is to identify the data portion of the mail messages. We can use the filter to display the data portion of the mails. The use of email protocol and data will display the packets with data. For example, use `pop || data-text-lines` to filter the mails with data using the POP3 protocol:

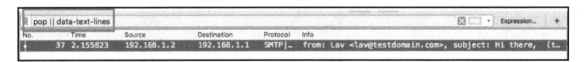

2. In the preceding screenshot, the data exchange between the specific endpoints is not so big. Based on the size, it appears to be a text message and does not carry any attachments, so we can ignore this:

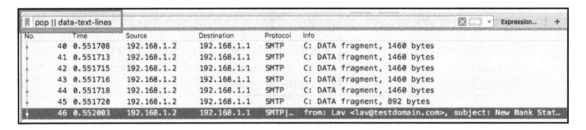

3. On the other hand, the previous capture shows that the data exchange is pretty big and it appears to carry an attachment.

4. Use follow the stream to narrow down the TCP flow. This will filter and list the mail exchange in clear text as follows:

```
250-ANANYAA-PC
250-SIZE 20480000
250-AUTH LOGIN
250 HELP
AUTH LOGIN
334 VXNlcm5hbWU6
bGF2QHRlc3Rkb21haW4uY29t
334 UGFzc3dvcmQ6
bGF2YW55YQ==
235 authenticated.
MAIL FROM:<lav@testdomain.com> SIZE=9224
250 OK
RCPT TO:<lav@testdomain.com>
250 OK
RCPT TO:<ana@testdomain.com>
250 OK
DATA
354 OK, send.
To: ana@testdomain.com, lav@testdomain.com
From: Lav <lav@testdomain.com>
Subject: New Bank Statements
Message-ID: <6d857d5e-c116-1f46-dfd3-0122d840ef1c@testdomain.com>
Date: Thu, 15 Feb 2018 10:03:20 -0500
User-Agent: Mozilla/5.0 (Macintosh; Intel Mac OS X 10.11; rv:52.0)
 Gecko/20100101 Thunderbird/52.6.0
MIME-Version: 1.0
Content-Type: multipart/mixed;
 boundary="----------0E047D05B9EF784947CC3546"
Content-Language: en-US

This is a multi-part message in MIME format.
--------------0E047D05B9EF784947CC3546
Content-Type: text/plain; charset=utf-8; format=flowed
Content-Transfer-Encoding: 7bit



--------------0E047D05B9EF784947CC3546
Content-Type: application/pdf;
 name="bank-statement.pdf"
Content-Transfer-Encoding: base64
Content-Disposition: attachment;
 filename="bank-statement.pdf"
```

In the preceding screenshot, we can see that this email carries a PDF file. Use the sender, receiver, subject, and related information to identify whether the mail is genuine. Alternatively, we can use other malware detection software to look for any issues in the attachment.

If a similar attachment is seen on multiple emails, identify the common sender and create a spam rule in the server to mark it as spam or filter such emails directly.

How it works...

Most email servers support spam and junk message detection, and dynamically create filter rules for such emails. Servers also support customizing such rules based on sender/receiver mail address, or based on domain and IP.

When the server receives a mail from an internal client using IMAP/POP3, or from an external server using SMTP, it checks the local filters and forwards it to the respective inbox if the rules allow it to do so. If any rule matches certain attributes or metadata in the mail, the server will filter the message.

On the email client, we can optionally have email-scanning software for more rigid security. Such software will perform additional checks on the client side and mark it as spam or malicious, and warn the user about it.

15
NetBIOS and SMB Protocol Analysis

In this chapter, we will cover the following recipes:

- NetBIOS name, datagram, and session services
- SMB/SMB2/SMB3 details and operation
- Different problems and how to analyze them
- Connectivity and performance problems
- Common problems with database traffic and steps to analyze
- Export SMB objects – how to use it

Introduction

One of the important things that you can use Wireshark for is application analysis and troubleshooting. When an application slows down, it can be because of the LAN (quite uncommon in a wired LAN), the WAN service (common due to insufficient bandwidth or high delay), or slow servers or clients (we will see this in the *Database traffic and common problems* section). It can also be due to slow or problematic applications.

The purpose of this chapter is to get into the details of how applications work, and provide some guidelines and recipes for isolating and solving these problems. In the first recipe, we will learn how to find out and categorize applications that work over our network. Then, we will go through various types of applications, see how they work, how the network influences their behavior, and what can go wrong.

In this chapter, we will learn how to use Wireshark in order to resolve and troubleshoot common applications that are used in an enterprise network, such as NetBIOS and SMB protocols.

Understanding the NetBIOS protocol

Network Basic Input/Output System (**NetBIOS**) is a set of protocols developed in the early 1980s for LAN communications, in order to provide services for the session layer (fifth layer in the OSI model). A few years later, it was adopted by Microsoft for their networking over LAN, and then it was migrated for working over TCP/IP (NetBIOS over TCP/IP—NBT), which is discussed in RFC 1001 and 1002.

In today's networks, NetBIOS provides three services:

- **Name service** (port 137) for name registration and name to IP address resolution. Also referred to as NetBIOS-NS.
- **Datagram distribution service** (port 138) for service announcements by clients and servers. Also referred to as NetBIOS-DGM.
- **Session service** (port 139) for session negotiation between hosts. This is used for accessing files, opening directories, and so on. Also referred to as NetBIOS-SSN.

NBNS is the service that registers and translates names to IP addresses. Registration happens when a client registers its name in the domain controller. The client sends a registration request and then gets a response of whether the registration is OK or the name is registered with another device. The Microsoft environment was implemented with WINS, and as most networks did not use it, it was later replaced by DNS. It works over UDP port 137.

NBDS is used for service announcements by clients and servers. With this service, devices on the network announce their names, services that they can provide to other devices on the network, and how to connect to these services. It works over UDP port 138.

NBSS is used to establish sessions between hosts, open or save files, and execute remote files and other sessions over the network. It works over TCP port 139.

There are additional protocols, such as **Server Message Block** (**SMB**), that run over NBSS for transaction operations and over NBDS for service announcement, spools for printer requests, and several others. Getting into the details of NetBIOS is beyond the scope of this book. If you are required to troubleshoot NetBIOS protocols, follow the instructions in this section and pay special attention to error messages and notes.

Understanding the SMB protocol

We have briefly discussed SMB in earlier sections, and have also seen relevant filters. Just to refresh, SMB is a protocol that is used for browsing directories, copying files, accessing services such as printers, and several other operations over the network. **Common Internet File System** (**CIFS**) is a form, or flavor, of SMB.

SMB runs on top of the session layer protocols such as NetBIOS as originally designed or can also run directly over TCP port `445`. SMB 2.0 was introduced by Microsoft in 2006 in Windows Vista, with the intention of reducing the commands and subcommands required in the SMB 1.0 protocol. Even though SMB 2.0 came out as a proprietary protocol, Microsoft published the standard to allow other systems to interoperate with their operating systems.

SMB 2.1 was released with Windows 7 and Server 2008 R2 with performance improvements compared to SMB 2.0.

SMB 3.0 (earlier referred to as SMB 2.2) was introduced with Windows 8 and Server 2012. SMM 3.0 has significant performance improvements (compared to earlier releases) in order to support virtualization occurring in the data center computing environment.

How it works...

SMB works in a client-server model, where the client makes specific requests to the server, and based on the requests, the server responds accordingly. Most of the requests are related to accessing filesystems, while other forms of requests involve **Inter-Process Communication** (**IPC**). IPC is a mechanism that facilitates different processes to communicate with each other, irrespective of them running on the same device or multiple devices across the network.

Analyzing problems in the NetBIOS/SMB protocols

In this chapter, we will get into some common problems with the NetBIOS suite of protocols, and we will learn how to try and solve them. Since the NetBIOS set of protocols is quite complicated, and there are hundreds of scenarios where things might go wrong, we will try to provide some guidelines for how to look for common problems and what might go wrong.

Getting ready

NetBIOS protocols work in Windows environments, along with macOS and Linux machines communicating with Windows. When facing problems such as instability, slow response times, disconnections, and so on in these environments, NetBIOS issues can be one of the reasons. When facing these problems, the tool for solving them is Wireshark. It will show you what is running over the network, and Windows tools will show you what runs on the clients and servers.

How to do it...

To try and find out what the problem could be, connect your laptop with Wireshark to the network and port-mirror the suspected clients or server as described here. In the following sections, we will see several scenarios for several problems.

There are many predefined filters that are used with NetBIOS. You can find them by clicking on the **Expression...** button, which is on the right-hand side of the **Display Filters** window:

- General NetBIOS commands start with `netbios`
- NetBIOS name service commands start with `nbns`
- NetBIOS datagram service commands start with `nbds`
- NetBIOS session service commands start with `nbss`
- SMB commands start with `smb` or `smb2`

General tests

First, take a general look at the network. Then, look for suspicious patterns:

1. Connect Wireshark to the network. Make sure the workstation running Wireshark is on the same broadcast domain as the clients that are having the problems.
2. Configure the display filter `nbns.flags.response == 0`. It will give you the NBNS requests. You will see many broadcasts, as shown in the following screenshot:

Filter:	nbns.flags.response == 0		▾	Expression... Clear Apply Save NBNS NBDS NBSS			
No.	Time	Source	Destination		Protocol	Length	Info
4994	0.000002	10.0.0.103	10.0.0.255	①	NBNS	110	Registration NB WORKGROUP<1e>
4997	0.749962	10.0.0.103	10.0.0.255		NBNS	110	Registration NB ETTI<20>
4998	0.000002	10.0.0.103	10.0.0.255		NBNS	110	Registration NB WORKGROUP<1e>
5057	10.255261	10.0.0.102	10.0.0.255	②	NBNS	92	Name query NB WPAD<00>
5075	0.763927	10.0.0.102	10.0.0.255		NBNS	92	Name query NB WPAD<00>
5088	0.512027	10.0.0.138	10.0.0.105		NBNS	92	Name query NBSTAT *<00><00><00><00><00>
5091	0.252327	10.0.0.102	10.0.0.255		NBNS	92	Name query NB WPAD<00>
5141	16.912745	10.0.0.105	10.0.0.255	③	NBNS	92	Name query NB YORASM-NDI<1c>
5144	0.749377	10.0.0.105	10.0.0.255		NBNS	92	Name query NB YORASM-NDI<1c>
5147	0.750008	10.0.0.105	10.0.0.255		NBNS	92	Name query NB YORASM-NDI<1c>
5265	4.215402	169.254.26.83	169.254.255.255	④	NBNS	92	Name query NB UM23.ESET.COM<00>
5287	0.744925	169.254.26.83	169.254.255.255		NBNS	92	Name query NB UM23.ESET.COM<00>
5297	0.749979	169.254.26.83	169.254.255.255		NBNS	92	Name query NB UM23.ESET.COM<00>
5298	0.751111	169.254.26.83	169.254.255.255		NBNS	92	Name query NB UM23.ESET.COM<00>

Figure 15.1: NBNS packet types

3. As you saw in the preceding screenshot, in the capture file you will see the following:

- **NBNS registration packets (1)**: In the examples, there are registrations with the names WORKGROUP and ETTI. The NBNS server will accept or reject the name registration by issuing a positive or negative name registration response to the requesting node. If none is received, the requesting node will assume it is OK.
- **NBNS queries (2, 3, and 4)**: Queries are sent for the name specified. If there is an NBNS server (this is the domain controller), you will see one of the following responses:
  - Requested name does not exist (code 3)
  - No error (code 0)

4. Make sure there is no registration or any other requests coming from addresses that start with 169.254 (5). These are **Automatic Private IP Addressing** (**APIPA**) addresses. This actually means that the PC is configured to accept addresses automatically (by DHCP) and it has not received one.

5. There are many announcement packets as well. These will be broadcast on UDP port 138. Here, you will see that every station announces its capabilities: workstation, server, print server, and so on. For example, you can see here that:

- 172.16.100.10 name is FILE-SRV, and it functions like a workstation, server, and SQL server (**1**)

- `172.16.100.204` name is `GOLF`, and it functions like a workstation, server, and a print queue server (**2**)

No.	Source	Destination	Protocol	Length	Info
10119	172.16.100.176	172.16.100.255	BROWSER	243	Host Announcement ZIVAK, workstation, Server, Windows for W
10179	172.16.100.119	172.16.100.255	BROWSER	243	Host Announcement MERAVT1, Workstation, Server, NT Workstat
10332	172.16.100.16	172.16.100.255	BROWSER	244	Host Announcement GNETAPP, Workstation, Server, NT Workstat
10424	172.16.100.96	172.16.100.255	BROWSER	243	Host Announcement HAGITA, Workstation, Server, NT Workstati
1047①	172.16.100.10	172.16.100.255	BROWSER	243	Host Announcement FILE-SRV, Workstation, Server, SQL Server
10542	172.16.100.94	172.16.100.255	BROWSER	243	Host Announcement ORNAP1, Workstation, Server, NT Workstati
1072②	172.16.100.204	172.16.100.255	BROWSER	264	Host Announcement GOLF, Workstation, Server, Print Queue Se
10721	172.16.100.204	172.16.100.255	BROWSER	264	Host Announcement GOLF, Workstation, Server, Print Queue Se
10766	172.16.100.124	172.16.100.255	BROWSER	243	Host Announcement ADIP, Workstation, Server, NT Workstation
10768	172.16.100.170	172.16.100.255	BROWSER	243	Host Announcement MICHALA, Workstation, Server, NT Workstat
10929	172.16.100.106	172.16.100.255	BROWSER	258	Domain/workgroup Announcement NDI, NT Workstation, Domain E

Filter: `tcp.port==138 or udp.port==138`   Expression... Clear Apply Save NBNS ▶   Host Announcing services   Announced services

```
⊞ Frame 10119: 243 bytes on wire (1944 bits), 243 bytes captured (1944 bits)
⊞ Ethernet II, Src: 3com_82:9a:c7 (00:50:da:82:9a:c7), Dst: Broadcast (ff:ff:ff:ff:ff:ff)
⊞ Internet Protocol Version 4, Src: 172.16.100.176 (172.16.100.176), Dst: 172.16.100.255 (172.16.100.255)
⊞ User Datagram Protocol, Src Port: netbios-dgm (138), Dst Port: netbios-dgm (138)
⊞ NetBIOS Datagram Service
⊞ SMB (Server Message Block Protocol)          NetBIOS
⊞ SMB MailSlot Protocol                        Protocol
⊞ Microsoft Windows Browser Protocol           Structure
```

Figure 15.2: NetBIOS service announcement

6. There are some worms and viruses that are using the NetBIOS name service to scan the network. Look for unusual patterns such as massive scanning, high broadcast rate, and so on.

7. Verify that you don't have too many broadcasts. 5 to 10 broadcast/minute/device are reasonable. More than this usually means a problem.

> There are hundreds of message scenarios you can see here. Use the Wireshark expert system, Google, and common sense to find out the problem.

Specific issues

Here are some issues and problems you might see during usual operations:

- Using SMB, which is the protocol that is used for browsing directories, copying files, and other operations over the network, you might see some error codes. The full list of error classes and codes is listed in Microsoft MSDN:

  `http://msdn.microsoft.com/en-us/library/ee441884.aspx` and `https://tinyurl.com/y7kuxygd`.

- Code 0 means STATUS_OK, which implies that everything works fine and there is no problem. Any other code should be examined.
- In the following example, you can see a message STATUS_ACCESS_DENIED. This is one of many error codes you should look for. In the example, access to \NAS01HOMEDIR on a server with an IP address that starts with 203 (full address hidden for security reasons) was denied.
- When you try to see the home directory by browsing it, Windows will usually show you an access denied message or something similar. This problem can happen when an application is trying to access a directory and cannot get access to it. In this case, you see an access denied message, a software communication problem message, or any other message the programmers have made for you. Using Wireshark in this case will get you to the exact error, and Google will show you the reason for it:

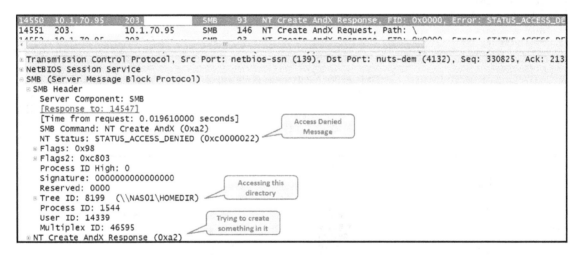

Figure 15.3: SMB error classes and codes—access denied

- In the next example, we see a status STATUS_MORE_PROCESSING_REQUIRED (2) that happened during session setup (1) on \NAS01SAMIM (3).
- Looking at the link mentioned earlier, we see that this is because on the designated named pipe, there is more data available to read.

- A short Google search tells us that it might indicate a credentials problem. Check with your system administrator:

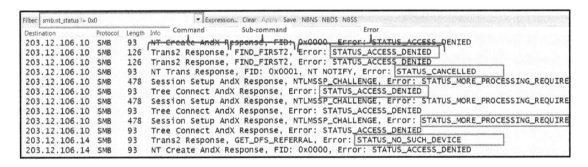

```
No.      Source        Destination    Protocol   Length  Info
23894  10.1.70.95  203.                SMB      478   Session Setup AndX Response, NTLMSSP_CHALLENGE, Error: STATUS_MOR
23800  10 1 70 95  203                 SMB      03    Tree Connect AndY Peronnse  Error: STATUS ACCESS DENIED

Internet Protocol Version 4, Src: 10.1.70.95 (10.1.70.95), Dst: 203.            (203.          )
Transmission Control Protocol, Src Port: netbios-ssn (139), Dst Port: nuts-dem (4132), Seq: 358564, Ack: 2252
NetBIOS Session Service
SMB (Server Message Block Protocol)
  SMB Header
    Server Component: SMB
    [Response to: 23893]
    [Time from request: 0.019370000 seconds]                          (1)
    SMB Command: Session Setup AndX (0x73)
    NT Status: STATUS_MORE_PROCESSING_REQUIRED (0xc0000016)           (2)
    Flags: 0x98
    Flags2: 0xc803
    Process ID High: 0
    Signature: 0000000000000000
    Reserved: 0000
    Tree ID: 0   (\\NAS01\SAMIM) (3)
    Process ID: 65279
    User ID: 16386
    Multiplex ID: 54339
  Session Setup AndX Response (0x73)
```

Figure 15.4: SMB error classes and codes—named pipe

- To see all SMB error messages, type the filter `smb.nt_status != 0x0`. You will get all error responses, as shown in the following screenshot:

```
Filter: smb.nt_status != 0x0                    ▼ Expression... Clear Apply Save NBNS NBDS NBSS
Destination      Protocol  Length  Info    Command        Sub-command        Error
203.12.106.10   SMB       93    NT Create AndX Response, FID: 0x0000  Error: STATUS_ACCESS_DENIED
203.12.106.10   SMB       126   Trans2 Response, FIND_FIRST2, Error: STATUS_ACCESS_DENIED
203.12.106.10   SMB       126   Trans2 Response, FIND_FIRST2, Error: STATUS_ACCESS_DENIED
203.12.106.10   SMB       93    NT Trans Response, FID: 0x0001, NT NOTIFY, Error: STATUS_CANCELLED
203.12.106.10   SMB       478   Session Setup AndX Response, NTLMSSP_CHALLENGE, Error: STATUS_MORE_PROCESSING_REQUIRE
203.12.106.10   SMB       93    Tree Connect AndX Response, Error: STATUS_ACCESS_DENIED
203.12.106.10   SMB       478   Session Setup AndX Response, NTLMSSP_CHALLENGE, Error: STATUS_MORE_PROCESSING_REQUIRE
203.12.106.10   SMB       93    Tree Connect AndX Response, Error: STATUS_ACCESS_DENIED
203.12.106.10   SMB       478   Session Setup AndX Response, NTLMSSP_CHALLENGE, Error: STATUS_MORE_PROCESSING_REQUIRE
203.12.106.10   SMB       93    Tree Connect AndX Response, Error: STATUS_ACCESS_DENIED
203.12.106.14   SMB       93    Trans2 Response, GET_DFS_REFERRAL, Error: STATUS_NO_SUCH_DEVICE
203.12.106.14   SMB       93    NT Create AndX Response, FID: 0x0000, Error: STATUS_ACCESS_DENIED
```

Figure 15.5: SMB error classes and codes—filtering errors

There's more...

In this section, I would like to show some examples to get a better understanding of the NetBIOS protocols.

Example 1 – application freezing

In the following screenshot, we see the reason for an application freeze:

No.	Time	Source	Destination	Protocol	Info
26562	362.699257	203.	10.1.70.95 ①	SMB	Tree Connect AndX Request, Path: \\NAS01\SAMIM
26563	362.717483	10.1.70.95	203	SMB	Tree Connect AndX Response, Error: STATUS_ACCESS_DENIED
26564	362.717635	203.	10.1.70.95 ②	SMB	Logoff AndX Request
26565	362.734572	10.1.70.95	203.	SMB	Logoff AndX Response
26572	362.853441	203.	10.1.70.95	TCP	nuts-dem > netbios-ssn [ACK] Seq=226260 Ack=359968 Win=
36000	482.813425	10.1.70.95	203.	TCP	netbios-ssn > nuts-dem [ACK] Seq=339967 Ack=226260 Win=
36001	482.813508	203.	10.1.70.95	TCP	[TCP Dup ACK 26572#1] nuts-dem > netbios-ssn [ACK] Seq=
44869	602.799670	10.1.70.95	203.	TCP	[TCP Keep-Alive] netbios-ssn > nuts-dem [ACK] Seq=35996
44872	602.800321	203.	10.1.70.95 ③	TCP	[TCP Keep-Alive ACK] nuts-dem > netbios-ssn [ACK] Seq=2
55372	722.786747	10.1.70.95	203.	TCP	[TCP Keep-Alive] netbios-ssn > nuts-dem [ACK] Seq=35996
55375	722.787380	203.	10.1.70.95	TCP	[TCP Keep-Alive ACK] nuts-dem > netbios-ssn [ACK] Seq=2
59751	798.181386	10.1.70.95	203.	NBSS	Session keep-alive
59758	798.390573	203.	10.1.70.95	TCP	nuts-dem > netbios-ssn [ACK] Seq=226260 Ack=359972 Win=
60622	816.812860	203.	10.1.70.95 ④	SMB	Tree Disconnect Request
60623	816.829093	10.1.70.95	203.	SMB	Tree Disconnect Response
60627	816.984481	203.	10.1.70.95	TCP	nuts-dem > netbios-ssn [ACK] Seq=226299 Ack=360011 Win=
64565	936.948575	10.1.70.95	203.	TCP	[TCP Keep-Alive] netbios-ssn > nuts-dem [ACK] Seq=36001
64568	936.949116	203.	10.1.70.95 ⑤	TCP	[TCP Keep-Alive ACK] nuts-dem > netbios-ssn [ACK] Seq=2
75087	1056.936316	10.1.70.95	203.	TCP	[TCP Keep-Alive] netbios-ssn > nuts-dem [ACK] Seq=36001
75088	1056.936568	203.	10.1.70.95	TCP	[TCP Keep-Alive ACK] nuts-dem > netbios-ssn [ACK] Seq=2
84066	1142.229579	10.1.70.95	203. ⑥	TCP	netbios-ssn > nuts-dem [RST, ACK] Seq=360011 Ack=226299

Figure 15.6: Error condition—application freeze

In the example, we make the following observations:

- A client with an IP address that starts with 203 is trying to connect to \NAS01SAMIM on a server with an IP address 10.1.70.95, and gets back a STATUS_ACCESS_DENIED error
- The server on 10.1.70.95 answers that the access is denied
- Since the application waits, TCP is holding the connection with keep-alive messages
- After a while, the client sends disconnect request that is approved by the server
- The application waits and TCP maintains the connection with keep-alive
- TCP closes the connection with RST (reset)

What the customer saw here was an application freeze.

Example 2 – broadcast storm caused by SMB

In one of my client's networks, I received an urgent call that a remote office was disconnected from the HQ. Some network details are as follows:

- The remote office addresses are on subnet 172.30.121.0/24, with a default gateway 172.30.121.254.
- The HQ addresses are on subnet 172.30.0.0/24. The connections between the remote offices and the HQ are with L3 IP-VPNs over an MPLS network.

To solve the problem, I did the following:

- I tried to ping the servers in the HQ. I got no response.
- I called the service provider that provides the lines to the center, and they said that on their monitoring system they didn't see any load on the line.
- I pinged the local router, 172.30.121.254, and got no response. This means that PCs on the LAN couldn't even get to their local router, which is their default gateway.
- I connected a Wireshark with port-mirror to the router port, and I saw something like the following screenshot:

No.	Time	Source	Destination	Protocol	Info
22	0.000002	172.30.121.1	172.30.121.255	SMB Mailslot	Write Mail Slot
23	0.000001	172.30.121.1	172.30.121.255	SMB Mailslot	Write Mail Slot
24	0.000001	172.30.121.1	172.30.121.255	SMB Mailslot	Write Mail Slot
25	0.000001	172.30.121.1	172.30.121.255	SMB Mailslot	Write Mail Slot
26	0.000002	172.30.121.1	172.30.121.255	SMB Mailslot	Write Mail Slot
27	0.000910	172.30.121.1	172.30.121.255	SMB Mailslot	Write Mail Slot
28	0.000002	172.30.121.1	172.30.121.255	SMB Mailslot	Write Mail Slot
29	0.000001	172.30.121.1	172.30.121.255	SMB Mailslot	Write Mail Slot
30	0.000001	172.30.121.1	172.30.121.255	SMB Mailslot	Write Mail Slot
31	0.000857	172.30.121.1	172.30.121.255	SMB Mailslot	Write Mail Slot

```
⊞ Frame 1: 277 bytes on wire (2216 bits), 277 bytes captured (2216 bits) on interface 1
⊞ Ethernet II, Src: Hewlett-_2b:5d:e3 (f4:ce:46:2b:5d:e3), Dst: Broadcast (ff:ff:ff:ff:ff:ff)
⊞ Internet Protocol Version 4, Src: 172.30.121.1 (172.30.121.1), Dst: 172.30.121.255 (172.30.121.255)
⊞ User Datagram Protocol, Src Port: netbios-dgm (138), Dst Port: netbios-dgm (138)
⊞ NetBIOS Datagram Service              ┐ SMB
⊞ SMB (Server Message Block Protocol)   ├ Mailslot
⊞ SMB Mailslot Protocol                 │ Protocol
⊞ Data (65 bytes)                       ┘
```

Figure 15.7: Error condition—broadcast storm

- I saw that a huge amount of packets were generated within microseconds (**1**) by a host with IP address 172.30.121.1. The packets are broadcast (**3**), and the service that generated them is Write Mail Slot (**5**), which is sent by the SMB Mailslot protocol (**4**).

- To get a picture of the number of packets, I used the I/O graphs feature. I got 5,000 packets per second, that generated 10 Mbps that blocked the poor old router port (changing the router port to 100 Mbps or 1 Gbps wouldn't help; it still would have been blocked.

- When I didn't find anything about it on Google or Microsoft, I started to stop services that I didn't know, keeping track of what happened with the broadcast after every change. Eventually, I found that the service that caused the problem was called `LS3Bcast.exe`. I stopped it and made sure it didn't come back, and that was it.

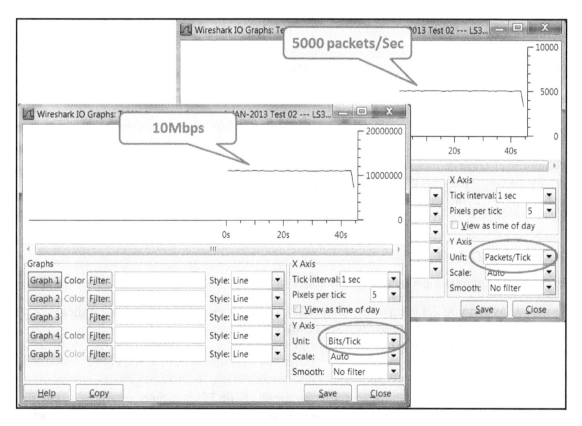

Figure 15.8: SMB broadcast storm—traffic rate

Analyzing the database traffic and common problems

Some of you may wonder why I have added this section here. After all, databases are considered to be a completely different branch in the IT environment. There are databases and applications on one side, and the network and infrastructure on the other side. This is correct, since we are not supposed to debug databases; there are DBAs for this. But with the information that runs over the network, we can see some issues that can help the DBAs with solving the problem.

In most cases, the IT staff will come to us first because people blame the network for everything. We will have to make sure that the problems are not coming from the network, and that's it. In a minority of the cases, we will see some details in the capture file that can help the DBAs with what they are doing.

Getting ready

When the IT team come to us complaining about a slow network, there are some things to do just to verify that it is not the case. Follow the instructions in the following section to make sure we avoid slow network issues.

How to do it...

In the case of database problems, follow these steps:

1. When you get complaints about slow network responses, start asking these questions to define the problem precisely:
    - Is the problem local or global? Does it occur only in the remote offices, or also in the center? When the problem occurs in the entire network, it is not a WAN bandwidth issue.
    - Does it happen the same for all clients? If not, there might be a specific problem that happens only with some users, because only these users are running a specific application that causes the problem.
    - Is the communication line between the clients and the server loaded? What is the application that loads them?

- Do all applications work slowly, or is it only the application that works with the specific database? Maybe some PCs are old and tired, or is it a server that runs out of resources?

2. When we are done with the questionnaire, let's start our work:

   1. Open Wireshark and start capturing packets. You can configure port-mirror to a specific PC, to the server, to a VLAN, or to a router that connects to a remote office in which you have the clients.

   2. Look at TCP events (expert info). Do they happen on the entire communication link, on specific IP address/addresses, or on specific TCP port number/numbers? This will help you isolate the problem and verify whether it is on a specific link, server, or application.

> When measuring traffic on a connection to the internet, you will get many retransmissions and duplicate ACKs to websites, mail servers, and so on. This is the internet. In an organization, you should expect 0.1 to 0.5 percent retransmissions. When connecting to the internet, you can expect much higher numbers.

3. If you see problems in the network, solve them as we learned in previous chapters. However, there are some network issues that can influence database behavior. In the following example, we see the behavior of a client that works with the server over a communication line with a roundtrip delay of 35 to 40 ms.

   1. We are looking at the TCP stream number eight (**1**), and the connection started with TCP SYN/SYN-ACK/ACK. I've set this as a reference (**2**). We can see that the entire connection took 371 packets (**3**).

No.	Time	Source	Destination	Protocol	Info
1840	*REF*	192.168.20.88	192.168.10.80	TCP	vfo > wv-csp-udp-cir [SYN] Seq=0 W
1844	0.013483	192.168.10.80	192.168.20.88	TCP	wv-csp-udp-cir > vfo [SYN, ACK] Se
1845	0.013496	192.168.20.88	192.168.10.80	TCP	vfo > wv-csp-udp-cir [ACK] Seq=1 A
1846	0.015710	192.168.20.88	192.168.10.80	TCP	vfo > wv-csp-udp-cir [PSH, ACK] Se
1847	0.044857	192.168.10.80	192.168.20.88	TCP	wv-csp-udp-cir > vfo [PSH, ACK] Se
1848	0.045057	192.168.20.88	192.168.10.80	TCP	vfo > wv-csp-udp-cir [PSH, ACK] Se
1849	0.075752	192.168.10.80	192.168.20.88	TCP	wv-csp-udp-cir > vfo [PSH, ACK] Se

Filter: tcp.stream eq 8 (**1**) Expression... Clear Apply Save NBNS NBDS NBSS

⊞ Frame 1930: 87 bytes on wire (696 bits), 87 bytes captured (696 bits)
⊞ Ethernet II, Src: Hewlett-_3e:54:e7 (00:0b:cd:3e:54:e7), Dst: Cisco_4f:4a:ec (00:60:47:4f:4
⊞ Internet Protocol Version 4, Src: 192.168.20.88 (192.168.20.88), Dst: 192.168.10.80 (192.16
⊞ Transmission Control Protocol, Src Port: vfo (1056), Dst Port: wv-csp-udp-cir (3717), Seq:
⊞ Data (33 bytes)

(**3**) File: "C:\Courses\Upstream Systems\PCAP Files\Example 0... | Packets: 6494 Displayed: 371 Marked: 0 Load time: 0:00.307 | Profile: Wireless

Figure 15.9: Following a TCP stream

2. The connection continues, and we see time intervals of around 35 ms between DB requests and responses:

No.	Time	Source	Destination	Protocol	Info
1981	35.833309	192.168.20.88	192.168.10.80	TCP	vfo > wv-csp-udp-cir [PSH, ACK] Se(
1982	35.869385	36mS 168.10.80	192.168.20.88	TCP	wv-csp-udp-cir > vfo [PSH, ACK] Se(
1983	35.869930	192.168.20.88	192.168.10.80	TCP	vfo > wv-csp-udp-cir [PSH, ACK] Se(
1984	35.905654	36mS 168.10.80	192.168.20.88	TCP	wv-csp-udp-cir > vfo [PSH, ACK] Se(
1985	35.906194	192.168.20.88	192.168.10.80	TCP	vfo > wv-csp-udp-cir [PSH, ACK] Se(
1986	35.944428	38mS 168.10.80	192.168.20.88	TCP	wv-csp-udp-cir > vfo [PSH, ACK] Se(
1987	35.953804	192.168.20.88	192.168.10.80	TCP	vfo > wv-csp-udp-cir [PSH, ACK] Se(

Figure 15.10: Database requests and responses—time interval

3. Since we have 371 packets travelling back and forth, 371 x 35 ms gives us around 13 seconds. Add to this some retransmissions that might happen and some inefficiencies, and this leads to a user waiting for 10 to 15 seconds and more for a database query.

4. In this case, you should consult with the DBA on how to significantly reduce the number of packets that run over the network; or you can move to another way of access, for example, terminal server or web access.

5. Another problem that can happen is that you will have a software issue that will be reflected in the capture file. If you have a look at the following screenshot, you will see that there are five retransmissions, and then a new connection is opened from the client side. It looks like a TCP problem, but it occurs only in a specific window in the software. It is simply a software procedure that stopped processing, and this stopped the TCP from responding to the client:

No.	Time	Source	Destination	Protocol	Info
					http > vrtp [ACK] Seq=1 Ack=59884 Wir
274	0.078889	192.168.3.50	192.168.200.227	TCP	http > vrtp [ACK] Seq=1 Ack=59884 Wir
275	0.380166	192.168.200.227	192.168.3.50	TCP	[TCP Retransmission] [TCP segment of
276	0.983678	192.168.200.227	192.168.3.50	TCP	[TCP Retransmission] [TCP segment of
277	2.195589	192.168.200.227	192.168.3.50	TCP	[TCP Retransmission] [TCP segment of
278	4.604757	192.168.200.227	192.168.3.50	TCP	[TCP Retransmission] [TCP segment of
279	9.432867	192.168.200.227	192.168.3.50	TCP	[TCP Retransmission] [TCP segment of
280	18.989050	192.168.200.227	192.168.3.50	TCP	rcts > http [SYN] Seq=0 Win=65535 Ler
281	18.994054	192.168.3.50	192.168.200.227	TCP	http > rcts [SYN, ACK] Seq=0 Ack=1 Wi
282	18.994085	192.168.200.227	192.168.3.50	TCP	rcts > http [ACK] Seq=1 Ack=1 Win=655
283	18.994264	192.168.200.227	192.168.3.50	TCP	[TCP segment of a reassembled PDU]
284	18.994280	192.168.200.227	192.168.3.50	TCP	[TCP segment of a reassembled PDU]
285	19.000271	192.168.3.50	192.168.200.227	TCP	http > rcts [ACK] Seq=1 Ack=537 Win=6

Figure 15.11: Following a TCP stream—retransmissions

How it works...

Well, how databases work is always a mystery to me. Our task is to find out how they influence the network, and this is what we've learned in this section.

There's more...

When you right-click on one of the packets in the database client to the server session, a window with the conversation will open. It can be helpful to the DBA to see what is running over the network.

When you are facing delay problems, for example, when working over cellular lines over the internet or over international connections, the database client to the server will not always be efficient enough. You might need to move to web or terminal access to the database.

An important issue is how the database works. If the client is accessing the database server, and the database server is using files shared from another server, it could be that the client-server works great, but the problems come from the database server to the shared files on the file server. Make sure that you know all these dependencies before starting with your tests.

And, most importantly, make sure you have very professional DBAs as friends. One day you will need them.

Exporting SMB objects

Exporting SMB objects is a simple feature for exporting SMB statistics.

Getting ready

To export HTTP objects, choose **File** | **Export Objects** | **SMB/SMB2**.

How to do it...

To export SMB objects, follow these steps:

1. You can use this feature when a capture is running, or you can run it on the captured file. You will get the following window:

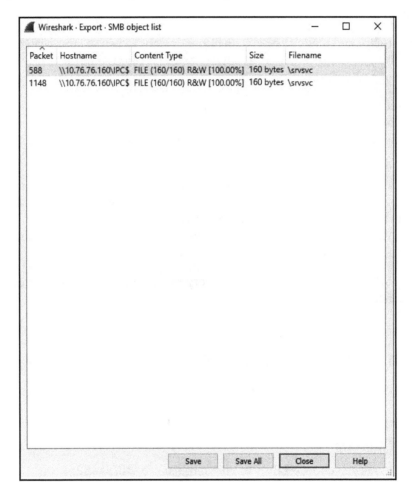

Figure 15.12: SMB—object export

2. From here, you can get a list of the servers that were accessed, including the files that were accessed in each one of them. You can see the packet number, hostname, content type (with operation mode, read or read/write), size, and filename.

3. You can use the **Save As** or **Save All** buttons for saving the data in a file.

4. In the **Content Type** column, you will see the following contents:
   - **FILE**: If the content that is accessed is a file served by the specified server(s).
   - **PIPE**: As we discussed in the earlier sections of this chapter, SMB is also used for IPC. For this IPC mechanism, the SMB system provides a named pipes service. For example, Microsoft's implementation of RPC over SMB operates using named pipes infrastructure. Details on named pipes is beyond the scope of this book, as is any other file discovered by Wireshark.

 For the export SMB objects feature to work, first go to TCP preferences and enable TCP packets reassembly (allow subdissector to reassemble TCP streams).

Once exported and saved successfully, you should see the data (file, pictures, or anything that is accessed using SMB) built by reassembling the packets.

How it works...

This feature scans SMB packets in the currently opened capture file or the running capture, takes reassembled objects, and lets you save them to a disk. The saved objects can then be opened with the proper viewer, or they can be executed, in the case of executable files, just by clicking on them. This feature can be helpful for various purposes, including eavesdropping and saving objects for backup (for example, files that were accessed via file sharing).

16
Analyzing Enterprise Applications' Behavior

In this chapter, we will cover the following recipes:

- Finding out what is running over your network
- Analyzing Microsoft Terminal Server and Citrix problems and protocols
- Analyzing database traffic and common problems
- Analyzing SNMP

Introduction

One of the important things that you can use Wireshark for is application analysis and troubleshooting. When the application slows down, it can be because of the LAN (quite uncommon in wired LAN), the WAN service (common due to insufficient bandwidth or high delay), or slow servers or clients (we will see this in TCP window problems). It can also be due to slow or problematic applications.

The purpose of this chapter is to get into the details of how applications work, and provide relevant guidelines and recipes for isolating and solving these problems. In the first recipe, we will learn how to find out and categorize applications that work over our network. Then, we will go through various types of applications to see how they work, how networks influence their behavior, and what can go wrong.

In this chapter, we will learn how to use Wireshark in order to resolve and troubleshoot common applications that are used in an enterprise network. These are Microsoft Terminal Server and Citrix, databases, and **Simple Network Management Protocol** (**SNMP**).

Finding out what is running over your network

The first thing to do when monitoring a new network is to find out what is running over it. There are various types of applications and network protocols, and they can influence and interfere with each other when all of them are running over the network.

In some cases, you will have different VLANs, different **Virtual Routing and Forwardings** (**VRFs**), or servers that are connected to virtual ports in a blade server.
Eventually, everything is running on the same infrastructure, and they can influence each other.

There is a common confusion between VRFs and VLANs. Even though their purpose is quite the same, they are configured in different places. While VLANs are configured in the LAN in order to provide network separation in the OSI layers 1 and 2, VRFs are multiple instances of routing tables to make them coexist in the same router. This is a layer 3 operation that separates between different customer's networks. VRFs are generally seen in service provider environments using **Multi-Protocol Label Switching** (**MPLS**) to provide layer 3 connectivity to different customers over the same router's network, in such a way that no customer can see any other customer's network.

In this recipe, we will see how to get to the details of what is running over the network, and the applications that can slow it down.

The term blade server refers to a server enclosure, which is a chassis of server shelves on the front and LAN switches on the back. There are several different acronyms for it; for example, IBM calls them blade center and HP calls them blade system.

Getting ready

When you get into a new network, the first thing to do is connect Wireshark to sniff what is running over the applications and protocols. Make sure you follow these points:

- When you are required to monitor a server, port-mirror it and see what is running on its connection to the network.
- When you are required to monitor a remote office, port-mirror the router port that connects you to the WAN connection. Then, check what is running over it.

- When you are required to monitor a slow connection to the internet, port-mirror it to see what is going on there.

In this recipe, we will see how to use the Wireshark tools for analyzing what is running and what can cause problems.

How to do it...

For analyzing who is talking, follow these steps:

1. Connect Wireshark using one of the options mentioned in the previous section.
2. You can use the following tools:
   - Navigate to **Statistics | Protocol Hierarchy** to view the protocols that run over the network and the percentage of the total traffic
   - Navigate to **Statistics | Conversations** to see who is talking and what protocols are used

3. In the **Protocol Hierarchy** feature, you will get a window that will help you analyze who is talking over the network. It is shown in the following screenshot:

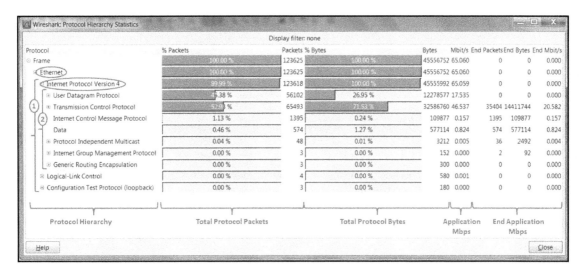

In the preceding screenshot, you can see the protocol distribution:

- **Ethernet**: IP, **Logical-Link Control** (**LLC**), and configuration test protocol (loopback)
- **Internet Protocol Version 4**: UDP, TCP, **Protocol Independent Multicast** (**PIM**), **Internet Group Management Protocol** (**IGMP**), and **Generic Routing Encapsulation** (**GRE**)

If you click on the + sign, all the underlying protocols will be shown.

To see a specific protocol throughput, click down to the protocols as shown in the following screenshot. You will see the application average throughput during the capture (HTTP in this example):

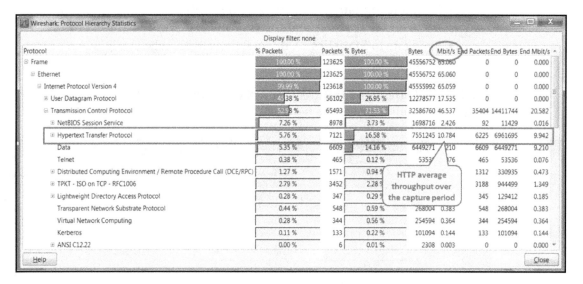

Clicking on the + sign to the left of HTTP will open a list of protocols that run over HTTP (XML, MIME, JavaScripts, and more) and their average throughput during the capture period.

There's more...

In some cases (especially when you need to prepare management reports), you are required to provide a graphical picture of the network statistics. There are various sources available for this, for example:

- **Etherape (for Linux)**: http://etherape.sourceforge.net/
- **Compass (for Windows)**:
  http://download.cnet.com/Compass-Free/3000-2085_4-75447541.html?tag=mn col;1

Analyzing Microsoft Terminal Server and Citrix communications problems

Microsoft Terminal Server, which uses **Remote Desktop Protocol** (**RDP**) and Citrix metaframe **Independent Computing Architecture** (**ICA**) protocols, are widely used for local and remote connectivity for PCs and thin clients. The important thing to remember about these types of applications is that they transfer screen changes over the network. If there, are only a few changes, they will require low bandwidth. If there many changes, they will require high bandwidth.

Another thing is that the traffic in these applications is entirely asymmetric. Downstream traffic takes from tens of Kbps up to several Mbps, while the upstream traffic will be at most several Kbps. When working with these applications, don't forget to design your network according to this.

In this recipe, we will see some typical problems of these applications and how to locate them. For the convenience of writing, we will refer to Microsoft Terminal Server, and every time we write Microsoft Terminal Server, we will refer to all applications in this category, for example, Citrix Metaframe.

Getting ready

When suspecting a slow performance with Microsoft Terminal Server, first check with the user what the problem is. Then, connect the Wireshark to the network with port-mirror to the complaining client or to the server.

How to do it...

For locating a problem when Microsoft Terminal Server is involved, start with going to the users and asking questions. Follow these steps:

1. When users complain about a slow network, ask them a simple question: Do they see the slowness in the data presented on the screen or when they switch between windows?

2. If they say that the switch between windows is very fast, it is not a Microsoft Terminal Server problem. Microsoft Terminal Server problems will cause slow window changes, picture freezes, slow scrolling of graphical documents, and so on.

3. If they say that they are trying to generate a report (when the software is running over Microsoft Terminal Server), but the report is generated after a long period of time, this is a database problem and not Microsoft Terminal Server or Citrix.

4. When a user works with Microsoft Terminal Server over a high-delay communication line and types very fast, they might experience delays with the characters. This is because Microsoft Terminal Server is transferring window changes, and with high delays, these windows changes will be transferred slowly.

5. When measuring the communication line with Wireshark:
   - Use I/O graphs to monitor the line
   - Use filters to monitor the upstream and the downstream directions
   - Configure bits per second on the y axis

6. You will get the following screenshot:

Wireshark IO Graphs: bitan test 17-AGU-2010 test with Citrix.pcap

Network slowdown

1Mbps communication line

2000000

1000000

0

360s   380s   400s   420s   440s   460s   480s   500s

Graphs

Upstream filter

Graph 1	Color	Filter:		Style:	Line	▼
Graph 2	Color	Filter:	ip.src==192.168.0.70 and tcp.port==2598	Style:	Line	▼
Graph 3		Filter:		Style:	Line	▼
Graph 4	Color	Filter:	ip.src==192.168.1.110 and tcp.port==2598	Style:	Line	▼
Graph 5	Color	Filter:		Style:	Line	▼

Downstream filter

X Axis
Tick interval: 1 sec ▼
Pixels per tick   5 ▼
☐ View as time of day

Y Axis
Unit: Bits/Tick   ▼
Scale: Auto   ▼
Smooth: No filter   ▼

Help   Copy   Save   Close

7. In the preceding screenshot, you can see a typical traffic pattern with high downstream and very low upstream traffic. Notice that the **Y-Axis** is configured to **Bits/Tick**. In the time between 485s and 500s, you see that the throughput got to the maximum. This is when applications will slow down and users will start to feel screen freezes, menus that move very slowly, and so on.

When a Citrix ICA client connects to a presentation server, it uses TCP ports 2598 or 1494.

8. When monitoring Microsoft Terminal Server servers, don't forget that the clients access the server with Microsoft Terminal Server and the servers access the application with another client that is installed on the server. The performance problem can come from Microsoft Terminal Server or the application.

9. If the problem is an Microsoft Terminal Server problem, it is necessary to figure out whether it is a network problem or a system problem:

- Check the network with Wireshark to see if there are any loads. Loads such as the one shown in the previous screenshot can be solved by simply increasing the communication lines.
- Check the server's performance. Applications like Microsoft Terminal Server are mostly memory consuming, so check mostly for memory (RAM) issues.

How it works...

Microsoft Terminal Server, Citrix Metaframe, and applications simply transfer window changes over the network. From your client (PC with software client or thin client), you connect to the terminal server; and the terminal server, runs various clients that are used to connect from it to other servers. In the following screenshot, you can see the principle of terminal server operation:

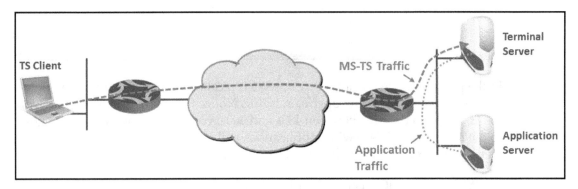

There's more...

From the terminal server vendors, you will hear that their applications improve two things. They will say that it improves manageability of clients because you don't have to manage PCs and software for every user; you simply install everything on the server, and if something fails, you fix it on the server. They will also say that traffic over the network will be reduced.

Well, I will not get into the first argument. This is not our subject, but I strongly reject the second one. When working with a terminal client, your traffic entirely depends on what you are doing:

- When working with text/character-based applications, for example, some **Enterprise Resource Planning (ERP)** screens, you type in and read data. When working with the terminal client, you will connect to the terminal server that will connect to the database server. Depending on the database application you are working with, the terminal server can improve performance significantly or does not improve it at all. We will discuss this in the database section. Here, you can expect a load of tens to hundreds of Kbps.
- If you are working with regular office documents such as Word, PowerPoint, and so on, it entirely depends on what you are doing. Working with a simple Word document will require tens to hundreds of Kbps. Working with PowerPoint will require hundreds of Kbps to several Mbps, and when you present the PowerPoint file with full screen (the *F5* function), the throughput can jump up to 8 to 10 Mbps.
- Browsing the internet will take between hundreds of Kbps and several Mbps, depending on what you will do over it. High resolution movies over terminal server to the internet-well, just don't do it.

Before you implement any terminal environment, test it. I once had a software house that wanted their logo (at the top-right corner of the user window) to be very clear and striking. They refreshed it 10 times a second, which caused the 2 Mbps communication line to be blocked. You never know what you don't test!

Analyzing the database traffic and common problems

Some of you may wonder why we have this section here. After all, databases are considered to be a completely different branch in the IT environment. There are databases and applications on one side and the network and infrastructure on the other side. It is correct since we are not supposed to debug databases; there are DBAs for this. But through the information that runs over the network, we can see some issues that can help the DBAs with solving the relevant problems.

In most of the cases, the IT staff will come to us first because people blame the network for everything. We will have to make sure that the problems are not coming from the network and that's it. In a minority of the cases, we will see some details on the capture file that can help the DBAs with what they are doing.

Getting ready

When the IT team comes to us complaining about the slow network, there are some things to do just to verify that it is not the case. Follow the instructions in the following section to make sure you avoid the slow network issue.

How to do it...

In the case of database problems, follow these steps:

1. When you get complaints about the slow network responses, start asking these questions:
    - Is the problem local or global? Does it occur only in the remote offices or also in the center? When the problem occurs in the entire network, it is not a WAN bandwidth issue.
    - Does it happen the same for all clients? If not, there might be a specific problem that happens only with some users because only those users are running a specific application that causes the problem.
    - Is the communication line between the clients and the server loaded? What is the application that loads them?
    - Do all applications work slowly, or is it only the application that works with the specific database? Maybe some PCs are old and tired, or is it a server that runs out of resources?

2. When we are done with the questionnaire, let's start our work:
    1. Open Wireshark and start capturing packets. You can configure port-mirror to a specific PC, the server, a VLAN, or a router that connects to a remote office in which you have the clients.
    2. Look at the TCP events (expert info). Do they happen on the entire communication link, on specific IP address/addresses, or on specific TCP port number/numbers? This will help you isolate the problem and check whether it is on a specific link, server, or application.

When measuring traffic on a connection to the internet, you will get many retransmissions and duplicate ACKs to websites, mail servers, and so on. This is the internet. In an organization, you should expect 0.1 to 0.5 percent of retransmissions. When connecting to the internet, you can expect much higher numbers.

3. If you see problems in the network, solve them as we learned in previous chapters. But there are some network issues that can influence database behavior. In the following example, we see the behavior of a client that works with the server over a communication line with a round trip delay of 35 to 40 ms.

4. We are looking at the TCP stream number 8 (**1**) and the connection started with TCP SYN/SYN-ACK/ACK. I've set this as a reference (**2**). We can see that the entire connection took 371 packets (**3**):

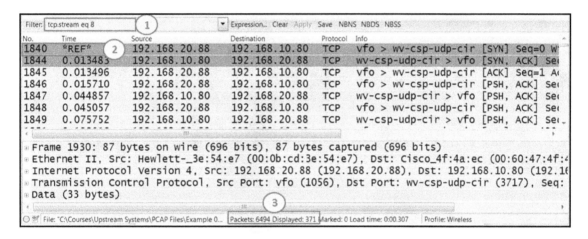

5. The connection continues, and we can see time intervals of around 35 ms between DB requests and responses:

6. Since we have 371 packets travelling back and forth, 371 x 35 ms gives us around 13 seconds. Add to this some retransmissions that might happen and some inefficiencies, and this leads to a user waiting for 10 to 15 seconds and more for a database query.

7. In this case, you should consult the DBA on how to significantly reduce the number of packets that run over the network, or you can move to another way of access, for example, terminal server or web access.

8. Another problem that can happen is that you will have a software issue that will reflect in the capture file. If you have a look at the following screenshot, you will see that there are five retransmissions, and then a new connection is opened from the client side. It looks like a TCP problem but it occurs only in a specific window in the software. It is simply a software procedure that stopped processing, and this stopped the TCP from responding to the client:

No.	Time	Source	Destination	Protocol	Info
		192.168.3.50	192.168.200.227	TCP	http > vrtp [ACK] Seq=1 Ack=59884 Wir
274	0.078889	192.168.3.50	192.168.200.227	TCP	http > vrtp [ACK] Seq=1 Ack=59884 Wir
275	0.380166	192.168.200.227	192.168.3.50	TCP	[TCP Retransmission] [TCP segment of
276	0.983678	192.168.200.227	192.168.3.50	TCP	[TCP Retransmission] [TCP segment of
2 ②	2.195589	192.168.200.227	192.168.3.50	T ①	[TCP Retransmission] [TCP segment of
278	4.604757	192.168.200.227	192.168.3.50	TCP	[TCP Retransmission] [TCP segment of
279	9.432867	192.168.200.227	192.168.3.50	TCP	[TCP Retransmission] [TCP segment of
280	18.989050	192.168.200.227	192.168.3.50	TCP	rcts > http [SYN] Seq=0 Win=65535 Ler
281	18.994054	192.168.3.50	192.168.200.227	T ③	http > rcts [SYN, ACK] Seq=0 Ack=1 Wi
282	18.994085	192.168.200.227	192.168.3.50	TCP	rcts > http [ACK] Seq=1 Ack=1 Win=655
283	18.994264	192.168.200.227	192.168.3.50	TCP	[TCP segment of a reassembled PDU]
284	18.994280	192.168.200.227	192.168.3.50	TCP	[TCP segment of a reassembled PDU]
285	19.000271	192.168.3.50	192.168.200.227	TCP	http > rcts [ACK] Seq=1 Ack=537 Win=6

How it works...

Well, how databases work was always be a miracle to me. Our task is to find out how they influence the network, and this is what we've learned in this section.

There's more...

When you right-click on one of the packets in the database client to the server session, a window with the conversation will open. It can be helpful to the DBA to see what is running over the network.

When you are facing delay problems, for example, when working over cellular lines over the internet or over international connections, the database client to the server will not always be efficient enough. You might need to move to web or terminal access to the database.

An important issue is how the database works. If the client is accessing the database server, and the database server is using files shared from another server, it can be that the client-server works great; but the problems come from the database server to the shared files on the file server. Make sure that you know all these dependencies before starting with your tests.

And most importantly, make sure you have very professional DBAs among your friends. One day, you will need them!

Analyzing SNMP

SNMP is a well-known protocol that is used to monitor and manage different types of devices in a network by collecting data and statistics at regular intervals. Beyond just monitoring, it can also be used to configure and modify settings with appropriate authorization given to SNMP servers. Devices that typically support SNMP are switches, routers, servers, workstations, hosts, VoIP Phones, and many more.

It is important to know that there are three versions of SNMP: SNMPv1, SNMPv2c, and SNMPv3. Versions v2c and v3, which came later, offer better performance and security.

SNMP consists of three components:

- The device being managed (referred to as managed device).
- SNMP Agent. This is a piece of software running on the managed device that collects the data from the device and stores it in a database, referred to as the **Managed Information Base (MIB)** database. As configured, this SNMP agent exports the data/statistics to the server (using UDP port 161) at regular intervals, and also any events and traps.
- SNMP server, also called **Network Management Server** (**NMS**). This is a server that communicates with all the agents in the network to collect the exported data and build a central repository. SNMP server provides access to the IT staff managing network; they can monitor, manage, and configure the network remotely.

It is very important to be aware that some of the MIBs implemented in a device could be vendor-specific. Almost all the vendors publicize these MIBs implemented in their devices.

Getting ready

Generally, the complaints we get from the network management team are about not getting any statistics or traps from a device(s) for a specific interval, or having completely no visibility to a device(s). Follow the instructions in the following section to analyze and troubleshoot these issues.

How to do it...

In the case of SNMP problems, follow these steps.

When you get complaints about SNMP, start asking these questions:

1. Is this a new managed device that has been brought into the network recently? In other words, did the SNMP in the device ever work properly?
   - If this is a new device, talk to relevant device administrator and/or check the SNMP-related configurations, such as community strings.
   - If SNMP configurations looks correct, make sure that the NMS's IP address configured is correct and also check the relevant password credentials.
   - If SNMP v3 is in use, which supports encryption, make sure to check encryption-related settings like transport methods.
   - If the setting and configuration looks valid and correct, make sure the managed devices have connectivity with the NMS, which can be verified by simple ICMP pings.
2. If it is a managed device that has been working properly and didn't report any statistics or alerts for a specific duration:
   - Did the device in discussion have any issues in the control plane or management plane that stopped it from exporting SNMP statistics? Please be aware that for most devices in the network, SNMP is a least-priority protocol, which means that if a device has a higher-priority process to work on, it will hold the SNMP requests and responses in the queue.
   - Is the issue experienced only for a specific device or for multiple devices in the network?
   - Did the network (between managed device and NMS) experience any issue? For example, during any layer 2 spanning-tree convergence, traffic loss could occur between the managed device and SNMP server, by which NMS would lose visibility to the managed devices.

As you can see in the following picture, an SNMP Server with IP address `172.18.254.139` is performing SNMP walk with a sequence of `GET-NEXT-REQUEST` to a workstation with IP address `10.81.64.22`, which in turn responds with `GET-RESPONSE`. For simplicity, the Wireshark filter used for these captures is SNMP.

The workstation is enabled with SNMP v2c, with community string public.

Let's discuss some of the commonly seen failure scenarios.

Polling a managed device with a wrong SNMP version

As I mentioned earlier, the workstation is enabled with v2c, but when the NMS polls the device with the wrong SNMP version, it doesn't get any response. So, it is very important to make sure that the managed devices are polled with the correct SNMP version.

Polling a managed device with a wrong MIB object ID (OID)

In the following example, the NMS is polling the managed device to get a number of bytes sent out on interfaces. The MIB OID for byte count is .1.3.6.1.2.1.2.2.1.16, which is ifOutOctets. The managed device in discussion has two interfaces, mapped to OID .1.3.6.1.2.1.2.2.1.16.1 and .1.3.6.1.2.1.2.2.1.16.2. When NMS polls the device to check the statistics for the third interface (which is not present), it returns a `noSuchInstance` error.

How it works...

As you have learned in the earlier sections, SNMP is a very simple and straightforward protocol and all its related information on standards and MIB OIDs is readily available in the internet.

There's more...

Here are some of the websites with good information about SNMP and MIB OIDs:

- Microsoft TechNet SNMP: `https://technet.microsoft.com/en-us/library/cc776379(v=ws.10).aspx`
- Cisco IOS MIB locator: `http://mibs.cloudapps.cisco.com/ITDIT/MIBS/servlet/index`

17
Troubleshooting SIP, Multimedia, and IP Telephony

In this chapter, you will learn about:

- The IP telephony principle and normal operation
- The SIP principle of operation, messages, and error codes
- Video over IP and RTSP
- Wireshark's feature for RTP stream analysis and filtering
- Wireshark's feature for VoIP call replay

Introduction

For transferring voice, video, or multimedia, we need perform two functions. The first one is to carry the media stream, which is mostly voice or video, and the second one is for signaling, which is to establish and terminate the call, to invite participants to the call, and so on. Two protocol suites were proposed over the years for signaling:

- The ITU-T suite of protocols, including H.323 as an umbrella protocol for the suite, H.225 for registration and address resolution, H.245 for control, and some others
- The IETF suite of protocols, including SIP as a signaling protocol (RFC 3261 with later updates) and **Session Description Protocol** (**SDP**) to describe the session parameters (RFC 4566)

The ITU-T set of protocols phased out in the last few years, and the majority of the applications today are using the IETF set of protocols, which we will be focusing on in this chapter. In the following diagram, you can see the structure of the IETF protocol suite.

For the stream transfer, both suites use RTP and RTCP (RFC 3550 with later updates). RTP is used for the media transfer, and RTCP is used for controlling the quality of the stream.

There are several protocols for transferring multimedia sessions over an IP-based network, as shown in the following diagram:

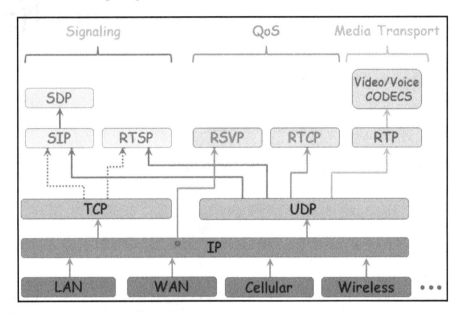

In this chapter, we will discuss different protocols and how to analyze audio and video streams using Wireshark.

IP telephony principle and normal operation

IP telephony is the concept of converting analog voice calls into IP packets and steering them over the IP network. Call signaling protocols such as SIP will be used to establish the call session between the endpoints and will then leverage **Real-Time Transport Protocol** (**RTP**) as the application layer protocol to transfer the media streams over the IP network. The audio (or video) packets will be encapsulated with RTP header and typically run over UDP.

In this recipe, we will see the normal operation of IP telephony and how RTP and RTCP are used for an end-to-end audio stream using Wireshark-based capture analysis.

Getting ready

As IP Telephony converts analog to digital calls, the captures can be done only on the IP part. Wireshark does not help capture any signals on the analog portion of the network.

How to do it...

RTP operation

Open the Wireshark capture and use the **Telephony** menu to navigate to **RTP** | **RTP Streams**, as shown in the following screenshot:

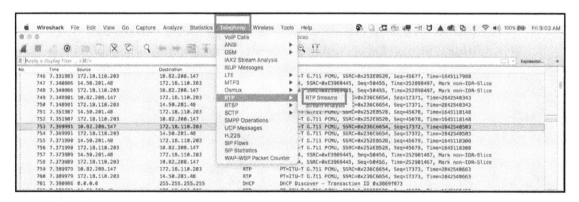

Selecting the preceding option will list all the RTP streams in a new pop-up window, as shown here:

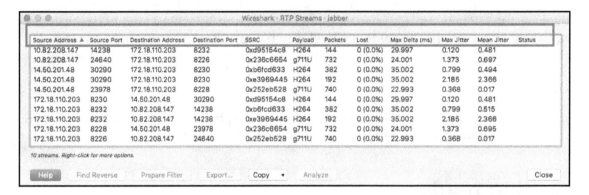

Source Address ▲	Source Port	Destination Address	Destination Port	SSRC	Payload	Packets	Lost	Max Delta (ms)	Max Jitter	Mean Jitter	Status
10.82.208.147	14238	172.18.110.203	8232	0xd95154c8	H264	144	0 (0.0%)	29.997	0.120	0.481	
10.82.208.147	24640	172.18.110.203	8226	0x236c6654	g711U	732	0 (0.0%)	24.001	1.373	0.697	
14.50.201.48	30290	172.18.110.203	8230	0xb6fcd633	H264	382	0 (0.0%)	35.002	0.799	0.494	
14.50.201.48	30290	172.18.110.203	8230	0xe3969445	H264	192	0 (0.0%)	35.002	2.185	2.366	
14.50.201.48	23978	172.18.110.203	8228	0x252eb528	g711U	740	0 (0.0%)	22.993	0.368	0.017	
172.18.110.203	8230	14.50.201.48	30290	0xd95154c8	H264	144	0 (0.0%)	29.997	0.120	0.481	
172.18.110.203	8232	10.82.208.147	14238	0xb6fcd633	H264	382	0 (0.0%)	35.002	0.799	0.515	
172.18.110.203	8232	10.82.208.147	14238	0xe3969445	H264	192	0 (0.0%)	35.002	2.185	2.366	
172.18.110.203	8228	14.50.201.48	23978	0x236c6654	g711U	732	0 (0.0%)	24.001	1.373	0.695	
172.18.110.203	8226	10.82.208.147	24640	0x252eb528	g711U	740	0 (0.0%)	22.993	0.368	0.017	

10 streams. Right-click for more options.

Help | Find Reverse | Prepare Filter | Export... | Copy ▾ | Analyze | Close

Each RTP stream will be listed in the following format:

- **Source Address**: The source IP address of the RTP stream endpoint. This can be IP Phone or a teleconference unit.
- **Source Port**: Source port of the UDP header. The session originator uses a locally unique random port as the source port.
- **Destination Address**: The destination IP address of the RTP stream endpoint.
- **Destination port**: The destination port of the UDP header. The session originator uses one of the ports from the RTP port range as the destination port. RTP uses a broad range of UDP ports to support concurrent calls. The port range is from 16384 to 32767.
- **SSRC**: Synchronization Source, which is an RTP stream identifier.
- **Payload**: RTP payload that defines the codec type used for the stream.
- **Additional Stream Data**: Additional details including the number of packets captured for each stream, lost packets, jitter/delay details, and so on.

Select the relevant stream from the pop-up window or use the follow the stream option:

```
▶ Frame 75: 214 bytes on wire (1712 bits), 214 bytes captured (1712 bits)
▶ Ethernet II, Src: Cisco_b7:17:0a (00:0b:45:b7:17:0a), Dst: Cisco_76:b5:12 (a4:4c:11:76:b5:12)
▶ Internet Protocol Version 4, Src: 14.50.201.48, Dst: 172.18.110.203
▶ User Datagram Protocol, Src Port: 23978, Dst Port: 8228
▼ Real-Time Transport Protocol
  ▶ [Stream setup by SDP (frame 72)]  ─────────────▶ Signaling Protocol used
    10.. .... = Version: RFC 1889 Version (2)
    ..0. .... = Padding: False
    ...0 .... = Extension: False
    .... 0000 = Contributing source identifiers count: 0
    1... .... = Marker: True
    Payload type: ITU-T G.711 PCMU (0)  ───────────▶ Audio Codec
    Sequence number: 45559
    [Extended sequence number: 45559]  ─────────────▶ RTP Sequence number
    Timestamp: 1645099108  ─────────────────────▶ RTP timestamp
    Synchronization Source identifier: 0x252eb528 (623818024)
    Payload: ffffffffffffffffffffffffffffffffffffffffffffffffff...
```

These are explained as follows:

- This was the screenshot of an RTP packet. Wireshark will highlight the packet number of the signaling protocol that setup this RTP packet.
- The payload field of RTP packet will describe the audio codec used. In the preceding packet, G711 is used as the audio codec.
- Each RTP packet will be included with a sequence number that will sequentially increment by 1 for each subsequent packets.
- RTP packet also carries the timestamp from the endpoint.
- The Sequence number and timestamp are used to measure the quality of service.

RTCP operation

Get the UDP port number of the RTP call flow and increment it by 1 and use the same to filter the associated RTCP packets. For example, if the UDP port is 24950 , which is used for RTP packets, UDP port 24951 will be used for RTCP packets.

```
▶ Frame 75: 214 bytes on wire (1712 bits), 214 bytes captured (1712 bits)
▶ Ethernet II, Src: Cisco_b7:17:0a (00:0b:45:b7:17:0a), Dst: Cisco_76:b5:12 (a4:4c:11:76:b5:12)
▶ Internet Protocol Version 4, Src: 14.50.201.48, Dst: 172.18.110.203
▼ User Datagram Protocol, Src Port: 23978, Dst Port: 8228
     Source Port: 23978
     Destination Port: 8228
     Length: 180
     Checksum: 0x72c5 [unverified]
     [Checksum Status: Unverified]
     [Stream index: 2]
▼ Real-Time Transport Protocol
  ▶ [Stream setup by SDP (frame 72)]
     10.. .... = Version: RFC 1889 Version (2)
     ..0. .... = Padding: False
     ...0 .... = Extension: False
     .... 0000 = Contributing source identifiers count: 0
     1... .... = Marker: True
     Payload type: ITU-T G.711 PCMU (0)
     Sequence number: 45559
     [Extended sequence number: 45559]
     Timestamp: 1645099108
     Synchronization Source identifier: 0x252eb528 (623818024)
     Payload: ffffffffffffffffffffffffffffffffffffffffffffffff...
```

The preceding screenshot is a capture of one of the RTP flows between endpoints 14.50.201.48 and 172.18.110.203 that uses UDP port 23978. The SSRC associated with this RTP flow is 0x252eb528. By using UDP port 23979, we can identify the associated RTCP packet for this flow:

```
▶ Frame 2069: 138 bytes on wire (1104 bits), 138 bytes captured (1104 bits)
▶ Ethernet II, Src: Cisco_b7:17:0a (00:0b:45:b7:17:0a), Dst: Cisco_76:b5:12 (a4:4c:11:76:b5:12)
▶ Internet Protocol Version 4, Src: 14.50.201.48, Dst: 172.18.110.203
  User Datagram Protocol, Src Port: 23979, Dst Port: 8229
▼ Real-time Transport Control Protocol (Sender Report)
  ▼ [Stream setup by SDP (frame 72)]
        [Setup frame: 72]
        [Setup Method: SDP]
     10.. .... = Version: RFC 1889 Version (2)
     ..0. .... = Padding: False
     ...0 0001 = Reception report count: 1
     Packet type: Sender Report (200)
     Length: 12 (52 bytes)
     Sender SSRC: 0x252eb528 (623818024)
     Timestamp, MSW: 3728372393 (0xde3a72a9)
     Timestamp, LSW: 3179194385 (0xbd7ea811)
     [MSW and LSW as NTP timestamp: Feb 23, 2018 10:59:53.740213874 UTC]
     RTP timestamp: 1645146724
     Sender's packet count: 298
     Sender's octet count: 47680
  ▼ Source 1
        Identifier: 0x236c6654 (594306644)
     ▼ SSRC contents
           Fraction lost: 0 / 256
           Cumulative number of packets lost: 0
        ▼ Extended highest sequence number received: 17549
           Sequence number cycles count: 0
           Highest sequence number received: 17549
        Interarrival jitter: 2
        Last SR timestamp: 1923794062 (0x72aac48e)
        Delay since last SR timestamp: 33685 (513 milliseconds)
▶ Real-time Transport Control Protocol (Source description)
```

In the preceding screenshot, the sender SSRC will match the SSRC of the RTP packet (`0x252eb528`). Sender report is a type of RCTP message that carries the telemetry details of the RTP flow. Ensure the following:

- **Fraction lost**: This is zero or well within the tolerance range. This counter shows the number of RTP data packets lost between the current and previous Sender report.
- **Cumulative number of packets lost**: This is zero or well within the tolerance range. This counter shows the total number of RTP data packets lost in this session.
- **Inter-arrival Jitter**: This is well within the range. This counter shows the jitter measurement of the received packets.

Any problem in the preceding counters may point us to an issue in the end to end call flow. More details on the use of RTCP and how it helps with feedback looping is explained in the *How it works...* section.

How it works...

IP telephony heavily leverages RTP and RTCP for end to end call flow. RTP is the application layer protocol used to transport the media flow (audio and video) between endpoints.

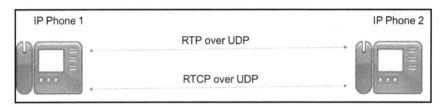

RTP principles of operation

RTP is used for carrying the media. Preceding RTP, we have various types of codec for voice and video compression. The following is the sample packet format of an RTP packet:

The RTP header carries details specific to the flow and the direction that can be used for session identification, resiliency and real-time jitter/delay measurement. RTP provides mechanisms for timing recovery, loss detection and correction, payload and source identification, and media synchronization.

RTP uses UDP as the transport layer protocol. In the following diagram, you see the RTP packet structure:

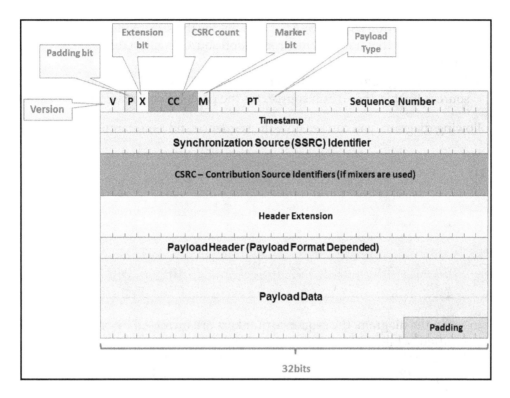

The fields in the header are as follows:

- **Version (V)**: This field indicates the RTP version
- **Padding (P)**: This field indicates that the packet contains one or more additional padding bytes at the end that are not part of the payload
- **Extension bit (X)**: This field indicates a fixed header that follows the standard header
- **CSRC count (CC)**: This field contains the number of CSRC fields that follow the fixed header
- **Marker (M)**: This field is used to indicate application events, for example video frame boundaries
- **Payload type**: This field identifies the format of the RTP payload to be interpreted by the receiving application
- **Sequence number**: This field is incremented by one for each RTP packet sent. Used by the receiver to detect packet losses
- **Timestamp**: This field reflects the sampling rate of octets in the RTP data stream

- **Synchronization source (SSRC)**: This field is the stream identifier that is chosen randomly so that no two synchronization sources within the same RTP session will have the same SSRC identifier
- **Contributing source identifiers list (CSRC)**: This field identifies the contributing sources (that is, the stream source) for the payload contained in this packet

In the following diagram, you can see how the sequence and timestamps mechanisms work:

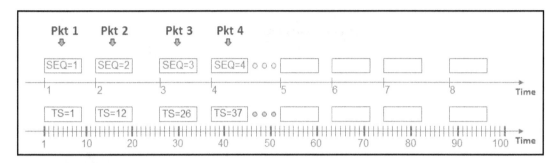

As we can see in the diagram, the sequence numbers are increased by one for each RTP packet transmitted, while timestamps increase by the time covered by a packet. Packet number 1, for example, will have both set to 1; packet 2 will have a sequence number of 2 and a timestamp of 12; and it goes on in this manner for the other packets. The receiver will receive the sequence numbers that tell him the order of the packets and timestamps that tell him the time at which they left the receiver. The receiver will use both to play back the received data.

The RTCP principle of operation

RTCP specifies reports that are exchanged between the source and destination of the session.

RTCP works in conjunction with RTP and is used by the endpoints to monitor the end-to-end quality of the RTP data packets and control the transmission by exchanging the information as reports. For each RTP streams, there will be an RTCP flow that is used to exchange different reports about the RTP stream. Reports contain statistics such as the number of RTP-PDUs sent, the number of RTP-PDUs lost, inter-arrival jitter, and so on. These reports can be used by applications to modify the sender's transmission rates and for diagnostic purposes.

RTCP has several report types, in which the sender and receiver update each other on the data that was sent and received. The following are a few RTCP packet types:

- Sender report (type 200)
- Receiver report (type 201)
- Source description (type 202)
- BYE (type 203)
- Application specific (type 204)

A detailed description of each types are available in RFC 3550. In the following screenshot, you can see an example of this, in which we see a sender report that tells the receiver how many packets and octets were sent, timestamp information, and other parameters that can be used by the receiver.

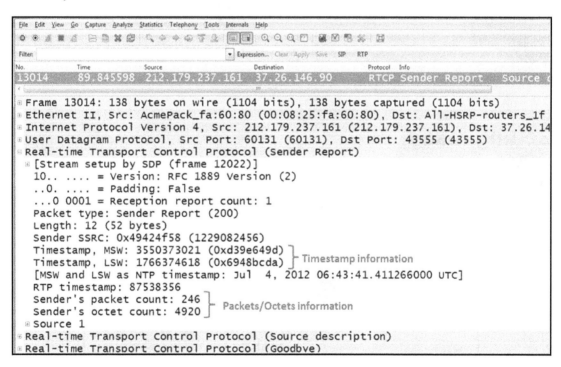

SIP principle of operation, messages, and error codes

Session initiation protocol or SIP (RFC 3261 and various extensions) is a signaling and control protocol that operates at application layer and responsible for creating, modifying, and terminating multimedia session between one or more participants. While sending SIP requests, the session parameters are sent via SDP (SDP, RFC 4566) which enable users to agree on a set of compatible media types between them. When sessions are created, the voice or video is carried by RTP and optionally controlled by RTCP.

SIP defines endpoints as **User Agents (UAs)**, and the process of creating a session involves UA negotiation in order to agree on a characterization of a session that they would like to create. For additional services such as locating session participants, registration, call forwarding, and others, SIP defines network hosts called servers to which UAs can send registrations, send invitations to sessions, and other requests.

In this recipe, we will discuss the signaling part of the protocol suite, which is SIP, and how to use Wireshark in order to verify the normal operation of SIP.

Getting ready

In order to establish, end-to-end call flow, SIP sessions may be created between different SIP endpoints.

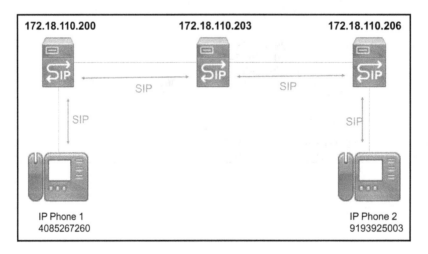

It is more optimal to perform the Wireshark capture in a switch or router that is common to multiple sessions. In the preceding topology, we performed the capture on `172.18.110.203` as it is the terminating node for two SIP sessions.

How to do it...

1. Open the Wireshark capture and use the **Telephony** menu to navigate the **SIP Flows**, as shown in the following screenshot:

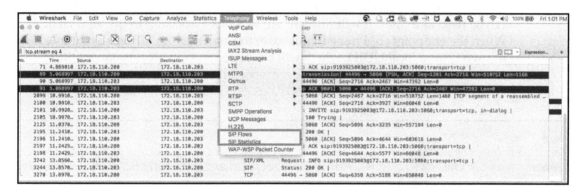

2. The **SIP Flow** option will list all the SIP flows in the packet capture in a new pop-up window. SIP Statistics will list all the SIP messages and the counts in the packet capture. The following is a screenshot of the pop-up window listing the SIP Flows in the capture:

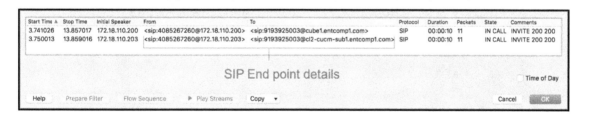

3. The preceding screenshot shows that there are two SIP flows. A cube or CCM with IP address `172.18.110.200` connected to UA with SIP number `4085267260` is initiating the SIP session to the cube with a host name of `cube1.entcomp1.com`.

4. Follow the relevant TCP stream for the SIP packet using the display filters and get the Flow Graph for the SIP flow by navigating to **Statistics | Flow Graph.**

5. Enable the **Limit to display filter** option to limit the flow graph only for the SIP flow. This will list all the SIP messages exchanged between the SIP endpoints as a graph for ease of analysis.

6. While following the TCP stream will only list a specific SIP session, local UUID can be used as a filter. It will filter all SIP sessions associated to the local UUID. When the endpoint (IP Phone in this case) triggers the first SIP session, it includes its own ID as a local UUID, which will be carried over in all subsequent SIP sessions along the path towards the remote endpoint. In our example, the local UUID of IP Phone 1 is `025ac8cd-0010-5000-a000-acbc3296f7dd`.

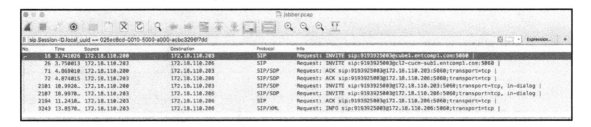

7. The preceding screenshot lists all the SIP sessions associated with the local UUID mentioned in the filter. As you can see there are two SIP sessions:
   - Session from `172.18.110.200` to `172.18.110.203`
   - Session from `172.18.110.203` to `172.18.110.206`

8. By navigating the Flow graph and limiting it to the display, we can see the SIP messages exchanged in each SIP session in the capture. The following is a sample graph for the SIP session in our topology:

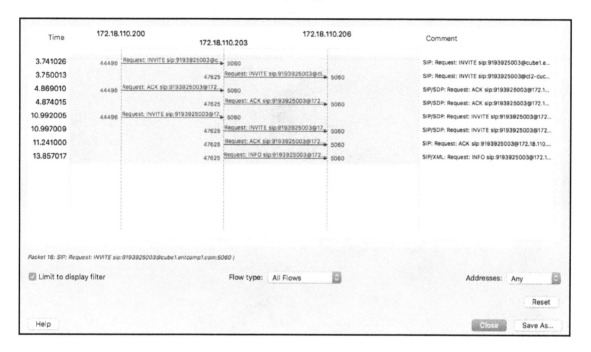

How it works...

1. When a UA desires to establish a multimedia session, it sends an INVITE method to the remote UA. In the following diagram, you can see an example of a basic call flow:

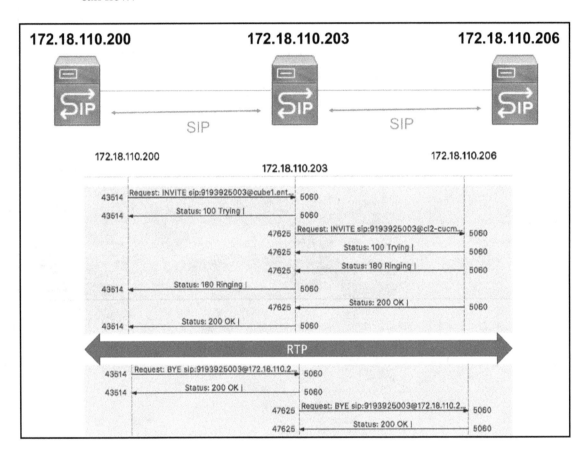

An end device in SIP is called UA. A user agent can initiate or receive a call. A UA can be an IP phone, video camera, software client, or any device or software that participates in an SIP session.

2. After `INVITE`, you should see **Trying, Session Progress, Ringing,** or a combination of them coming from the other side

3. We can see here how the session progress between the initiator on **172.18.110.200** and the responder on **172.18.110.203**:
   - The **INVITE** method is sent from the session initiator. This will always be the first packet that starts the conversation.
   - The responder answers with **Trying** (code **100**), **Session progress** (code **183**), and after three seconds with **Ringing** (code **180**). Then it answers with **OK** (code **200**), meaning that the handset was picked up.

4. In the preceding topology, there are multiple CUBEs in between that help to establish end to end call flow

5. The CUBE or switch `172.18.110.200` on the left sends an **INVITE** request to switch `172.18.110.203`

6. The switch `172.18.110.203` replies with the SIP **Trying** message.

7. The switch sends an **INVITE** to the CUBE or switch `172.18.110.206` on the right.

8. The switch `172.18.110.206` sends **Trying** (code **100**), and then the session progresses (code **183**) to the switch.

9. When `172.18.110.203` receives **Ringing** from `172.18.110.206`, it in turn sends **Ringing** message to `172.18.110.200`.

10. The destination endpoint sends **SIP 200 OK** to the communications manager at `172.18.110.206` when the call is answered. The **SIP 200 OK** message carries SDP content in the message body. The SDP provides information about RTP UDP port number and the list audio and video codec offered by the destination end point (also referred to as SDP Offer). The **SIP 200 OK** message traverses SBC (`172.18.110.203`), communication manager (`172.18.110.200`) and reaches the origination endpoint.

```
▼ Session Initiation Protocol (200)
  ▼ Status-Line: SIP/2.0 200 OK
      Status-Code: 200
      [Resent Packet: False]
  ► Message Header
  ▼ Message Body
    ▼ Session Description Protocol
        Session Description Protocol Version (v): 0
      ► Owner/Creator, Session Id (o): CiscoSystemsCCM-SIP 22971 1 IN IP4 172.18.110.206
        Session Name (s): SIP Call
      ► Connection Information (c): IN IP4 14.50.201.48
      ► Bandwidth Information (b): TIAS:384000
      ► Bandwidth Information (b): AS:384
      ► Time Description, active time (t): 0 0
      ▼ Media Description, name and address (m): audio 25944 RTP/AVP 9 124 0 8 116 18 101
          Media Type: audio
          Media Port: 25944
          Media Protocol: RTP/AVP
          Media Format: ITU-T G.722
          Media Format: DynamicRTP-Type-124
          Media Format: ITU-T G.711 PCMU
          Media Format: ITU-T G.711 PCMA
          Media Format: DynamicRTP-Type-116
          Media Format: ITU-T G.729
          Media Format: DynamicRTP-Type-101
```

11. In the preceding sample screenshot, the SDP message instructs to use UDP port `25944` for the RTP audio stream. In addition, it includes other details such as the codec supported.

```
▼ Session Initiation Protocol (ACK)
  ▶ Request-Line: ACK sip:9193925003@172.18.110.206:5060;transport=tcp SIP/2.0
  ▶ Message Header
  ▼ Message Body
    ▼ Session Description Protocol
        Session Description Protocol Version (v): 0
      ▶ Owner/Creator, Session Id (o): CiscoSystemsSIP-GW-UserAgent 4483 9483 IN IP4 172.18.110.203
        Session Name (s): SIP Call
      ▶ Connection Information (c): IN IP4 172.18.110.203
      ▶ Time Description, active time (t): 0 0
      ▼ Media Description, name and address (m): audio 8260 RTP/AVP 0 101
          Media Type: audio
          Media Port: 8260
          Media Protocol: RTP/AVP
          Media Format: ITU-T G.711 PCMU
          Media Format: DynamicRTP-Type-101
      ▶ Connection Information (c): IN IP4 172.18.110.203
      ▶ Media Attribute (a): rtpmap:0 PCMU/8000
      ▶ Media Attribute (a): rtpmap:101 telephone-event/8000
      ▶ Media Attribute (a): fmtp:101 0-15
      ▶ Media Description, name and address (m): video 8262 RTP/AVP 126
      ▶ Connection Information (c): IN IP4 172.18.110.203
      ▶ Bandwidth Information (b): TIAS:320000
      ▶ Media Attribute (a): rtpmap:126 H264/90000
      ▶ Media Attribute (a): fmtp:126 profile-level-id=42E01F;packetization-mode=1;max-fs=3600
        Media Attribute (a): recvonly
      ▶ Media Attribute (a): label:11
      ▶ Media Attribute (a): content:main
```

12. The origination endpoint selects one of the audio codes and sends the selected codec and its RTP port number information (also referred to as SDP answer) in the SIP ACK to its communication manager (`172.18.110.200`). This `SIP ACK` message traverses SBC (`172.18.110.203`), communication manager (`172.18.110.206`) and reaches the destination endpoint. Upon receiving the ACK, the destination endpoint starts sending RTP packets at port `8260`. It will also receive RTP packets at port `25944`.

13. When the user hangs up the call, **SIP BYE** message will be exchanged between the SIP devices to terminate the call signaling session.

14. If an error message is received at any stage, the connection will not be established.

Don't forget that SIP works over UDP. And since UDP does not open any connection to the other side before sending the request, it can be possible that a request will not arrive to the destination simply because of a network reachability problem. For this reason, when you don't get a response, it could be that the INVITE simply didn't get to the destination because of a network problem.

SIP error codes are listed in the following tables, along with their possible reasons. Unless mentioned otherwise, the codes are defined in RFC 3261.

1xx codes – provisional/informational

The 1xx codes or provisional/informational codes are those where the received request is still in process, and the receiver notifies the sender about it. They are described in detail in the following table:

Code	Event name	Reason
100	Trying	The request has been received and accepted by the server, and an action is being taken for this call.
180	Ringing	The UA that received the call is alerting the end user. This is the message that is sent back to the client while doing so.
181	Call forward	The call is being forwarded to another destination.
182	Queued	The called party is temporarily unavailable, and the server saves the message for later delivery.
183	Session progress	The session is being handled by the receiving server. Additional details on the call progress can be conveyed in the message header.

2xx codes – success

The 2xx codes or the success codes indicate that the action was successfully received, understood, and accepted. They are described in detail in the following table:

Code	Event name	Reason
200	Ok	The request has been accepted, processed, and succeeded
202	Accepted	The request has been accepted for processing, but its processing has not been completed (RFC 3265)

3xx codes – redirection

The 3xx codes indicate that a redirection action needs to be taken in order to complete the request. They are described in detail here:

Code	Event name	Reason
300	Multiple choices	The address in the request was resolved to several choices, and the accepting server can forward it to one of them. The UA can use the addresses in the contact header field for automatic redirection, or confirm it with the sender before redirecting the message.
301	Moved permanently	The user could not be located at the address in the Request URI, and the requesting client should try at the address provided in the contact header field. The sender should update its local directories with the change.
302	Moved temporarily	The requesting client should retry the request at the new address/addresses provided in the contact header field.
305	Use proxy	The requested resource must be accessed through the proxy, whose address is given by the contact field.
380	Alternative service	The call was not successful, so the recipient sends this response for alternative services to be made available on the receiver. These services are described in the message body.

4xx codes – client error

The 4xx codes or client errors indicate that the request contains bad syntax or cannot be fulfilled in this server. They are described in the following table:

Code	Event name	Reason
400	Bad request	The request couldn't be processed due to syntax error.
401	Unauthorized	The request that was received requires user authentication. Usually the client will ask the user for it.
402	Payment required	This is reserved for future use.
403	Forbidden	The server has understood the request, but is refusing to perform it. The client should not try it again.

404	Not found	The server notifies the client that the user does not exist in the domain specified in the Request URI.
405	Method not allowed	A method sent by the client is not allowed to be used by it. The response will include an `allow` header field to notify the sender which methods he is allowed to use.
406	Not acceptable	The resource identified by the request is only capable of generating response entities that have unacceptable content characteristics according to the `accept` header field sent in the request.
407	Proxy authentication required	The client must authenticate with a proxy server.
408	Request timeout	The server couldn't respond during the expected time. The client may send the request again after a while.
410	Gone	The requested resource is no longer available at the server, and the forwarding address is not known. This condition is considered to be permanent.
413	Request entity too large	The server is refusing to process a request because the request entity's body is larger than what the server is able or willing to process.
414	Request-URI too long	The server is refusing to service the request because the Request URI is longer than what the server is able or willing to interpret.
415	Unsupported media type	The server is refusing to process the request because the message body of the request is in a format that is not supported by the server.
416	Unsupported URI scheme	Request URI is unknown to the server, and therefore, the server cannot process the request.
420	Bad extension	The server did not understand the protocol extension received from the client.
421	Extension required	The UA that received the request requires a particular extension in order to process it, but this extension is not listed in the supported header field of the request.
423	Interval too brief	The server is rejecting the request because the expiration time of the resource refreshed by the request is too short.

424	Bad location information	This response code indicates a rejection of the request due to its location contents. This indicates malformed or unsatisfactory location information (RFC6442).
428	Use Identity header	It is sent when a verifier receives an SIP request that lacks an Identity header in order to indicate that the request should be re-sent with an Identity header (RFC4474).
429	Provide referrer identity	This provides referrer identity (RFC3892).
433	Anonymity disallowed	This indicates that the server refused to satisfy the request because the requestor was anonymous (RFC5079).
436	Bad identity info	This response is used when there is bad information in the Identity-Info header (RFC4474).
437	Unsupported certificate	This is used when the verifier cannot validate the certificate referenced by the URI in the Identity-Info header (RFC4474).
438	Invalid identity header	This is used when the verifier (the receiver UA) receives a message with an Identity signature that does not correspond to the digest-string calculated by the verifier (RFC4474).
470	Consent needed	This is the response to a request that contained a URI list in which at least one URI was such that the relay had no access permissions (RFC5360).
480	Temporarily unavailable	The caller's end system was contacted successfully, but the caller is currently unavailable.
481	Call/transaction does not exist	The receiving UA received a request that does not match any existing transaction or dialog.
482	Loop detected	The server has detected a loop.
483	Too many hops	The server received a request that contains a Max-Forwards header field that equals zero.
484	Address incomplete	The server received a request with an incomplete Request-URI.

485	Ambiguous	The Request-URI was unclear. The response may contain a listing of possible addresses in the Contact header fields.
486	Busy here	The caller's end system was contacted successfully, but the caller is currently unable or unwilling to take additional calls by this end system.
487	Request terminated	The request was terminated by a BYE or CANCEL request.
488	Not acceptable here	Specific resources addressed by the Request-URI are not accepted.
491	Request pending	The receiving UA had a pending request.
493	Undecipherable	The request contains an encrypted MIME body, which cannot be decrypted by the recipient.

5xx codes – server error

The 5xx codes or server error codes indicate that the server failed to fulfill an apparently valid request. They are described in detail in this table:

Code	Event name	Reason
500	Server internal error	An unexpected condition prevented the server from fulfilling the request
501	Not implemented	The functionality that requested to fulfill the request is not supported by the server
502	Bad gateway	A gateway or proxy received an invalid response from the downstream server it accessed while attempting to fulfill the request
503	Service unavailable	The server is temporarily unable to process the request due to temporary overloading or maintenance of the server
504	Server time out	The server processing the request has sent the request to another server in order to process it, and the response did not arrive on time
505	Version not supported	The server does not support the SIP protocol version that is used in the request

513	Message too large	The server was unable to process the request since the message length is too long

6xx codes – global failure

The 6xx codes or global failure codes indicate that the request cannot be fulfilled at any server. They are described in detail in the following table:

Code	Event name	Reason
600	Busy everywhere	The recipient's end system was contacted successfully, but the user is busy and does not wish to take the call at this moment
603	Decline	The receiving UA was successfully contacted, but the user explicitly does not wish to or cannot participate
604	Does not exist anywhere	The server has authoritative information that the user indicated in the Request URI, which does not exist anywhere
606	Not acceptable	The US was contacted successfully, but some aspects of the session description described by SDP were not acceptable

Video over IP and RTSP

As per the internet report published by internet Society, more than 70% of global consumer internet traffic is IP video traffic. In the world of entertainment and education, video content is very prevalent and leverages the maturity of IP network by using IP as transport media for video content delivery. Various codecs are used to encode the video content into bit streams and use RTP as the transport protocol for end-to-end video data delivery.

The video traffic can be streaming video or can be a one-to-one video call. While in either of the cases, RTP is used as the protocol for video data packets, different control plane signaling protocols can be used to establish the video call sessions. For example:

- SIP can be used as the signaling protocol for video calls
- RTSP can be used as signaling protocol for streaming video.

In this recipe, we will discuss about both the options and see how Wireshark can be used to analyze the normal operation.

Getting ready

Port mirroring to capture the packet can be done either on the client side or on the server side. Connect Wireshark close to the endpoint and capture the packets for analysis.

How to do it...

SIP signaling protocol:

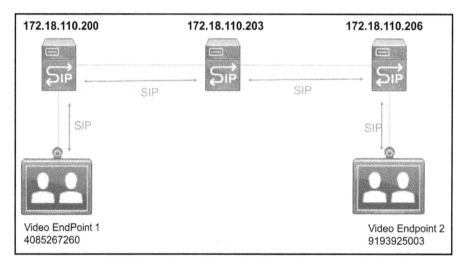

When SIP is used as the signaling protocol, the messages exchanged between the endpoints and any CUBE or SIP proxy along the path are exactly the same as explained in the *How it works...* section of SIP Principle of Operation, Messages, and Error codes. Additional details exchanged between the endpoints when video calling is enabled are explained here:

1. When the endpoints are enabled to make video calls, the SDP messages carry not only the RTP information for the audio stream but also the RTP information for video streams.

```
▼ Session Initiation Protocol (200)
  ▷ Status-Line: SIP/2.0 200 OK
  ▷ Message Header
  ▼ Message Body
    ▼ Session Description Protocol
        Session Description Protocol Version (v): 0
      ▷ Owner/Creator, Session Id (o): CiscoSystemsCCM-SIP 22374 1 IN IP4 172.18.110.206
        Session Name (s): SIP Call
      ▷ Connection Information (c): IN IP4 14.50.201.48
      ▼ Bandwidth Information (b): TIAS:384000
          Bandwidth Modifier: TIAS [Transport Independent Application Specific maximum]
          Bandwidth Value: 384000 b/s
      ▼ Bandwidth Information (b): AS:384
          Bandwidth Modifier: AS [Application Specific (RTP session bandwidth)]
          Bandwidth Value: 384 kb/s
      ▷ Time Description, active time (t): 0 0
      ▷ Media Description, name and address (m): audio 23978 RTP/AVP 9 124 0 8 116 18 101           ──────→ RTP stream info for
      ▷ Media Attribute (a): rtpmap:9 G722/8000                                                              audio
      ▷ Media Attribute (a): rtpmap:124 iSAC/16000
      ▷ Media Attribute (a): rtpmap:0 PCMU/8000
      ▷ Media Attribute (a): rtpmap:8 PCMA/8000
      ▷ Media Attribute (a): rtpmap:116 iLBC/8000
      ▷ Media Attribute (a): maxptime:20
      ▷ Media Attribute (a): fmtp:116 mode=20
      ▷ Media Attribute (a): rtpmap:18 G729/8000
      ▷ Media Attribute (a): fmtp:18 annexb=no
      ▷ Media Attribute (a): rtpmap:101 telephone-event/8000
      ▷ Media Attribute (a): fmtp:101 0-15
      ▼ Media Description, name and address (m): video 30290 RTP/AVP 126 97                        ──────→ RTP stream info for
          Media Type: video                                                                               video
          Media Port: 30290
          Media Protocol: RTP/AVP
          Media Format: DynamicRTP-Type-126
          Media Format: DynamicRTP-Type-97
      ▷ Bandwidth Information (b): TIAS:384000
      ▷ Media Attribute (a): rtpmap:126 H264/90000
      ▷ Media Attribute (a): fmtp:126 profile-level-id=42801E;packetization-mode=1;level-asymmetry-allowed=1
      ▷ Media Attribute (a): rtpmap:97 H264/90000
      ▷ Media Attribute (a): fmtp:97 profile-level-id=42801E;packetization-mode=0;level-asymmetry-allowed=1
      ▷ Media Attribute (a): imageattr:* recv [x=640,y=480,q=0.50]
      ▷ Media Attribute (a): content:main
```

2. In the preceding screenshot, it can be observed that the SDP message carries Media Description details for both audio and video stream. It also signals the use of H.264 as the video codec.

3. The SDP message instructs to use UDP port `23978` for audio stream and UDP port `30290` for Video stream.

```
▶ Frame 116: 63 bytes on wire (504 bits), 63 bytes captured (504 bits)
▶ Ethernet II, Src: Cisco_b7:17:0a (00:0b:45:b7:17:0a), Dst: Cisco_76:b5:12 (a4:4c:11:76:b5:12)
▶ Internet Protocol Version 4, Src: 14.50.201.48, Dst: 172.18.110.203
▶ User Datagram Protocol, Src Port: 30290, Dst Port: 8230
▼ Real-Time Transport Protocol
  ▶ [Stream setup by SDP (frame 72)]
    10.. .... = Version: RFC 1889 Version (2)
    ..0. .... = Padding: False
    ...0 .... = Extension: False
    .... 0000 = Contributing source identifiers count: 0
    0... .... = Marker: False
    Payload type: H264 (126)
    Sequence number: 50377
    [Extended sequence number: 50377]
    Timestamp: 252700497
    Synchronization Source identifier: 0xe3969445 (3818296389)
▶ H.264
```

4. Upon receiving the SDP message, the video endpoint will use UDP port `30290` for RTP video stream. As seen in the preceding screenshot, H.264 codec is used for the video payload encoding.

Real-time streaming protocol:

As like SIP messages, RTSP also uses SDP message to instruct the RTP audio/video stream information.

1. Open the Wireshark capture and filter the RTSP packets using **rtsp** as display filter.
2. Get the RTSP Flow Graph by navigating to the **Statistics** and **Flow Graph** option.

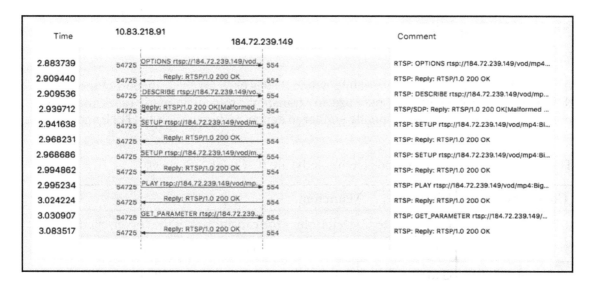

3. The Flow graph will list the RTSP messages exchanged between the client and the media server. In the preceding screenshot, the client 10.83.218.91 establishes RSTP session with 184.72.239.149.

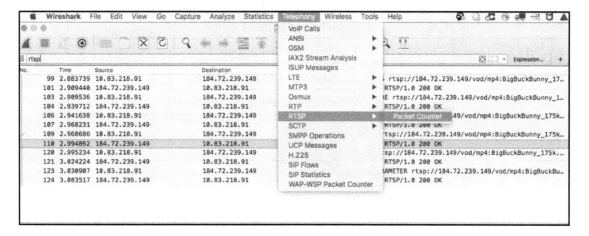

4. Navigate to **Telephony** and **RTSP** and **Packet Counters** to list the different RTSP messages received.

5. More details on the normal operation of RSTP are available in the *How it works...* section.

How it works...

Real-time streaming protocol:

As with SIP (which is used for signaling, while RTP is used for the transport of the media), the streams controlled by RTSP may use any transport protocol; in many cases, they also use RTP. The protocol is intentionally similar in syntax and operation to HTTP and uses the same syntax.

The most common RTSP methods (commands) are (C-Client, S-Server).

Command	Direction	Function
OPTIONS	C to S or S to C	Determines the capabilities of the server/client
DESCRIBE	C to S	Gets a description of the media stream
GET_PARAMETERS	C to S	Retrieves the value for parameters in the URI
ANNOUNCE	C to S or S to C	Announces a new session's description
SETUP	C to S	Creates a media session
PLAY	C to S	Starts media delivery
RECORD	C to S	Starts media recording
PAUSE	C to S	Pauses media delivery
REDIRECT	S to C	Redirects to another server
TEARDOWN	S to C	Performs immediate teardown

The response categories are:

Code series	Type	Meaning
1xx	Informational	Request received, continue with processing
2xx	Success	The action was successfully received, understood, and accepted
3xx	Redirection	Further action must be taken in order to complete the request
4xx	Client error	The request contains bad syntax or cannot be fulfilled
5xx	Server error	The server failed to fulfill an apparently valid request

1. The client `10.83.218.91` will establish an RTSP session over TCP port `554`.

```
▶ Frame 99: 211 bytes on wire (1688 bits), 211 bytes captured (1688 bits)
▶ Ethernet II, Src: Apple_96:f7:dd (ac:bc:32:96:f7:dd), Dst: BelkinIn_62:62:ff (c0:56:27:62:62:ff)
▶ Internet Protocol Version 4, Src: 10.83.218.91, Dst: 184.72.239.149
▶ Transmission Control Protocol, Src Port: 54725, Dst Port: 554, Seq: 1, Ack: 1, Len: 145
▼ Real Time Streaming Protocol
  ▼ Request: OPTIONS rtsp://184.72.239.149/vod/mp4:BigBuckBunny_175k.mov RTSP/1.0\r\n
      Method: OPTIONS
      URL: rtsp://184.72.239.149/vod/mp4:BigBuckBunny_175k.mov
    CSeq: 2\r\n
    User-Agent: LibVLC/2.2.1 (LIVE555 Streaming Media v2014.07.25)\r\n
    \r\n
```

2. Once the session is established, the client sends an RTSP request message with the OPTIONS method and the resource requested. In the preceding screenshot, The requested resource is `mp4:BigBuckBunny_175k.mov` from `184.72.239.149`.

3. The server replies with RTSP 200 OK. The RTSP Response message is also used to carry the capabilities. The response will carry the CSeq number from the Request message.

```
▶ Frame 103: 237 bytes on wire (1896 bits), 237 bytes captured (1896 bits)
▶ Ethernet II, Src: Apple_96:f7:dd (ac:bc:32:96:f7:dd), Dst: BelkinIn_62:62:ff (c0:56:27:62:62:ff)
▶ Internet Protocol Version 4, Src: 10.83.218.91, Dst: 184.72.239.149
▶ Transmission Control Protocol, Src Port: 54725, Dst Port: 554, Seq: 146, Ack: 235, Len: 171
▼ Real Time Streaming Protocol
   ▼ Request: DESCRIBE rtsp://184.72.239.149/vod/mp4:BigBuckBunny_175k.mov RTSP/1.0\r\n
       Method: DESCRIBE
       URL: rtsp://184.72.239.149/vod/mp4:BigBuckBunny_175k.mov
     CSeq: 3\r\n
     User-Agent: LibVLC/2.2.1 (LIVE555 Streaming Media v2014.07.25)\r\n
     Accept: application/sdp\r\n
   \r\n
```

4. The client now sends the RTSP Request message with the DESCRIBE method for the resource in the URI. This is used to retrieve the content description or media object from the server. The CSeq number is incremented by 1 for each subsequent Request message.

```
▶ Frame 104: 990 bytes on wire (7920 bits), 990 bytes captured (7920 bits)
▶ Ethernet II, Src: BelkinIn_62:62:ff (c0:56:27:62:62:ff), Dst: Apple_96:f7:dd (ac:bc:32:96:f7:dd)
▶ Internet Protocol Version 4, Src: 184.72.239.149, Dst: 10.83.218.91
▶ Transmission Control Protocol, Src Port: 554, Dst Port: 54725, Seq: 235, Ack: 317, Len: 924
▼ Real Time Streaming Protocol
  ▼ Response: RTSP/1.0 200 OK\r\n
       Status: 200
     CSeq: 3\r\n
     Server: Wowza Streaming Engine 4.7.3.02 build21313\r\n
     Cache-Control: no-cache\r\n
     Expires: Thu, 22 Feb 2018 01:08:08 UTC\r\n
     Content-length: 590
     Content-Base: rtsp://184.72.239.149/vod/mp4:BigBuckBunny_175k.mov/\r\n
     Date: Thu, 22 Feb 2018 01:08:08 UTC\r\n
     Content-type: application/sdp
     Session: 1785054106;timeout=60
     \r\n
  ▼ Session Description Protocol
       Session Description Protocol Version (v): 0
     ▶ Owner/Creator, Session Id (o): - 1785054106 1785054106 IN IP4 184.72.239.149
       Session Name (s): BigBuckBunny_175k.mov
     ▶ Connection Information (c): IN IP4 184.72.239.149
     ▶ Time Description, active time (t): 0 0
     ▶ Session Attribute (a): sdplang:en
     ▶ Session Attribute (a): range:npt=0- 596.458
     ▶ Session Attribute (a): control:*
     ▶ Media Description, name and address (m): audio 0 RTP/AVP 96
     ▶ Media Attribute (a): rtpmap:96 mpeg4-generic/48000/2
     ▶ Media Attribute (a): fmtp:96 profile-level-id=1;mode=AAC-hbr;sizelength=13;indexlength=3;indexdeltalength=3;config=1190
     ▶ Media Attribute (a): control:trackID=1
     ▶ Media Description, name and address (m): video 0 RTP/AVP 97
     ▶ Media Attribute (a): rtpmap:97 H264/90000
     ▶ Media Attribute (a): fmtp:97 packetization-mode=1;profile-level-id=42C01E;sprop-parameter-sets=Z0LAH/tkDxWhAAAADAEAAAAwDxYuS,aMuMsg==
     ▶ Media Attribute (a): cliprect:0,0,160,240
     ▶ Media Attribute (a): framesize:97 240-160
     ▶ Media Attribute (a): framerate:24.0
     ▶ Media Attribute (a): control:trackID=2
```

5. The server will reply with RTSP 200 OK. This response will carry the SDP with session and content-related information. The SDP instructs the use of Dynamic-RTP type 96 for RTP audio stream and Dynamic-RTP type 97 for RTP video stream.

6. Unlike the SIP session, where the RTP port information will be exchanged using SDP, RTSP uses the SETUP method for this purpose. The client will send a Request message with the SETUP method and carry the UDP port for RTP audio stream.

```
▶ Frame 106: 271 bytes on wire (2168 bits), 271 bytes captured (2168 bits)
▶ Ethernet II, Src: Apple_96:f7:dd (ac:bc:32:96:f7:dd), Dst: BelkinIn_62:62:ff (c0:56:27:62:62:ff)
▶ Internet Protocol Version 4, Src: 10.83.218.91, Dst: 184.72.239.149
▶ Transmission Control Protocol, Src Port: 54725, Dst Port: 554, Seq: 317, Ack: 1159, Len: 205
▼ Real Time Streaming Protocol
  ▼ Request: SETUP rtsp://184.72.239.149/vod/mp4:BigBuckBunny_175k.mov/trackID=1 RTSP/1.0\r\n
      Method: SETUP
      URL: rtsp://184.72.239.149/vod/mp4:BigBuckBunny_175k.mov/trackID=1
    CSeq: 4\r\n
    User-Agent: LibVLC/2.2.1 (LIVE555 Streaming Media v2014.07.25)\r\n
    Transport: RTP/AVP;unicast;client_port=50960-50961
    \r\n
```

7. In the preceding screenshot, the client signals that UDP port 50960 is assigned for RTP audio stream and 50961 for RTCP traffic.

8. A similar request with the SETUP method will be exchanged for RTP video stream as well.

9. Upon receiving RTSP 200 OK from the server, it will send other methods such as PLAY to start the audio/video streams.

There's more...

RFC 7826 proposes RTSP v2.0; that obsoletes the RTSP v1.0 defined in RFC 2326.

Wireshark features for RTP stream analysis and filtering

Wireshark has various inbuilt features that are very useful in analyzing the RTP audio and video streams. In this recipe, we will discuss the features and how to use it for troubleshooting purposes.

Getting ready

When there is a problem on a specific client, connect Wireshark to the client port with a port mirror. When there is a problem with all clients, connect Wireshark to a common switch connecting all the clients.

How to do it...

1. Open the Wireshark capture and use the **Telephony** menu to navigate to **RTP | RTP Streams**, as shown in the following screenshot:

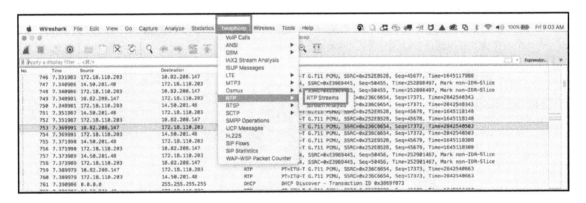

2. This will result in a pop-up window listing all the RTP streams available in the capture.

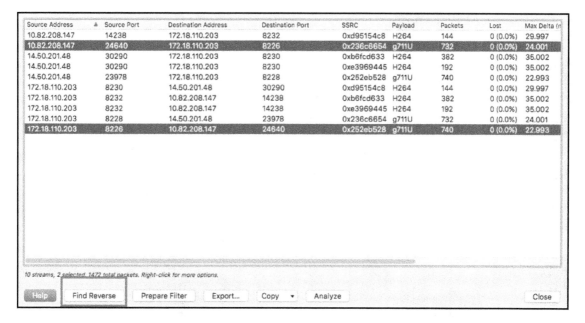

Source Address	▲ Source Port	Destination Address	Destination Port	SSRC	Payload	Packets	Lost	Max Delta (n
10.82.208.147	14238	172.18.110.203	8232	0xd95154c8	H264	144	0 (0.0%)	29.997
10.82.208.147	24640	172.18.110.203	8226	0x236c6654	g711U	732	0 (0.0%)	24.001
14.50.201.48	30290	172.18.110.203	8230	0xb6fcd633	H264	382	0 (0.0%)	35.002
14.50.201.48	30290	172.18.110.203	8230	0xe3969445	H264	192	0 (0.0%)	35.002
14.50.201.48	23978	172.18.110.203	8228	0x252eb528	g711U	740	0 (0.0%)	22.993
172.18.110.203	8230	14.50.201.48	30290	0xd95154c8	H264	144	0 (0.0%)	29.997
172.18.110.203	8232	10.82.208.147	14238	0xb6fcd633	H264	382	0 (0.0%)	35.002
172.18.110.203	8232	10.82.208.147	14238	0xe3969445	H264	192	0 (0.0%)	35.002
172.18.110.203	8228	14.50.201.48	23978	0x236c6654	g711U	732	0 (0.0%)	24.001
172.18.110.203	8226	10.82.208.147	24640	0x252eb528	g711U	740	0 (0.0%)	22.993

10 streams, 2 selected, 1472 total packets. Right-click for more options.

| Help | Find Reverse | Prepare Filter | Export... | Copy ▾ | Analyze | Close |

3. Choose the relevant stream to analyze and use **Find Reverse** to identify the RTP stream in reverse direction between the endpoints.

4. Use **Prepare Filter** to filter all RTP packets in both forward and reverse direction. Alternately, use **Analyze** to analyze the forward and reverse RTP streams. Clicking on **Analyze** will popup a new window with metrics on forward and reverse direction.

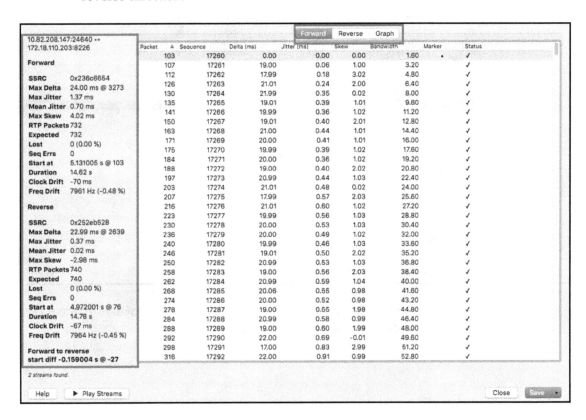

5. Different tabs are available that list the metrics associated with forward and reverse RTP streams. As shown in the preceding screenshot, RTP streams will be analyzed to list the jitter, delay, and packet loss for both forward and reverse direction streams...

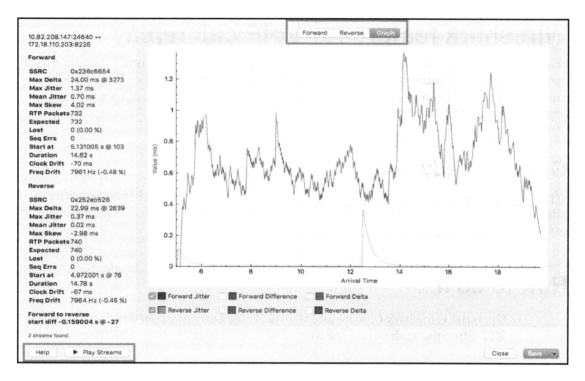

6. The preceding screenshot is a sample graph for a specific RTP stream that highlights the jitter in forward and reverse direction of the stream.

How it works...

Irrespective of the call signaling protocol used, most of the current audio and video streams use RTP as the application layer protocol. RTP protocol provides reliability by sequencing the packets at application layer and helps to control jitter and delay by forwarding audio and video payload as small chunks in each RTP packets.

More details on how the RTP stream works are available in the *IP Telephony principle and normal operation* section in this chapter.

Wireshark feature for VoIP call replay

Wireshark is augmented with an audio playback feature that encodes the RTP audio stream and plays the actual audio content. Play Streams is used for this purpose. This option merges the audio stream from both forward and reverse directions and allows the user to listen to the actual conversation.

Getting ready

When there is a problem on a specific client, connect Wireshark to the client port with a port mirror. When there is a problem with all clients, connect Wireshark to a common switch connecting all the clients.

How to do it...

1. Open the Wireshark capture and use the **Telephony** menu to navigate to **RTP | RTP Streams**, as shown in the following screenshot:

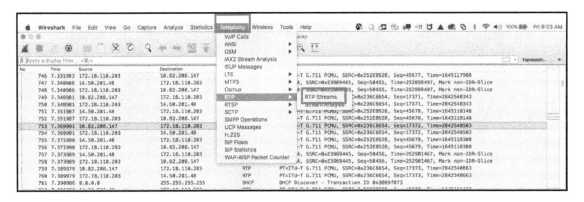

2. Choose the relevant RTP audio stream and the associated reverse stream. Now use analyze to combine the streams from both directions. This will pop up as a different window, as shown here:

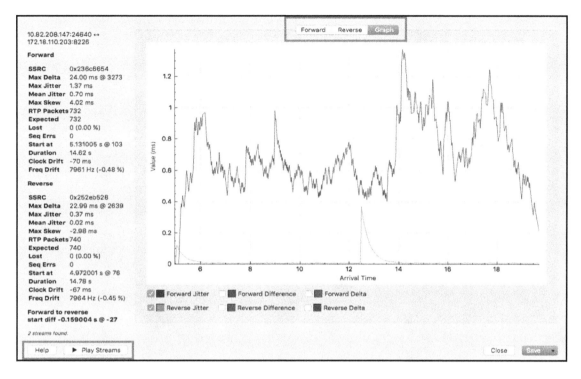

3. Use the **Play Stream** and listen to the actual audio content.
4. Wireshark RTP playback does not work for RTP video stream. So it cannot be used to view video content.

How it works...

Wireshark interprets the audio codec used to encode the audio stream and leverages the same to decode the audio file content. Wireshark will save the RTP audio streams using G711 codec as an .au file format that allows us to play back the captured conversation.

There's more...

Currently, Wireshark natively supports playback of RTP audio streams with G711 codec. If the codec used for the audio stream is G729, it does not play. Use the following procedure to convert G729: https://wiki.wireshark.org/HowToDecodeG729

18
Troubleshooting Bandwidth and Delay Issues

In this chapter, you will learn about:

- Measuring network bandwidth and application traffic
- Measuring jitter and delay using Wireshark
- Analyzing network bottlenecks, issues, and troubleshooting

Introduction

The performance of end-to-end services and applications heavily depends on various network parameters such as bandwidth, delay, jitter, and packet loss. There are various SLA constraints for different types of end applications. For example, applications that involve large file exchange, such as file transfer applications (FTP, TFTP), are very sensitive to bandwidth and packet loss, while on the other hand, media applications such as voice and video traffic are very sensitive to delay and jitter.

Measuring the performance of an end application varies depending on the SLA constraints of the end application, and therefore we need to measure different network parameters.

In this chapter, we will learn how to measure these network parameters, how to check for network problems caused by them, and how to solve these when possible.

Measuring network bandwidth and application traffic

One of the primary responsibilities of a network operator is to monitor the network and bandwidth utilization. This may be for various business purposes, such as:

- Ensuring that low-priority or scavenger traffic is not choking the network and making business-critical traffic suffer
- Ensuring that the WAN provider is able to provide the committed traffic rate on the access circuit
- Use the result for capacity planning to upgrade or downgrade the bandwidth

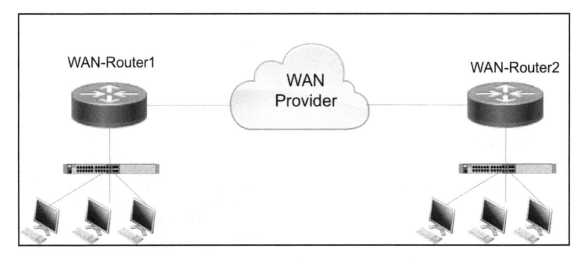

Figure 19.1: WAN topology

In most of the troubleshooting and analysis recipes we have discussed so far, the data capture will be done as close as possible to the application endpoints. In order to measure WAN circuit utilization, we may need additional consideration to measure the bandwidth accurately. In the preceding topology, **WAN-Router1** may be connected through a 1 Gbps interface to a WAN provider, but the **Committed Access Rate** (**CAR**) can be much lower (such as 10 Mbps). Normally, WAN providers will have traffic rate limiting enabled in the inbound direction to limit the traffic to 10 Mbps, and drop any excess traffic. So, performing packet capture on the **WAN-Router1** side may not be accurate. On the other hand, the customer may implement features such as traffic shaping, which allows them to buffer the traffic and ensure that the outbound traffic from WAN router to provider does not exceed the CAR. So, depending on how the network is deployed, packet capture will need to be done at the appropriate position.

In this recipe, we will discuss how to use Wireshark to measure the WAN circuit bandwidth and analyze different application traffic utilizations.

Getting ready

Depending on how the network is deployed, we may need to identify and position the packet capture tools at the relevant locations:

- If traffic shaping is enabled, we can capture the packet in the outbound direction on WAN routers
- If traffic shaping is not enabled, we can capture the packet in the inbound direction on the WAN provider or on remote WAN routers

How to do it...

To measure the bandwidth on a WAN circuit, we may need to pump some traffic at a rate close to the bandwidth to test whether the circuit can handle it or not. There are different traffic generator tools available such as iPerf, IXIA, and Spirent that can be used to pump different types of traffic. Other open source traffic generators such as Scapy, tcpreplay, or playcap can also be used to generate traffic.

To identify the average bandwidth utilization, follow these steps:

1. Select **Summary** from **Statistics**:

Display
Display filter: none
Ignored packets: 0

Traffic	Captured	Displayed	Marked
Packets	175391	175391	0
Between first and last packet	55.323 sec		
Avg. packets/sec	3170.284		
Avg. packet size	1289.011 bytes		
Bytes	226081014		
Avg. bytes/sec	4086531.946		
Avg. MBit/sec	32.692		

The output will list the number of packets captured, **Avg. MBit/sec**, **Avg. packet size**, and so on.

2. It also allows us to view the summary for a specific flow or set of flows by using the filter. To get a summary of selective flows, use the display filter to filter the stream(s) and then use **Statistics | Summary**:

Display
Display filter: tcp.stream eq 133
Ignored packets: 0

Traffic	Captured	Displayed	Marked
Packets	175391	110782	0
Between first and last packet	55.323 sec	10.537 sec	
Avg. packets/sec	3170.284	10513.801	
Avg. packet size	1289.011 bytes	1327.361 bytes	
Bytes	226081014	147047699	
Avg. bytes/sec	4086531.946	13955608.982	
Avg. MBit/sec	32.692	111.645	

The preceding is an example output for a specific TCP stream.

3. A more detailed view of the maximum bandwidth available on the circuit can be gained by using the I/O graph. From **Statistics**, select **IO Graphs**:

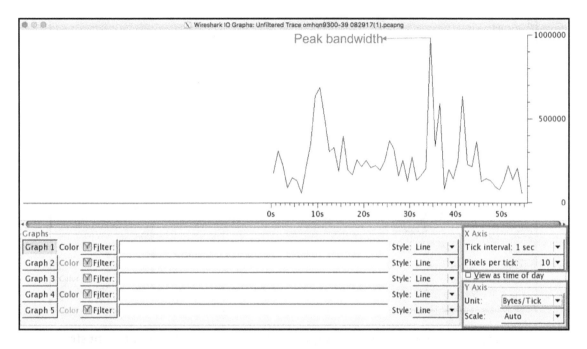

4. By default, the graph will show the overall performance of all captured packets. The **X Axis** and **Y Axis** can be modified:

   - The **X Axis** defines the tick interval, the interval at which the **Y Axis** will be measured. The granularity of this interval can be set from 10 minutes to 1 millisecond.

   - The **Y Axis** defines the unit in which the performance is measured. The measurement is termed the number of packets, bytes, or bits in each tick (**X Axis**).

   - In the preceding example, the **X Axis** is set to a **Tick interval** of **1 sec** and the **Y Axis** is set to **Bytes/Tick**. So the measurement value is bytes/sec.

   - Choosing the **View as time of day** option will list the actual time of day when the packet was captured. This is a very useful tool to identify the actual time of day when a spike in traffic throughput is observed in the graph.

5. Multiple graphs can be created that list different streams to identify the bandwidth utilization based on streams:

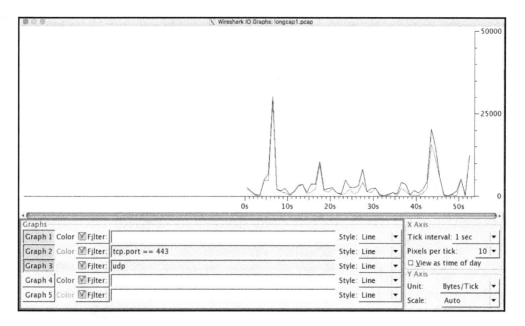

The preceding is an example output with different graphs for different stream(s).

6. To identify the end user or application that is consuming most of the bandwidth, the top talking endpoint can be listed. From **Statistics**, go to **Endpoints**:

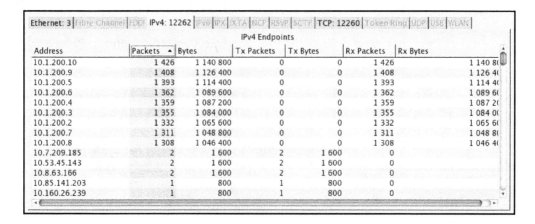

This lists all the endpoints based on the number of packets/bytes sent and received. It helps to identify the top talking endpoints.

7. Precise flow-specific details can be seen by using the conversation statistics option. From **Statistics**, go to **Conversations**:

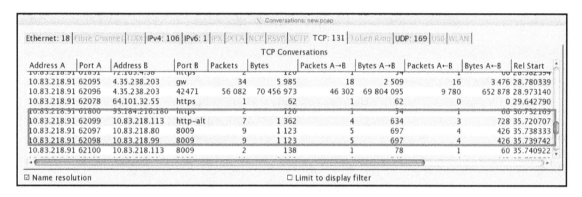

The preceding screenshot shows flow-specific conversations, duration of the flow, number of packets exchanged, and so on.

How it works...

There are three different definitions related to network traffic utilization, and distinguishing between them is critical to understanding network bandwidth utilization:

- **Speed**: Maximum amount of traffic that can traverse the circuit or link.
- **Bandwidth**: Maximum amount of traffic (bits per second) that is allowed to traverse the link. By default, the bandwidth will be equal to the speed of the link.
- **Throughput**: Effective end application traffic (bits per second) that is transferred between the application endpoints.

The speed of a link (and so the bandwidth) varies depending on various factors, including the type of link, CAR offered by the provider, and local configuration. By default, most network devices will be able to forward traffic at line rate, which is the maximum supported bandwidth on the respective link.

In recent deployments, it is common to see Gigabit Ethernet as the last mile access connection from WAN routers to service providers. The speed of the Gigabit Ethernet will be 1 Gbps, but the bandwidth can vary depending on the CAR provided by the service provider.

Even if a WAN router is capable of sending traffic at line rate of the link, the service provider will ensure that the traffic does not exceed the CAR.

There's more...

Any network device will use the **first in, first out** (**FIFO**) queuing mechanism to forward traffic out of the circuit. So if there is too much scavenger traffic, it is possible that such low-priority traffic may consume all bandwidth and cause the business-critical traffic to suffer. This can be avoided by deploying **Quality of Service** (**QoS**) in the network. QoS changes the queuing mechanism from FIFO to priority-based queuing, preventing scavenger or low-priority traffic from consuming all bandwidth and thereby ensuring that business-critical traffic will always be prioritized.

Measurement of jitter and delay using Wireshark

Jitter and delay are characteristics that can significantly influence various network applications. To monitor jitter and delay on a communication line, you can use simple or graphical ping tools that will show you the line characteristics. Wireshark, on the other hand, does not measure the end-to-end delay but the influence that it has on the network traffic, the interframe delay, and how it influences applications.

In this recipe, we will see how to use Wireshark tools to monitor these parameters, and in the next recipe we will see how to find out problems caused by parameters.

Getting ready

To monitor delay on a communication line, first use the `ping` command to get a feel for the line, and then configure the port mirror to the port you want to monitor.

How to do it...

To monitor interframe delay, follow these steps:

1. From **Statistics**, select **IO Graphs**.
2. To monitor the time between frames in a specific stream of data, follow these steps:
   1. Click on a packet in the TCP or UDP stream
   2. Click on **Follow TCP Stream** or **Follow UDP Stream**
   3. Copy the displayed filter string (numbered **1** in the following screenshot)
3. From **Statistics**, open **IO Graphs**.
4. In **IO Graphs**, in the **Y Axis** part (lower-right corner of the window), select **Advanced...** (numbered **2** in the following screenshot).
5. Copy the TCP stream number (numbered **1** in the following screenshot) to the filter window in the I/O graph (numbered **3** in the following screenshot):

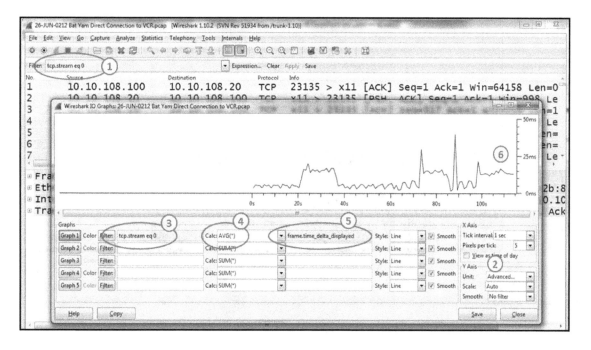

6. Select **AVG(*)** (numbered **4** in the preceding screenshot).
7. Configure the filter `frame.time_delta_displayed` (numbered **5** in the preceding screenshot).
8. In the graph (numbered **6** in the preceding screenshot), you see the time between frames in milliseconds.
9. By navigating to **Statistics | TCP Stream Graph | Round Trip Time Graph** you will get the same results, as shown in the following graph:

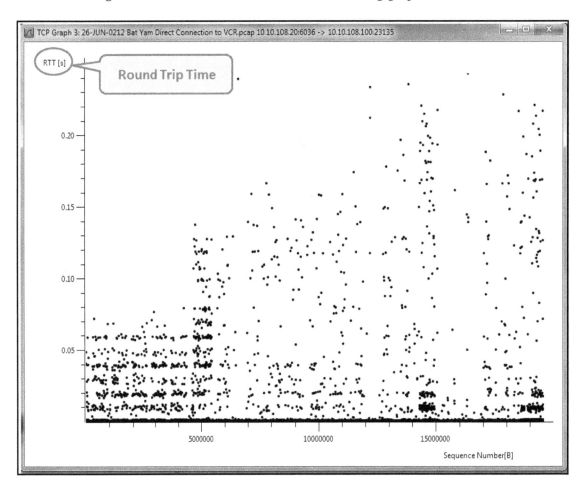

10. In the illustration, we see that the RTT varies between values that are lower than 10 milliseconds and up to 200-300 milliseconds.

11. To measure delays in layer 4, use the `tcp.analysis.ack_rtt` TCP filter, which will give you the time that it takes to acknowledge every received packet.

How it works...

The software simply captures packets over the line and shows you the time difference between them. It is important to note that there is a delay or jitter, but we will not see where it is coming from.

Delay is the time that it takes a packet to get from one end of the network to the other. It is usually referred to as RTT. Delay can be measured with the simple ping or Graphical Ping tools. Delay is measured in seconds, milliseconds, microseconds, and so on.

Jitter in IP networks measures the variations in delay. For example, if we have an average delay of 100 ms, and it varies between 80 milliseconds and 120 milliseconds, the jitter is 20 percent.

There's more...

Graphical Ping tools are available for free on many websites. You can use, for example, `http://www.colasoft.com/download/products/download_ping_tool.php`.

Analyzing network bottlenecks, issues, and troubleshooting

The problems and troubleshooting discussed in the previous recipes are mostly related, and may result in networking bottleneck issues. Any misbehaving link or router introducing a delay, or a network design with poor capacity planning, may result in bandwidth bottleneck issues, causing end-to-end application performance to suffer.

In this recipe, we will see how to use Wireshark to analyze bottleneck issues.

Getting ready

In order to identify bottleneck issues, we may need to reiterate the capture at multiple locations for analysis and bottleneck isolation. Ideally, packet capture at endpoints will be a good start to identify the application traffic that is impacted, and we then use other tools, such as the ping utility, to possibly narrow down the capture points.

How to do it...

1. Filter the capture to display the DNS resolution packets for the application server and check the average time for resolution. This can be viewed by filtering the DNS packets and getting the I/O graph:
   - Check whether the number of DNS packets is within the threshold that the DNS server can handle. If not, a DNS server upgrade needs to be considered.
   - Check whether the time delta for resolution is within the threshold. Any delay in resolution will introduce a delay in end application session establishment:

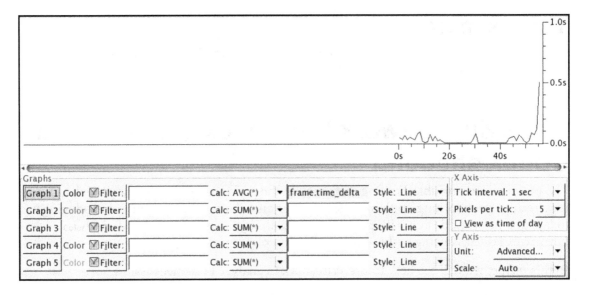

The preceding graph is the I/O graph of DNS packets used to check the delay in name resolution.

2. Check that the WAN bandwidth utilization is within the threshold at its peak and during normal business hours. Use the steps defined in the *Measuring network bandwidth and application traffic* section to identify the bandwidth utilization on the LAN and WAN side. The procedure defined in this section can be used to not only identify the bandwidth utilization, but also to check whether the utilization is due to business-critical traffic or scavenger traffic:

   • If the capture shows the WAN bandwidth utilization is completely utilized and the traffic is mostly business-critical, you may need a bandwidth upgrade.

   • If the capture shows the WAN bandwidth utilization is completely utilized and the traffic is not business-critical, it may need additional queuing and QoS mechanisms to rate limit the non-critical traffic.

3. Check whether any transit link (LAN, WAN) is suffering from high delay/jitter issues. More details on how to perform this is explained in *Measurement of jitter and delay using Wireshark* section. Capture showing a link delay in seconds is completely abnormal:

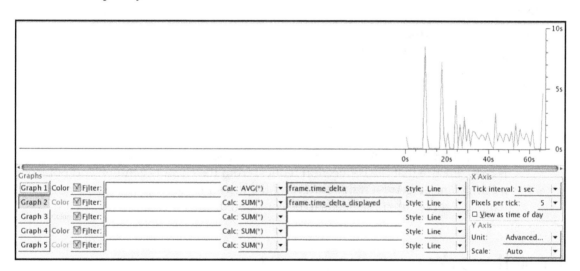

The preceding I/O graph shows a link with a peak delay as high as 10 seconds, and an average of more than 1 second. Traffic over such a link will be heavily impacted and it may need additional link-level troubleshooting (checking the power, fiber cleaning, and so on).

4. Check whether the application server is hitting any scale issues. This can be done by checking the number of concurrent sessions at peak and normal times and whether the number of sessions is within the threshold that the server can handle.

5. Check the endpoints graph to identify the number of concurrent sessions:

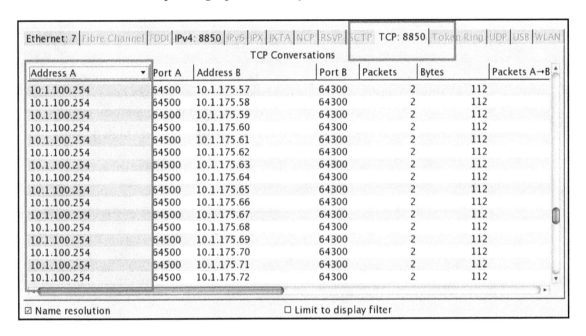

Address A		Port A	Address B	Port B	Packets	Bytes	Packets A→B
10.1.100.254		64500	10.1.175.57	64300	2	112	
10.1.100.254		64500	10.1.175.58	64300	2	112	
10.1.100.254		64500	10.1.175.59	64300	2	112	
10.1.100.254		64500	10.1.175.60	64300	2	112	
10.1.100.254		64500	10.1.175.61	64300	2	112	
10.1.100.254		64500	10.1.175.62	64300	2	112	
10.1.100.254		64500	10.1.175.63	64300	2	112	
10.1.100.254		64500	10.1.175.64	64300	2	112	
10.1.100.254		64500	10.1.175.65	64300	2	112	
10.1.100.254		64500	10.1.175.66	64300	2	112	
10.1.100.254		64500	10.1.175.67	64300	2	112	
10.1.100.254		64500	10.1.175.68	64300	2	112	
10.1.100.254		64500	10.1.175.69	64300	2	112	
10.1.100.254		64500	10.1.175.70	64300	2	112	
10.1.100.254		64500	10.1.175.71	64300	2	112	
10.1.100.254		64500	10.1.175.72	64300	2	112	

Ethernet: 7 | Fibre Channel | FDDI | IPv4: 8850 | IPv6 | IPX | JXTA | NCP | RSVP | SCTP | **TCP: 8850** | Token Ring | UDP | USB | WLAN

TCP Conversations

☑ Name resolution   ☐ Limit to display filter

In the preceding list, the number of concurrent sessions to server 10.1.100.254 is 8850. Ensure that the connection request from the client is genuine and not from a compromised server. If this is beyond the threshold of what the server can handle, a server upgrade needs to be considered.

How it works...

This recipe explains how Wireshark can be used to troubleshoot networking bottleneck issues. The working mechanism may vary depending on the type of traffic in the network. Ideally, the flow is a combination of different protocols. For example, a client that is trying to establish a session with the application server will use a name resolution protocol such as DNS to identify the IP address of the end server.

Once the IP address is received, it may send TCP SYN to establish a TCP session if the transport protocol is TCP (for example, HTTP or FTP). If the transport protocol for the application is UDP (for example, QUIC), it will simply send the application request over UDP packets. The server, upon receiving the request, will pump the data over the network towards the client.

Any network devices (L2 switches and routers) will forward the traffic over the best path. Depending on the availability of equal cost paths, the router may load balance different flows over different paths.

There are different factors that come into the picture for end-to-end performance. End application server processing capability and memory play a key role in session handling and data transfer. Network capacity planning plays a key role in end-to-end data transfer between different clients and servers.

There's more...

There are various network telemetry collection features available that can be used to collect network data periodically from all or selected network devices to have a holistic view of network performance. This will be very useful for capacity planning. The basic features that can be used, and are available across many platforms, are as follows:

- Cisco Netflow:
    - `http://www.cisco.com/en/US/products/ps6601/products_ios_protocol_group_home.html`
    - `http://www.ietf.org/rfc/rfc3954.txt`
- Juniper J-Flow:
    - `http://www.juniper.net/techpubs/software/erx/junose82/swconfig-ip-services/html/ip-jflow-stats-config2.html`
- sFlow:
    - `http://www.ietf.org/rfc/rfc3176.txt`

19
Security and Network Forensics

In this chapter, we will cover the following recipes:

- Discovering unusual traffic patterns
- Discovering MAC-based and ARP-based attacks
- Discovering ICMP and TCP SYN/port scans
- Discovering DoS and DDoS attacks
- Locating smart TCP attacks
- Discovering brute force and application attacks

Introduction

Information security is one of the most fascinating areas in information systems, and its purpose is to secure the organization's systems against internal and external attacks, which can come in various patterns. These attacks can come from the internet or from the internal network, and as such, they all come through the network; therefore, they can be monitored with Wireshark (and other similar tools).

To monitor the network against malicious traffic, we must first understand what constitutes normal traffic and define the base line of the traffic rate, it's pattern, and so on. We can then try to find out how malicious traffic is short of being normal traffic according to it. Among unusual traffic, we might see an ARP, IP, or TCP scanning; DNS responses without queries; unusual TCP flags; unknown IP addresses or port numbers whose purpose is not known to us, and so on.

It is also important to understand the difference between security problems and networking problems, and to distinguish between them. For example, an ICMP scan can be a malicious software scanning the network or even a management software that discovers the network. A TCP SYN scan can be a worm or a software bug. We will elaborate on these in each of the recipes.

In this chapter, we will start by differentiating between normal and unusual network traffic and then understand the various types of attacks, where they come from, and how to isolate and solve them.

Discovering unusual traffic patterns

In this recipe, we will learn what usual and unusual traffic patterns are and how to distinguish between them.

Getting ready

The first thing is to locate Wireshark. There are several options for this:

1. When you suspect an attack that comes from the internet, locate Wireshark after the firewall (**1**), and when you suspect that it crosses the firewall, locate it before (**2**).
2. When you suspect malicious traffic coming from a remote office, port-mirror traffic coming on the central line before (**3**) or after (**4**) the router. In this case, you can filter the suspicious traffic with IP networks to see patterns from different offices in order to isolate the problematic office.
3. You can also port-mirror the traffic in the remote office before (**7**) or after (**6**) the routers.
4. When a PC or a server is the suspect, port-mirror its port on the switch (**8**).

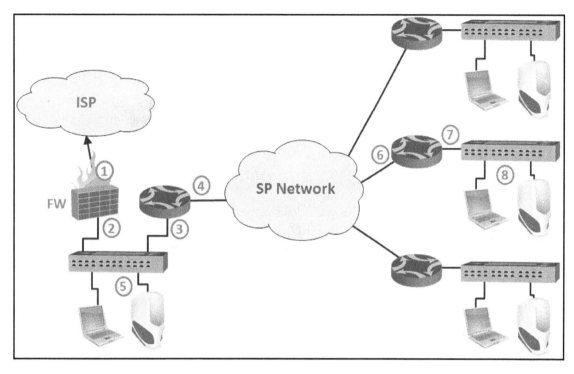

Figure 19.1: Wireshark locations

Now, we will try to see which types of traffic we should look out for, which types of traffic are normal, and which traffic should be followed.

Before starting with the tests, make sure that you have an updated topology of the network that includes these things:

- Servers' IP addresses and LANs' IP address ranges
- Routers, switches, and other communication equipment's IP addresses and topology
- Security device firewalls, **Intrusion Detection Systems (IDSs)/Intrusion Prevention Systems (IPSs)**, **Web Application Firewalls (WAFs)**, database and application firewalls, antivirus systems, and any other device that has an IP address and generates, filters, or forwards network traffic
- What applications work over the network, including TCP/UDP port numbers and IP addresses of software

How to do it...

When you monitor internal traffic in your organization, the following things should be checked:

- Traffic that is generated from known addresses (in the organization):
    - **Normal**: This is the traffic from known addresses and address ranges
    - **Suspicious**: This is the traffic from/to addresses that you don't know

- Applications and port numbers:
    - **Normal**: This includes standard port numbers, 80 (HTTP), 137/8/9 (NetBIOS), 3389 (RDP), 20/21 (FTP), 25110 (Mail), 53 (DNS), and so on. Be sure of the applications that run over the network, and verify that these are the only port numbers that you see.
    - **Suspicious**: This includes unusual port numbers, that is, port numbers that do not belong to applications that run on server (for example, RDP packets to web server).

- TCP patterns:
    - **Normal**: TCP SYN/SYN-ACK/ACK indicates a connection establishment. Single reset (RST) indicates a fast connection tear-down. FIN/FIN-ACK packets indicate a regular tear-down of a connection, standard packets, and acknowledgments.
    - **Suspicious**: Lots of SYN packets that go to single or multiple destinations or coming from multiple sources (usually in a scan pattern that will be described later in this chapter), unusual flag combinations (RST/FIN, URG), and so on.

- Massive traffic to single or multiple sites that you don't know about:
    - **Normal**: Traffic patterns are usually not of fixed bandwidth. When you save or open files, browse the internet, send or receive mails, or access a server with RDP, you see ups and downs.
    - **Suspicious** (in some cases): Fixed bandwidth patterns can indicate that someone is connected to your device, but it can also indicate that someone is listening to radio over the internet (100-150 Kbps), watching video (in some cases), and so on. When you see a fixed bandwidth pattern of traffic, check what it is. A fixed bandwidth pattern is illustrated in the following screenshot:

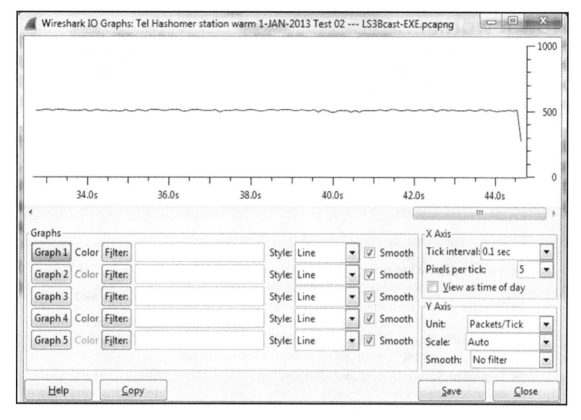

Figure 19.2: Fixed bandwidth pattern

- Broadcasts:
    - **Normal**: NetBIOS broadcasts, ARP broadcasts (not too many), DHCP (not too many), application broadcasts (usually once every several seconds or more), and so on
    - **Suspicious**: Tens, hundreds, thousands, or more broadcasts per second per device
- DNS queries and responses:
    - **Normal**: A standard query-response pattern up to several tens per second per client, occasionally
    - **Suspicious**: Massive number of DNS queries and/or responses, responses without queries, and so on

How it works...

Network forensics is quite the same as what you see in crime scene investigation dramas. Something is going wrong; so, you go to the crime scene (this is your network) and look for evidence (the traces that are left in the network).

What you look for are the things that do not match the crime scene (your network), things that are left behind (unusual traffic patterns), fingerprints, and DNA (patterns that can identify the attacker).

In the following recipes, we will look at the details of various types of attacks and abnormalities that can indicate that a crime was committed, and we will see how to isolate the problems and solve them.

Some common attacks that can come from the network are:

- **Viruses**: These are small programs that attack your computer and try to cause damage. Viruses should be discovered and fixed by antivirus software.
- **Worms**: These are usually programs that attempt to replicate themselves across the network. They have a major impact on resource consumption, for example, bandwidth consumption and CPU load. The important thing is that the moment you fix the problem, everything will go back to normal.
- **Denial of Service (DoS) and Distributed DoS (DDoS)**: These are attacks that deny access to network resources. These types of attacks are usually very easy to discover since they have a distinct behavior that can be located easily.
- **Man-in-the-middle attacks**: These are attacks in which the attacker intercepts messages and then retransmits them. In this way, the attacker can eavesdrop on the traffic or change it before it gets to the destination.
- **Scanning**: There are various types of scans ranging from simple ICMP scans that usually are a form of DDoS, TCP scans that send, for example, SYN requests on various port numbers in order to try and open connections to services running on a server, and also application scans that try to connect to applications running on your servers.
- **Application-layer attacks**: These are attacks that target applications on your servers by intentionally causing a fault in a server's operating system or applications.

In the following recipes, we will see each one of them (and some more).

There's more...

An important indication that something went wrong is when a server, a PC, a communication link, or any other entity on the network becomes slow, without any logical reason. For example:

- When a server becomes slow, check for hardware and software issues. Check for network problems, and also whether someone is attacking it.
- When a link from a remote office to the center becomes slow, it can be because of the load (constant or sudden), but it can also be because of an attack that blocks it (usually DOS/DDoS).
- When a PC becomes slow, it can be because it is doing something that you know about, but there is not just one possibility. Check for the things you don't know.

It is important to mention here that there are various systems that protect us from attacks; a few of them are listed as follows:

- **Firewalls**: They protect against unauthorized traffic getting into specific areas. Firewalls can be located on the connection to the internet, before the organization servers, between organization areas, and even as personal firewalls on every PC.
- **Network Access Control** (**NAC**): These systems allow only authorized users to connect to the network. When connecting an unauthorized device to the network, you will see that the link on the device will be turned on and immediately off, and the unauthorized device will be blocked on the MAC layer.
- **IDS/IPS**: These systems can identify intrusion patterns and block them. There are usually two lines of defense here—one at the ISP network and one at the customer premises. IDS/IPS can be a dedicated device located between the firewall and the internet or an additional software on the firewall.
- **WAF, application firewalls, database firewalls, and other application protection devices**: This group of products are layer-7 protection devices that look inside the applications and forward or block application layer attacks.
- **Web filters and mail filters**: These are devices that scan mail and/or web content and forward only those messages and traffic that are allowed.

The features mentioned just now can come as different devices, software on VMs, or features on the same device.

See also

In this recipe, we talked about some security components. Some examples are:

- **Firewalls**: Checkpoint (`www.checkpoint.com`), Juniper SSG series (`http://www.juniper.net/us/en/products-services/security/ssg-series/`), Cisco ASA series (`http://www.cisco.com/en/US/products/ps5708/Products_Sub_Category_Home.html`), and many others.

- **NAC**: In this category, you have, for example, Forescout (`http://www.forescout.com/solutions/network-access-control/`) and Enterasys (`http://www.enterasys.com/company/literature/nac-ds.pdf`).

- **IDS/IPS**: In this category, we have, for example, the Juniper IDP device series (`http://www.juniper.net/us/en/products-services/security/idp-series/`) and the Checkpoint software blade for the firewall (`http://www.checkpoint.com/products/ips-software-blade/`).

- **WAF**: Here we have, for example, Imperva (`http://www.imperva.com/products/wsc_web-application-firewall.html`) and F5 (`http://www.f5.com/glossary/web-application-firewall/`). Database firewalls are available, for example, form Oracle (`http://www.oracle.com/us/products/database/security/audit-vault-database-firewall/overview/index.html`).

- **Web and mail filters**: Here we have, for example, McAfee (`http://www.mcafee.com/au/products/email-and-web-security/index.aspx`), Bluecoat (`http://www.bluecoat.com/security-policy-enforcement-center`), and Websense (`http://www.websense.com/content/Home.aspx`).

Discovering MAC-based and ARP-based attacks

There are various types of layer 2 MAC-based attacks and layer 2/3 ARP-based attacks that can be easily discovered by Wireshark. These attacks are usually caused by scanners (described in the next recipe) and man-in-the-middle attacks. In this recipe, we will see some typical attack patterns and their meanings.

Getting ready

When viewing too many ARP requests on a network or when seeing non-standard MAC addresses in the network, connect Wireshark with a port-mirror to their source and start the capture.

How to do it...

To look for ARP/MAC-based attacks, follow these steps:

1. Connect Wireshark to any port on the network.
2. Look for massive ARP broadcasts. Since ARP requests are broadcasts, they will be distributed in the entire layer 2 network (that is, on a single VLAN). In the following screenshot, you can see a typical ARP-scan pattern. It's important to note that this ARP scan can be an application that works this way, for example, SNMP software that discovers the network and router that use gratuitous ARP. It is a problem only if it comes from an unidentified source.

Time	Source	Destination	Protocol	Info	
0.000217	HonHaiPr_c7:8e:73	Broadcast	ARP	who has 10.0.0.239?	Tell 192.168.43.191
0.000194	HonHaiPr_c7:8e:73	Broadcast	ARP	who has 10.0.0.242?	Tell 192.168.43.191
0.000184	HonHaiPr_c7:8e:73	Broadcast	ARP	who has 10.0.0.243?	Tell 192.168.43.191
0.000194	HonHaiPr_c7:8e:73	Broadcast	ARP	who has 10.0.0.246?	Tell 192.168.43.191
0.000183	HonHaiPr_c7:8e:73	Broadcast	ARP	who has 10.0.0.247?	Tell 192.168.43.191
0.000412	HonHaiPr_c7:8e:73	Broadcast	ARP	who has 10.0.0.240?	Tell 192.168.43.191
0.000067	HonHaiPr_c7:8e:73	Broadcast	ARP	who has 10.0.0.241?	Tell 192.168.43.191
0.000116	HonHaiPr_c7:8e:73	Broadcast	ARP	who has 10.0.0.244?	Tell 192.168.43.191
0.000385	HonHaiPr_c7:8e:73	Broadcast	ARP	who has 10.0.0.250?	Tell 192.168.43.191
0.000092	HonHaiPr_c7:8e:73	Broadcast	ARP	who has 10.0.0.245?	Tell 192.168.43.191
0.000044	HonHaiPr_c7:8e:73	Broadcast	ARP	who has 10.0.0.248?	Tell 192.168.43.191
0.000264	HonHaiPr_c7:8e:73	Broadcast	ARP	who has 10.0.0.249?	Tell 192.168.43.191
0.496923	HonHaiPr_c7:8e:73	Broadcast	ARP	who has 10.0.0.212?	Tell 192.168.43.191

Figure 19.3: ARP scan pattern

3. There are also some suspicious MAC patterns. You can identify them when you see:
    - Two identical MAC addresses with different IP addresses. It can be two IP addresses configured on the same network adapter, which is OK, but it can also be an attack pattern in which someone has changed its MAC address to the MAC address of a server (can be performed nearly in every adapter.)

- The case mentioned above can also indicate a man-in-the-middle attack as mentioned in the ARP poisoning and the man-in-the-middle attack's section in `Chapter 10`, *Network Layer Protocols and Operations.*

How it works...

ARP sends broadcasts to the network asking for the MAC address of a specific IP destination. Anything that does not follow this pattern should be considered malicious.

There's more...

ARP requests can also come from the SNMP software that discovers the network (auto-discovery feature), the DHCP server that sends gratuitous ARP, and so on. Whenever you see ARP scanning something, it is not necessarily a problem; the question is who sends them? You can find more information on the ARP process in `Chapter 10`, *Network Layer Protocols and Operations.*

Discovering ICMP and TCP SYN/port scans

Scanning is the process of sending packets to network devices in order to see who is answering the ping requests, to look for listening TCP/UDP ports, and to find out which types of resources are shared on the network, including system and application resources.

Getting ready

A scanning attack is usually detected by users complaining about slow network responses, by management systems that discover an unusual load on servers or communication lines, or when the attack is implemented by **Security Information and Event Management Systems (SIEM)** that identify suspicious usage patterns. In these cases, locate the Wireshark with a port-mirror as close as possible to the area that you suspect is infected, and start the capture.

How to do it...

To discover the problem, follow these steps:

1. Start Wireshark with capture on the interface that is close to the problem:
   - If the line to the internet becomes slow, port-mirror the line
   - If a server becomes slow, port-mirror the server
   - If remote offices become slow, port-mirror the lines to them

2. If you see that Wireshark does not respond, it is probably because you have a very strong attack that generates thousands or more packets per second; so, Wireshark (or your laptop) cannot process them. In this case, stop Wireshark (with *Ctrl* + *Alt* + *Del* in Windows, the `kill` command in Unix if necessary, or *Force Quit* in Apple Mac) and configure it to capture multiple files (described in the start capturing data section in `Chapter 1`, *Introduction to Wireshark Version 2*).

3. There are various patterns that you might see, all of them with the same behavior—massive scanning, ICMP or TCP in most of the cases, but also other types. The best way to understand is to see them with some examples.

4. In the following diagram, you see a network that was under attack. Users from all the remote sites complained about a very slow network. They were all accessing servers on the center on the left-hand side of the diagram.

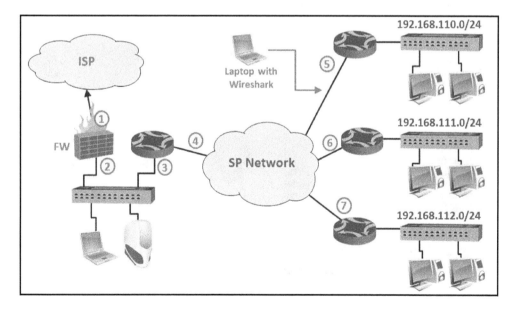

Figure 19.4: Wireshark location—slowness at remote sites

What I got when I connected Wireshark to a remote site (as illustrated) was many ICMP requests (3) coming from the LAN 192.168.110.0 (1) to random destinations (2). Was it random?

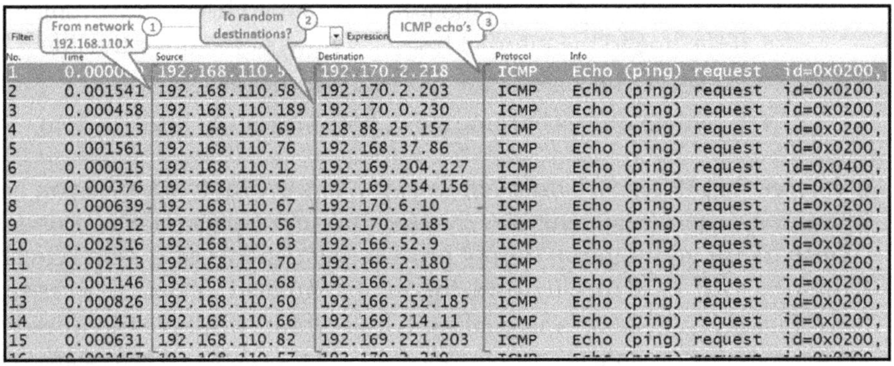

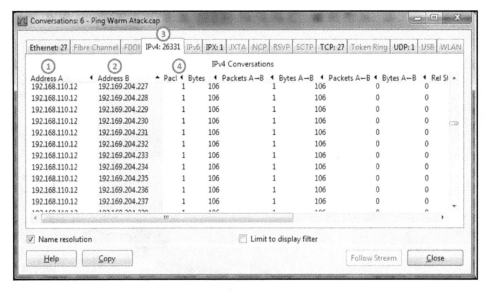

Figure 19.5: ICMP scan to random destination

Also, look at the time between the packets. If scanned, it will usually be very short.

When you go to **Statistics | Conversations**, you will see something interesting:

Figure 19.6: ICMP Scan to random destination—traffic conversations

When we sort the table by address A (**1**), we see a pattern of ICMP requests coming from various addresses on the network `192.168.110.0` (here, we see a very small part of it, that is, `192.168.110.12` scans the network).

This worm simply scans the network with ICMP requests. The moment someone answers, the worm infects him/her also, and after a few minutes, all communication lines are blocked with ICMP requests going out of the remote offices.

Conclusion

When you see a massive number of pings scanning on a communication channel or link, that is, thousands or more pings, check for the problem. It can be the SNMP software discovering the network, but it can also be a worm that will flood your communication line or server links (or both).

5. Another common type of scan is the TCP-SYN scan. In this case, the attacker scans random TCP ports with TCP-SYN packets, waiting for someone to answer with SYN-ACK. The moment it happens, there are two options:
    - The attacker will continue to send SYN packets and receive the SYN-ACKs, thus leaving many half-open connections on the device under attack
    - The attacker will answer with ACK, thus initiating the connection, and leave it open as in DoS/DDoS attacks or try to harm the device under attack with this connection

6. The TCP-SYN scan will look like one of the patterns in the following screenshots:
    - You will see many SYN packets without any response from the node under attack

						The Attacker	Node under attack		SYN Scan

Filter: ip.addr==173.194.66.116   ▾ Expression... C   Apply Save

No.	Time	Source	Destination	Protocol	Info
17984	0.000061	192.168.43.191	173.194.66.116	TCP	50991 > 714 [SYN] Seq=0 Win=1024 Len=0 MS
17985	0.000083	192.168.43.191	173.194.66.116	TCP	50990 > 11110 [SYN] Seq=0 Win=1024 Len=0
17986	0.000064	192.168.43.191	173.194.66.116	TCP	50990 > 1198 [SYN] Seq=0 Win=1024 Len=0 N
17987	0.000071	192.168.43.191	173.194.66.116	TCP	50990 > 50300 [SYN] Seq=0 Win=1024 Len=0
17988	0.000067	192.168.43.191	173.194.66.116	TCP	50990 > 5002 [SYN] Seq=0 Win=1024 Len=0 N
17989	0.000070	192.168.43.191	173.194.66.116	TCP	50990 > 6002 [SYN] Seq=0 Win=1024 Len=0 N
17990	0.000063	192.168.43.191	173.194.66.116	TCP	50990 > 9081 [SYN] Seq=0 Win=1024 Len=0 N
18109	0.794487	192.168.43.191	173.194.66.116	TCP	50991 > 6788 [SYN] Seq=0 Win=1024 Len=0 N
18110	0.000160	192.168.43.191	173.194.66.116	TCP	50990 > 15742 [SYN] Seq=0 Win=1024 Len=0
18111	0.001761	192.168.43.191	173.194.66.116	TCP	50991 > 79 [SYN] Seq=0 Win=1024 Len=0 MSS
18112	0.001911	192.168.43.191	173.194.66.116	TCP	50991 > 1805 [SYN] Seq=0 Win=1024 Len=0 N

Figure 19.7: TCP SYN attack—no response

- You will see many SYN packets when a TCP RST packet is sent as a response to each one of them. This is usually when you have a firewall on the device that is under attack or will be attacked.

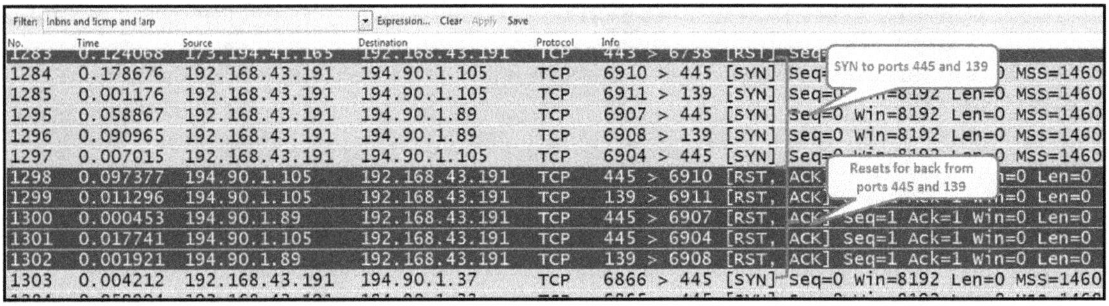

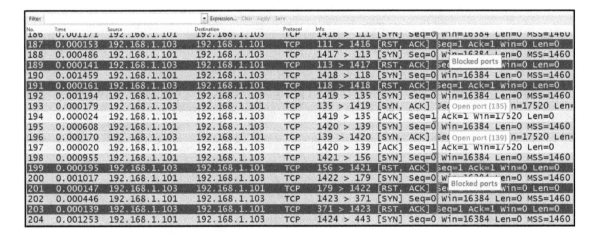

Figure 19.8: TCP SYN attack - connection reset

- You can also have consecutive SYN and RST packets. When there is a port number that is opened, you will see the complete SYN/SYN-ACK/ACK when the scanner opens a connection to the victim. This is illustrated in the following screenshot:

Figure 19.9: TCP session initiation—three-way handshake

7. Always look for unusual traffic patterns. Too many ICMP requests, for example, are a good indication of scanning. Look for multiple ICMP requests to clients, ICMP timestamp request, ICMP in ascending or descending order, and so on. These patterns can indicate malicious scanning.

- When you suspect a scan, click on the title of the destination (address), and you will get the packet list sorted by the destination address. In this way, it will be easier to see the scan patterns.
- In the following screenshot, you see an example of this scenario:

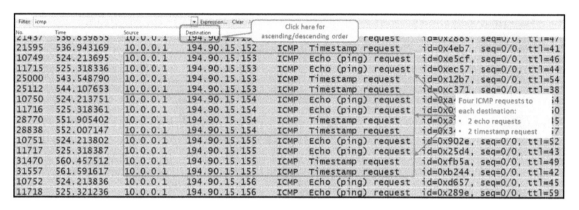

Figure 19.10: ICMP requests—malicious scan

8. In the case of application scanning, you can have various types of scans:

- **NetBIOS**: This looks for massive scanning of NetBIOS ports
- **HTTP**: This looks for SYN requests to HTTP port 80 with HTTP requests later on
- **SMTP**: This looks for massive scanning on the TCP port 25
- **SIP**: This looks for massive requests on port 5060

Other types of applications are scanned according to their port numbers

How it works...

The majority of scanners work in several steps: ARP scanning, ICMP, and then TCP or UDP. The principle is simple:

- If the scanner is on the LAN, it sends an ARP broadcast to the entire LAN.
- The scanner sends ICMP requests. Some of the ICMP requests will be answered.
- When someone answers the ARP or ICMP request, it goes up to TCP and UDP and starts scanning the layer 4 ports. When the scanner finds out that a port is open, it starts with application scanning.
- In application scanning, the scanner sends commands to the applications, trying to get the application to answer, and, in this way, trying to break into it.

There's more...

Most of the modern intrusion detection/prevention systems (IDS/IPS) in the last several years know how to deal with ICMP scans, TCP SYN scans, and various types of scans that generate massive traffic of standard, well-known attack patterns. In case you have such a system and you connect to the internet with an ISP that has their systems, you are probably protected from these simple types of attacks.

These systems usually work in two ways:

- NetFlow/Jflow-based IDS/IPS that identifies massive traffic coming from several sources; they neutralize it by blocking it or changing the routing tables to disable these packets from getting to the ISP network.
- Content-based IDS/IPS. It looks at the traffic patterns and accordingly decides whether to forward it or not.

Attacks coming from the internal network are not filtered by the external devices, and therefore, are even more common. There are more sophisticated types of attacks that will be discussed in the *Smart TCP attacks* recipe later in this chapter.

The way to prevent attacks coming from the internet is to connect through an ISP with efficient IDS/IPS systems along with using one of your own. The way to prevent attacks coming from the internal network is to implement organizational security policy along with appropriate protection software, such as antivirus and personal firewalls.

See also

In the previous section, I mentioned the issue of organizational security policy, that is, how to implement a set of rules for securing your organization. Further information on this subject is widely available on the internet. Some interesting websites that cover this are:

- http://www.cert.org/work/organizational_security.html
- http://www.praxiom.com/iso-17799-4.htm
- http://www.sans.org/reading-room/whitepapers/policyissues/1331.php
- http://www.sans.org/security-resources/policies/

Discovering DoS and DDoS attacks

Denial of Service (DoS) and **Distributed Denial of Service (DDoS)** are attacks that intend to deny users from accessing network services. Services that can be denied to the users are:

- **Communication lines**: This will usually be done by generating traffic that floods and blocks the communication line
- **Applications and services (web services, mail services, and so on)**: This will usually be done by loading a server to a point at which it will not be able to serve clients' requests

DoS/DDoS attacks can be a result of scanning that we talked about in the previous recipe. The difference is that DoS/DDoS is a scan that slows down a server or a network in a way that denies the user access.

In this recipe, we will see some common DoS/DDoS patterns, and learn how to identify and block them.

Getting ready

DoS/DDoS are usually discovered when one of the network resources, that is, communication lines or servers become very slow or are not functioning.

When you identify such a resource, connect Wireshark with a port-mirror to this device and start packet capture. In this recipe, we will go through some common DoS/DDoS attacks and their signatures.

How to do it...

Connect Wireshark to the network with a port-mirror to the port of the resource that you suspect is exposed to DoS/DDoS. Usually, it will be a server that becomes very slow, a communication line that becomes very loaded, or any other resource that stops functioning or becomes very slow.

- When a communication line becomes very slow, for example, a connection to the internet, connect Wireshark with a port-mirror to this line.
  - Try to locate where the traffic comes from.
  - I've port-mirrored the server, and this is what I got:

			Ascending source ① addresses		A single Internet ② destination address		SYN packets are ③ generated to port 6000	
Filter:					pression... Clear Apply Save			
No.	Time	Source		Destination		Protocol	Info	
1	0.000000	1.1.164.98		94.23.71.12		TCP	44129 > 6000 [SYN] Seq=0 Win=16384 Len=0	
2	0.000011	1.1.164.99		94.23.71.12		TCP	44130 > 6000 [SYN] Seq=0 Win=16384 Len=0	
3	0.000011	1.1.164.100		94.23.71.12		TCP	44131 > 6000 [SYN] Seq=0 Win=16384 Len=0	
4	0.000011	1.1.164.101		94.23.71.12		TCP	44132 > 6000 [SYN] Seq=0 Win=16384 Len=0	
5	0.000012	1.1.164.102		94.23.71.12		TCP	44133 > 6000 [SYN] Seq=0 Win=16384 Len=0	
6	0.000011	1.1.164.103		94.23.71.12		TCP	44134 > 6000 [SYN] Seq=0 Win=16384 Len=0	
7	0.000011	1.1.164.104		94.23.71.12		TCP	44135 > 6000 [SYN] Seq=0 Win=16384 Len=0	
8	0.000011	1.1.164.105		94.23.71.12		TCP	44136 > 6000 [SYN] Seq=0 Win=16384 Len=0	
9	0.000011	1.1.164.106		94.23.71.12		TCP	44137 > 6000 [SYN] Seq=0 Win=16384 Len=0	
10	0.000012	1.1.164.107		94.23.71.12		TCP	44138 > 6000 [SYN] Seq=0 Win=16384 Len=0	
11	0.000011	1.1.164.108		94.23.71.12		TCP	44139 > 6000 [SYN] Seq=0 Win=16384 Len=0	
12	0.000011	1.1.164.109		94.23.71.12		TCP	44140 > 6000 [SYN] Seq=0 Win=16384 Len=0	

Figure 20.11: TCP SYN attack—sourced from different IP address

- We see source addresses in ascending order, generating traffic to the internet address 94.23.71.12.

When you look at the time column that is configured with time since the previously displayed packet, you see that there are 11-12 microseconds between the frames. When you see TCP-SYN coming at this rate, something is wrong. Check out what it is!

- Since the source addresses were unknown, I checked their MAC address. What I got was:

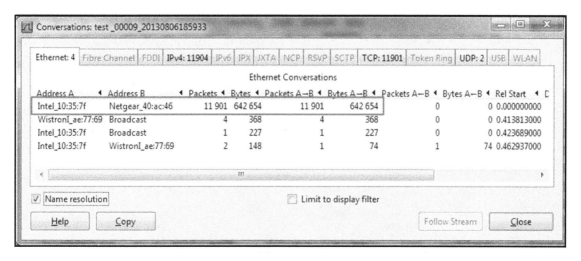

Figure 19.12: TCP SYN attack—Traffic Conversations

- The problem was that all source addresses came from a single MAC address. So I checked their MAC addresses, and all IP addresses came from a single MAC address: the MAC address of the server.

> Check for SYN scans, and verify which IP and MAC addresses they are coming from. It could be that a worm is generating source addresses that are not the addresses of the host.

- Another example can be a simple SYN scan that comes from a single attacker, as seen in the next illustration. Look for SYN and watch the port numbers that they are scanning. You might see:
    - No response
    - Reset packet
    - SYN-ACK response

- There can be various consequences of this type of attack:
  - In case of no response or reset response, the attacked server is functioning well. If the server answers with a SYN-ACK response, it might be a risk to the server.
  - The risk is that if too many connections are opened (SYN/SYN-ACK/ACK) or half-opened (SYN/SYN-ACK), the server might get slow due to these connections.
  - You can see a typical TCP SYN attack in the following screenshot. A SYN attack becomes DoS/DDoS when it blocks a communication line or loads a server to the point that it stops functioning.

No.	Time	Source	Destination	Protocol	Info
55371	0.000025	10.0.0.103	10.0.0.10	TCP	33928 > 1080 [SYN] Seq=0 Win=1024 Len=0 MSS=1460
55372	0.000025	10.0.0.103	10.0.0.10	TCP	33928 > 1082 [SYN] Seq=0 Win=1024 Len=0 MSS=1460
55373	0.000025	10.0.0.103	10.0.0.10	TCP	33928 > 15003 [SYN] Seq=0 Win=1024 Len=0 MSS=146
55374	0.000034	10.0.0.103	10.0.0.10	TCP	33928 > 6567 [SYN] Seq=0 Win=1024 Len=0 MSS=1460
55375	0.000025	10.0.0.103	10.0.0.10	TCP	33928 > 458 [SYN] Seq=0 Win=1024 Len=0 MSS=1460
55376	0.000026	10.0.0.103	10.0.0.10	TCP	33928 > 8383 [SYN] Seq=0 Win=1024 Len=0 MSS=1460
55377	0.000035	10.0.0.103	10.0.0.10	TCP	33928 > 2100 [SYN] Seq=0 Win=1024 Len=0 MSS=1460
55378	0.000025	10.0.0.103	10.0.0.10	TCP	33928 > 1721 [SYN] Seq=0 Win=1024 Len=0 MSS=1460
55379	0.000025	10.0.0.103	10.0.0.10	TCP	33928 > 8994 [SYN] Seq=0 Win=1024 Len=0 MSS=1460
55380	0.000025	10.0.0.103	10.0.0.10	TCP	33928 > 6699 [SYN] Seq=0 Win=1024 Len=0 MSS=1460
55381	0.000025	10.0.0.103	10.0.0.10	TCP	33928 > 10616 [SYN] Seq=0 Win=1024 Len=0 MSS=146
55382	0.000025	10.0.0.103	10.0.0.10	TCP	33928 > 2381 [SYN] Seq=0 Win=1024 Len=0 MSS=1460
55383	0.000024	10.0.0.103	10.0.0.10	TCP	33928 > 55555 [SYN] Seq=0 Win=1024 Len=0 MSS=146
55384	0.000025	10.0.0.103	10.0.0.10	TCP	33928 > 8193 [SYN] Seq=0 Win=1024 Len=0 MSS=1460
55385	0.000026	10.0.0.103	10.0.0.10	TCP	33928 > 10001 [SYN] Seq=0 Win=1024 Len=0 MSS=146
55386	0.000025	10.0.0.103	10.0.0.10	TCP	33928 > 5904 [SYN] Seq=0 Win=1024 Len=0 MSS=1460

Figure 19.13: TCP SYN DDoS attack

How it works...

DoS is an attack that denies the use of a network service. The way it does this is by causing the device under attack to allocate hardware resources (CPU, memory, and so on) to the attacker so that nothing is left to the users.

DoS is when there is an attack on a network resource. Distributed DoS is when the attack is coming from multiple sources.

There's more...

DoS/DDoS attacks are sometimes hard to discover since they can simulate a real situation. For example:

- Ping scans that can also come for management systems
- HTTP GET requests that are the normal requests that are accepted by web servers
- SNMP GET request

These and many others should be monitored for their quantity and sources in order to discover a problem. In the following screenshot, we see what we get when we follow a specific TCP stream.

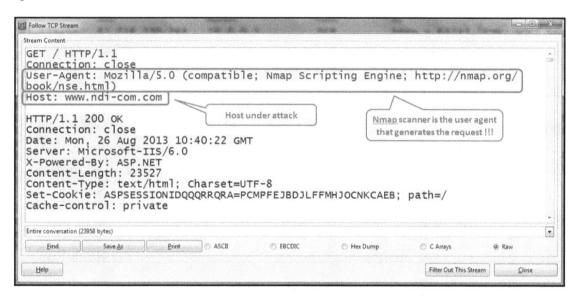

Figure 19.14: TCP SYN DDoS attack

Locating smart TCP attacks

Another type of attack is when you send unknown TCP packets, hoping that the device under attack will not know what to do with them and hopefully pass them through. These types of attacks are well known, and blocked by most of the modern firewalls that are implemented in networks today; but still, I will inform you about them in brief.

Getting ready

What I usually do when I get to a new network is to connect my laptop to the network and see what is running over it. First, I just connect it to several switches and see the broadcasts. Then I configure a port-mirror to critical servers and communication lines and look what is running over it.

To look for unusual traffic, port-mirror the communication links and central servers, and check for unusual traffic patterns.

How to do it

The traffic patterns you should look for are:

- **ACK scanning**: Multiple ACKs are sent usually to multiple ports in order to break the existing TCP connections

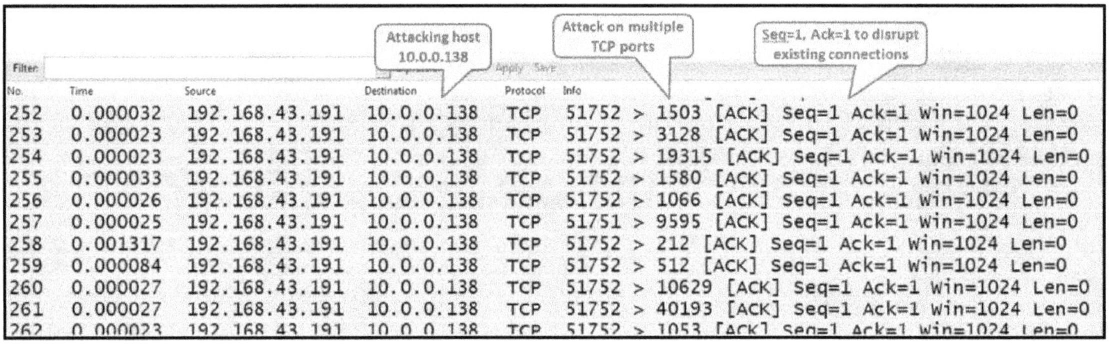

Figure 19.15: TCP ACK scanning

- **Unusual flag combinations**: This refers to anything with a URG flag, FIN and RST, SYN-FIN, and so on. Unusual flag combinations are not the usual SYN, FIN or RST, with or without ACK. In the following screenshot, you see an example of this scenario. The operations FIN/PSH/URG are together called Xmas scan.

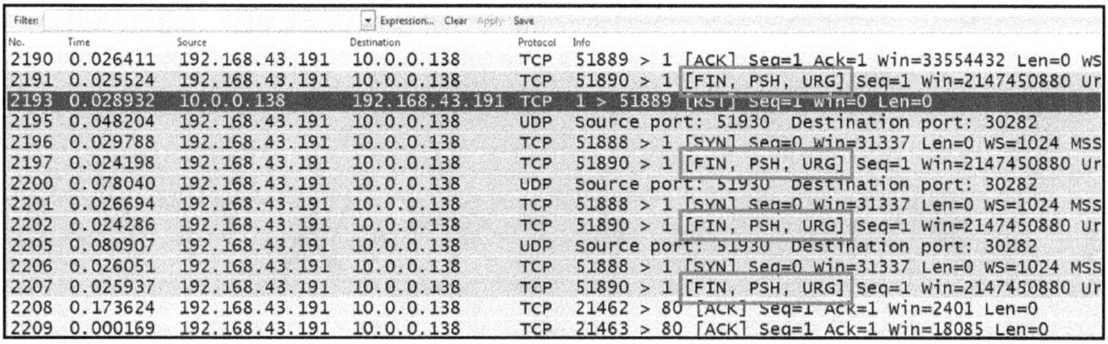

Figure 19.16: TCP unusual flag combinations

TCP scans with all flags set to zero. This scan is called **null scan**.

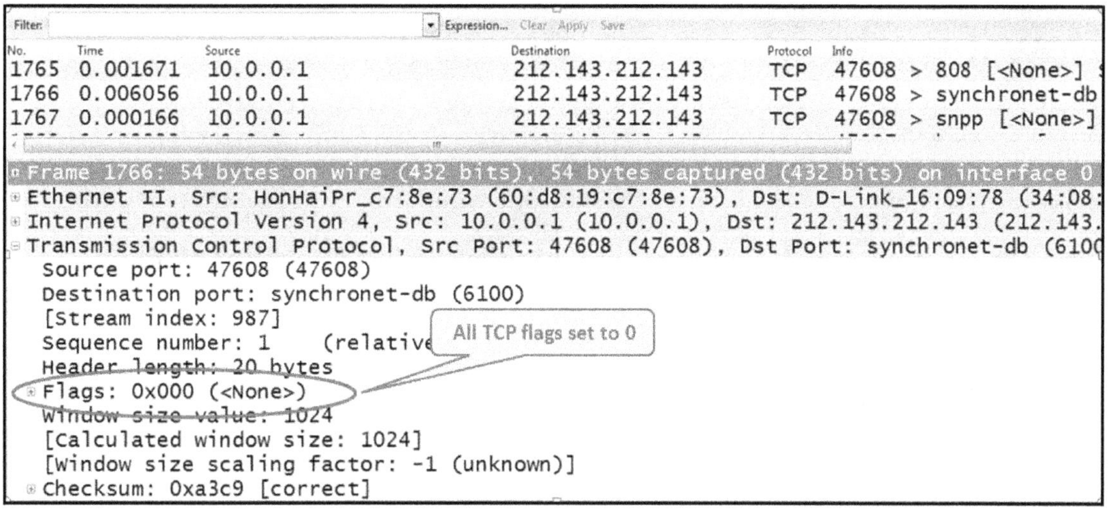

Figure 19.17: TCP null scan

- **Massive FIN-ACK scanning**: Large number of packets with FIN and ACK flags set to one are sent to multiple ports in order to cause them to be closed or just to flood the network

No.	Time	Source	Destination	Protocol	Info
1133	0.092435	10.0.0.1	212.143.212.143	TCP	50948 > 545 [FIN, ACK] Seq=1 Ack=1 Win=1024 Len=0
1134	0.000199	10.0.0.1	212.143.212.143	TCP	50948 > 2005 [FIN, ACK] Seq=1 Ack=1 Win=1024 Len=0
1135	0.000156	10.0.0.1	212.143.212.143	TCP	50948 > 57294 [FIN, ACK] Seq=1 Ack=1 Win=1024 Len=0
1136	0.018944	10.0.0.1	212.143.212.143	TCP	50948 > 1455 [FIN, ACK] Seq=1 Ack=1 Win=1024 Len=0
1137	0.000237	10.0.0.1	212.143.212.143	TCP	50948 > 9040 [FIN, ACK] Seq=1 Ack=1 Win=1024 Len=0
1138	0.000125	10.0.0.1	212.143.212.143	TCP	50948 > 25734 [FIN, ACK] Seq=1 Ack=1 Win=1024 Len=0
1139	0.000178	10.0.0.1	212.143.212.143	TCP	50948 > 20221 [FIN, ACK] Seq=1 Ack=1 Win=1024 Len=0
1140	0.000108	10.0.0.1	212.143.212.143	TCP	50948 > 11110 [FIN, ACK] Seq=1 Ack=1 Win=1024 Len=0
1141	0.000070	10.0.0.1	212.143.212.143	TCP	50948 > 45100 [FIN, ACK] Seq=1 Ack=1 Win=1024 Len=0

Figure 19.18: TCP FIN-ACK scan

How it works...

There are many types of TCP scans based on the assumption that when we send target RST or FIN flags (with or without an ACK) that scan various port numbers, we will cause the target to close connections, and when we send unusual combinations of flags to it, it will make the target busy. This will cause it to slow down and drop the existing connections.

Most of these scans are well known and well protected against firewalls and intrusion detection/prevention systems.

There's more...

You can also configure predefined filters to catch these types of attacks, but the best thing to do while suspecting such an event is to go through the captured data and look for unusual data patterns.

See also

- For scan types, go to the NMAP.org web page: `http://nmap.org/book/man-port-scanning-techniques.html`

Discovering brute force and application attacks

The next step in network attack is to understand the various types of brute force attacks. A brute force attack is a trial-and-error method used to obtain information from the victim, for example, trying to find organizational servers, user directories, and to crack passwords.

Getting ready

Brute force attacks will usually not produce non-standard loads on the network, and the way they are discovered is usually by IDS systems or when there is a suspicion that someone is trying to hack into the network. In this recipe, we will learn how to identify typical brute force attacks.

How to do it...

When you suspect a brute force on the network, follow these steps to locate it.

1. Connect Wireshark with a port-mirror to the port in the server that you suspect is under attack.
2. For DNS brute force attacks, look for DNS queries that are asking for common names under your domain. For example, in the following screenshot, you can see a scan for ISP servers. We can see DNS queries to common names such as DNS (**1**) and DNS (**2**) a record for IPv4 (**2**) and a record for IPv6 (**3**), and intranet—a record for IPv4 (**4**) and a record for IPv6 (**5**).
    - In the case of `dns.icomm.co` (**1**), we got a reply; in all other cases, we did not.

- Many queries with no response can not only indicate a DNS brute attack, but also indicate someone who is looking for a server that does not exist. Look at the source address to see where it is coming from.

No.	Time	Source	Destination	Protocol	Info
7749	0.127587	10.0.0.1	10.0.0.138	DNS	Standard query 0x0001 AAAA sip.icomm.com
7750	0.023064	10.0.0.138	10.0.0.1	DNS	Standard query response 0x0001
7751	0.128110	10.0.0.1	10.0.0.138	DNS ①	Standard query 0x0001 A dns.icomm.com
7752	0.026680	10.0.0.138	10.0.0.1	DNS ①	Standard query response 0x0001 A 81.199.199.199
7755	0.124379	10.0.0.1	10.0.0.138	DNS	Standard query 0x0001 AAAA dns.icomm.com
7756	0.023907	10.0.0.138	10.0.0.1	DNS	Standard query response 0x0001
7757	0.127113	10.0.0.1	10.0.0.138	DNS ②	Standard query 0x0001 A ns2.icomm.com
7758	0.023341	10.0.0.138	10.0.0.1	DNS ②	Standard query response 0x0001 No such name
7759	0.005137	10.0.0.1	10.0.0.138	DNS	Standard query 0x0001 AAAA corp.icomm.com
7760	0.000190	10.0.0.1	10.0.0.138	DNS	Standard query 0x0001 AAAA whois.icomm.com
7761	0.000640	10.0.0.1	10.0.0.138	DNS	Standard query 0x0001 AAAA ns2.icomm.com
7762	0.001602	10.0.0.138	10.0.0.1	DNS ③	Standard query 0x0001 AAAA ns2.icomm.com
7763	0.023563	10.0.0.138	10.0.0.1	DNS ③	Standard query response 0x0001 No such name
7764	0.088002	10.0.0.1	10.0.0.138	DNS ④	Standard query 0x0001 A intranet.icomm.com
7765	0.024316	10.0.0.138	10.0.0.1	DNS ④	Standard query response 0x0001 No such name
7766	0.134785	10.0.0.1	10.0.0.138	DNS ⑤	Standard query 0x0001 AAAA intranet.icomm.com
7767	0.023727	10.0.0.138	10.0.0.1	DNS ⑤	Standard query response 0x0001 No such name

Figure 19.19: DNS brute force attack

3. Another brute force attack to watch out for is HTTP trying to find resources on the server.
   - To look for HTTP scanning, look for the scanner's signature in the packet details, as seen in the following screenshot.

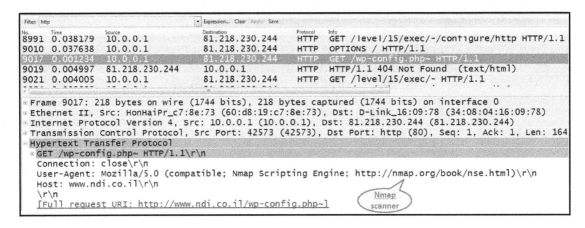

Figure 19.20: HTTP brute force attack—finding resources

- Also, look for too many HTTP error messages. Some examples are illustrated in the following screenshot. Choose **Statistics** | **HTTP** | **Packet Counter** | **PC**. If you get too many error messages, check their source.

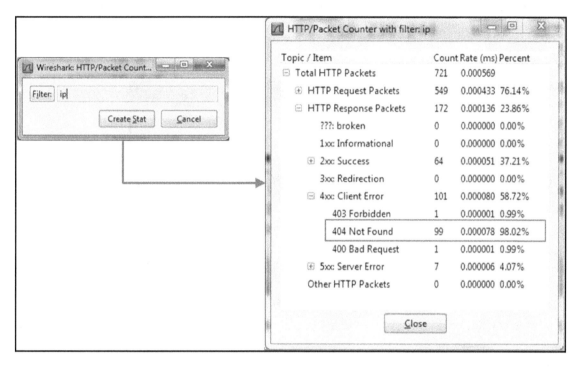

Figure 19.21: HTTP error messages and source

How it works...

Brute force attacks are trial-and-error attacks that send requests to the destination, hoping that some of them will be answered. Since most of these requests will be denied (if you've configured you servers properly), a large amount of **Not Found** messages, forbidden messages, and other error codes can be some of the signs of such an attack.

There's more...

To discover HTTP error codes, configure the display filter `http.response.code >= 400`. The same applies to SIP and any protocol that uses HTTP-like codes. To find known scanners, you can simply use the **Edit** | **Find** packet feature and look for common scanner names. In the following screenshot, you can see an example for Nmap, which is one of the common ones. We chose the string **nmap.org** (1) in **Packet bytes** (2).

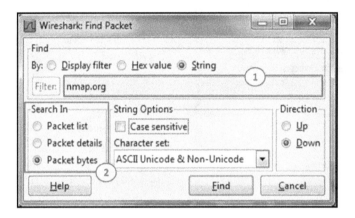

Figure 19.22: Filtering to discover HTTP errors

And this is what we got:

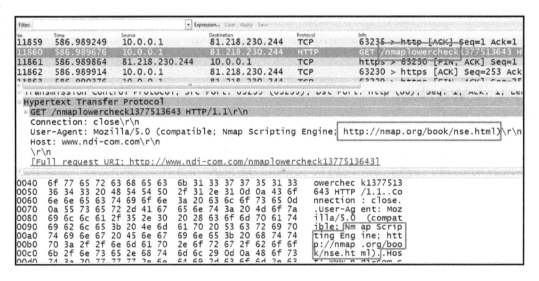

Figure 19.23: Discovering HTTP error codes

Another important issue in a brute force attack is when the attacker tries to guess the password in order to break into a server.

In the following screenshot, you see what happens when an attacker tries to break into a well-protected FTP server.

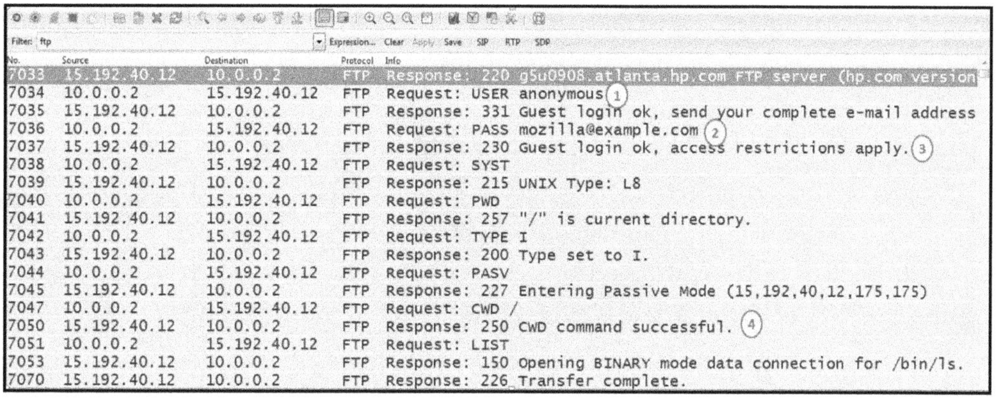

Figure 19.24: User breaking an FTP server

Since it is FTP, the first trial is with username `anonymous` (1). A password chosen by the attacker (2). The login is, of course, approved (3) and the attacker gets in (4).

In the following screenshot, you see what happens when the attacker tries other usernames that are not authorized.

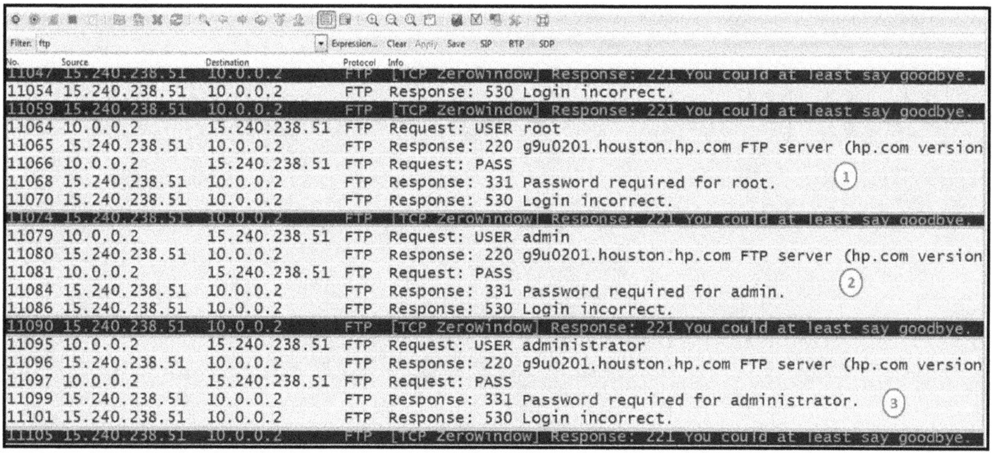

Figure 19.25: User breaking FTP server—invalid usernames

Here, you can see that the attacker is trying to log in with the usernames **root** (1), **admin** (2) and **administrator** (3).

The attacker is blocked, and the server sends a **TCP Zero-Window** message and even answers by displaying **you could at least say goodbye**.

Index